A NOTE FROM THE AUTHORS

If you are holding this book in your hands, you are most likely a high school student searching for a way to have world history make sense. Perhaps AP World History is your first exposure to the Advanced Placement program and the demands of college-level work. Perhaps you are overwhelmed by the prospect of studying more than of 10,000 years of history for a three-hour exam. Many of us who teach AP World History also have been overwhelmed with the awesome scope of this course.

Remember that hundreds of thousands of high school students have already gained college credit for AP World History since the first exam. Most have been high school sophomores. Their success can be your success if you master the skills and themes of world history. Kaplan review books have provided students an edge on AP exams for many years. The practical strategies for success on the AP World History exam provide the focus for this book. The AP World History course is like no other, and this review book is tailored to its specific demands.

This year, you will most likely spend many hours reading, writing, and studying world history. You are to be commended for rising to this challenge. Years from now, you will understand the world better from having studied its past. Despite all of the hard work, do not lose sight of what makes people love world history: the fascinating stories of people much like us doing extraordinary things during extraordinary times.

Best of luck,

Jennifer Laden
Patrick Whelan

RELATED TITLES

AP Biology

AP Calculus AB & BC

AP Chemistry

AP English Language & Composition

AP English Literature & Composition

AP Environmental Science

AP European History

AP Macroeconomics/Microeconomics

AP Physics B & C

AP Psychology

AP Statistics

AP U.S. Government & Politics

AP U.S. History

AP World History

SAT Premier with CD-Rom

SAT Strategies, Practice, and Review

SAT Subject Test: Biology E/M

SAT Subject Test: Chemistry

SAT Subject Test: Literature

SAT Subject Test: Mathematics Level 1

SAT Subject Test: Mathematics Level 2

SAT Subject Test: Physics

SAT Subject Test: Spanish

SAT Subject Test: U.S. History

SAT Subject Test: World History

AP® WORLD HISTORY

2015

Jennifer Laden

Patrick Whelan

PUBLISHING

New York

Published by Kaplan Publishing, a division of Kaplan, Inc.
395 Hudson Street
New York, NY 10014

Printed in the United States of America

10 9 8 7 6 5 4 3 2 1

ISBN-13: 978-1-61865-264-5

TABLE OF CONTENTS

PART THREE: AP WORLD HISTORY REVIEW

PART FOUR PRACTICE TESTS

ACCESSING YOUR ONLINE COMPANION

Welcome to *AP World History 2015*!

The online companion provides one-month access to Grockit. Grockit is a comprehensive, personalized platform for AP test-like question practice and review.

Track Your Skill Data: Analyze and track your performance based on content area, difficulty, and time spent on each question.

Target Your Weaknesses: Grockit continually learns as you learn, and targets you with the material you need to work on most.

Study with Peers and Friends: Collaborate and compete with peers or learn from expert instructors.

REGISTER YOUR ONLINE COMPANION USING THESE SIMPLE STEPS

1. Go to http://goto.grockit.com/textbook/ap/.

2. Follow the on-screen instructions. Please have a copy of your book available.

Good luck with your studies!

ABOUT THE AUTHORS

Jennifer Laden is the District Supervisor for Secondary Social Studies in the Harrison Central School District in Harrison, New York, and taught social studies at Fox Lane High School in Bedford, New York from 1996 to 2009, where she developed the AP World History program. She has also served as a reader and table leader for the AP World History exam.

The author would like to acknowledge her students for their inspiration and insight; her colleagues, Andrea Keating and Christine Tierney, for their collaboration; her co-author, Patrick Whelan, for his encouragement and guidance; and her husband, Tom Murphy, and children, Eamonn and Doran, for their limitless support.

Patrick Whelan has taught history at Saint Stephen's Episcopal School in Bradenton, Florida, since 1988, where he helped develop the AP World History program. He has been a reader and/or table leader for the AP World History exam since its inception in 2002.

The author would like to acknowledge all of the teachers and students who have so enriched his life: his parents, who taught him that his worth is more than what can be measured on a test, his wife and sons, who continue to demonstrate the importance of love, and his co-author, Jennifer Laden. His AP World History classes have been of great assistance and have reminded him of why he enjoys teaching high school history.

Charles Hart currently teaches at Korea International School in Seoul, Korea and has been a facilitator and reader for College Board in all three AP history disciplines. He has been a table leader in World History since 2004 and has conducted weeklong summer workshops in that discipline in 12 different states.

Emily Millians has taught in Fairfax County Public Schools since 1998 and helped to establish the AP World program in the district. She has been a reader and table leader for the AP World History exam since 2003.

Dominique Craft has taught history since 2007, and is currently a faculty member at Shorecrest Preparatory School in St. Petersburg, Florida. She currently teaches AP World History and Ancient and Medieval Civilizations and advises student researchers in Shorecrest's Global

Scholars' Initiative program. She earned her masters degree in Education Leadership at Columbia University in 2013.

John Maunu has taught at Grosse Ile High School, Michigan since 1973, currently on-line classroom mentor at Grosse Ile High and AP World History consultant at Cranbrook/Kingswood Schools, West Bloomfield, Michigan. John teaches AP World History workshops nationally, is a Reader/Table Leader for AP World History since 2004, co-moderator for AP College Board World History teacher community, and Digital Resources editor for World History Connected on-line Journal.

KAPLAN PANEL OF AP EXPERTS

Congratulations—you have chosen Kaplan to help you get a top score on your AP exam.

Kaplan understands your goals and what you're up against—achieving college credit and conquering a tough test—while participating in everything else that high school has to offer.

You expect realistic practice, authoritative advice, and accurate, up-to-the-minute information on the test. And that's exactly what you'll find in this book, as well as every other in the AP series. To help you (and us!) reach these goals, we have sought out leaders in the AP community. Allow us to introduce our experts:

AP WORLD HISTORY EXPERTS

Jay Harmon teaches AP World History at The Woodlands Christian Academy in Houston, Texas. He has been a question leader or table leader since the inception of AP World History in 2002 and served on its test development committee for three years. He has worked as a College Board consultant and has broad experience with AP United States History and AP European History as well as AP World History.

Lenore Schneider teaches AP World History at New Canaan High School in New Canaan, Connecticut. She has been a table leader at the AP readings since 2002. She helped set the benchmarks for AP World History and also served on the test development committee for AP European History for three years. She has consulted with the College Board at numerous workshops and institutes.

Part One

THE BASICS

CHAPTER 1: INSIDE THE AP WORLD HISTORY EXAM

"World History"—even the title of the course seems overwhelming. At first glance, it seems like a course on the entire world for all of recorded time. But such a course would be impossible. Anyone teaching a world history course, therefore, must decide what to include and what to leave out.

The people who write the AP World History exam face the same dilemma. As a student studying for the AP exam, you need to know how to separate the important stuff to know from the not-so-important stuff. This book will guide you through that process.

You should know that this course has a completely different approach than the typical history course. AP World History deals more with the **connections** between issues in history than the facts of everything that has happened in world history. The **big picture** is much more important than the small details. In some ways, this organization makes your job easier; in others, it makes your job more difficult.

OVERVIEW OF THE TEST STRUCTURE

The material tested on the exam is divided into six chronological periods.

Time Period	Weight on Exam
8000 BCE to 600 BCE	5%*
600 BCE to 600 CE	15%*
600 to 1450 CE	20%
1450 to 1750 CE	20%
1750 to 1900 CE	20%
1900 to the present	20%

* Even though these are considered two separate periods on the AP, they are combined for the purposes of the review chapter and tests in this book. The periods 8000 BCE to 600 BCE and 600 BCE to 600 CE are grouped into a single time frame of "up to 600 CE."

The College Board uses the designation BCE (**Before the Common Era**) and CE (**Common Era**) instead of BC and AD. The dates themselves are otherwise the same; 1492 CE is the same as 1492 AD. This abbreviation system is not difficult to understand, but might be confusing if you have never seen it before.

Often, teachers speed through the 20th century in a rush to finish the material before the exam date. In your review, you may want to emphasize more modern history to compensate.

You may also notice that the exam covers material up to the present. In case you think that your studying should also include current events, do not worry. The exam is written a few years before it is administered to students. You will *not* need to know any specific material that has occurred in the *very recent past*.

REGIONS TESTED ON THE EXAM

Almost all parts of the world are covered on the AP World History exam, though some areas are covered more extensively than others. Asia, for instance, receives much more attention than Australia.

The overwhelming majority of the World History exam deals with those areas outside of Europe, such as Asia, Africa, and Latin America. The questions that address European history account for at most 30% of the exam. The College Board offers a separate AP European History exam.

In addition, U.S. history is not emphasized on the World History AP exam, except when it involves relationships with other areas of the world and with issues that involve larger global processes.

EXAM FORMAT

Multiple-choice	70 questions	55 minutes	50% of the exam
Free-response essays	3 questions	130 minutes	50% of the exam

QUESTION TYPES

There are two types of questions on the exam: multiple-choice and free-response essays.

MULTIPLE-CHOICE QUESTIONS

The multiple-choice questions have four possible responses (A through D). The 70 questions are arranged in chronological clusters or groups in the first 40 or so questions and then repeat the sequence to the number 70. You don't need to shift your mind from African prehistory to the Cold War to the Mongol invasions for consecutive questions. Some of the questions may also cover material that crosses chronological boundaries.

Many questions will contain visual materials, such as maps, charts, graphs, illustrations, and pictures. Other questions may be based on quotations from historical sources. Occasionally, two multiple-choice questions may be drawn from a longer quotation or a more complex visual source.

FREE-RESPONSE ESSAYS

There are three types of free-response essay questions. Each essay allows for the same amount of writing time and counts the same for the final score. Note, however, that there are **no mandatory stop times for each essay.** If you spend 90 minutes on the document-based essay, your other two essays are bound to be sloppy. Bring a watch, and consciously budget your time.

Essay Type	Time Allotted	Scoring Weight
Document-based essay	10 minutes reading 40 minutes writing	33.3% of the essay section; 16.7% of the whole test
Continuity and Change-Over-Time essay	40 minutes writing	33.3% of the essay section; 16.7% of the whole test
Comparative essay	40 minutes writing	33.3% of the essay section; 16.7% of the whole test

Unlike the other AP history exams, AP World History does not provide you with a choice among several questions. You must answer the questions provided. You may, however, have some flexibility within each question. For example, you may be able to answer a Continuity and Change-Over-Time or a Comparative essay question by using information about two regions of the world out of several regions that are listed.

World History Themes

In defining what the AP exam should include, the College Board highlights five specific themes in world history—all dealing with the big picture of world history. These themes form the building blocks of the course, and they help the College Board decide what to put into the test. Knowing these themes will help you focus on certain areas for studying.

Theme 1

Interactions between people and the environment
Includes: demography and disease; migration; patterns of settlement; technology

> In other words: **How does the environment shape human societies, and how do humans shape the environment?**

Theme 2

Development and interaction of cultures
Includes: religions; belief systems, philosophies, and ideologies; science and technology; the arts and architecture

> In other words: **How do people express themselves, and what is the impact of ideas?**

Theme 3

State-building, expansion, and conflict
Includes: political structures and forms of governance; empires; nations and nationalism; revolts and revolutions; regional, transregional, and global structures and organizations

> In other words: **How do people govern themselves, and how do these processes lead to conflict?**

Theme 4

Creation, expansion, and interaction of economic systems
Includes: agricultural and pastoral production; trade and commerce; labor systems; industrialization; capitalism and socialism

> In other words: **How do human societies use their environments to produce, distribute, and consume goods and services?**

Theme 5

Development and transformation of social structures
Includes: gender roles and relations; family and kinship; racial and ethnic constructions; social and economic classes

> In other words: **How do human societies group their members socially, and how do these groupings affect people's lives?**

HISTORICAL THINKING SKILLS

In addition to the five major themes of world history, the College Board has identified four historical thinking skills that are tested on the exam.

HISTORICAL THINKING SKILL 1

Crafting Historical Arguments from Historical Evidence in World History

> In other words: **using historical sources to support your thoughts on what happened in the past.**

HISTORICAL THINKING SKILL 2

Applying Chronological Reasoning Skills to World History

> In other words: **using cause and effect, change and continuity, and the division of historical periods to analyze what happened in the past.**

HISTORICAL THINKING SKILL 3

Applying Comparison and Contextualization Skills to World History

> In other words: **using similarities and differences among regions and how the story of one region fits into the larger picture of history to better interpret what happened in the past.**

HISTORICAL THINKING SKILL 4

Applying Historical Interpretation and Synthesis to World History

> In other words: **using the different perspectives concerning history and the wide variety of types of sources to better understand the complexity of what happened in the past.**

APPLYING HISTORICAL THINKING SKILLS

How can you apply this list of skills to your studying? It comes down to understanding the exam better. A multiple-choice question might use a quotation to test how you are able to analyze historical interpretation; another question might ask you to identify the correct statement comparing two cultures. Both of these types of questions assess your ability with the historical thinking skills.

The free-response essay section uses the historical thinking skills as much as the multiple-choice section. All of the essays, for example, ask you to construct arguments, which is the first historical thinking skill. One essay deals specifically with change and continuity over time, and another deals specifically with making comparisons among societies. The document-based essay heavily emphasizes point of view, diversity of interpretations, and putting diverse ideas into historical context. Knowing why the questions are written helps you decode what is being asked.

HOW THE EXAM IS SCORED

The multiple-choice and free-response sections each count for 50% of your total exam score. The actual grading process and formula are more complicated.

MULTIPLE-CHOICE SECTION

Scores are based on the number of questions answered correctly. **There is no penalty for incorrect answers.** No points are awarded for leaving a question blank. Therefore, you should answer every question, even if you have to guess.

Often, you can use the process of elimination to rule out at least one of the four possible responses. The odds are more in your favor if you can narrow it down to two or three responses. Use your best judgment, make an educated guess, and move on quickly to the next question.

The answers for the 70 multiple-choice questions are scored by machine. A weighted score for this first section comes from multiplying the number of correct responses by 0.8571. The weighted scores range from 0 to 60. Any score less than zero is rounded up to zero.

[Number Correct (Out of 70)] × 0.8571 = Multiple-Choice Section Score

FREE-RESPONSE SECTION

The essays are scored by hand, meaning that real people read and evaluate them. College and high school world history teachers come together at a central reading site and are guided through the specific standards for each essay question. A great deal of effort is taken to ensure consistency so that all essays are scored fairly and with the same set of standards.

Each essay is scored on a 10-point system, from 0 to 9. Each essay score is multiplied by 2.2222; all essay scores are then added together to get a total weighted free-response score between 0 and 60.

(Question 1 score × 2.2222)
+
(Question 2 score × 2.2222)   = **Free-Response Section Score**
+
(Question 3 score × 2.2222)

FINAL AP SCORE

For your composite score, the scores from both sections of the exam are added together.

Multiple-Choice Section Score (out of 60 points)
+   = **Composite Score (out of 120 points)**
Free-Response Section Score (out of 60 points)

Neither you nor your school will ever see your composite score, however. That score is converted into a scale of 1 through 5. See page 271 for a conversion chart.

AP Score	Recommendation	2013 AP World History Grade Distribution
5	Extremely well qualified	5.9%
4	Well qualified	13.7%
3	Qualified	29.4%
2	Possibly qualified	30.2%
1	No recommendation	20.90%

How do these AP scores convert to college credit? That depends. Each college department sets its own AP policy. Scores of 3, 4, and 5 are accepted for college credit at the majority of American colleges and universities; some of the most competitive schools accept only scores of 4 or 5.

HOW AP SCORING IS DIFFERENT

You may be accustomed to tests that score on a straight percentage basis. In other words, on a 25-question test, 5 wrong would be an 80 percent or a B-minus. Ten wrong out of 25 would be barely passing with 60 percent.

The AP exams do *not* work this way. For one thing, the questions tend to be much more difficult than non-AP questions. Students can do well even if they miss quite a few multiple-choice questions.

The difficulty of the multiple-choice questions depends on the options presented. On some questions, it can be quite difficult to make a distinction between two, even three answer choices. Thus, the process of eliminating clearly incorrect responses is critical. On the most difficult questions, if you can get down to two possibly correct answers, you are doing well. On the AP exam, many of the questions that you get right will be educated guesses.

You may also notice that the types of questions on the AP World History exam are different from other kinds of tests. Very few questions ask for the detailed recall of specific events, dates, or people. Even the testing of historical vocabulary is done within the context of higher-level, thought-provoking questions. The questions tend to reflect the world history themes and habits of mind discussed earlier. Questions concerning technology, social structure, and the impact of interactions among societies receive greater emphasis on the World History AP exam than they might on other kinds of history exams.

REGISTRATION AND FEES

If you are taking an AP World History course at your high school, registering for the AP exam is easy. Just talk with your teacher and your school's AP coordinator about signing up. Make sure that your name is on the AP exam order list that your AP coordinator sends in March.

If you are home schooled or are not in a school that offers AP courses, you can still take the exam. Call AP Services at (888) 225-5427 or (212) 632-1780 for a list of schools in your area where you can take the exam. Then contact the AP coordinator at one of the schools identified by the College Board for a place on the exam day.

The College Board makes accommodations if you have a documented disability. These may include extended time, large-print exams, use of a word processor, and other necessary accommodations. If you have a need for these sorts of special accommodations, see your AP coordinator.

At the date of printing, the cost of the exam was $89, and $119 at schools and testing centers outside of the United States. For students with acute financial need, the College Board offers a $26 or $28 credit, depending on the state. In addition, most states offer exam subsidies to cover all or part of the remaining cost for eligible students. To learn about other sources of financial aid, contact your AP coordinator.

For more information on the AP Program and the World History exam, contact AP Services:

Phone: (888) 255-5427 or (212) 632-1780
Email: apstudents@info.collegeboard.org
Website: https://apstudent.collegeboard.org/home

ADDITIONAL RESOURCES

The best starting place to find information about the AP World History and the AP exams in general is at the official College Board Student website: www.student.collegeboard.org.

The major world history textbook companies also run valuable websites that can be used for review and getting additional information.

Pearson Longman *World Civilizations*
www.pearsonhighered.com/educator/product/World-Civilizations-The-Global-Experience-Combined-Volume/9780205659562.page

McGraw-Hill *Traditions and Encounters*
glencoe.mcgraw-hill.com/sites/2222555555/student_view0/

Prentice Hall *The World's History*
cwx.prenhall.com/bookbind/pubbooks/spodek2/

Houghton Mifflin *The Earth and Its People*
college.hmco.com/history/world/bulliet/earth_peoples/3e/students/

CHAPTER 2: STRATEGIES FOR SUCCESS: IT'S NOT ALWAYS HOW MUCH YOU KNOW

HOW TO APPROACH THE MULTIPLE-CHOICE SECTION

The AP World History multiple-choice section consists of 70 questions to be completed in 55 minutes. As noted before, there is no penalty for incorrect answers so guessing is encouraged. There are four answer choices for each question. Questions come from all six periods and can deal with specific countries and regions, global situations, or a single topic, such as the basic knowledge of a religion. Questions are often comparative both within and across time frames. There are examples of art or architecture to analyze as well as graphs, charts, and maps. Some questions deal with **periodization**—why a particular time period started or ended.

Although there is no hard rule for how the test is organized, it generally cycles through each of the six periods at least twice. The questions are ranked as easy, medium, and difficult with no distinct pattern to their appearance. A basic strategy for scoring well on this test is to NOT do it linearly, that is, taking each question one at a time and answering each one in order. The best strategy is to do the following:

- Answer all the questions that you know and are sure about first.

- If you can eliminate at least two answer choices and the topic is familiar, mark the question by circling the question number and move on.

- If you look at the question and do not remember the topic, mark the question with an X and move on.

- Go back through the test and answer the questions you marked by circling the question number. Try to eliminate at least two choices, then take your best educated guess as to the answer.

- Go back a third time to answer the questions you marked with an X. Again, try to eliminate at least two choices, and take an educated guess.

Here are some tips for doing well on the multiple-choice section:

- The easiest question may be the last one! Go through all the test questions!

- Move quickly but thoroughly through the test. Don't linger on any one question for more than 30 seconds or so.

- If you skip a question, make sure that you skip that line on the answer grid sheet as well.

- If you finish with time left, go back and check your answers and check to make sure you have gridded in all responses correctly.

- DO NOT change an answer you have made unless you are absolutely sure that your initial attempt is incorrect. Research shows that your first answer is usually the correct one.

- When eliminating distracters (wrong choices) look for choices that are out of time period, out of region, or not related to specific categories (the question asked for economic factors, the distracter mentions law codes).

EXAMPLES OF MULTIPLE-CHOICE QUESTIONS

1. A key development in the advancement of civilization during the Neolithic Era was the

    (A) use of fire.
    (B) development of porcelain.
    (C) development of settled agriculture.
    (D) invention of iron tools.

The correct answer is (C), the development of settled agriculture. Man's use of fire (A) long predates the Neolithic Era, and porcelain (B) and iron tools (D) were developed long after the Neolithic Era. This question is an example of general information required of a specific time period.

2. All of the following cities relied on monsoon seasonal winds for trade EXCEPT

    (A) Kilwa.
    (B) Alexandria.
    (C) Sofala.
    (D) Calicut.

The correct answer is (B), Alexandria, which is located in the Mediterranean. The monsoon seasonal winds influenced trade in the Indian Ocean. Kilwa (A) and Sofala (C) are Swahili city-states on the east coast of Africa, and Calicut (D) is a port city in India, all of which were impacted by monsoon winds. This question is an example of specific information required about a general trade region. Note that geographic knowledge of where important trade cities is required.

3. Which of the following empires was based on a different economic and military foundation than the others?

   (A) Napoleonic
   (B) British
   (C) Portuguese
   (D) Dutch

The correct answer is (A), the Napoleonic Empire. The French Empire of Napoleon relied on continental agriculture and trade and the strength of its armies. The other empires represented by choices (B), (C), and (D) were all maritime based.

HOW TO APPROACH THE ESSAY SECTION

The essay section inspires the most dread in the minds of students taking the AP World History exam. Knowing the structure, and especially how the essays will be scored can give you a substantial advantage.

The three essays are written together during the second part of the exam. All of the essays go into the same pink booklet. Your proctor will *not* tell you to move from one essay to the next—you must do this on your own. A total of 130 minutes is the time allotted for reading, organizing, and writing all three questions.

The three essays can be done in any order. Almost everyone chooses to answer the document-based question (DBQ) first. The second question is an essay that asks a continuity and change-over-time question (CCOT); the third is a comparison question (COMP). Depending on your comfort level with the specific questions, you may want to do the last two essays in a different order than they are listed on the exam.

Pace yourself during this section, so you do not rush through the essays too quickly or, even worse, run out of time. Plenty of students write full and detailed responses to the first essay but are able only to put down a few sentences for the last essay. Partial essays, not surprisingly, do not receive high scores.

Try to write as neatly and as legibly as you can. It is understood that your essays are drafts. Scratch-outs, inserted lines with arrows, and other working thoughts are perfectly acceptable. Try not to use unusual abbreviations, shorthand symbols such as & or @, or texting spelling. If the reader cannot understand the symbol or texting spelling, it will be ignored and you might not gain a point. You must write an *essay* for each question. Bullet notes, diagrams, or simple lists of information are not considered essay formats and will be ignored by the reader.

HOW TO APPROACH THE DOCUMENT-BASED QUESTION

The first of the three essays is the document-based question (DBQ). This essay **asks you to be a historian**; it will ask a specific question, provide a bit of historical background, and then present 4 to 10 related documents. Essentially, you are the historian who will take these sources and draw conclusions based on your skills of historical analysis. The DBQ evaluates historical understanding at its purest: the task is not to remember facts but to organize information in an analytical manner.

Many students panic once they see the DBQ because they do not know much about the topic—the question and the documents often cover something well outside of the mainstream of their high school class. The test writers do this on purpose. Outside knowledge is not needed for the DBQ. You may bring in outside information if you wish, but there is no need to mention facts other than those found in the documents provided.

The other two essays on the exam will evaluate your knowledge of history, but the DBQ evaluates your ability to work with historical material. Consequently, writing the DBQ is a skill that can be learned much like any other skill.

ORGANIZING YOUR ESSAY IN 10 MINUTES

The entire 130-minute essay time is divided into two parts: the first 10 minutes is reading and organizing time, during which you may not write in the pink essay booklet, and the last 120 minutes is the essay writing period. Spend that first 10 minutes working solidly on the DBQ, since that is the essay that requires the most reading and preparation time.

First, read the question. Underline the words that are most related to your task. Let's look at a sample question:

> Using the following documents, analyze how the Ottoman government viewed ethnic and religious groups within its empire for the period 1876–1908. Identify an additional document and explain how it would help you analyze the views of the Ottoman government.

All of the documents that follow will relate to the time period and the place, so you do not need to underline 1876–1908 or Ottoman government. You are being asked how the Ottoman government **viewed ethnic and religious groups** within its empire. An essay that dealt with how the groups viewed the Ottoman Empire would miss the point.

AP EXPERT TIP

Take a couple of seconds to read the instructions for the DBQ and each of the other essays. These list the tasks that you must accomplish to score high. Use these instructions as a checklist.

In the DBQ, you will always be asked to provide and explain examples of another type of document. This task is important.

Second, read the historical background that often follows the question. Since the College Board does not expect you to bring in outside information, the background paragraph sets the historical scene so that you understand the most basic aspects of the topic before you begin. Perhaps you know a great deal about late Ottoman imperial history. More likely, you will need a few sentences to bring you up to speed before you start looking at the documents themselves.

Be careful, though. Quoting from the historical background paragraph in your essay is not recommended. Essays that have material from the historical background repeated in the first paragraph tend to do poorly. The task of the DBQ is to answer the question by using the documents—not by using the historical background.

> In the middle of the 19th century, the Ottoman Empire started liberal reforms that granted civil rights to subjects of their empire. The Ottoman government, which was also known as the Sublime State, ruled over a diverse set of ethnic and religious groups. In 1908, nationalist reformers known as the Young Turks created a new style of government.

Third, read the documents. Most of the first 10 minutes of the reading period will be used looking at the documents and organizing them into groups for analysis. Each of the 4 to 10 documents will have a number above a box. Inside the box will be information on the source of the document, which is very important as you will see later, and the document itself.

Documents can be of many different sorts. Written documents are usually excerpts of much longer pieces that have been edited specifically for the exam. They could be from personal letters, hidden journals, official decrees, public speeches, or propaganda posters. Obviously, the nature of the source should guide you in how you analyze the document. Documents can also be pictures, photographs, maps, charts, and graphs.

Often, students have a harder time analyzing visual and graphic sources than the written sources. Even so, use all of the documents in your essay, treating the nonwritten sources with the same attention as the written ones.

All of the essay questions will be presented in a green booklet. Feel free to write notes in the green booklet as you read the documents. Nothing in the green booklet is read as part of the essay scoring. Feel free to underline important words in both the source line and the document itself. Use the generous margins for notes that will help you group the documents with other documents and discuss their points of view.

Jot down notes about the background of the authors in the margins. Information about the authors' social class, education, occupation, and gender may be important in the essay. On the bottom of the document, write a short phrase that summarizes the basic meaning of the

AP EXPERT TIP

You will have to use black or blue ink to write your essays. If you are used to writing in pencil or typing, practice writing in ballpoint pen. Use a comfortable pen—one with a finger cushion and a wide diameter.

document, its purpose (why it was written), and possibly, a missing piece of evidence that could relate to the document. If the document is a speech, the missing evidence could be the perception of those listening to the speech. If the document is a government declaration, the missing evidence could be information about how effectively the declaration was carried out. It is also helpful to pause after reading all of the documents to consider evidence that would provide a more complete understanding of the issue. Then you can suggest an additional document.

Once you have finished reading and have made short notes of all of the documents, **reread the question.** Note again what the question asks. If you have not done so already, mark which documents address the different issues that the question asks. Group the documents by their similarities. Can you draw enough conclusions at this point to organize an analytical thesis?

At the end of the 10-minute reading period, the proctor will announce that students may open their pink booklets and begin writing the essays. If you have not yet finished reading and organizing the essay, take a few more minutes to finish up. A few students might be ready to write before the end of the 10-minute reading period, but most find that 10 minutes is just about right.

CORE POINT SCORING

For fairness and ease of scoring, the essays for AP World History are evaluated using what is called a "core scoring method" that comes from scoring rubrics. Each essay is scored on a 10-point system from 0 to 9, with 9 being the best.

With the DBQ, the first 7 points are awarded for doing specific tasks. These are called the "basic core" points. Up to an extra 2 points ("expanded core" points) may be awarded after all of the essential core points are met.

For the DBQ, the basic core points are as follows:

Points	Task
1	Has an acceptable thesis
1	Addresses all of the documents and demonstrates understanding of all or all but one
2	Supports thesis with appropriate evidence from all or all but one of the documents
(1)	(Supports thesis with appropriate evidence from all but two documents)
1	Analyzes point of view in at least two documents

1	Analyzes documents by grouping them in two or three ways depending on the question
1	Identifies and explains the need for one type of appropriate additional document or source
7	Subtotal for all basic core points
2	Possible expanded core points
9	Total possible points for the DBQ

Your goal for the DBQ is to get all 7 basic core points. If you make all of your core points, you will have a much better chance of doing well on the whole exam.

Expanded core points reward excellence in those essays that have met all of their basic core points. More on the expanded core later. First, let's look at an example of a DBQ before learning how to earn your basic core points.

Using the following documents, analyze how the Ottoman government viewed ethnic and religious groups within its empire for the period 1876–1908. Identify an additional document and explain how it would help analyze the views of the Ottoman Empire.

Historical Background: In the middle of the 19th century, the Ottoman Empire started liberal reforms that granted civil rights to subjects of their empire. The Ottoman government, which was also known as the Sublime State, ruled over a diverse set of ethnic and religious groups. In 1908, nationalist reformers known as the Young Turks created a new style of government.

DOCUMENT 1

Source: Adapted from Abdolonyme Ubicini and Pavet de Courteille, *The Present State of the Ottoman Empire*, a guide concerning the Ottoman Empire published in Western Europe, 1876.

FIGURES ON NATIONALITIES WITHIN THE OTTOMAN EMPIRE

Ethnic Group (Total population) Percentage of Empire	Subgroup	Subgroup Population
Turkish group (14,020,000) 49.1%	Ottoman Turks	13,500,000
	Turkomans	300,000
	Tatars	220,000
Greco-Latin group 3,520,000 12.3%	Greeks	2,100,000
	Kutzo-Vlachs	220,000
	Albanians	1,200,000
Slavic group (4,550,000) 15.9%	Serbo-Croatians	1,500,000
	Bulgarians	3,000,000
	Cossacks	32,000
	Lipovans	18,000
Persian group (3,620,000) 12.7%	Armenians	2,500,000
	Kurds	1,000,000
	Other Persians	120,000
Semites (1,611,000) 5.6%	Jews	158,000
	Arabs	1,000,000
	Other Semites	453,000
Other groups (1,232,000) 4.3%		

Total Population of the Ottoman Empire: 28,553,000

DOCUMENT 2

Source: The Ottoman Constitution, 23 December 1876.

Art. 1. The Ottoman Empire comprises present territory and possessions, and semidependent provinces. It forms an indivisible whole, from which no portion can be detached under any pretext whatever.

Art. 4. His Majesty the Sultan, under the title of "Supreme Caliph," is the protector of the Muslim religion. He is the sovereign and emperor of all the Ottomans.

Art. 8. All subjects of the empire are called Ottomans, without distinction whatever faith they profess; the status of an Ottoman is acquired and lost according to conditions specified by law.

Art. 9. Every Ottoman enjoys personal liberty on condition of noninterfering with the liberty of others.

Art. 11. Islam is the state religion. But, while maintaining this principle, the state will protect the free exercise of faiths professed in the Empire, and uphold the religious privileges granted to various bodies, on condition of public order and morality not being interfered with.

DOCUMENT 3

Source: Mr. Owen Davis, from a lecture at a British Congregational Church "Those Dear Turks," 1st November 1876.

Unfortunately for the peace of mankind, it has happened that the Turk is placed in a position where it is impossible to ignore him, and almost equally impossible to endure him; while by his origin, habits, and religion, he is an Asiatic of Asiatics, he is by irony of fate established in a position where his presence is a ceaseless cause of misery to millions of Christian people.

DOCUMENT 4

Source: Hagop Mintzuri, an Armenian baker's apprentice, from his book *Istanbul Memoirs 1897–1940*, commenting about the military guards accompanying the sultan's arrival at a mosque for ceremonial prayers at the end of the fast of Ramadan.

First the Albanian guards, dressed in violet knee-breeches, who were not soldiers or police and did not speak Turkish, would fill the upper part of our market square. Then would come the Arab guards of the sultan, dressed in red salvar and adorned with green turbans. These too, did not speak Turkish and they would fill the road. Finally the Palace Guard of the sultan, chosen exclusively from Turks who were tall, sporting their decorations on their chests, would take up their positions as an inner ring in front of the Albanians and Arabs.

DOCUMENT 5

Source: Suleyman Husnu Pasha (Pasha is a title of distinction within the Ottoman Empire), former high adviser to the sultan, commenting on the ethnic and religious diversity in Iraq, 7 April 1892.

The elements belonging to the official faith and language of the state are in a clear minority whereas the majority falls to the hordes of the opposition.

DOCUMENT 6

Source: Ahmed Cevdet Pasha, respected Ottoman statesman and historian, undated official memorandum.

The Sublime State rests on four principles. That is to say, the ruler is Ottoman, the government is Turkish, the religion is Islam, and the capital is Istanbul. If any of these four principles were to be weakened, this would mean a weakening of one of the four pillars of the state structure…The Sublime State is a great structure made up of various peoples and strata; all of these constituent elements are held together by the sacred power of the Caliphate. Because the only thing uniting Arab, Kurd, Albanian, and Bosnian is the unity of Islam. Yet, the real strength of the Sublime State lies with the Turks. It is an obligation of their national character and religion to sacrifice their lives for the House of Osman until the last one is destroyed. Therefore it is natural that they be accorded more worth than other peoples of the Sublime State.

DOCUMENT 7

Source: Proclamation by the Young Turks, 1908.

3. It will be demanded that all Ottoman subjects having completed their twentieth year, regardless of whether they possess property or fortune, shall have the right to vote.

5. Every citizen will enjoy complete liberty and equality, regardless of nationality or religion, and be submitted to the same obligations. All Ottomans, being equal before the law as regards rights and duties relative to the State, are eligible for government posts, according to their individual capacity and their education. Non-Muslims will be equally liable to the military law.

DO YOU HAVE A THESIS?

You have one chance to make a good first impression. Usually, an AP reader can tell within the first few sentences whether or not an essay is going to be strong. A few essays strongly recover after a poor start, but first impressions matter. Consequently, nothing is more important in the first paragraph than the clear statement of an analytical thesis.

Different kinds of writings demand different types of opening paragraphs. In English class, you may learn a style of essay writing that asks for general background information in a first paragraph. On a DBQ, however, you do not have much time. The reader is most interested in seeing a strong thesis as soon as possible.

Your thesis can be more than just one sentence. With the compound questions often asked by the DBQ, two sentences might be needed to complete the idea. To count for the basic core point, the thesis needs to include specific information that responds to the question. Many students think they have written a thesis but actually have not; their opening paragraphs are just too general and unspecific.

The thesis is that part of your essay that 1) specifically addresses the terms of the question and 2) sets up the structure for the rest of your essay. Let's use the specific question.

> "For the period 1876–1908, analyze how the Ottoman government viewed ethnic and religious groups within its empire."

THESIS STATEMENTS THAT DON'T WORK

The following statement is not an acceptable thesis; it is far too vague. It says very little about how the essay is structured.

> There were many ways in which the Ottoman government viewed ethnic and religious groups.

The next statement paraphrases the historical background and does not address the question. It would not receive credit for being a thesis.

> The Ottoman government brought reforms in the constitution of 1876. The empire had a number of different groups of people living in it, including Christians and Muslims who did not practice the official form of Islam. By 1908 a new government was created by the Young Turks and the sultan was soon out of his job.

This next sentence gets the question backward: You are being asked for the government's view of religious and ethnic groups, not the groups' view of the government. Though the issue of point-of-view is very important, this statement would not receive a basic core point.

> People of different nationalities reacted differently to the Ottoman government depending on their religion.

AP EXPERT TIP

Your thesis can be in the first or last paragraph of your essay, but it cannot be split between the two. Many times your original thesis is too simple to gain the point. A good idea is to write a concluding paragraph that might extend your original thesis. Think of a way to restate your thesis, adding information from your analysis of the documents.

The following paragraph says a great deal about history but it does not address the substance of the question. It would not receive a basic core point because of its irrelevancy.

> Throughout history, people around the world have struggled with the issue of political power and freedom. From the harbor of Boston during the first stages of the American Revolution to the plantations of Haiti during the struggle to end slavery, people have battled for power. Even in places like China with the Boxer Rebellion, people were responding against the issue of westernization. Imperialism made the demand for change even more important, as European powers circled the globe and stretched their influences to the far reaches of the known world. In the Ottoman Empire too, people demanded change.

THESIS STATEMENTS THAT DO WORK

Now we turn to thesis statements that do work. These two sentences address both the religious and ethnic aspects of the question. They describe *how* these groups were viewed.

> The Ottoman government took the same position on religious diversity as it did on ethnic diversity. Minorities were servants of the Ottoman Turks, and religious diversity was allowed as long as Islam remained supreme.

This statement answers the question in a different way, but is equally successful.

> Government officials in the Ottoman Empire were able to send out the message that all people in the empire were equal regardless of religion or ethnicity, yet the reality was that the Turks and their version of Islam were superior.

DO YOU UNDERSTAND THE DOCUMENTS PROPERLY?

With the core point system of scoring, the readers award points based on what the essays accomplish. They do not remove points if an essay is off-task, written poorly, or wrong. There is one exception, however. In the DBQ, you must demonstrate that you understand the documents being used. If your essay makes more than one major misinterpretation, the basic core point cannot be earned.

A major misinterpretation is one that misses the basic intent of the document. If you wrote that the Proclamation of the Young Turks (Document 7) was a

---

AP EXPERT TIP

Remember, if you ADD another paragraph or statement after writing a conclusion—that becomes your conclusion. Draw a line from any information added after the conclusion with an arrow to just before your conclusion. This keeps your conclusion valid.

movement away from ethnic and religious equality, then that misinterpretation would be a major error.

If, instead, you wrote that the Ottoman Empire survived for decades after the Proclamation of the Young Turks in 1908, the statement would be wrong (the Ottoman Empire collapsed after World War I) but would not be a misinterpretation of the document. All of the documents could still count as being understood properly.

Be careful, especially with visual and graphic documents. Students tend to misinterpret these nonwritten documents more than traditional written documents.

Do You Use Evidence to Support Your Thesis?

These core points strike at the basic idea of the DBQ. The documents present a case for answering the question. Your ability to use those documents to answer the question is the focus of the essay. Use the documents to analyze, and you will earn this basic core point.

If the essay supports the thesis with appropriate evidence from all or all but one of the documents, then the essay earns 2 basic core points. If it uses evidence from all but two of the documents, then 1 basic core point is earned.

As you are writing your essay, check off each document in your green booklet as you use it. Writing under time pressure, you may forget to mention one or two. Also remember to include the documents that are in graphic or visual formats. Students often forget to analyze these to the same degree that they do written sources.

To receive this core point, the documents need to be used as part of the analysis. In other words, do you mention something about a document that helps to answer the question? If a document is only mentioned in a list, it will not count for this point. For example, "The Ottoman Empire looked down on ethnic and religious minorities, as seen in documents 3, 4, and 5." If documents 3, 4, and 5 were not analyzed further, this essay would not receive the basic core points for supporting the thesis with appropriate evidence.

How should essays refer to the documents? Any of the following ways could count for the evidence core points. Your essay could:

1. Refer to the document number directly in the sentence: "As shown by document 7, the Young Turks believed that all ethnic and religious groups should be treated equally."

2. Refer to the document within parentheses at the end of the sentence: "The Young Turks believed that all ethnic and religious groups should be treated equally (Document 7)."

> ### AP EXPERT TIP
>
> For charts and graphs, pay particular attention to the title and to the factors delineating the information in the visual. This will help you interpret the document. For pictures, remember that all pictures are taken for a reason and reflect the point of view of the photographer and/or the subject. Notice details in the background or foreground that can help you interpret them.

3. Refer to information presented in the line of source attribution: "As shown by The Proclamation of the Young Turks in 1908, the Young Turks believed that all ethnic and religious groups should be treated equally."

4. Combine the last two techniques: "As shown by The Proclamation of the Young Turks in 1908, the Young Turks believed that all ethnic and religious groups should be treated equally (Document 7)." **(best option)**

5. Give no attribution: "The Young Turks believed that all ethnic and religious groups should be treated equally." **(worst option)**

Merely summarizing the documents is the easiest way to miss these basic core points. You must link the document to the question, not just repeat what the document says. For example, the following paragraph might not count as evidence in support of the thesis:

> Document 1 is a chart with numbers for the different nationalities within the Ottoman Empire. Turks are 49.1% of the population. There are a lot of other groups listed too. The total population is about 28 million people. In document 2 the constitution says that the Sultan is the religious authority and the sovereign. It also says that Islam is the state religion and that 'the state will protect the free exercise of faiths professed in the Empire, and uphold the religious privileges granted to various bodies.'

This summary does not provide any analysis. It states simply *what* the documents say; it does not describe *how* the documents show government views toward ethnic and religious groups. The task of the essay is to answer the question by analyzing.

The following paragraph would help earn the basic core point for evidence in support of the thesis:

> Document 1 is a chart that clearly demonstrates the ethnic diversity of the Ottoman Empire at the time of the new constitution. The Turks were a minority at 49.1% of the population, even though they controlled the government of the Ottoman Empire. The Constitution of 1876 (Document 2) also reinforces the idea that the empire was formed of various ethnicities and religions. It formally states that all people are granted equality, and that all religions answer to the same law. However, this document reflects the law from the point of view of high government officials. It therefore demonstrates only the legal rules, rather than the day-to-day reality in the empire.

Another easy way to miss core points is by not having a strong thesis. How can you use document evidence to support the thesis if the thesis itself is weak? Your essay should be organized enough so that the reader can see how each document fits into the analysis presented in the thesis. Using the same terms that are mentioned in the thesis is a good way to make the links between the evidence and the thesis more apparent.

DO YOU DISCUSS THE POINT OF VIEW OF THE DOCUMENTS?

Generally, more essays do not get point of view (POV) than any other basic core point. So be warned: POV is an important and difficult task. It will separate the mediocre essays from those that do very well. As with any of the other basic core qualities, if an essay does not contain point of view, the highest score it can earn is 6. Your goal is to earn a 7 or above.

Your essay will need to mention aspects of POV for at least two documents in order to receive the basic core point for POV.

So what is point of view? Essentially, POV is the analysis of why a certain person composed the material for the document. What is the author's (or the document's) "angle"? Comments in your essay that explore the motivations for the documents often count as POV. In addition, comments relating to the reliability of a source relate to that source's POV.

You cannot just say that an author is biased or prejudiced to receive the point for point of view. You must state why or indicate an impact or desired effect of the document.

Ask these questions in order to earn the core point for POV:

1. Does the occupation of the author give the document more or less reliability? For example, government officials may overstate or exaggerate information for political, state, or personal reasons.

2. Does the social class, religion, national background, or gender of the author influence what is mentioned in the document?

3. Does the type of document influence the content of what is said? A journal entry or private letter might be more candid about a topic than a public address that is meant to be persuasive. A political cartoon by definition is exaggerated and meant to convey a certain message, whereas a photograph may accurately represent what was in front of the camera for a shot, but could be staged and framed to only capture a certain perspective.

4. Does the timing of the document influence the message? Recollections and memoirs written long after an event may not have the same reliability as first-hand materials done immediately afterward.

5. Does the intended audience skew the message of a source? If a document is meant to be read by the sultan, it has a different POV than one written for a European audience.

6. Describing the tone of the document can also count for POV—if the document is sarcastic, triumphant, haughty, etc. Using tone for POV can be more subtle and is best used with other descriptions of POV.

Merely attributing the document's source by repeating the source material from the document is not enough to earn the POV point. The source material, however, gives you clues as to what you could say relating to POV.

Using our sample DBQ on the Ottoman government's view of ethnic and religious groups, let's examine different examples of POV. You may want to go back to review the documents in the sample DBQ. The following statements may all count for point of view:

For Document 1:

- "The census of national groups within the Ottoman Empire was compiled for Western European readers, which may make it more reliable in counting ethnic minorities than one published for a Turkish distribution." (intended audience and reliability)

- "The figures on nationalities provide a detailed picture of the population at the beginning of the sultan's reign but do not show how the population groups changed over time." (timing of the document)

- "The numbers in these census figures might be inexact because of the difficulty of counting widely dispersed people over a hundred years ago. The numbers seem rounded and may be educated guesses." (reliability)

For Document 2:

- "The Constitution of 1876 reflects the official governmental laws and may not accurately represent the reality within the empire." (type of document)

- "The Constitution was most likely written by high government officials, who may have wanted the Ottoman Empire to seem more enlightened than it actually was." (background of the authorship)

- "The Constitution's protection of rights may have been an attempt to calm the masses during a sensitive time of transition." (timing)

For Document 3:

- "Mr. Davis's speech may demonstrate anti-Muslim feelings that Europeans held at that time." (background of author and tone)

- "This speech given to a Christian group far away from the Ottoman Empire may be biased against the Ottoman government since the Ottomans were not in the mainstream of Western European society." (audience and reliability)

- "As a speech given in a British church, this document may have exaggerated the problems of the Ottoman government's treatment of Christians for dramatic effect." (type of document)

For Document 4:

- "As an Armenian, Mintzuri was very aware of the different ethnic groups representing the sultan's guard." (background of the author)

- "Since this recollection was published in Mintzuri's memoirs years after the event, the details may be inexact." (type of document)

- "As a lower-class baker's apprentice, Mintzuri may have had strong feelings about his low position in society and consequently recorded the arrangement of guards as a ranking based on status." (occupation of author)

For Document 5:

- "Suleyman Husnu Pasha, who had a title of distinction, was a former advisor to the sultan. Husnu's occupation had an effect on his opinion since he probably knew more about the conditions of the empire." (occupation of the author)

- "Since Suleyman Husnu Pasha was in political exile at the time of this document, he may have been more open about the situation in Iraq since he was not officially a part of the government." (background of the author)

- "Suleyman Husnu Pasha seems to hold a bias against the ethnic and religious minorities in Iraq, calling them 'hordes of the opposition.' This bias may have come from Husnu's loyalty to the official version of Islam and the Turkish language." (tone and background of author)

For Document 6:

- "As a respected Ottoman statesman, Ahmed Cevdet Pasha was representing the official government views toward the different ethnic groups in the empire." (occupation of the author)

- "Since Cevdet's comments were in the form of an official memo, this document reveals the view of someone close to the power center of the Ottoman Empire." (type of document)

- "Most likely Ahmed Cevdet Pasha was a Turk and a Muslim and therefore would look more favorably on the role of Muslims and Turks within the Ottoman Empire." (background of author)

For Document 7:

- "The Young Turks, as a revolutionary group of reformers, wanted the support of ethnic minorities. Consequently, they demanded complete liberty and equality in this proclamation to the people." (type of document, intended audience, and authorship)

- "The Young Turks wanted a new style of government. As a result they called on values different from those that had been practiced by the Ottoman officials." (background of authors)

- "Since this proclamation came in 1908 at the end of the sultan's rule, the message is more democratic and progressive than seen previously." (timing of document)

Some of the statements seem more sophisticated than others. Some of the statements may actually contradict each other. Even so, describing point of view is a skill that must be demonstrated for at least two documents.

Essays that use POV in a sophisticated manner and use it consistently are rewarded with expanded core points, if every other basic core point has been earned.

DO YOU GROUP THE DOCUMENTS TOGETHER IN YOUR ANALYSIS?

Historians analyze material by pulling together similar pieces of evidence, and in writing your DBQ, so should you. The documents naturally come together into groups for analysis. Within each of your body paragraphs, group the documents. Essays that successfully have two or three groupings, depending on the question, earn this core point.

Do not work with documents in isolation, since a group cannot have just one document. A common mistake is for students to describe each document in order, by paraphrasing what it says. This "listing" format is deadly to good performance on the DBQ.

Earlier were two paragraphs that served as examples of how to use and how not to use evidence to support your thesis. Let's look at these paragraphs again to see how effectively they group documents.

- "Document 1 is a chart with numbers for the different nationalities within the Ottoman Empire. Turks are 49.1% of the population. There are a lot of other groups listed too. The total population is about 28 million people. In document 2 the constitution says that the Sultan is the religious authority and the sovereign. It also says that Islam is the state religion and that 'the state will protect the free exercise of faiths professed in the Empire, and uphold the religious privileges granted to various bodies.'"

- "Document 1 is a chart that clearly demonstrates the ethnic diversity of the Ottoman Empire at the time of the new constitution. The Turks were a minority at 49.1% of the population, even though they controlled the government of the Ottoman Empire. The Constitution of 1876 (Document 2) *also reinforces* the idea that the empire was formed of various ethnicities and religions. It formally states that all people are granted equality, and that all religions answer to the same law. However, this document reflects the law from the point of view of high government officials. It therefore demonstrates only the legal rules, rather than the day-to-day reality in the empire."

In example 1, the documents are discussed independently. In example 2, they are discussed together.

How you group documents is a matter of personal opinion. Typical groupings include:

- Chronological timing of the documents (grouped by time periods of the documents)
- Class, gender, occupation, and ethnicity of the documents' authors
- Purpose or intended audience of the documents (grouped by who was supposed to read the document)
- Attitude and tone of the documents (favorable or unfavorable to a certain issue or group)

- Aspects covered by the documents (economic, political, social, or religious)
- Geographic areas represented by the documents
- Type of documents (pictures, charts, written documents, transcripts of speeches)

For example, you could group the documents in the following ways:

By document type and intended audience:

- Official proclamations/constitutions (Documents 2 and 7)
- Ottoman internal correspondence (Documents 4 and 5)
- Documents intended for non-Ottoman audiences (Documents 1 and 3)

By attitudes toward ethnic and religious minorities:

- Documents that show inclusion (Documents 2, 4, and 7)
- Documents that show division (Documents 3, 4, 5, and 6)

By focus on types of groups:

- Documents that focus on religious groups (Documents 2, 3, 5, 6, and 7)
- Documents that focus on ethnic groups (Documents 1, 4, 6, and 7)

You can group documents in a variety of ways. A single document can even be used in more than one group within an essay. You are encouraged to group documents in as many appropriate ways as possible.

> **AP EXPERT TIP**
>
> Notice that a comparison is used to indicate that the documents are related and thus a grouping. Using comparisons tells the reader that you are analyzing documents, not just listing them.

ORGANIZING YOUR DOCUMENTS

A simple way to organize your grouping is to indicate why you are grouping documents together in your topic sentence. For example: "The Ottoman Constitution of 1876 (Document 2) and the Proclamation of the Young Turks (Document 6) both indicate that the Ottoman rulers wanted to ensure that all of their subjects understood that they were equal before the law. In the Ottoman Constitution, subjects are _____, while in the Proclamation of the Young Turks, subjects are _____." Make sure that when you list two or more documents in a grouping sentence you actually address each document. If you forget to actually use the document, it will cost you the core point for not using all of the documents.

DO YOU SUGGEST AND EXPLAIN THE NEED FOR AN ADDITIONAL DOCUMENT?

When doing research, historians continuously ask the question, Where else could valuable information be found on this topic? Historians are in constant search of new areas of inquiry and new sources to explain the past. Since the DBQ is the essay that asks you to be a historian, your essay needs to provide suggestions for additional documents that could be useful in answering the question. These suggestions should not be types of documents that are *already* present in the DBQ, but rather the "missing voice" not already included in the list of documents.

For this task, you do not need to be very specific; you do not even need to mention a specific document. All you need to do is mention a type of document that could be useful in answering the question asked. The readers of the AP essay do not expect that high school students would have knowledge of hidden documents in some archive that might shed light on this topic. General statements involving hypothetical types of documents would be fine, *even if* they do not really exist.

Just as important as mentioning a potentially useful additional type of document is describing *why* it would be useful. To earn this basic core point, therefore, you need to include mention of an additional document and an explanation about why it would be useful in analyzing the question. Unfortunately, students frequently mention a type of additional document without describing why.

For our sample DBQ, examples of additional documents could be:

- A document from the sultan himself since he represents the central power of the Ottoman Empire

- Official orders from the Ottoman government on how to treat different ethnic and religious subjects, since such a document could show how the government implemented its policies

- A chart showing statistics of religious diversity within the empire that would help describe the position of the official faith within the empire

- A speech or article from a Young Turk on his attitude toward the Ottoman government that would help show the differences in thought between reformers and officials

- A document from a religious leader within the Ottoman Empire that would provide a sense of how official religious policies were perceived by the religious communities themselves

- A map showing the distribution of different ethnic groups within the Ottoman Empire, which would help illustrate the divisions faced by this multi-ethnic country

Any of these responses or any combination of these would receive a basic core point for the additional document(s). Other potential responses would also be counted if their importance could be explained.

Be careful: Mentioning a type of document that already exists disqualifies the statement. For our sample DBQ, mentioning a document from a person outside of the Ottoman Empire would not count since document 3 is written from a British perspective. Nor would mentioning a document from an ethnic or religious minority within the Ottoman Empire count, since document 4 is written by an Armenian in Istanbul. To make sure that you get this basic core point, you may want to mention two or three different types of additional documents and why each would be useful.

Often students mention an additional document at the end of the essay. Discussion of the additional document can take place anywhere in the essay. Often, the most sophisticated essays will have the discussion of the additional documents as part of the body of the essay.

DO YOU GO BEYOND THE BASIC REQUIREMENTS?

Your goal for the DBQ is to earn all 7 basic core points. Students who earn scores of 7 are well on track for success. But what about the additional 2 points—the expanded core points—which would elevate your essays even further above the norm? For those, you must first have earned all 7 of the basic core points.

Earning expanded core points is not as straightforward as earning basic core points. For the basic core, either your essay has a thesis or it does not. Either your essay analyzes documents through grouping or it does not. And so on.

For the expanded core, several indicators of excellence may come into play. For instance, an essay that earns expanded core points might:

- Have a highly sophisticated thesis
- Show deep analysis of the documents
- Use documents persuasively in broad conceptual ways
- Analyze point of view thoughtfully and consistently
- Identify multiple additional documents with sophisticated explanations of their usefulness
- Bring in relevant outside information beyond the historical background provided

Expanded core points are awarded to essays that do the tasks of the basic core really well. Instead of just having an acceptable thesis or just two references to point of view, an essay would have an outstanding thesis and refer to point of view with almost every document.

Knowledge of outside information is not required for the DBQ. If you have some basic knowledge of the period, however, incorporate that information into your essay. For our sample DBQ, you may know that one of the leaders of the Young Turks was Mustafa Kemal Attaturk, who later became the leader of the Republic of Turkey. Or you may know that officials of the Ottoman Empire committed mass murder against the Armenians during World War I. Neither of these ideas needs to be mentioned in order to do well on the DBQ, yet if they were included, your essay would be set apart from the rest and would likely earn extra expanded core points (as long as your essay met the other basic core point criteria).

Readers have the option of awarding 2, 1, or 0 expanded core points. Even essays that earn the highest score of 9 might not be perfect, but they have done the tasks of the DBQ very well.

FINAL NOTES ON HOW TO WRITE THE DBQ

The following list of items applies specifically to the DBQ. More general essay-writing hints appear later in this chapter.

Do:

- Take notes in the margins during the reading period relating to the background of the speaker and his or her possible point of view

- Assume that each document provides only a snapshot of the topic—just one perspective

- Look for connections between documents for grouping

- Mark off documents that you use in the green booklet so that you do not forget to mention them

- Refer to the authorship of the documents as you are writing, not just the document numbers

- Mention additional documents and the reasons why they would help further analyze the question

- Mark off each part of the instructions for the essay as you accomplish them

- Use visual and graphic information in non-text based documents

Don't:

- Repeat information from the historical background in your essay

- Assume that the documents are universally valid rather than presenting a single perspective

- Spend too much time on the DBQ rather than moving on to the other two essays

- Write the first paragraph before you have a clear idea of what your thesis will be

- Ignore part of the question

- Structure the essay with just one paragraph

- Underline or highlight the thesis (this may be done as an exercise for class, but on the test it looks juvenile)

HOW TO APPROACH THE CONTINUITY AND CHANGE-OVER-TIME QUESTION

The continuity and change-over-time (CCOT) question **asks what has changed and what has not.** Here, you must be as detailed as possible with your knowledge of the material. Being good at historical interpretation is not enough; you also need to know history.

ORGANIZING YOUR ESSAY IN 5 MINUTES

The CCOT question includes a definite time span for analysis. The time span may have the same division dates as the main structural periods for the course: 8000 BCE, 600 CE, 1450 CE, 1750 CE, 1900 CE, and the present. Start by reading the question. Underline the parts that are most important for your essay. Let's look at an example:

> Analyze the continuities and changes in social structure in ONE of the following regions between 1900 and the present.
>
> • Russia
>
> • China

For this example, you may want to underline the term *social structure* and the dates *between 1900 and the present.* To adequately answer this question, you need to have a good handle on what "social structure" actually means. Vocabulary is not tested on the AP exam, but knowing how to define terms can make a big difference in interpreting the questions. You would be in trouble with this question if you did not know what social structure meant.

For world history, **social structure** refers to the ways in which a society might organize relations between people. Such structures might include different gender roles for women and men, different ways that social classes interact, different racial and ethnic groups, and different patterns for family and work. One of the themes of the AP course is "development and transformation of social structure." As these themes form the building blocks for the course, fluency with these ideas and their applications will help you decode what the questions are asking.

Continuity refers to those aspects that remained the same during the entire stretch of the time period. In this way, it is the *opposite* of the word **change.**

The best way to organize your thoughts for the CCOT question is to construct a crude time line in the green question booklet. Remember that the readers do not look at the green booklet when scoring—they look only at the pink answer booklet. Putting together a time line might take a minute or two, but it is helpful. Let's look at a sample time line for the Russian response.

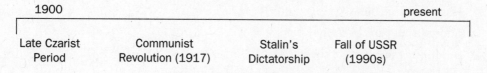

1900   present

Late Czarist   Communist   Stalin's   Fall of USSR
Period   Revolution (1917)   Dictatorship   (1990s)

As is, this time line is inadequate. Though it mentions some of the great division points in 20th-century political history, it does not address social structure. A discussion of social structure is the main point of the essay, so if your essay response included only political issues, you would be responding to a question that had not been asked. In that case, your score would drop dramatically.

In your time line notes, you will want to write about social changes that happened. How did gender, family, work, and class structures change? You may remember that communism brought about huge changes in women's legal status and equality or that many people were persecuted because of their social class, especially during Stalin's dictatorship. Collective farming and the changes in work patterns resulting from the forced industrialization under Stalin would also be good information to note, especially since they represented a sharp change from the peasant labor system from before the revolution. Recent changes after the collapse of the U.S.S.R. involved capitalist work patterns and a social structure modeled on Western ideas.

Your time line and notes might start out as follows, but you would add information as you think of them.

1900			present
Late Czarist Period	Communist Revolution (1917)	Stalin's Dictatorship	Fall of USSR (1990s)
Peasant labor for rich landlords	Women's equality and revolutionary involvement	Labor thru collectives Persecution by social class	Capitalist labor Western influence

So far, the notes have provided several examples of changes, but nothing yet for continuity. **Do not forget to mention what has stayed the same.** Jot down at least two ideas for continuities throughout this time period—perhaps that Russian and Soviet society did not allow women to rise to the highest positions of power and that common working-class people suffered low standards of living throughout the time period.

CORE POINT SCORING

The CCOT question uses a 7-point basic core point system, with an additional expanded core of 2. The 7 points of the basic core are divided among five tasks: two of the tasks count for 2 core points, with a partial credit of 1 point awarded in some instances.

Points	Task
1	Has acceptable thesis
2	Addresses all parts of the question
(1)	(Addresses most parts of the question)
2	Substantiates thesis with appropriate historical evidence

(1)   (Partially substantiates thesis with appropriate historical evidence)

  1   Uses relevant world historical context effectively to explain continuity and change over time

__1__ Analyzes the process of continuity and change over time

  7   Subtotal for all basic core points

__2__ Possible number of points earned for the expanded core

  9   TOTAL possible points for the CCOT

As was the case for the DBQ, the goal for your performance on the CCOT should be to meet all of the core points. Excellent essays may earn points beyond the basic core, but those that earn 7 points are very good indeed.

DO YOU HAVE A THESIS?

Your initial task is to present a clear thesis statement. Do not simply restate the question. Instead, mention specifics about continuity and change. A strong thesis will deal with both what changed and what stayed the same. Since this essay is based on chronological reasoning, the thesis also must reference the time span of the question. Let's continue with our sample question.

> Analyze the continuities and changes in social structure in ONE of the following regions between 1900 and the present.
>
> • Russia
>
> • China

THESIS STATEMENTS THAT DON'T WORK

As common as it may be, the following statement is worthless as a thesis. It lacks the specificity required to set up the analysis in the essay.

> There are many ways that Russia changed between 1900 and the present and many things that stayed the same.

The phrase "There are many" is a terrible way to start an essay; it indicates weak writing and weak analysis. Avoid this kind of sentence construction.

The three-way divided thesis presented next is typically a good way to structure the analysis of an AP essay, yet here, it fails on two counts: It mentions neither social structure nor continuities. It would likely not receive credit as a thesis.

> Russia changed most dramatically as a result of the Communist Revolution, the dictatorship of Stalin, and the collapse of the Soviet Union.

This next thesis is simply incorrect. To count as a thesis, the statement must be correct. You should find at least one major social issue that stayed the same. The claim that "no continuities exist" is a cop-out.

> Russian society changed from a country of horrible poverty during the Czarist time
> to one of perfect equality and general prosperity under the rule of Stalin. Nothing
> remained the same, so no continuities existed during this time period.

The next thesis deals with changes and continuities outside of the time period from 1900 to the present. Serf emancipation occurred in Russia in 1861, and Czarist rule ended in 1917. Also notice that this statement and the two previous statements do not make reference to the dates or the time span of the question.

> With the emancipation of the serfs, Russian society shifted from one based on
> forced labor to one based on modern wage labor. Strict Czarist rule remained the same.

Although this next statement would receive credit as a thesis, the essay would likely be headed for problems. Stick to material on either Russia or China—not both.

> Social structure in both China and Russia changed most dramatically from 1900
> to the present because of the role of communism. The condition of lower-class workers,
> however, remained the same in both China and Russia.

THESIS STATEMENTS THAT DO WORK

A successful thesis statement has specific information on both changes and continuities:

> Three aspects of society changed dramatically in Russia between 1900 and the
> present: gender roles, work patterns, and class structure. An important continuity
> would be the condition of the working class.

DO YOU ADDRESS ALL PARTS OF THE QUESTION?

The CCOT question often requires the analysis of change and continuity. If an essay neglects one of these two aspects—almost always, *continuity* is the one left out—then it may not receive the full 2 points. Neglecting to mention **what stays the same** may be a tragic pitfall.

To correctly analyze continuity, you must consider the entire time span of the question, in this case, from 1900 to the present. The continuities mentioned in the essay must apply for the whole period. The following thesis statement, for instance, does not address continuity for the periods 1900 to 1917 and 1991 to the present.

> During the time of the Soviet Union, a continuity would be that the government
> officially proclaimed social equality. The reality, however, was social inequality.

Our sample question asks only for the analysis of social structure. If it had asked instead, "analyze the changes and continuities in social and *political* structure," then you would need to address both items to receive the full 2 points. A CCOT question can ask for two, even three, areas of analysis. Remember to cover them all.

Also important is the issue of setting chronological boundaries. Each CCOT essay has a starting date and an ending date. A description of the background situation for a given area at the time of the starting date is helpful for understanding how things later change. For our sample question, a paragraph on Russian social structure in 1900 would frame the discussion that followed.

> Russian society in 1900 existed much as it had for centuries. The largest social class was the enormous peasant class, who toiled on land owned mostly by landlords. The Czar was at the top of the social structure, followed by the nobles. The Russian Orthodox Church provided the social glue that held all of the classes together. On the eve of World War I, factories were beginning to change the social dynamics of urban areas, where the working class was heavily exploited. Within Russian society women had few rights and almost no ability to demonstrate political leadership.

This discussion would work best as a second paragraph, directly following the thesis/introductory paragraph. It sets up the analysis that is to come later about the changes and continuities of Russian society. Similarly, a paragraph near the end of the essay about the situation at *present* would serve as a sophisticated balance to the whole essay.

Do You Use Enough Facts to Support Your Thesis?

For the DBQ, no outside knowledge is required. For the CCOT, however, this is not the case. A strong essay must have facts. If it has many facts, it will earn 2 basic core points. If it has a few facts, it will earn 1 point.

How many facts are needed and what counts as a fact completely depends on the question. For our sample question, material must relate to social structure. Facts on politics, the revolutions, or the economy would not count unless they were linked to a discussion of social structure. In addition, the facts must be correct and within the chronological boundaries of the question.

Many people think of *historical facts* as names, dates, and events of history— "Columbus sailed the ocean blue in 1492." Though these things indeed count as facts, specific statements that relate to the question count as well. For example:

> Women participated in many aspects of the Communist Revolution.

> Workers received little to no material benefits from Stalin's drive to industrialize the Soviet Union.

AP EXPERT TIP

A good rule of thumb is to have at least three or more facts related to changes and three or more facts related to continuities. Aim for eight total facts and you will most likely score both points.

> The Orthodox Church lost its position of prominence in Russian society when the communists took control.

> In recent years, Russian society has been structured with more capitalist values.

All of these statements are correct and relevant to the question; they all deal with social structure. As such, they would count as facts.

Statements that are incorrect certainly do not help your score, but neither do they count against you in terms of core points. As with information outside of the time boundaries or statements that don't address the precise question, errors don't necessarily count against your score. Even essays that earn the top score of 9 may have small factual errors. Avoid errors, to be sure, but understand that a factual misstatement won't sink your chances at a good score.

Do You Discuss the Global Context of the Changes and Continuities?

When answering the CCOT question, you must explain how events in one area relate to the big picture; that is, you need to discuss the global context of the changes and continuities.

The global context point can be earned by effectively showing:

- Connections to global processes
- Interactions among regions

A simple statement is all that is required to earn this basic core point. Any of the following statements would be considered accurate:

> After World War II, the Soviet Union forced Eastern European countries to adopt communist social structure.

(Interaction among regions)

> Social roles in the former Soviet Union changed dramatically during the early 1990s as part of a worldwide movement away from communism.

(Connection to global process)

At some point during your essay, you must **think big**. The CCOT question is designed to focus on large global issues such as trade, technology, culture, social systems, and migrations. Making connections to global processes should come as a natural part of writing about the topic.

Do You Analyze the Changes Over Time and the Continuities?

Analysis is a critical skill when writing college-level essays. Analysis means asking *why* the changes and continuities occurred. The skill it requires involves a deeper kind of thinking than simply remembering facts to support a thesis.

Analysis works best when it is integrated into the body paragraphs. Readers do not typically look to the thesis statement for the analysis core point, though a strong thesis should indeed have some analysis.

For our question on the changes and continuities of Russian or Chinese social structures, think about *why* some conditions changed and why others stayed the same. Since analysis asks *why*, your essay should include the word *because*: "This is significant because…" "This changed over time because…"

Following are some examples of analysis:

> Social structure changed the most in Russia after the Russian Revolution because the new Soviet leaders adopted many of the ideas of sexual equality and class equality found in Karl Marx's writings. The social structures changed again at the end of the 20th century when the Soviet Union collapsed, and Russian society rapidly rushed toward free-market capitalism.

> The working class in Russia and the Soviet Union had low standards of living throughout the 20th century because any economic gains were focused elsewhere, such as on the military and the ruling elite. Even after the collapse of the Soviet Union, the working class was still poor because of the underdeveloped Russian economy.

> Rapid industrialization was the major cause of why Soviet society changed so much in the middle decades of the 20th century.

(This sentence does not include *because*, but it does explain the cause of industrialism.)

Do You Go Beyond the Basic Requirements?

Once a CCOT essay has met all 7 basic core points, it is eligible for up to 2 additional points. These points are awarded for excellence above the basic core point standards. Indicators of excellence might include the following:

- A clear and analytical thesis
- An abundance of evidence
- Particularly sophisticated connections to global processes
- Clear chronology with the use of dates associated with events
- Links to a rich variety of events, ideas, and trends
- Deep and even coverage of all parts of the question
- A thorough discussion of continuity in addition to change

> **AP EXPERT TIP**
>
> The scoring rubric for both the CCOT and comparative essays tells readers that information in the thesis cannot be used for other points on the essay.

FINAL NOTES ON HOW TO WRITE THE CCOT

Do:

- Read the question several times so that you understand the tasks required
- Draw a quick time line in order to organize your thoughts
- Write a thesis statement that uses the terms of the question while providing analysis
- Describe in a paragraph the situation at the starting point of the time span
- Focus on continuities, not just changes
- Make sure the continuities cover the entire time span of the question
- Bring in a discussion of the big-picture context of these changes through global processes
- Mention facts—remember, content is king

Don't:

- Discuss events that are not related to the question
- Include long sections of material outside the time span of the question
- Focus only on changes and not on continuities
- Include continuities that apply only to one part of the time span

HOW TO APPROACH THE COMPARATIVE QUESTION

By the last essay of this exam, most students are exhausted. At best, their hands are tired. At worst, they have not managed their time well and have only a few minutes to complete a task that counts for one-sixth of their entire score.

As a result, the third essay is often the weakest of the group. It does not need to be this way. The comparative question (the COMP) **asks what is the same and what is different.** It requires a task familiar to historians and nonhistorians alike: analyzing similarities and differences. As a student, you should be used to making comparisons—whether it is comparing teachers or comparing Coke and Pepsi. Unlike the CCOT, which focuses on changes and continuities across time, the COMP focuses on similarities and differences between areas.

By the time you reach the COMP, take a deep breath, stretch out your arms, wiggle your fingers, and dive into it with the best that you have. Your handwriting may be messier than it was on the DBQ, but fortunately AP readers are accustomed to reading all sorts of handwriting. Consequently, don't take the time to rewrite an essay to make it look more presentable—an essay cannot earn points for neatness and cannot lose points for sloppiness.

Even so, try to make your essay as neat as possible: If you have sloppy handwriting, don't abbreviate words. If you are a poor speller, do not disguise the problem by writing difficult words with a few letters at the beginning and then a scribble. Moreover, don't include too many arrows that point to inserted sentences elsewhere in the essay—they just make the whole essay less readable.

ORGANIZING YOUR ESSAY IN 5 MINUTES

Typically, the COMP asks you to analyze a broad historical issue or issues for two areas of the world. Often, several areas are listed, and you have a choice. If given a choice, pick those areas you know the most facts in relation to the question.

As always, underlining and note-taking are important. Even a few notes jotted down in the green booklet can make your essay more focused. Let's look at an example:

Compare and contrast the dynamics of trade in TWO of the following regions for the periods mentioned:

- China during the Qin and Han dynasties (third century BCE to third century CE)

- The Mediterranean during the Roman Empire (first century BCE to fourth century CE)

- Mesoamerica during the Mayan Empires (fourth century CE to 11th century CE)

- South America during the Incan Empire (13th century CE to 16th century CE)

CORE POINT SCORING

The COMP is scored in much the same way as the CCOT—up to 7 basic core points in five task areas. Though the essays are fundamentally different, several of the tasks are the same.

Points	Task
1	Has acceptable thesis
2	Addresses all parts of the question
(1)	(Addresses most parts of the question)
2	Substantiates thesis with appropriate historical evidence
(1)	(Partially substantiates thesis with appropriate historical evidence)
1	Makes at least one relevant, direct comparison between or among societies
1	Analyzes at least one reason for a similarity or difference
7	Subtotal for all basic core points
2	Possible number of points earned for the expanded core
9	TOTAL possible points for the COMP

> ### AP EXPERT TIP
>
> COMP questions often ask you to provide information about specific regions like the Mediterranean or Mesoamerica. You should familiarize yourself with the regions and their empires, countries, etc., as outlined in the AP World History course description. Note that the question does not indicate specific political entities during the time frames. You are expected to know based on the time frames indicated that the first region would be the Qin and Han dynasties, the second region the Roman Empire, the third region the Mayan Empire, and the fourth region the Incan Empire.

Do You Have a Thesis?

For our sample essay, a thesis must compare both the similarities and differences for trade for two areas. Our example again:

> Compare and contrast the dynamics of trade in TWO of the following regions for the periods mentioned:
>
> - China during the Qin and Han dynasties
>   (third century BCE to third century CE)
> - The Mediterranean during the Roman Empire
>   (first century BCE to fourth century CE)
> - Mesoamerica during the Mayan Empire
>   (fourth century CE to 11th century CE)
> - South America during the Incan Empire
>   (13th century CE to 16th century CE)

Thesis Statements That Don't Work

The following statement discusses technology instead of trade. It most likely would not receive a basic core point for the thesis. Even so, the facts are good.

> In Mayan culture the elites used a form of hieroglyphic writing to keep records while elites in the Incan society used a complex method of knot tying called quipu to keep records.

The next statement uses all four areas instead of selecting two of the four. It demonstrates wasted effort.

> In both the Mayan and Incan societies, trade occurred mostly within their empire by land. For the Chinese and Roman societies trade occurred by land with the Silk Road, but also by water.

Thesis Statements That Do Work

The thesis statement does not need to be sophisticated. It just needs to cover differences and similarities for both areas in trade and technology.

> Trade dynamics in the Roman Empire centered around the Mediterranean Sea. In China, however, they used rivers for trade. Both societies used water routes to transport goods.

You will notice that this statement is three sentences long. If a thesis is usually defined as one sentence, you may ask how can this count as the thesis? For the purposes of scoring COMP essays, the readers know that a question of this complexity might require a long thesis.

This next example answers the question with greater sophistication and discusses the reasons behind the similarities and differences.

> The greatest similarity between the Han and the Roman Empires involved trade since both were linked by the Silk Road and both used the structures of empire to support transportation projects. The greatest difference was in the types of items traded by each civilization.

DO YOU ADDRESS ALL PARTS OF THE QUESTION?

To earn the full 2 basic core points, an essay on our sample question should do all of the following. To earn 1 point, it should do two of the three items.

- Address the issue of the dynamics of trade for both areas
- Provide an accurate similarity between the two areas
- Provide an accurate difference between the two areas

The biggest challenge with earning the points for this task is **mentioning similarities**. Remember that for the purposes of the AP World History exam, the term *compare* means **both** similarities and differences.

You may want to make a checklist so that all of the tasks of the question are addressed. A list for our sample question might look like this:

- Trade for Maya
- Trade for China
- Similarities for trade
- Differences for trade

Making this kind of list will help guide you to answering the question thoroughly. The information you provide, however, needs to be accurate. Also, the material that you provide to support the thesis may not count again for this task.

DO YOU USE ENOUGH FACTS TO SUPPORT YOUR THESIS?

Knowing facts about your topic is critical for scoring well on the COMP. Two points are awarded if an essay mentions several correct facts about both areas. One point may be earned if the facts are minimal or deal almost entirely with one area.

Information that is incorrect obviously does not receive credit as facts. And material not pertaining to the question does not receive credit. For our sample question, the essay's information would need to concern trade dynamics and/or technology in order to count as a fact.

AP EXPERT TIP

Evidence does not
have to be evenly
distributed between
the two regions. But
you do have to have
at least one piece of
evidence for each
region. A strong essay
will have at least four
comparisons: two
differences and two
similarities or any
combination of three
and one.

The following would count as facts for the sake of the basic core scoring:

- The Incan road system facilitated trade from one region of the empire to another.
- Roman ships carried wheat, wine, and olive oil throughout the Mediterranean Sea area.
- Mayan city-states traded among each other for mostly elite items such as feathers and slaves.
- Chinese trade expanded dramatically through the Silk Road during the Han dynasty.

If you mentioned that gunpowder was transferred by Chinese trade, the statement would not receive credit as a fact—gunpowder was developed around the 10th century in China, significantly later than the time of the Han dynasty. Since the question is specific in its time frame, the facts need to fit.

Likewise, mention of political accomplishment—a unified China under one dynasty, let's say—would not count unless it was related to a larger discussion of trade dynamics.

DO YOU MAKE A SOLID COMPARISON BETWEEN THE SOCIETIES?

This basic core point should be easy to earn. In writing a comparative essay, you should be making plenty of direct comparisons. Essays that make at least one relevant and substantial direct comparison between the two societies earn this basic core point. To earn the point, the comparison cannot be found in the thesis.

Many students, however, write essays in which the comparisons are indirect. Their flawed essays start with an introductory thesis paragraph and are followed by paragraphs about the first area, followed by entirely separate paragraphs about the second area. Perhaps these essays have plenty of facts and even address most parts of the question, but they never get around to making a substantial direct comparison.

Direct comparisons should go beyond just a statement of a simple similarity or difference. They should refer to both regions by name and mention a substantial comparison.

The way to avoid that kind of organizational problem is to **weave comparisons within each paragraph**. For our sample question, we have paragraphs on technology in which both regions are discussed—similarities and differences. The same could be done with trade dynamics. When both areas are addressed simultaneously, the essay is more likely to make direct comparisons.

DO YOU ANALYZE THE REASONS FOR THE SIMILARITIES AND DIFFERENCES?

Analysis is crucial for building a sophisticated COMP essay. One basic core point is awarded to essays that state clear reasons why the similarities or differences existed. This analysis must go beyond simply listing the items in common or the differences.

The following statements may earn the basic core point for analysis on the COMP:

> The Romans and Incas had elaborate roads because both had empires that stretched across vast territories.

> Rome was located on the Mediterranean Sea, consequently its trade was water-based to a great extent. The Incan Empire differed since its location within Mesoamerica meant that its trade was not as focused on water travel.

DO YOU GO BEYOND THE BASIC REQUIREMENTS?

If your essay scores all 7 basic core points, it is eligible for up to 2 expanded core points. Essays that earn those expanded points may include some or all of the following indicators:

- A clear and analytical thesis

- An abundance of evidence

- Comparisons related to larger global processes

- Clear mention of similarities as well as differences

- Explanations for the reasons why the differences and similarities existed

- Frequent and consistent direct comparisons between areas

- Comparisons made within regions in addition to between areas

These indicators show a kind of sophistication that separates the truly great essays from the merely acceptable ones.

FINAL NOTES ON HOW TO WRITE THE COMP

Do:

- Treat the COMP question with the same degree of focus as the other two essays. All three essays are worth the same number of points

- Use all of the 130 minutes for organizing and writing the essays

- Select regions for which you have the most factual information

- Write a thesis that addresses all aspects of the question

- Make a checklist of tasks that must be completed
- Include both similarities and differences between the two areas
- Use comparative words and phrases to join ideas together
- Write paragraphs in which both areas are discussed together
- Mention plenty of facts for both areas
- Analyze why the similarities and differences occur

Don't:

- Rewrite complete essays—rarely is the extra time investment worth it (this rule goes for all three essays!)
- Favor one area to the exclusion of the other
- Mention facts that are not focused on the topic of the question
- Discuss each area in isolation

STRESS MANAGEMENT

The high school AP program is intended to provide rigorous college-level course material. AP World History, in particular, deals with high-level analytical connections between different places and times. This is hard work.

But what if your AP class is not up to par? Maybe it is enrolled with more students than the teacher can effectively teach. Maybe the textbook resources are not at the college level or do not reflect the topics covered on the exam. What if your teacher is not thoroughly trained for teaching AP World History?

Certainly, if you are in this situation, you are at a disadvantage. But this does not mean that you cannot succeed. Thousands of students succeed with the AP exams despite having subpar AP classes—or no AP class at all.

You, too, can succeed, but it will take extra work and diligence. Much of this work will need to be done through your own independent study.

You have already taken the first step. The review book in your hands provides detailed information about the exam and the course. Read over its chapters several times, especially those chapters that cover unfamiliar aspects of the course. Take the Diagnostic Test and full-length practice tests and analyze the results. This book should not be considered as a replacement for a rigorous AP course, but it can certainly help solidify content knowledge and skills.

Second, you will need a quality college-level textbook. A good one will have about 1,000 densely packed pages of writing, documents, and illustrations. For recommended textbooks and their support websites, see the list on page 10.

Third, you can use the resources of the Internet to help you connect to the class websites of top college professors of world history. Often, college professors will post their lecture notes and assignments online. Following these notes can help you supplement a less-than-perfect situation in your own classroom. You can also learn more about the AP World History exam by examining www.student.collegeboard.org. The official AP World History course description, which includes information about what students are expected to know for the exam, can be downloaded in pdf format on the AP website.

Finally, you may want to create a study group with other students who are in the same situation as you. Divide the review tasks and help share review notes. Use the world history themes and chronological periods listed in chapter 1 to help organize responsibilities. Have a fixed agenda when the group meets so that the gatherings will be more productive.

COUNTDOWN TO THE TEST

Preparation for the AP World History exam should be an ongoing process from the beginning of your class to the day before the exam. **Six weeks before** the exam—which is about the time for Spring Break for most high school students—review should begin in earnest. Spend one week on each of the sections in Part 3 that correspond to the chronological divisions of the course.

The **week or two before** the exam, fill the gaps in your preparation. Perhaps the material at the start of the course has faded from your memory. Perhaps you never had a solid grasp of gender structure among different societies. Perhaps you did not cover the history of Latin America thoroughly the first time. Find your weaknesses and make them your strong points. This review book, along with your textbook, will help provide the missing content.

Chart out a plan of attack. Be realistic, however, and don't overextend yourself. Your review will not be as effective if you are losing a great deal of sleep studying for the AP World History exam. Certainly, part of your strategy before test day should be to practice exam questions. Use the questions in this book to become more confident with the concept of pacing. You will also want to work ahead on projects for classes other than AP World History so that your schedule is as clear as possible right before the test.

The **day before** the exam, shift your studying strategy. Instead of reading content, you may want to look over the pictures, maps, and illustrations in your textbook. Or you may want to read over the guidelines for the essay questions listed earlier in this book.

> ## AP EXPERT TIP
>
> Create a list of key terms like *nation-state* and even common words like *commerce,* and quiz yourself on their meanings. This is not an exam you can cram for. There is literally too much information. As indicated, start reviewing early—at least six weeks out. A glossary appears in the back of this book.

AP EXPERT TIP

If your teacher
or school offers
extracurricular review
sessions, try to attend
them. If your school
doesn't, there may
be a school nearby
that does. Ask if you
can attend. Some
schools or districts
run a practice exam.
Attending a full-
session practice
exam is one of the
best ways to prepare,
as it makes sure you
understand the rigor
of taking this 3+ hour
exam and allows you
to practice your time
management skills.

Retire early the night before the exam. Sleep well—but don't get more sleep than normal. Eat healthy food for dinner and for breakfast the next morning. Follow a normal routine. In the morning, read a few pages of a favorite piece of literature to get your mind moving in a thoughtful direction.

On the day of the exam, avoid unnecessary anxiety. Arrive early. Most likely the exam will not be in the same place as your classroom. Know where the room is located and when the test is starting.

Keep your distance from other students who are freaked out; they will only make you more anxious.

Keep your cell phone far away from the exam room. The Educational Testing Service has strict policies prohibiting the use and even the possession of cellular telephones during the AP exam and during the break. New advances in text messaging and photo messaging have created problems with test security and cell phones. Nothing would be worse than having your exam score disqualified for a breach of the rules.

You will not be allowed to drink or eat during the exam. You will be given a short break between the multiple-choice and essay sections. This break would be a good time for a light snack.

Make sure to bring the following items:

- A watch or other timepiece (without an alarm)
- A number 2 pencil with a good eraser
- A dark pen (black is best)
- An extra pencil and pen
- Photo ID
- Your Social Security number (or other government-issued identification number)

Right before you step into the exam room, you may want to stretch your muscles. The increased blood flow will help you think better, and the more limber muscles will make sitting in a chair for three hours more comfortable.

PACING DURING THE TEST

The AP World History exam is a timed test. Your strategy during the exam should be to use all available time without leaving anything out. During the exam, you should be very aware of the passage of time. On the multiple-choice section, do not linger over any questions. Either guess after using the process of elimination, or circle the question and leave it for later. Check frequently as you bubble in answers so that the numbers for the questions and the numbers for the answers match. Remember, you can write in and mark up all of the exam question booklets.

Also be sure during the multiple-choice section that you don't rush through the questions without reading or thinking about them thoroughly. Nobody can leave the exam room before the full 55-minute session, and no advantage is gained by being the first person done. Likewise, don't be distracted by people who seem to be finishing faster. You have 55 minutes; use the time to its best potential.

If you finish a few minutes before the end of the multiple-choice section, go back to review those questions that you left blank. But be careful: most students run into problems when they change answers from an earlier response. Your first intuition is more likely to be correct. Answer all of the questions on the multiple-choice section, since there is no penalty for incorrect responses.

Pacing is equally important on the essay section. The first 10 minutes is designated as a reading period, in which you may not write in the answer booklet. Use this time for reading and organizing for your DBQ essay.

THINKING AHEAD

Glance at the CCOT and COMP questions. If you recognize one, quickly jot down evidence before writing the DBQ. Your brain will unconsciously process information while you are doing the DBQ, and when you get to the other two essays you will already have a head start.

The three essays can be done in any order. All three call for an equal amount of time and have equal weight in the final score. Shoot for 40 minutes on each. Spending much less than 40 minutes writing the DBQ is not advised; it is so complex that it requires the full amount of time. The CCOT and the COMP can also be very complex. Rushing through these often leads to incomplete essays and lower scores.

If you have time remaining, read over the essay questions again to make sure that you have answered every aspect of them. Only when you have written all that you can should you go back and read over your essays. Spelling errors and grammatical problems do not lower an essay's score. Even so, you should correct any problems that you encounter. A simple cross-out is fine; blotting out errors with lots of ink just looks messy.

AP EXPERT TIP

Review your DBQ
to ensure that you
have used all the
documents, have at
least two groupings,
at least two POVs, and
at least one additional
document. Look at
the CCOT for both
change and continuity
and the COMP for
both similarities and
differences.

The last piece of advice deals with conclusions. Both English and history teachers emphasize the importance of conclusions for strong essay writing. Strong, sophisticated conclusions certainly leave AP readers with good impressions of the essays just before they mark the score. A thoughtful conclusion can never hurt an essay. If you don't think that your thesis paragraph is strong enough, write another paragraph as a conclusion with more specificity and analysis than your first one.

On the other hand, many conclusions don't help AP World History essays nearly as much as one might expect. Your most important task when writing these essays is to have all of the indicators for the basic core scoring. If you have only a few minutes remaining, spend the time writing a solid body paragraph of factual analysis. The last paragraph should not rehash what has been said earlier in the essay. Such conclusions are not all that valuable since an idea can only receive credit once.

The most valuable conclusions are ones that contain an analytical thesis or that include analysis that was lacking in the rest of the essay; a DBQ conclusion that mentions two possible additional documents; the CCOT conclusion that makes a solid point about continuities across the time period; the COMP conclusion that has a direct relevant comparison between societies. You might be able to tie the whole essay together for the first time at the very end. These conclusions are extremely useful.

Part Two

DIAGNOSTIC TEST

AP WORLD HISTORY DIAGNOSTIC TEST

The Diagnostic Test is a brief multiple-choice exam to help you identify your strengths and weaknesses in AP World History. The goal is to help you determine the areas that you should focus on while studying. The questions are drawn from all areas covered on the actual AP World History exam.

To score your Diagnostic Test, go through the answers once you have completed the exam. Add up the number of questions you answered correctly and those you answered incorrectly.

If you score well, you are in terrific shape. Keep doing what you are doing. If you didn't score that high, you have some studying to do. This book should help a great deal.

DIAGNOSTIC TEST ANSWER GRID

To score your Diagnostic Test, count the number of questions you got right. To set this equal to a score out of 100, divide the number of questions you got right by 70. Then multiply that number by 100. The approximate score range is as follows:

80–100 (extremely well qualified)

60–79 (well qualified)

50–59 (qualified)

40–49 (possibly qualified)

0–39 (no recommendation)

1. A B C D	19. A B C D	37. A B C D	55. A B C D
2. A B C D	20. A B C D	38. A B C D	56. A B C D
3. A B C D	21. A B C D	39. A B C D	57. A B C D
4. A B C D	22. A B C D	40. A B C D	58. A B C D
5. A B C D	23. A B C D	41. A B C D	59. A B C D
6. A B C D	24. A B C D	42. A B C D	60. A B C D
7. A B C D	25. A B C D	43. A B C D	61. A B C D
8. A B C D	26. A B C D	44. A B C D	62. A B C D
9. A B C D	27. A B C D	45. A B C D	63. A B C D
10. A B C D	28. A B C D	46. A B C D	64. A B C D
11. A B C D	29. A B C D	47. A B C D	65. A B C D
12. A B C D	30. A B C D	48. A B C D	66. A B C D
13. A B C D	31. A B C D	49. A B C D	67. A B C D
14. A B C D	32. A B C D	50. A B C D	68. A B C D
15. A B C D	33. A B C D	51. A B C D	69. A B C D
16. A B C D	34. A B C D	52. A B C D	70. A B C D
17. A B C D	35. A B C D	53. A B C D	
18. A B C D	36. A B C D	54. A B C D	

DIAGNOSTIC TEST

Section I: Multiple-Choice Questions

Time: 55 Minutes
70 Questions

Directions: Each of the following questions or incomplete statements is followed by four suggested answers or completions. Select the one that is best in each case and then fill in the corresponding oval on the answer sheet.

1. Which of the following aspects did the Harrapan, Shang, and Sumerian civilizations have in common?

   (A) Horse-drawn plows
   (B) River-based settlements
   (C) Urban centers of over 100,000 people
   (D) Pastoral-based economy

2. The biggest environmental problem for ancient Mesopotamia was

   (A) deforestation
   (B) polluted drinking water
   (C) volcanic eruption
   (D) loss of soil fertility

3. Both early Christianity and Mahayana Buddhism shared which of the following religious ideas?

   (A) Personal salvation
   (B) Sacramental worship
   (C) Sacrificial offerings
   (D) Physical reincarnation

4. Cross-Asian trade of the first two centuries of the Common Era (CE)

   (A) used sleds to cross frozen areas of northern Asia
   (B) linked Polynesian islands to the urban centers of the Near East
   (C) relied on cowry shells as mediums of exchange
   (D) linked the Roman Empire with Chinese textile producers

5. Which of the following represents the greatest change in the Chinese political state during the reign of Emperor Qin Shihuangdi (third century BCE)?

   (A) Use of Confucian principles
   (B) Acceptance of Buddhism
   (C) Establishment of the civil service exams
   (D) Centralization of rule

GO ON TO THE NEXT PAGE

6. The Swahili language illustrates which of the following aspects of African civilization during the 1200s and 1300s CE?

   (A) Lack of linguistic diversity in Africa

   (B) Growth of West African empires

   (C) Connection to Arab and Asian trade routes

   (D) Continuity of Egyptian culture

7. In which of the following regions did the Mongols remain as a political force more than 200 years following their conquest?

   (A) Persia

   (B) Russia

   (C) China

   (D) Northern India

8. The Gothic movement in European architecture required which of the following new medieval technological innovations?

   (A) Concrete molds

   (B) Pointed arches

   (C) Wooden scaffolding

   (D) Glass blowing

9. The main factor for the population drop of both Egypt and China during the mid-1300s was

   (A) foreign invasion

   (B) desertification

   (C) famine

   (D) disease

10. The greatest territorial expansion of the Muslim religion occurred

   (A) during Muhammad's life

   (B) within the first 100 years after Muhammad's death

   (C) in areas that had been previously Christian

   (D) along a north-south geographic orientation

11. How did Aztec religion differ from the religion of earlier Mesoamerican civilizations, such as the Toltec and Maya?

   (A) The Aztec worship focused on fertility gods whereas Toltec and Mayan worship focused on gods of creation and destruction.

   (B) Missionaries converted the Aztecs to Christianity but had not been active among the Toltec and Maya.

   (C) The Aztecs expanded the role of human sacrifice from what the Maya had previously practiced.

   (D) The Aztecs were monotheistic, worshiping only Quetzalcoatl, whereas the Toltec and Maya were polytheistic.

12. The majority of African slaves taken from Africa in the 1600s and 1700s were shipped to

   (A) Western Europe

   (B) British and French colonies in North America

   (C) British and French colonies in the Caribbean

   (D) Spanish and Portuguese colonies in Central and South America

GO ON TO THE NEXT PAGE

13. Which of the following events created economic conditions that motivated Christopher Columbus's voyage in 1492?

    (A) The fall of Constantinople's trade routes to the Turks

    (B) The voyages of Vasco DaGama to India

    (C) The adoption of silver currency in Spain

    (D) The creation of sugar plantations off the African coast

14. The majority of people living in Russia in the 1600s were

    (A) free peasants

    (B) boyars

    (C) Mongols

    (D) serfs

15. Peter the Great of Russia and Attaturk of Turkey shared a

    (A) commitment to Islam

    (B) goal of westernization

    (C) desire to spread democratic values

    (D) hope of achieving a warm-water port

16. The French Revolution and the American Revolution were similar in that both

    (A) involved a violent reign of terror against members of the upper class

    (B) started because of anger over taxation

    (C) had the lowest members of the working class attain political power

    (D) changed the religious structure of the country

17. The first large-scale industrial factories in Western Europe were established to produce

    (A) refined food items

    (B) ceramics

    (C) textiles

    (D) weapons

18. A Marxist historian would most likely see which of the following as a primary mover of historical events?

    (A) Technological innovation

    (B) Scholarship and intellectualism

    (C) Class conflict

    (D) Interaction among societies

19. The economic changes of the Meiji Restoration in Japan were most influenced by

    (A) Chinese merchants

    (B) German and British industrialists

    (C) Portuguese and Dutch traders

    (D) the increased power of the Samurai

20.

Justice

The cartoon shown from the British magazine *Punch* (1857) relates to which of the following ideas?

    (A) Women's ability to serve in the military

    (B) The inferiority of Africans as compared to the British

    (C) The importance of female modesty for British women

    (D) The need to retaliate against the Sepoy Rebellion in India

GO ON TO THE NEXT PAGE

21. Which of the following conflicts motivated the international community to form the United Nations?

    (A) The creation of Israel
    (B) The Cold War
    (C) World War I
    (D) World War II

22. Over the last four decades of the 20th century, the political structure of most Latin American countries changed

    (A) from democracy to communism
    (B) from communism to military dictatorship
    (C) from European colonial rule to independence
    (D) from dictatorship to democracy

23. Cambodia in the 1970s and Rwanda in the 1990s both experienced

    (A) communist revolution
    (B) genocidal violence
    (C) European invasion
    (D) hyperinflation

24. Which of the following diseases increased as a result of changing lifestyles during the late 20th century?

    (A) Heart disease
    (B) Cholera
    (C) Malaria
    (D) Tuberculosis

25. What impact did the Chinese communist revolution of 1949 have with regard to gender roles?

    (A) Husbands and wives were told to share responsibilities of child rearing and housekeeping.
    (B) Women were encouraged to marry at a younger age.
    (C) Men became more prominent as a result of communist ideology.
    (D) Foot-binding and arranged marriages were eliminated.

26. The primary characteristic of the Neolithic "Revolution" is

    (A) settled communities
    (B) the control of fire
    (C) humans living in monogamous relationships
    (D) the domestication of animals

27. The term "Revolution" is in quotation marks in reference to the Neolithic event because

    (A) there is evidence to suggest it never happened
    (B) revolutions only refer to political events, and this was a cultural event
    (C) the term "revolution" suggests an event that happened suddenly, whereas the Neolithic phase happened over thousands of years
    (D) it took place in several different parts of the world at the same time, but those events were independent of each other

GO ON TO THE NEXT PAGE

28.

Source: Manuscript copied by 'Alî ibn Hasan al-Hûfî al-Qâsimî in Cairo in 1456, now preserved in the Bodleian Library in Oxford. (Mss. Pococke 375 fol. 3v-4,)

This 12-century map by Al-Idrisi was made in or at

(A) southern Asia

(B) northern Europe

(C) the eastern terminus of the Silk Road

(D) Andalusia

29. One of the main reasons the Chinese government suspended its voyages of discovery in the 15th century was because

(A) the Europeans had already reached the New World.

(B) it feared the navy was leaving the country vulnerable to attack.

(C) it was concerned about the precious metal draining out of the treasury.

(D) it decided to use China's resources to construct the Grand Canal.

30. Use this chart to answer the question that follows.

SLAVE POPULATION AND SUGAR PRODUCTION

Colony	Year	Slave Population	Tons of Sugar Produced
BARBADOS (British)	1712	42,000	6,343
	1757	63,600	7,068
	1792	64,300	9,025
JAMAICA (British)	1703	45,000	4,782
	1730	74,500	15,972
	1754	130,000	23,396
	1789	250,000	59,400
SAINT-DOMINGUE (French)	1764	206,000	60,000
	1776	240,000	76,000
	1789	452,000	70,313
	1791	480,000	78,696
CUBA (Spanish)	1774	44,300	10,000
	1792	85,900	18,571
	1817	199,100	43,415

What event impacted sugar production in the French colony?

(A) The Haitian Revolution

(B) The Enlightenment

(C) The French Revolution

(D) The American purchase of Louisiana

31. A Marxist historian would be most interested in studying

(A) the relationship between imperialism and capitalism

(B) the findings of Charles Darwin and the theories of Herbert Spencer

(C) relationships between males and females

(D) the characteristics of Stone Age civilization

GO ON TO THE NEXT PAGE

32. Which of the following is true of the Chinese Revolution (1911) and the Mexican Revolution (1821)?

    (A) Both were prompted by external invasion

    (B) Both were endorsed by religious leaders

    (C) Both were inspired by the teachings of Karl Marx

    (D) Both were motivated by a desire to more fairly distribute land ownership

33. Which of the following stories was written 4,000 years ago and describes a king's quest to achieve immortality?

    (A) *The Rig Veda*

    (B) The *Upanishads*

    (C) The legend of Quetzalcoatl

    (D) *The Epic of Gilgamesh*

34. What discouraged mechanization in imperial Rome?

    (A) The existence of a proud and dominant landowning class

    (B) The ability to trade agricultural products for manufactured products

    (C) The existence of abundant slave labor

    (D) The absence of natural resources

35. Trade brought which two faiths to Southeast Asia in the post-classical era?

    (A) Christianity and Buddhism

    (B) Judaism and Hinduism

    (C) Buddhism and Christianity

    (D) Islam and Hinduism

36. What comparisons can be made between the politics and cultures of Renaissance Italy and the Abbasid dynasty?

    (A) Both political structures admired the artistic accomplishments of the other

    (B) Both cultures copied the artistic talents of the other

    (C) As each was a terminus of the Silk Road, they were able to share each other's cultural values

    (D) In both cultures, political fragmentation went hand in hand with cultural creativity

37. The two most profitable products produced by slave labor in the New World were

    (A) tobacco and sugar

    (B) corn and silver

    (C) coffee and tea

    (D) pepper and gold

38. On the eve of WWI, a characteristic common to both Russia and Japan was

    (A) the countries were becoming more and more democratic

    (B) each country saw a dramatic increase in the size of its middle class

    (C) rapid industrialization

    (D) an equitable redistribution of land ownership

GO ON TO THE NEXT PAGE ▷

39. The commonality shared by Abraham and Ikhnaton is

    (A) both men founded monotheistic faiths

    (B) both men were conquered by the Babylonians

    (C) both men led armies that defeated the Persians

    (D) although they ruled in different countries, both men married sisters from a family in Nubia

40. The most significant difference between the political leadership in Han China and that of Mauryan India is

    (A) the Chinese recognized a meritocracy

    (B) Mauryan India was a theocracy

    (C) Han China was a monarchy

    (D) China aggressively sought to extend its boundaries, whereas Mauryan India did not

41. At the end of the first millennium CE, the manufacturing center of the world was

    (A) the Middle East

    (B) East Asia

    (C) South Asia

    (D) Europe

42. The practice of mercantilism encouraged colonialism in the Atlantic World by

    (A) offering European kingdoms the opportunity for military glory

    (B) promoting the movement of raw materials and finished products across the Atlantic Ocean

    (C) urging the migration of European aristocrats to the New World

    (D) helping religious leaders spread the Christian faith

43.

The instrument shown would have most likely be used by a(n)

(A) artisan

(B) sailor

(C) soldier

(D) mathematician

44. What region of the world most actively discouraged interaction on the global scene in the 17th and 18th centuries?

(A) Latin America

(B) Africa

(C) Europe

(D) East Asia

45. Though the global slave trade decreased in the 19th century, it saw an increase in volume in

(A) Africa

(B) South Asia

(C) the Caribbean

(D) isolated islands in the Mediterranean

GO ON TO THE NEXT PAGE ⟩

46. The basic ideological difference between Karl Marx and Vladimir Lenin is that

(A) Marx believed revolution would originate with the agricultural class, while Lenin believed it would start with the industrial worker

(B) Marx believed revolution would begin with a spontaneous eruption by industrial workers but Lenin believed a nucleus of leadership was required to provide the spark

(C) Marx believed revolution could only happen in an urbanized nation, while Lenin believed it could only happen in an agricultural society

(D) Marx believed females should remain in a subordinate role, while Lenin believed they should perform an equal role in the development of the communist state

47. Which classical civilization had the greatest impact on the scientists and thinkers of Dar al-Islam?

(A) Han China
(B) Greece
(C) Rome
(D) Mali

48. The Mughal and Ottoman empires shared the common trait of

(A) being a Muslim empire in the Middle East

(B) possessing a monarchy that could trace its heritage to Muhammad

(C) having been defeated by Alexander the Great

(D) being created by nomadic horsemen

49. Use this chart to answer the following question.

BRITISH SUGAR CONSUMPTION, 1700–1770

	British Population	British Sugar Imports (lbs.)	Annual Per Capita Consumption (lbs.)
1700	6,122,000	28,000,000	4.6
1710	6,352,000	30,050,000	4.7
1720	6,253,000	47,310,000	7.6
1730	6,183,000	68,620,000	11.1
1740	6,153,000	72,201,000	11.7
1750	6,336,000	76,150,000	12.0
1760	8,000,000	110,210,000	13.8
1770	8,500,000	137,920,000	16.2

From this chart, what can we assume was happening in the Americas?

(A) France, Holland, and Britain were fighting for control of the colonies.

(B) Many scientists were migrating to the colonies and becoming dentists.

(C) There was a growing demand for slaves in the Americas.

(D) Britain was refining the sugar and sending it back to the Americas as rum.

50. Nineteenth-century western liberals identified the role of women as

(A) mothers of morality
(B) voters
(C) equally qualified for professional occupations
(D) barefoot and pregnant

GO ON TO THE NEXT PAGE ▷

51. The two primary reasons for the dramatic rise in world population in the 20th century were

    (A) an increased birth rate and an increased fertility rate

    (B) the elimination of malaria and small pox

    (C) a reduction in war and new types of food imported from the Americas

    (D) the Green Revolution and improvements in public health

52. Which of the following figures doesn't fit in chronologically with the other three?

    (A) Socrates

    (B) Siddhartha Gautama

    (C) Confucius

    (D) Muhammad

53. Marco Polo and Ibn Battuta

    (A) were both Muslims

    (B) both attempted to convert the so-called infidel to their faiths

    (C) never returned to their native lands

    (D) were both world travelers

54. The "Price Revolution" of the 16th century resulted in

    (A) massive unemployment in Europe and the Americas

    (B) a reduction in trade across the Atlantic Ocean

    (C) inflation in Europe

    (D) deflation in Europe

Answer these two questions based on your knowledge of history and the following quotation:

The Celestial Court has pacified and possessed the territory within the four seas. Its sole aim is to do the utmost to achieve good government and to manage political affairs, attaching no value to strange jewels and precious objects. The various articles presented by you, O King, this time are accepted by my special order to the office in charge of such functions in consideration of the offerings having come from a long distance with sincere good wishes. As a matter of fact, the virtue and respect of the Celestial Dynasty having spread far and wide, the kings of the myriad nations come by land and sea with all sorts of precious things. Consequently there is nothing we lack, as your principal envoy and others have themselves observed. We have never set much store on strange and ingenious objects, nor do we need any more of your country's manufacturers . . . .

—*Emperor Qianlong's letter to George III, 1793*

—From The Emperor Qianlong's "Mandates" in *Annals and Memoirs of the Court of Peking*, by E. Backhouse and J. P. P. Bland, London, 1914

55. The term "Celestial Court" references which 18th-century Chinese governmental belief system?

    (A) A belief in filial piety

    (B) The concept of the Middle Kingdom

    (C) Civil examinations

    (D) The Four Noble Truths

GO ON TO THE NEXT PAGE

56. Despite Emperor Qianlong's belief that the West had nothing to offer the Celestial Court, in the decades following, which two products would China demand from Western traders?

(A) Oil and cannons

(B) Opium and corn

(C) Silk and porcelain

(D) Opium and mechanical clocks

57. A major similarity between Mao Zedong and Mohandas Gandhi was that

(A) both sought the support of the peasant class

(B) both practiced civil disobedience

(C) they each relied on the support of the British Empire for the success of their revolutions

(D) both followed the philosophies of Vladimir Lenin

58. Which of the following is an inaccurate statement about the similarities between the pre-Columbian Aztec and Incan empires?

(A) They had an extensive trade network with each other

(B) They both practiced human sacrifice

(C) They both practiced military conquest of surrounding people

(D) They both worshiped their leader as a god

59. The Japanese equivalent of the French medieval knight was the

(A) samurai

(B) daimyo

(C) shogun

(D) emperor

60. The essential difference between Japanese and Chinese emperors was

(A) Japanese emperors were considered figurehead

(B) Chinese emperors were considered gods

(C) only Japanese emperors passed the position down to the oldest son

(D) Chinese emperors were not allowed to marry

61. What common characteristic is true of many mid- to late–20th-century leaders seeking decolonization in Africa?

(A) They were white

(B) They were trained by terrorist organizations outside the African continent

(C) They spent time in prison

(D) They attended communist indoctrination schools in Cuba

62. What belief is described by the following characteristics:

- Loyalty to ruler

- Filial obedience to father

- Respect for elders

- Chastity for wives

(A) Nihilism

(B) Social Darwinis

(C) Confucianism

(D) Brahminism

63. Prior to the Voyages of Discovery, the region the Middle East primarily traded with was

(A) Africa

(B) the Americas

(C) Europe

(D) South Asia

GO ON TO THE NEXT PAGE

Read these two accounts of the death of Montezuma and answer the questions that follow.

Account by Hernán Cortés in a letter to King Charles V of Spain.

Montezuma, who with one of his sons and many other chiefs who had been captured at the beginning, was still a prisoner, asked to be carried to the roof of the fort where he could speak to the captains and the [Aztec] people, and cause the war to cease. I had him taken thither, and when he reached the parapet on the top of the fort, intending to speak to the people who were fighting there, one of his own subjects struck him on the head with a stone with such force that within three days he died. I then had him taken out, dead as he was, by two of the Indian prisoners, who bore him away to his people; but I do not know what they did with him . . . .

Account by Diego Duran, written 60 years after the event took place.

The "Chronicle" tells us that once the Spanish had fled from Mexico [a temporary setback] and those who had remained behind had been killed, the Aztecs entered the chambers of Montezuma in order to treat him more cruelly than they had dealt with the Spaniards. There they found him dead with a chain about his feet and five dagger wounds in his chest. Near him lay many noblemen and great lords who had been held prisoner with him. All of them had been slain shortly before the Spaniards abandoned the building.

64. The most significant inconsistency between these two accounts is in the question of

(A) who killed Montezuma
(B) what happened to Montezuma's dead body
(C) how the Spanish king would react to the death of Montezuma
(D) whether or not Montezuma's son survived the ordeal

65. Cortés and his small army were able to defeat the Aztec Empire because

(A) the Spanish conquistadors defeated the Aztec army at the pitched Battle of Tenochtitlan
(B) many unhappy native groups allied with the Spanish
(C) intrigue and deceit enabled the Spanish to gain the upper hand
(D) disease grew rampant

66. Which of the following castas suffered the lowest status in colonial Latin America?

(A) Creole
(B) Gens de couleur
(C) Mestizo
(D) Peninsulare

67. Which economic priority was made by both India and China in the years after WWII?

(A) Land redistribution
(B) Dam construction
(C) Industrial development
(D) Limitations on family size

GO ON TO THE NEXT PAGE

68.

The artifact identified above would most likely be found

(A) in pre-Columbian America

(B) among the Inuit of North America

(C) among the Pacific Islanders

(D) in ancient Egypt

69. What was the major difference among British, American, and Japanese industrialization?

(A) British industrialization encouraged the development of monopolies

(B) Japanese industrialization was sponsored, subsidized, and controlled by the state

(C) American industrialization was heavily subsidized by foreign investors

(D) Japanese and American industrialists exploited the natural resources of their own countries, whereas Britain exploited the resources of other countries

70. Which individual would have most likely made the following statement?

"I contend we are the first race of the world and that the more of the world that we inhabit the better it is for the human race. I contend that every acre added to our territory means the birth of more of us who otherwise would not be brought into existence."

(A) A French revolutionary in 1792

(B) A Russian Marxist in 1917

(C) A British imperialist in 1885

(D) A Chinese communist in 1949

IF YOU FINISH BEFORE TIME IS CALLED, YOU MAY CHECK YOUR WORK ON THIS SECTION ONLY. DO NOT TURN TO ANY OTHER SECTION IN THE TEST.

STOP

SECTION II
Part A: Document-Based Question

Mandatory reading period: 10 minutes
Suggested writing time: 40 minutes

This DBQ is a practice activity. The actual question on the exam may be longer.

Directions: The following question is based on the accompanying Documents 1 to 10. (The documents have been edited for the purpose of this exercise.)

This question is designed to test your ability to work with and understand historical documents. Write an essay that:

- Has a relevant thesis and supports that thesis with evidence from the documents.

- Uses all of the documents.

- Analyzes the documents by grouping them in as many appropriate ways as possible; does not simply summarize the documents individually.

- Takes into account the sources of the documents and analyzes the authors' points of view.

- Explains the need for at least one additional type of document.

You may refer to relevant historical information not mentioned in the documents.

What are the similarities and differences between the revolution that lead to the formation of the Republic of Turkey in 1923 and the 1979 revolution in Iran? Identify one additional type of document and explain how it would help your analysis of this comparison.

Historical Background: In the early 1920s, the Ottoman Empire was still reeling from its defeat in WWI and internal strife was rampant. Outside forces brought about the dissolution of the empire through the Treaty of Sèvres (1920), and a nationalistic spirit, led by the charismatic general Kemal Atatürk, prompted the establishment of the Republic of Turkey, the new nation recognized internationally by the Treaty of Lausanne (1923).

From 1953 to 1979, a secular pro-Western regime controlled the people of Iran. Islamic forces developed and steadily became increasingly dissatisfied with pro-Western influence. In 1979, Shah Mohammad Reza Pahlavi was driven from power and replaced by Islamic fundamentalist Ayatollah Khomeini.

GO ON TO THE NEXT PAGE

DOCUMENT 1

Source: Tevfik Fikret, poet and founder of the modern Turkish literary style who was jailed several times by Ottoman authorities (1898)

> Once more a stubborn mist has swathed your horizons . . .
> A dusty, fearsome darkness, which the eye
> Takes care not to pierce, for it is afraid.
> But for you this deep, dark veil is right and fitting,
> This veiling becomes you well, O scene of evil deeds . . . .
> Yes, veil yourself, O tragedy, veil yourself, O city;
> Veil yourself and sleep forever, whore of the world!

DOCUMENT 2

Source: Francis McCullagh, a Western correspondent, observed the opening of Turkey's Parliament shortly before the fall of Sultan Abdul Hamid (1908)

A figure seemed to cross the sunlight, the silence of death fell on the crowded room: Abdul Hamid had entered. To do justice to the dramatic appearance of the mysterious chief of Islam, I should have been born a Turk and then I would have been awe-stricken, perhaps, by the memories of this Presence, by the recollection of the sultans whose flags floated on three continents and four seas, who ruled from the Adriatic to the Persian Gulf, from the Carpathians to the Nile, and for whom prayers were offered up from thirty kingdoms. Not having been born a Turk, I could only see a tottering old man, bent, ashy-faced, weary, and with a way of shuffling instead of walking which made him look ten years older than he really was.

GO ON TO THE NEXT PAGE

DOCUMENT 3

Source: Statements made by Kemal Atatürk, president of modern Turkey (speeches delivered between 1921 and 1927)

(1921) If we must define our government sociologically, we would call it a "people's government." . . . We are toiling people, poor people, who work to save their lives and independence. We are men who follow a principle that entitles us, in order to preserve this right and safeguard our independence, to struggle as a whole nation against the imperialism that seeks to crush and the capitalism that seeks to swallow our very nationhood.

(1924) The decline of the Ottomans began when, proud of their triumphs over the West, they cut their ties with European nations. This was a mistake which we will not repeat.

(1927) Can a civilized nation tolerate a crowd of people who let themselves be led by the nose by sheikhs, dervishes, and the like . . . and who trust their faith and their lives to fortunetellers, magicians, witch-doctors, and writers of amulets?

DOCUMENT 4

Source: Halide Edib was a Turkish novelist who broke with Atatürk's autocratic methods in 1925 and emigrated to the United States, where this excerpt was written in 1929.

In 1928, the clause in the Turkish constitution which declared Islam the state religion was abolished . . . . In the foreign press this act of the dictatorship was criticized very severely on the ground that it amounted to the abolition of religion in Turkey. The criticism was not only superficial but inaccurate. If religion, in the best sense, is in danger of losing its hold on the people in Turkey, this is due not to an act of governmental interference in its favor but to governmental interference against it. The men who sponsored this measure, may or may not have been atheists, but the measure itself does not do away with religion. No secular state can logically have a state-sponsored religion. The removal of this clause from the Turkish constitution was therefore in true and necessary accord with the nature of the new Turkish state at its last stage of secularization.

GO ON TO THE NEXT PAGE

DOCUMENT 5

Source: Image circulated around the world of Kemal Atatürk dancing with his daughter on the occasion of her marriage in Istanbul, 1929. (Getty)

GO ON TO THE NEXT PAGE ⇨

DOCUMENT 6

Source: Ayatollah Murtada Mutahhari, a leader of the Iranian Revolution (1979)

Experts on political affairs acknowledge that after passing through a period of mental crisis the Muslims are once again struggling to reestablish their "Islamic identity" against the challenges of the capitalist West and the communist East. The current Iranian movement is not restricted to any particular class or trade union. It is not only a laborer, an agrarian, a student, an intellectual, or a bourgeois movement. Within its scope fall one and all in Iran, the rich and the poor, the man and the woman, the school boy and the scholar, the artisan and the peasant, the clergy and the teacher, one and all. The awakened Islamic conscience of our society has induced it to search for Islamic values. This is the conscience of the cumulative enthusiasms of all classes of people, including some of the heretofore dissident groups, which has galvanized them into one concerted upsurge.

DOCUMENT 7

Source: A New Year's message delivered to the Iranian people by Ayatollah Khomeini, 1980

God Almighty has willed—and all thanks are due to him—that this noble nation be delivered from the oppression and crimes inflicted on it by a tyrannical government and from the domination of the oppressive powers, especially America, the global plunderer, and that the flag of Islamic justice wave over our beloved land. It is our duty to stand firm against the superpowers, as we are indeed able to do, on condition that the intellectuals stop following and imitating either the West and the East, and adhere instead to the straight path of Islam and the nation. We are at war with international communism no less than we are struggling against the global plunderers of the West . . . .

DOCUMENT 8

Source: V.S. Naipaul, traveler in Iran at the time of the Iranian Revolution (1981)

The election [I saw] was for an "Assembly of Experts," who would work out an Islamic constitution. Khomeini had advised that priests should be elected. Experts were necessary because an Islamic constitution couldn't simply be adopted. No such thing existed or had ever existed. An Islamic constitution was something that had to be put together, and it had to be something of which the Prophet would have approved. That was where the priests came in. They might not have ideas about a constitution . . . but with their knowledge of the Koran and the doings of the prophet, the priests would know what was non-Islamic . . . .

GO ON TO THE NEXT PAGE

DOCUMENT 9

Source: Turkish Press, commenting on a visit by Iranian President Hashemi Rafsanjani, who had been invited to Turkey by the leader of the Islamist Party, 1996

President Rafsanjani was accompanied by his daughter Faezeh Rafsanjani, president of the Iranian Olympic Committee and minister of sports. Asked by Turkish officials what she thought of Ankara, she said that it reminded her of Tehran in the last years of the shah.

DOCUMENT 10

Source: Image distributed worldwide of American hostages being paraded outside the U.S. compound in Tehran by their Iranian captors in 1979 while onlookers shouted, "Death to Jimmy Carter" and "Yankee, go home." (Getty)

IF YOU FINISH BEFORE TIME IS CALLED, YOU MAY CHECK YOUR WORK ON THIS SECTION ONLY. DO NOT TURN TO ANY OTHER SECTION IN THE TEST.

 STOP

Part B: Continuity and Change-Over-Time Question

Suggested writing time: 40 minutes

Directions: You are to answer the following question. You should spend five minutes organizing or outlining your essay. Write an essay that:

- Has a relevant thesis and supports that thesis with appropriate historical evidence.

- Addresses all parts of the question.

- Uses historical context to show continuity and change over time.

- Analyzes the process of continuity and change over time.

Prompt: Choose one of the following regions and discuss the continuities and changes in the political impact of belief systems between 8000 BCE and 600 CE. Be sure to offer specific examples.

- East Asia

- the Middle East

- Southeast AsiaPart

Part C: Comparative Question

Suggested writing time: 40 minutes

Directions: You are to answer the following question. You should spend five minutes organizing or outlining your essay. Write an essay that:

- Has a relevant thesis and supports that thesis with appropriate historical evidence.

- Addresses all parts of the question.

- Makes direct, relevant comparisons.

- Analyzes relevant reasons for similarities and differences.

Prompt: Compare trading patterns in TWO of the following regions between 1450 and 1750.

- Atlantic World

- Indian Ocean

- Mediterranean Sea

- China seas

IF YOU FINISH BEFORE TIME IS CALLED, YOU MAY CHECK YOUR WORK ON THIS SECTION ONLY. DO NOT TURN TO ANY OTHER SECTION IN THE TEST.

DIAGNOSTIC TEST: ANSWER KEY

1.	B	19.	B	37.	A	55.	B
2.	D	20.	D	38.	C	56.	D
3.	A	21.	D	39.	A	57.	A
4.	D	22.	D	40.	A	58.	A
5.	D	23.	B	41.	B	59.	A
6.	C	24.	A	42.	B	60.	A
7.	B	25.	D	43.	B	61.	C
8.	B	26.	A	44.	D	62.	C
9.	D	27.	C	45.	A	63.	D
10.	B	28.	D	46.	B	64.	A
11.	C	29.	D	47.	B	65.	B
12.	D	30.	C	48.	D	66.	B
13.	A	31.	A	49.	C	67.	C
14.	D	32.	D	50.	A	68.	A
15.	B	33.	D	51.	D	69.	B
16.	B	34.	C	52.	D	70.	C
17.	C	35.	D	53.	D		
18.	C	36.	D	54.	C		

DIAGNOSTIC TEST: ASSESS YOUR STRENGTHS

Question	Chapter
1	Chapter 3: Up to 600 CE
2	Chapter 3: Up to 600 CE
3	Chapter 3: Up to 600 CE
4	Chapter 3: Up to 600 CE
5	Chapter 3: Up to 600 CE
6	Chapter 4: 600 to 1450 CE
7	Chapter 4: 600 to 1450 CE
8	Chapter 4: 600 to 1450 CE
9	Chapter 4: 600 to 1450 CE
10	Chapter 4: 600 to 1450 CE
11	Chapter 5: 1450 to 1750 CE
12	Chapter 5: 1450 to 1750 CE
13	Chapter 5: 1450 to 1750 CE
14	Chapter 5: 1450 to 1750 CE
15	Chapter 5: 1450 to 1750 CE
16	Chapter 6: 1750 to 1900 CE
17	Chapter 6: 1750 to 1900 CE
18	Chapter 6: 1750 to 1900 CE
19	Chapter 6: 1750 to 1900 CE
20	Chapter 6: 1750 to 1900 CE
21	Chapter 7: 1900 CE to Present
22	Chapter 7: 1900 CE to Present
23	Chapter 7: 1900 CE to Present
24	Chapter 7: 1900 CE to Present
25	Chapter 7: 1900 CE to Present
26	Chapter 3: Up to 600 CE
27	Chapter 3: Up to 600 CE
28	Chapter 4: 600 to 1450 CE
29	Chapter 4: 600 to 1450 CE
30	Chapter 5: 1450 to 1750 CE
31	Chapter 7: 1900 CE to Present
32	Chapter 6: 1750 to 1900 CE and Chapter 7: 1900 CE to Present
33	Chapter 3: Up to 600 CE
34	Chapter 3: Up to 600 CE
35	Chapter 4: 600 to 1450 CE
36	Chapter 4: 600 to 1450 CE and Chapter 5: 1450 to 1750 CE

37	Chapter 5: 1450 to 1750 CE
38	Chapter 7: 1900 CE to Present
39	Chapter 3: Up to 600 CE
40	Chapter 3: Up to 600 CE
41	Chapter 4: 600 to 1450 CE
42	Chapter 5: 1450 to 1750 CE
43	Chapter 5: 1450 to 1750 CE
44	Chapter 5: 1450 to 1750 CE and Chapter 6: 1750 to 1900 CE
45	Chapter 6: 1750 to 1900 CE
46	Chapter 7: 1900 CE to Present
47	Chapter 4: 600 to 1450 CE
48	Chapter 4: 600 to 1450 CE and Chapter 5: 1450 to 1750 CE
49	Chapter 6: 1750 to 1900 CE
50	Chapter 7: 1900 CE to Present
51	Chapter 4: 600 to 1450 CE
52	Chapter 4: 600 to 1450 CE and Chapter 5: 1450 to 1750 CE
53	Chapter 4: 600 to 1450 CE
54	Chapter 5: 1450 to 1750 CE
55	Chapter 6: 1750 to 1900 CE
56	Chapter 6: 1750 to 1900 CE
57	Chapter 7: 1900 CE to Present
58	Chapter 4: 600 to 1450 CE
59	Chapter 4: 600 to 1450 CE
60	Chapter 4: 600 to 1450 CE
61	Chapter 7: 1900 CE to Present
62	Chapter 3: Up to 600 CE
63	Chapter 4: 600 to 1450 CE
64	Chapter 5: 1450 to 1750 CE
65	Chapter 5: 1450 to 1750 CE
66	Chapter 6: 1750 to 1900 CE
67	Chapter 7: 1900 CE to Present
68	Chapter 4: 600 to 1450 CE
69	Chapter 6: 1750 to 1900 CE
70	Chapter 6: 1750 to 1900 CE

ANSWERS AND EXPLANATIONS

SECTION I

MULTIPLE-CHOICE ANSWERS

1. B

Many AP World History questions will ask you to pick out similarities among several different societies. In this case, early civilizations developed around rivers so that the water could be used for irrigating fields: the Yellow (Huang He) River for the Shang, the Tigris and Euphrates Rivers for the Sumerians, and the Indus for the Harrapans. Because each of these early civilizations was agricultural, they did not have pastoral economies. Horses were not used regularly as plow animals until proper yokes were created much later. Only the Sumerian civilization had urban centers approaching 100,000 people.

2. D

Any major early civilization relied on the fertility of the soil to achieve its population density. With the type of farming practices and irrigation used by the Mesopotamians, the soil lost its fertility over time, especially because the evaporating water from irrigation left behind salt residue that dramatically reduced soil fertility over time.

3. A

Mahayana Buddhism, known as the "greater vehicle," places special emphasis on the greater accessibility of salvation for its followers. Early Christianity, though different in its beliefs and practices, also shared this personal sense of salvation. Early Christians believed in resurrection, not reincarnation, unlike Buddhists.

4. D

The Silk Road of the first centuries of the Common Era involved both land and sea trade from the Han Empire to the west, reaching as far as the eastern end of the Roman Empire. The primary items traded by the Chinese included silk and spices. In exchange, they received finished goods and other luxury items.

5. D

Emperor Qin Shihuangdi, who established the Qin dynasty, is famous for his self-proclaimed title of "first emperor" of China. Emperors had actually existed before, but none had established extensive centralized rule, with aspects of law, military defense, and even written script becoming more regulated by the central government. He ruled using a philosophical system called Legalism, which is considerably different from both Confucianism and Buddhism. The civil service exam came later.

6. C

Swahili developed as a blended language in the cities on the east coast of Africa that traded with Arab merchants and others who participated in the Indian Ocean trade system. Its development shows the connection that Africa had with the rest of the Indian Ocean basin. Africa had a huge amount of linguistic diversity. A common tongue facilitated trade.

7. B

All of the areas listed were conquered by Mongol troops. The Golden Horde of Russia, however, had some loose political influence in Russia until 1480 CE when Ivan the Great stopped paying tribute to the Mongols. By that time, Mongol influence in other regions had long passed.

8. B

The design of Gothic architecture needed pointed arches to transfer the weight of the roof and ceiling from the walls to supporting buttresses. With the weight off of the walls, taller structures could be built with stained glass windows. All of the other technologies listed had been around since at least the classical age.

9. D

The bubonic plague, otherwise known as the Black Death, was a worldwide pandemic of the mid-1300s. It caused the population of China, Egypt, and Western Europe to fall dramatically. Although the time period also experienced warfare and famine, neither had the demographic impact as did disease.

10. B

By the early 700s CE, the span of Islam reached from the Iberian Peninsula of modern-day Spain and Portugal in the west to the Indus River in the east. At the time of Muhammad's death in 632 CE, the Islamic areas were limited to Arabia. Many of the areas that were converted were Christian, but the majority of the population was to the east, which was not primarily Christian.

11. C

Aztec religion was highly influenced by the earlier Toltec and Mayan religions. All three of them practiced polytheism with gods of fertility as well as gods of creation and destruction. Indeed many of the gods were the same. The Aztecs, however, took the previous religious practice of human sacrifice to another level, making blood sacrifice to a much larger degree than either the Toltec or Maya had.

12. D

The largest portion of people who traveled on the Middle Passage from Africa went to Brazil (about 40%). Other major areas include Spanish colonies on the mainland and Spanish and French colonies on the islands of the Caribbean. North Americans accounted for less than 5 percent of the total African slave immigrants to the Americas.

13. A

The prime economic motive for Christopher Columbus's initial voyage was to discover a new route to the East Asian spice markets. Trade routes that had previously existed had traveled over land through Byzantine territories. After the conquest of Constantinople in 1453, the supply of Asian trade goods in Western Europe declined sharply.

Interest in using the New World as a place for silver mining and sugar plantations occurred after Columbus's initial voyage to what he thought was Asia. Vasco DaGama traveled to India in 1494, after Columbus's trip. This resulted in greater religious unity in Spain but was not the prime economic motive for exploration.

14. D

Russian society was structured around large agricultural estates run by the nobility, who were known as boyars, and the Russian Orthodox Church. The estates were farmed by the forced labor of serfs, who accounted for the vast majority of the population. Free peasants became a big factor in Russia after the emancipation of the serfs in 1861.

15. B

Both rulers wanted to westernize and modernize their countries. Though Turkey was a Muslim country, Attaturk saw Islamic institutions as backward and introduced Western ideas and institutions. He wanted to take power away from religious authorities. Peter the Great was strongly opposed to democratic reforms, but did dream of westernizing and establishing a warm-water port.

16. B

The initial motive for the American Revolution involved what the revolutionaries considered intolerable taxation through the Stamp Act, the Townshend Act, and the Tea Act. A primary grievance for the Third Estate in France involved the unequal tax burden due to the exemption of the First and Second Estates. Political power, especially in the American Revolution, did not flow to the working class, and many men without property were denied the right to vote until many years after the revolution. The American Revolution did witness violence against people loyal to Britain, but this terror was not directed specifically to aristocrats. In fact, the American Revolution was instigated by the wealthiest classes.

17. C

The first factories of Britain in the 1700s were created to spin thread and yarn and then later weave textiles. Mills had been set up in the Caribbean to refine sugar before, but the needs of production meant that sugar could not be refined in Britain.

18. C

According to Karl Marx and Friedrich Engels, history follows a path determined by the struggle of social classes. Their theory of dialectical materialism dictates that all history comes from the struggle between competing social classes. Class conflict will end only after revolution and the establishment of communism.

19. B

Japan came out of isolation and pursued a rapid course of industrialization and westernization starting in the 1860s. During this time, the Meiji officials hired a large number of consultants from Germany and Britain. The Samurai lost power.

20. D

This illustration shows the female figure "Justice," as seen by the title and the scales on her shield, slaying dark-skinned people. The *Punch* cartoon corresponds to the time of the Sepoy Mutiny. In 1857, native troops of the British army in India mutinied and killed many British soldiers, East India Company officials, and their families. The reaction in Britain was outrage. Thousands of British troops were deployed to northern India to regain control, and the British government took a more direct form of colonial rule.

21. D

The United Nations was formed in 1945 as a result of World War II. Fifty-one countries started the international organization. They committed to maintaining international peace and security, developing friendly relations among nations, and promoting social progress.

22. D

In 1960, most Latin American countries had some form of dictatorship. Democracy, where it existed, was not complete or fully expressed. Only Cuba was forming what would become a communist-style government. In 2000, almost all countries in the Western Hemisphere, with the notable exception of Cuba and Haiti, had a functioning democracy. Most European colonial control in Latin America ended in the early 1800s.

23. B

The Khmer Rouge rule by the dictator Pol Pot led to the systematic murder of about two million people in Cambodia during the mid-1970s. In 1994, one million people in Rwanda were murdered systematically in violence directed toward ethnic Tutsis.

24. A

Rates of heart disease have increased dramatically in developed countries because of changing lifestyles and increased longevity. Cholera, malaria, and tuberculosis are all diseases associated with poverty and underdevelopment.

25. D

Revolutionary time periods generally involve great changes in women's social roles. In no place is this truer than in China. The Chinese communist revolution of Mao Zedong eliminated forced marriages, granted equal rights to divorce, and made foot-binding illegal. Women were encouraged to become active leaders in the Communist Party, but they did not become army generals. Official concepts of equal rights often did not translate into more equitable roles within the household.

26. A

Settled communities came into existence through the development of agriculture. (B) and (C) existed before the Neolithic Revolution and (D) appeared well after the development of settled communities.

27. C

Revolutions are not limited to the political sphere and there is plenty of evidence to suggest this one happened in different parts of the world (though at different times). However, the term "revolution" suggests sudden change; that was not the case in the development of agriculture and settled communities.

28. D
Al-Idrisi was a Muslim cartographer; Andalusia (present-day southern Spain) was at that time part of Dar al-Islam.

29. D
Zheng He's voyages predated the journeys of Christopher Columbus and there was no precious metal drain out of China at that time. Though China was pestered by Japanese pirates, the desire to connect two major river valleys and improve agriculture was a dominant reason to place the global voyages on hold.

30. C
The Haitian Revolution would not have directly influenced Saint-Domingue, nor would the American purchase of Louisiana. Though the Enlightenment may have impacted those slaves who came in contact with its ideals, the turmoil of the French Revolution had a more dramatic and real impact on sugar production.

31. A
A Marxist historian would be interested in the conflicts created by the capitalist and imperialist drives of the haves versus the have-nots far more than he would the opinions of Charles Darwin and Herbert Spencer (Social Darwinism), survival techniques in the Stone Age, or gender relations.

32. D
Neither country was seriously threatened by external invasion. Religious leaders played a minor role in the Chinese Revolution and the Mexican Revolution predates Marx. However, revolutionary leaders in both countries did use land distribution as a rallying cry.

33. D
In *The Epic of Gilgamesh*, the royal hero unsuccessfully travels the world searching for the secret of immortality. *The Rig Veda* and the

Upanishads are both sacred Hindu texts, and Quetzalcoatl is a Mesoamerican deity.

34. C
Imperial Rome had the resources to mechanize but the presence of cheap labor erased the need to find more efficient methods of production.

35. D
The post-classical era (600–1600 CE) saw both Islam and Hinduism spread into Southeast Asia via the vehicle of trade. Buddhism had been introduced to the region by merchants at a much earlier date. Christian merchants had no influence on the region during this time period.

36. D
Because the artistic styles were so different, the two had little respect for each other's accomplishments, and Renaissance Italy was not a terminus of the Silk Road. However, the artistic and cultural accomplishments of both civilizations live down through the ages, despite the fact that both encompassed a confederation of semi-autonomous or autonomous states.

37. A
Although silver and gold were the most profitable by weight, over the 350-year period of active slavery in the New World, tobacco and sugar produced far more profit for their investors. The profitability of corn and pepper pale by comparison.

38. C
By the beginning of WWI, Russia and Japan were becoming increasingly autocratic, with growing gaps between wealthy and poor. Land distribution would not become an issue in Japan until much later in the century. Both nations were, however, experiencing large and rapid industrialization.

39. A
Abraham founded Judaism and Ikhnaton originated the short-lived monotheistic faith worshiping Aten in Egypt.

40. A

Han China made use of a civil service examination system but Mauryan India did not. Though Mauryan leadership respected local religious beliefs, they were not the leaders of the faith. Both empires sought to extend their boundaries, and both were monarchies.

41. B

Europe could hardly be considered a manufacturing center in the year 1000 CE, and the Middle East was more of a trading center than a manufacturing center. Though South Asia enjoyed comparative peace and prosperity at this time, it was more of an agricultural society than a manufacturing arena. Production of manufactured goods, though hardly an industrial revolution, was centered in China.

42. B

The economic concept of mercantilism is centered around the idea of European countries using raw products imported from colonies to keep citizens employed while producing a finished product that is eventually sold to other countries or back to the colonies. Though answers (A), (C), and (D) happened, they are not directly related to mercantilism.

43. B

This is an astrolabe, used by sailors to determine latitude through the position of the stars.

44. D

Although Latin America was not happy with its colonial status, it officially encouraged interaction with global markets and global politics. Africa was so fragmented at that time that it's difficult to make any generalizations about it. Of course, Europe's venture into the global scene perhaps peaked at this time. East Asia, led by China and Japan, actively and officially sought to exclude foreign interaction.

45. A

The actions of the Belgian government in 19th-century Congo and the Afrikaners in South Africa demonstrate the increased slave activity in the African continent.

46. B

The most fundamental difference between the two ideologues was how revolution would begin. Though both men agreed it needed the discontent fomented by an industrial working class, Marx thought there would be a spontaneous eruption and Lenin believed the workers needed leadership to choreograph the process.

47. B

The Greek thinkers—from mathematicians to physicians—had a dramatic impact on the thinkers of the Muslim world in the years before the modern world began. Mali and Han China influenced the Arabic world in other ways, but only sporadically when it came to the realm of science. The contributions of the Roman Empire in this regard fell far short of what Greece offered.

48. D

Nomadic tribesmen from the steppes of Central Asia created both empires over a span of 300 years. Neither empire could trace its ancestry to Muhammad, and Alexander the Great preceded these peoples by about 1500 years.

49. C

While these three countries may have been competing for land and power in the Americas, this chart does not reflect that. (D) is wrong because the Americas typically sent rum to Britain. (C) is the correct answer because the increased demand for sugar in Europe would result in an increased demand for cheap labor on the sugar plantations. (My apologies for even offering (B) as a choice.)

50. A

(B) and (C) would be seen by 19th-century citizens as radical ideas; (D) was identified as a more moderate reality. Liberals in the West at that time identified women as "keepers of the flame" of morality whose role was to raise sound future citizens.

51. D

Neither the birth rate nor the fertility rate increased; malaria is still a public health issue today. New foods from the Americas helped the population grow in the 16th and 17th centuries but were a part of the normal routine by the 20th century. However, by bringing new standards of productivity to food staples and improved methods of health measures, the Green Revolution dramatically reduced the infant mortality rate, insuring that greater numbers of people would reach their childbearing years.

52. D
Muhammad lived during the early seventh century CE, while the other three predate the fifth century BCE.

53. D
They were both world travelers but Battuta initiated his travels as a haj while Polo was motivated by trade. Conversion was not a primary goal for either and both made it back to their respective homelands. Marco Polo was Christian.

54. C
The influx of precious metals into Europe as a result of the Columbian Exchange resulted in an increase in coinage and an increase in prices (which also stimulated investment, production, and mercantilistic practices).

55. B
The Chinese believed their civilization was the center of the universe, where perfection had been achieved.

56. D
That opium was in demand is well documented, but it's also true that the Chinese were fascinated by mechanical clocks. Oil was not needed in abundance and silk and porcelain were exported. Corn was already well established on Chinese farms by this time.

57. A
Mao did not practice civil disobedience; both he and Gandhi were trying to expunge foreign influence from their land. While Mao supported the ideals of Lenin, Gandhi did not. Both leaders needed peasant support to accomplish their goals.

58. A
(B), (C), and (D) are similarities between the Aztecs and Incans but both limited trade to within their respective regions.

59. A
The samurai was Japan's warrior class; the daimyo, emperor, and shogun were different levels of rulers.

60. A
Chinese emperors exerted substantial real authority while the power in Japan lay in the hands of the samurai warrior class.

61. C
The vast majority were black and had spent time in the jails built by their colonial overseers. Though some may have had communist sympathies, few sought the aid of Cuba.

62. C
Nihilism was a 19th-century philosophy stating life is without meaning, Social Darwinism applied Darwin's theory of evolution to a racial pecking order, and Brahmanism was a precursor to Hinduism that called for a strict caste system.

63. D
At that time, the Americas were not yet in the global loop and Europe neither demanded a sufficient amount of goods from outside the continent nor provided goods the rest of the world wanted. Africa provided some goods in demand by the Middle East, but South Asia was the Middle East's largest trade partner in the years preceding the Voyages of Discovery.

64. A
Because the Spanish crown would be concerned about the death of a monarch, the question of who killed Montezuma was an issue in these two conflicting passages.

65. B
The Aztecs were successful in part because they avoided a pitched battle; the Aztecs were defeated

before disease could exact its terrible toll. Though intrigue was a factor, the conquerors' ability to gain the aid of disgruntled local groups was the biggest factor in their ultimate victory.

66. B
The gens de couleur were free people of color (mixed race black and white) and suffered the lowest status; the three other castas enjoyed some measure of Spanish heritage.

67. C
Dam construction and family size limitation became priorities in China but not India; land distribution was not given high priority status in either country, but both nations succeeded in industrializing their economies.

68. A
This is a quipu, used, among other things, as a counting tool by the Incans.

69. B
The zaibatsu of Japan were large cartels encouraged by the state.

70. C
The "we" in this quotation refers to the Europeans. Statements like this were often used to justify the practice of imperialism during that time period.

Section II

Part A: Document-Based Question: Strong Sample Response

The Middle East is no stranger to revolution in the 20th century. Two worth comparing are the creation of a secular government in Turkey at the end of WWI and the Iranian Revolution in 1979. Though these revolutions are similar in that they both happened in countries with a strong Muslim presence and a rising nationalistic pride, there are also significant differences. While one country rejected the West and embraced a government run by theologians, the other actively courted Western influence and went out of its way to separate church and state.

The majority of the people in Turkey and Iran are Muslim. This fact is initially a similarity between the two countries, but the revolutions that took place in each country harnessed this reality differently. In Document 2 we see a foreign correspondent (obviously saying what his pro-Western foreign audience wants to hear in the politically charged pre-WWI years) referencing the "Sick Man of Europe" and Document 4 declaring Islam to be no longer the state religion of Turkey. Of course, Ataturk (Document 3) is going to discourage Islam's voice in the matters of state. The leaders of the Iranian Revolution, on the other hand, while recognizing the Muslim domination, would have a different view the religion's role. In Document 6, one Ayatollah speaks to an "Islamic identity" while the other in Document 7 talks about the "flag of Islamic justice." Clearly, the early leadership in the Iranian Revolution seeks to reject Western values and embrace a traditional Islamic presence. This could not be more apparent than Document 8, showing the need for clerical input as Iran creates its new constitution. Iran's rejection of the West is most apparent in the image displayed in Document 10, an image designed to charge emotions in both the Middle East and the West. However, that image is offset by the subtle persuasion of Document 5, an elegant affair dominated by Western appearances. Thus, we see an Islamic similarity in these two revolutions but distinctions in that Iran melded religion and government together while Turkey separated the two. Another helpful document would be the viewpoint of an outsider observed while the revolution is happening in Turkey. Naipaul (Document 8) remains aloof from the passions of the Iranian Revolution yet is writing while the events are churning. McCullagh on the other hand (Document 2) seems to have an agenda and is describing events a decade before the Turkish Revolution would begin. To balance Naipaul's comments, let's hear from a dispassionate outsider commenting on the events in Turkey while they are happening.

Another similarity is that both revolutions fed off rising nationalistic spirits. Iran used this spirit to condemn the corruption of a puppet state propped up by the West and Turkey used this spirit to bury the Ottoman Empire. A Turkish poet in Document 1, no doubt reacting to his imprisonment by Ottoman officials, called for an awakening of this Turkish pride. Both Ataturk and the Ayatollah speak to how their revolution is a people's revolt: Ataturk in Document 3 speaks of the "toiling people" and Mutahhari in Document 6 refers to the "cumulative enthusiasm" of the movement. Clearly, both Ataturk and Mutahhari have the need to "cheerlead" their followers to the successful culmination of their revolutions Though her comments are perhaps prompted by her need to appease and validate those who appointed her to the presidency of Iran's Olympic Committee (a largely figurehead position), Rafsanjani (Document 9) suggests that perhaps Turkey is on the threshold of another revolution. Her statement only serves to highlight the nationalistic pride that she feels her own revolution has already accomplished. A good additional document to counter the views of Rafsanjani would be from a Turkish government official visiting the Muslim-controlled state of Iran. Such an additional document would help us better understand Turkish attitudes toward Iran. It is interesting to note that while each revolution had different attitudes toward the West, they were uniform in their condemnation of the communist world. Ataturk (Document 3) offers a de facto rejection as he embraces the West and Khomeini (Document 7) openly declares war on communism.

So, we have two revolutions separated by about 60 years but together in that they both border the Arab world. The revolutions are similar in that they happened in Muslim countries and appealed to the nationalistic spirit of their citizens but differed in how religion impacted their government and how they chose to relate to the Western world.

The student gets 1 thesis point and 3 points for demonstrating understanding of all the documents and using all of them as evidence to support his/her thesis. The student also gets 1 point for demonstrating at least two points of view and another point for justifying the need for a specific additional document.

The three groups provided are the reference to the presence of Islam in both countries (Documents 2, 3, 4, 6, 7, and 8), the manner in which both countries reacted to the West (Documents 3, 4, 5, 6, 7, 9, and 10), and the role religion played in the goals of the revolutions (Documents 2, 3, 4, 6, 7, and 8). A fourth grouping would be the use of documents 3 and 7 to show how both revolutions were similar in their condemnation of the communist world.

The student is to be commended on his/her ability to discover similarities and differences within particular topics—e.g., growing nationalistic spirits within each country "harnessed this reality differently." This student should also be rewarded for a sophisticated thesis, creative use of the documents, bringing in outside information, and several points of view, as well as calls for additional documents. This student receives a total score of 9.

WEAK SAMPLE RESPONSE

There are two revolutions in the 20th century that had remarkable similarities and remarkable differences. By looking at the revolutions individually, we will be able to see these comparisons.

Documents 1-5 speak to the revolution in Turkey. Led by charismatic General Kemal Ataturk, the revolution was successful in separating Turkey from the Ottoman Empire. Document 1 is asking for Turkey to awaken from its Ottoman coma. Document 2 describes the thoughts of a European journalist on the state of political affairs in Turkey. Document 3 has the leader Ataturk telling the people of Turkey what they can expect from the new government and Document 4 has a Turk expelled from his homeland criticizing the new government. Finally, Document 5 shows Ataturk dancing at his daughter's wedding.

Documents 6-10 talk about the revolution in Iran. All of these revolutions rip on the United States. Documents 6 and 7 are from the same person, Ayatollah, and in them he is singing the praises of the new revolution while condemning the West. Document 8 describes the Iranian government as they set up their new constitution and Document 9 describes an Iranian's thoughts as she visits Turkey. Finally, the last document, 10, shows how mean the people of Iran can be.

The only similarity is that both countries had revolutions in the 20th century and the only difference is that the Turks are humane while the Iranians are mean.

There is no thesis in either the introduction or the conclusion as there are no qualifiers identifying the similarities and differences. This student gets no points for understanding the documents as he/she misidentifies Documents 6 and 7 and misunderstands Document 4. The student's interpretation of Document 10 displays a dangerous bias. Dividing the documents geographically does not constitute grouping and does not meet the need to identify a minimum of three groups. There is no reference to a point of view and no identification of an additional document. This essay receives a score of zero.

PART B: CONTINUITY AND CHANGE-OVER-TIME QUESTION: STRONG SAMPLE RESPONSE

For most of the 8000 BCE to 600 CE time period, animistic religious practices had only a local impact on governance in Southeast Asia. However, with the development of emerging trade patterns between Southeast Asia and regions that would later be called India and China that began in the sixth century BCE, we see the organized faiths of Buddhism and Hinduism playing a significant role in the development of stronger and larger kingdoms in this part of the world.

Throughout this time, animistic religious practices were dominant. In fact, the organized faiths of Buddhism and Hinduism only gained a foothold in Southeast Asia after accepting some venerable animistic practices (such as worshiping river gods). Animism celebrates nature spirits and these beliefs encourage respect for nature at the expense of any human deities. Thus the authority of rulers was weakened as they were expected to pay homage to the sun and snakes. This meant local authorities were unable to extend their authority beyond small boundaries.

However, this would change with the development of trade between neighbors to the north and west that would begin in the sixth century BCE. As the maritime version of the Silk Road began to expand into Southeast Asia, merchants did not just bring goods to trade: they brought ideas. Hinduism came from India and Buddhism came from both India and China. Though these two faiths sometimes conflicted with each other (i.e. the competition over Angkor Wat), they both brought a unifying force that many rulers were able to harness. Both religions endorsed the idea of monarchical rule, affording a divine legitimacy for their throne. The epic stories of the faiths endorsed the idea of a ruler who was also a deity: the Bhagavad Gita speaks to a virtuous ruler pointing to how all should rule and Buddha provides a role model for similar behaviors. Each of these faiths enabled aggressive leaders to gain control of larger and larger pieces of territory, all in the name of Shiva. Devout followers were expected to follow Buddhist practices and obediently accept what was happening. Sanskrit from India institutionalized the change and the new rulers called themselves "rajas." The best example of this would be the kingdom of Funan (significant in what is today Vietnam and Cambodia) to the later years of this time period.

For most of the 8000 BCE to 600 CE time period an animistic belief system would have a disunifying impact on governance in Southeast Asia. Rulers seeking to use religion to legitimate their claim to power would have a difficult time using sun and river gods in a predominantly agricultural setting. But trade brought more of an urban setting and as the distant merchants brought the established faiths of Hinduism and Buddhism, they also brought a legitimacy that would be harnessed by local leaders, who became regional leaders, who would establish kingdoms. However, whether the leader was a raja or a local chieftain, to gain the support of the local populace he still had to respect the local animistic beliefs of the populace.

This is a fine essay, receiving a score of 8. The strength of the essay lies in its organization and thesis. There is plenty of evidence, although more analysis would be helpful, and as it stands there is only one piece of evidence supporting continuity.

WEAK SAMPLE RESPONSE

Many religions have been formed in the Middle East, especially during the time period of 8000 BCE to 600 CE. It is only fair to expect they would have had a dramatic impact on the lives of the people in this part of the world. Though the people of this region would evolve from placing their destiny in several gods to placing their destiny in only one God, they remained loyal to the belief that gods could protect them from harm.

Abraham is generally thought of as the founder of monotheism. Before him, people assigned gods to all types of conditions: sun gods and river gods to help in the harvesting of the grain, fertility gods to ensure offspring, and gods to guarantee the return of a prodigal son. All this changed when Abraham and Moses "saw the light" and passed the message along to the masses. No longer did human heads have to be connected to snakes or birds. Now, humanity could worship something created in his image!

Others followed suit. Ihknaten unsuccessfully attempted to get the people of 15th century BCE to pay homage to the super-god Aten but the statues were destroyed when Ihknaten died. Zoroastriansm in the eastern border of this region also practiced monotheism, although historians disagree as to when it made a first appearance. Descendants of the followers of Abraham called themselves Jews and a millennium and a half later, one Jew would proclaim himself to be the Son of God, giving birth to a new religion called Christianity.

A new faith was just being formed at the end of the time period: Islam. It would have the most remarkable impact on this region and others.

So, religion in this part of the world would evolve from the worship of snakes and birds to the worship of one omnipotent supernatural being. From Abraham, to Zoroaster, to Ihknaten, to Jesus, to Mohammad we see believers in this part of the world change from worshiping nature to worshipping a protector. Throughout all this time, people needed to believe in something.

Sadly, this student gets zero points for this essay. Though the student has some knowledge of history, he/she doesn't use it to answer the question. There is no point for thesis because the student doesn't direct the thesis toward the theme of political impact of belief systems. Though he/she has much evidence, some is inaccurate and there is no evidence pointing to religious beliefs and governance (not even the student's reference to Ikhnaten will work). Because there is no world historical context, there are no analysis points.

PART C: COMPARATIVE QUESTION: STRONG SAMPLE RESPONSE

The years 1450-1750 were a dynamic time for the development of new trade patterns as the world was becoming truly global. For the first time, the Western Hemisphere was interacting with Afro-Eurasia. In comparing trade patterns during this time between the Atlantic World and trade patterns in East Asia, similarities and differences abound. To begin, Europe was the major protagonist for developing trade patterns in both regions. However, whatever relationship was created between Europe and the New World would be an entirely new project at the beginning of this time frame. Europe's relationship with East Asia, however distant and inefficient, had existed for hundreds of years prior to the 15th century. For these reasons, the similarities in trade patterns between these two regions lay principally in Europe's role as leading the attempt to control the trade patterns. The differences lie in the reality that a trade pattern already existed in the Old World (Afro-Eurasia) and East Asia enjoyed the status quo.

By the middle of the 15th century, many factors had prompted Europe to look for other means to gain products from the Far East. The fall of Constantinople and recent maritime discoveries had encouraged Europeans to become more curious and entrepreneurial about the direct imports of luxuries from far away. All this led to the discovery of new lands and exploitation was soon to follow.

A dramatic similarity in the trade pattern of both regions was the leadership provided by Europe. Had there been no Europe, it may have been a long time before the Western Hemisphere would have ever met the Eastern Hemisphere. In both the Atlantic World and East Asia (the China Seas), Europe would begin the development of trade by exploiting the resources of both regions and finish the time period by attempting to apply the mercantilistic practice of establishing a favorable balance of trade. The resources exploited in the Americas would be precious metals, timber, sugar, and other foodstuffs. The resources exploited in East Asia included spices, silk, and porcelain. To gain these products and establish hegemony in both regions, Europe established such entrepôts as Lima and New Amsterdam in the Atlantic World and Capetown and Macau on the way to East Asia.

Despite the above similarities in trade patterns between the two regions, there were glaring differences. Most obvious is the degree of European success in each region. Europe was far more successful at subjugating the peoples of the Americas than they were in East Asia. Because East Asia already had a thriving trade network and because of the dramatic distance between East Asia and Europe, the effect was that during this time period Europe would never be able to dominate trade affairs but hopefully only accommodate the economic needs of East Asia. In fact, Japan and China typically found European attempts to trade with them tiresome and a nuisance and for a period cut off attempts to trade. While the sword and the germ would subjugate the Americas to the will of the Europeans, the size, distance, and immunities of the East Asian cultures prevented such foreign dominance. What's more, the established civilizations in East Asia yawned at the products Europeans had to sell. Japan built a cocoon and the Middle Kingdom more or less said sell me something, I dare you. What evolved was that while Europe developed a dramatic favorable balance of trade with the Americas (exporting precious metals) the reverse happened with its trade to China. The only payment China would accept was silver or gold. Finally, by the end of this time period, Europe found a replacement in opium. It is ironic that the New World imported addictive products to Europe (sugar, tobacco, rum) while Europe delivered addictive products (opium) to East Asia. It is also interesting to note that Europe shipped goods to both regions (slaves and opium) and raises questions of morality today.

Trade patterns in the Atlantic World and in the China Seas during the time frame 1450-1750 were similar in that Europe was the common denominator in provoking and developing global trade. However, the distinctions lie in the level of success. Europe only began to dominate East Asian affairs after this time frame had expired. Throughout this time period, Europe approached East Asia on bended knee and said "please."

This student has a solid command of history. All components in the basic core are present here and this student is awarded two points from the expanded core because of solid evidence, and an abundance of analysis and comparisons. Final score: 9.

WEAK SAMPLE RESPONSE

There were many similarities and differences in trading patterns in the Mediterranean Sea and trade patterns in the Atlantic world between 1450 and 1750. The basic similarity was that they relied upon boats to transport the goods and the main difference was in the products shipped.

The ships that traversed both bodies of water were basically the same. They relied upon the wind for movement and utilized the compass and astrolabe to effectively arrive at their destination. Sailors were motivated in their work by receiving a percentage of the profit. Of course, traveling across the ocean was more dangerous but the opportunity for greater profit still motivated them.

It was the distinction in what was shipped across these bodies of water that provided the biggest difference. Because the Mediterranean is smaller, more products were shipped and the products tended to be more diverse. Products coming from Africa, the Middle East and the Far East included such luxury items as carved elephant tusks, silks, spices, rice, and leather products. Products delivered could either be luxury items or items for mass consumption because the cost of shipping was cheap. Shipping across the Atlantic was more expensive because it was longer and more dangerous. For this reason, they shipped expensive goods, like gold and silver.

This student received one point for a minimal amount of evidence and one point for addressing differences within the body of the essay. There is no point for the thesis because citing "boats to transport the goods" as a similarity is obvious. There are no direct comparisons and there is no analysis. There is a great deal of inaccurate information.

HOW TO MAKE THIS BOOK WORK FOR YOU BASED ON THE RESULTS OF YOUR DIAGNOSTIC TEST

First, you should know that only one-half of the composite score for the AP World History exam will be multiple choice. The three essays are equally important and potentially easier to master with preparation. No matter what your results on the Diagnostic Test, you should review the essay exam format and expectations carefully.

How you interpret your Diagnostic Test score depends on your situation. How soon is the exam? If you took the Diagnostic Test in the fall or winter, you are likely to score lower than if you took the test in early May. Analyze the types of questions that you missed.

The Diagnostic Test is arranged into five time frames that correspond to the periods covered on the exam. (Remember: For the purpose of the review chapter and tests in this book, the periods 8000 BCE to 600 BCE and 600 BCE to 600 CE are grouped into a single time frame of "up to 600 CE.") If you missed several questions in one or two chronological periods, you may want to focus your preparation there. Also, if a certain type of question tripped you up, for example questions on social structures, then you may want to focus your preparation on that theme.

This review book can help. Part Three breaks down each of the chronological periods and reviews the content by topic. Look over these chapters, paying special attention to your weaknesses. Each chapter in Part Three includes practice questions to sharpen your understanding.

Part Four provides more testing practice: two complete exams with 70 multiple-choice questions and three essays. You will be ready to take these full-length exams after the bulk of your review. Set a time and a place for taking these full-length practice exams under test-like conditions without interruptions or distractions.

Part Three

AP WORLD HISTORY REVIEW

THINK LIKE A HISTORIAN

For each time period of the course, you need to **think like a world historian**. You should be able to identify the big picture ideas. Imagine yourself looking down upon the Earth and physically seeing the global developments. You could see the increase in trade, the growth of empires, the spread of religions, or the movement of people.

What would these visible changes look like? Those are your **big picture ideas**. For each time period, try to focus in on 5 to 10 big picture ideas. Before you answer any multiple-choice or essay questions dealing with that time period, first go through the list of big picture ideas in your head. Then tackle the question. Each of the five content chapters in Part Three starts with two sections that should help you focus on the big picture. The first is "If you only learn X things in this chapter." Read these over before you start, to get a sense of what is most important in the chapter that follows. Next is a section called "The Big Picture." This section provides an overview of the time period through the five themes of AP World History.

Reviewing multiple-choice and essay questions at the end of each chapter will help you understand your strengths and weaknesses for each time period.

For the sample essay questions, feel free to use as much paper as needed. For all three of those questions on the real test, you will be given 16 pages of paper.

CHAPTER 3: UP TO 600 CE

IF YOU ONLY LEARN FIVE THINGS IN THIS CHAPTER . . .

1. From the simplest barter system to long journeys along trade routes, the exchange of goods and ideas shaped this period and led to further change throughout the world. Important trade routes like the Silk Road, Indian Ocean, and Mediterranean Sea shaped development.

2. Once people began to settle and gradually organize into early civilizations, the discovery of agriculture began to change their lives at a more rapid pace.

3. As humans organized themselves in families, gender roles emerged. With the development of agriculture, the division of labor further deepened these divisions. These gender roles were reinforced by religious systems and governmental systems.

4. During this period, major world religions developed and spread, shaping the civilizations they encountered. Religions and belief systems such as Hinduism, Buddhism, Confucianism, and Daoism (Asia), and Christianity and Judaism (Europe, Asia) influenced large numbers of people throughout the period.

5. Civilizations emerged that had organized governments, complex religions, social structures, job specialization, public works, systems of writing, and arts and architecture. These civilizations grew into larger and more complicated governmental organizations such as empires, *i.e.*, Rome, Han, and Gupta.

THE BIG PICTURE

Most of the core developments that shape our world today began during this time period: government, religion, trade, and social structure, just to name a few.

1. Interactions between people and the environment

   In other words: **How does the environment shape human societies, and how do humans shape the environment?**

Farming: The Neolithic Revolution was a world-altering event. With the discovery of agriculture, people's lives began to change at a more rapid pace. Alternatively, people living in the steppes developed pastoral nomadism.

The use of metals: From the development of copper to bronze and then to iron, the use of metallurgy allowed humans to develop stronger and more efficient weapons and tools.

2. Development and interaction of cultures

   In other words: **How do people express themselves, and what is the impact of ideas?**

Religions: People always had questions about natural events, the afterlife, ethics, and the like, and religion played the role of the answer man. During this period, major world religions developed and spread, which shaped the civilizations they encountered.

Writing: As civilizations developed, so did the need to keep records and further communicate systems of writing.

Artistic Expression: Around the world, people expressed themselves through the arts: from the earliest cave paintings to great works of architecture.

3. State-building, expansion, and conflict

   In other words: **How do people govern themselves?**

Cooperation: Along with agriculture, humans began to settle down in larger groups, and this facilitated the need to cooperate and get along with each other.

Cities: Once a surplus of food could be grown, not all people needed to farm their own food, and those surpluses needed to be protected. This enabled the rise of cities, in which job specialization could occur and larger populations could be maintained.

Civilizations: From these first cities, civilizations emerged that had organized governments, complex religions, social structures, job specialization, public works, systems of writing, and arts and architecture. Over time, these early civilizations grew larger and more complex.

Governments: Most early governments were nonrepresentative monarchies or oligarchies. Representative forms of government such as democracies and republics were uncommon.

Empires: Many civilizations expanded their original area of one state and conquered surrounding neighbors to build an empire.

4. Creation, expansion, and interaction of economic systems

   In other words: **How do economic developments affect the world?**

Trade: From the simplest barter system to long journeys along the Silk Road, the exchange of goods and ideas shaped this period and led to further change throughout the world. To respond to this growth in trade, systems of currency were developed. As a result of this interaction, religions, ideas, and technology spread from one area to another.

5. Development and transformation of social structures

In other words: **How do people identify themselves socially, and what roles do men and women have?**

Social Stratification: The accumulation of a food surplus allowed some members of society to do things other than farm. This led to job specialization and the beginnings of social class structures based on economic roles, *i.e.*, aristocrats (nobles), artisans (craftsmen or tradesmen), peasants.

Gender Roles: As humans organized themselves in families, gender roles emerged. With the development of agriculture, the division of labor further deepened these divisions. In almost all cultures outside of Africa, women were excluded from positions of power, a condition also known as patriarchy. In most cultures, women had some protective rights, but in others, patriarchal societies emerged. This patriarchy was often reinforced by organized religion.

STUDY STRATEGY

As we look at more specific information for this unit, be aware of the theme the information is addressing. Also note changes and continuities and why the change or continuity occurred.

WHY THIS PERIODIZATION?

It is important to understand why historians view history through the use of periodization and to understand that there is no one right way to organize history. For the purposes of our course, world history has been divided into six chronological units. The first period counts for 5% of the exam and covers world history up to 600 BCE. The second period, from 600 BCE to 600 CE, counts for 15% of the exam. In this book, we combine these first two periods in this chapter, since each of the other four periods counts for 20% of the exam.

Around 600 BCE, the first classical empires emerge. By 600 CE, many of the classical empires of the world had collapsed. The recovery from this collapse will kick off our next unit (600 to 1450 CE).

BCE AND CE

AP World History qualifies dates as BCE (**Before the Common Era**) and CE (**Common Era**). BCE refers to the same time as BC (Before Christ), and CE refers to the same time as AD (Anno Domini, "in the year of our Lord").

GEOGRAPHIC REGIONS: WHERE IN THE WORLD AM I?

You will not be asked on the AP exam to fill in a blank map of the world, so don't worry, but you should know your basic geographic regions and hemispheres. Also, it is important to develop a sense of geography, as shown in the AP World History course description.

STUDY SUGGESTION

When you are reading about a given situation, try to visualize where in the world those developments are taking place. Alternatively, reproduce a blank world map and take notes as you read in the proper geographic region.

North America

Historic example: British, French, and Spanish colonies

Modern example: Canada, United States, Mexico

Latin America

Historic example: Spanish and Portuguese colonies in North, Central, and South America

Modern example: Brazil, Haiti, Mexico

Mesoamerica

Historic example: Olmec, Maya, Aztec

Modern example: Mexico and Central America

Western Europe

Historic example: Charlemagne's Carolingian Empire

Modern example: England, France, Spain, Italy

Eastern Europe

Historic example: parts of the Byzantine Empire

Modern example: Poland, Western Russia

Central Asia

Historic example: Tamerlane's Empire

Modern example: Kazakhstan, Uzbekistan

East Asia

Historic example: Han dynasty

Modern example: China, Japan, North and South Korea

West Asia or Middle East

Historic example: Ottoman Empire

Modern example: Iran, Iraq

South Asia

Historic example: Gupta Empire

Modern example: India, Pakistan

Southeast Asia

Historic example: Malay sailors

Modern example: Vietnam, Indonesia

Oceania

Historic example: Polynesian Migration

Modern example: Australia, New Zealand

Sub-Saharan Africa

Historic example: Kingdom of Mali, Swahili city-states

Modern example: Democratic Republic of the Congo, Kenya, South Africa

Western Hemisphere

The Americas

Eastern Hemisphere

Europe, Asia, Africa, Oceania

EARLY HUMANS

HUMAN MIGRATIONS OUT OF AFRICA

By far the longest period of human history involved the Paleolithic or early Stone Age people, when all humans lived in small bands as hunter-gathers. Almost everything that we know of these first humans comes to us from archeological evidence. By examining their bones and the remains of their campsites, we get clues about how they lived.

Small groups of ***Homo sapiens*** spread out of East Africa through the Middle East to Asia and Europe about 100,000 years ago. Groups also crossed over to what is now New Guinea and Australia when sea levels were lower because of Ice Age glaciers. Similarly, groups entered the Americas through an Ice Age land connection with Siberia. About 15,000 years ago, humans lived in almost all of the habitable regions of the world.

TOOLS OF PALEOLITHIC HUMANS

Early humans developed a variety of tools that have been found by archeologists. **Projectile points** for spears and arrows and bladed tools such as axes and knives helped these early humans take advantage of various resources. Other tools, such as harpoons and needles for sewing clothes, were adapted to the different environmental zones.

Paleolithic humans also used fire as a tool. Fire protected people against dangerous animals at night; it helped keep people warm, especially when used with clothing made of animal fur and hides; and it helped with cooking.

Although no documents exist as proof, historians believe that spoken **language** developed as another important innovation of Paleolithic humans. The coordination of a band of people for hunting big game, such as mastodons, would require that people be able to communicate through language.

PALEOLITHIC SOCIETY

Early humans traveled in nomadic groups of a few dozen hunter-gatherers. These groups were likely formed around kinship and were fairly self-sufficient. Although the evidence is slight, historians believe that these small bands of people exchanged ideas, valuable possessions, and mates with each other.

A few planned burial sites of Paleolithic people have been excavated. The items buried with the dead and also the elaborate artwork of the cave paintings indicate that Paleolithic people put a great deal of importance on the natural world. Most likely they were **animist** in their religious beliefs. In other words, they believed that spirit forces that lived in the natural world influenced events in their lives.

DEVELOPMENT OF AGRICULTURE

THE NEOLITHIC REVOLUTION: AN EXPERIMENT WITH SEEDS LEADS TO FARMING

Early man lived for thousands of years hunting animals and gathering roots and plants. Around 8000 BCE, a dramatic breakthrough in human history called the **Neolithic Revolution** changed the way people lived. It might have been called the Neolithic *transition*, though, since it took hundreds, if not thousands, of years of change before an agricultural economy took hold.

The discovery of agriculture, most likely made by women who were experimenting with seeds they had gathered, allowed people to change the way they lived. The first farmers used **slash-and-burn agriculture**, in which they would slash the bark and burn the trees to the ground. The problem was that although the land was initially very fertile, it lost much of that fertility after a few years. This caused people to migrate to new areas, helping to facilitate the spread of agriculture to new areas. A second great discovery was the **breeding of animals**. With these skills, people could now remain in one place.

Different crops were domesticated in different regions of the world depending on the plants that were available. Agriculture emerged at very different times as well. Grains such as wheat and barley were first grown in what is called the fertile crescent of Southwest Asia. Rice and soybeans were first grown in East Asia along the Yangzi and Huang He Rivers. Yams and sorghum grew in sub-Saharan Africa. People in Southeast Asia farmed taro and bananas. Maize, beans, and potatoes were grown in the Americas. From these places of independent agricultural transformation, the knowledge of how to farm crops and raise animals spread.

MORE STABILITY = MORE PEOPLE

Now that humans had settled, many changes could occur. Even though farming was a lot more work (the average hunter and gatherer only worked four hours a day to find food), it was also a lot more stable. With stability came population increase. Hunters and gatherers had very small families, but now that the moving had stopped, families could be larger. Just look at these numbers.

Time	World Population
10,000 BCE	4 million
5000 BCE	5 million
3000 BCE	14 million
2000 BCE	27 million
1000 BCE	50 million
500 BCE	100 million

LIFE IN A NEOLITHIC VILLAGE

Early farmers began to organize themselves in a more permanent way through the formation of villages. This permanence allowed for the development of new technologies: farming tools such as the hoe, for instance. As farmers experimented, they began to develop a **surplus** of food, and once a surplus was developed, **job specialization** was required. Not everyone needed to be a farmer; other jobs such as metalsmith, miller, brewer, trader, and priest provided services for the farmers—and the farmers could provide them food.

With the beginning of privately owned land, a wealthier class emerged. The ownership of this land equaled economic power. This land was kept in the families' hands and passed down from generation to generation, and with this, social classes emerged. It was the wealthiest in the community who desired luxury items, which could be traded with other communities.

For the Neolithic people, nature meant life or death. They had to learn the changes of the seasons based on the position of the sun, moon, and stars. Religiously, their main goal was to ensure fertility—both theirs and the land's. Religious beliefs centered on the life cycle of birth, growth, death, and regenerated life. Clay figurines of gods and goddesses have been unearthed that reflect these beliefs.

The Neolithic Revolution also had consequences for **gender roles**. Men were working in the fields and herding the animals, which required them to be outside the home. On the other hand, women performed such jobs as caring for the children, weaving cloth, and making cheese from milk, all of which required them to be in the home. Over time, the work outside the home was perceived as more important, and men began to take a more dominant role in the gender relationship.

EARLY INVENTIONS IN METAL AND TRANSPORTATION

In Neolithic villages, three main craft industries developed and became essential elements of almost all human agricultural societies: pottery, metallurgy, and textiles. The earliest metal used was **copper** for jewelry and simple tools. It was later heated to become more workable and was made into knives, axes, hoes, and weapons. Copper was the foundation for the later developments of tools and weapons made from bronze and iron.

Around 3000 BCE, Mesopotamian metalworkers discovered a mixture, or alloy, of copper and tin that was much harder than copper alone. This alloy, called **bronze**, was made into weapons such as swords, spears, axes, shields, armor, and tools such as bronze-tipped plows that significantly changed warfare and agriculture. Although copper is a fairly common ore, tin is relatively rare. Long-distance trade routes developed around the need for tin. Sometime around 1000 BCE, iron tools and weapons were first developed. Metalworkers discovered that when carbon was added to iron, it became much stronger. As iron is much more common than tin, it was more affordable to lower classes with resultant changes in warfare and, in some places like Greece, politics. Knowledge of metalworking spread throughout Mesopotamia, the Mediterranean region, into Africa, and across to Asia.

The exact origin of the **wheel** is unknown, but we do know that Before they were more formally organized (around 3200 BCE), Sumerians used wheeled carts for several centuries. The wheel allowed for the transport of heavier loads and much longer-distance travel and trade. This important technology spread like wildfire and within a few centuries was the standard means of overland transport everywhere but the Americas, where the absence of suitable draft animals meant it had no economic value.

Often, pastoralist people helped spread new technologies since they came in contact with a number of settled agricultural communities. Weapons from these nomads, such as iron blades and chariots, transformed warfare.

AN ALTERNATIVE WAY OF LIFE—NOT EVERYONE BECOMES A FARMER

Pastoral nomadism was another lifestyle that developed at this time. Pastoral nomads depended on their herd for survival and traveled to find grassland or **steppe** land required for their herds to graze. The steppe land of Central Asia had grass that grew where there was not much rainfall, so it was better suited for grazing animals than for farming crops. Pastoralists, however, may have adversely affected the environment when they overgrazed their animals on these fragile grasslands.

Pastoral nomadism was not a step toward a life of farming; it was quite unique. It was a complicated and advanced lifestyle in which nomads literally lived off their animals. Geography usually determined who would be a pastoralist and who would be a farmer.

Life could be quite difficult for these early pastoralists, and in response, they developed fighting skills, using both offensive and defensive military tactics to defend their herds. It was the interaction between the pastoralists and the settled people that caused much of the development in this and other time periods.

THE FIRST CIVILIZATIONS

Farming communities often developed along river banks. As the river banks flooded and carried silt onto the land, the land became more fertile. The river also allowed for transportation and communication.

Living near these large rivers required a larger amount of cooperation, because the flooding had to be controlled. Flood control techniques and irrigation projects were soon developed. Such cooperation among these first civilizations led to the development of the first urban centers or cities. These large, densely populated, permanent settlements shared many common characteristics:

- Diverse people
- Specialization—people with different jobs
- Social stratification—some people had more status than others
- Trade

Like the development of farming, the development of cities was a gradual process. Early cities were larger than Neolithic towns and villages, and had more intense specialization, professional craftsmen, professional managers (such as governors and tax collectors), and professional cultural specialists (priests, etc.). Cities had a large economic center called the **marketplace**, which was extremely influential to the surrounding regions. The marketplace became the center of political, military, and economic control.

These cities often led to the growth of more complex societies. These societies often had the following in common:

- Food surplus—such as storable grain crops
- Cities—such as Ur and Babylon
- Specialization—such as artisans and scribes
- Trade—such as transregional trade between Mesopotamia and Indus Valley
- Social stratification—such as with elites and lower classes
- Organized government—such as Assyria and Shang dynasty
- Complex religions—such as Egyptian religious belief
- Written language—such as cuneiform and hieroglyphs
- Arts/architecture—such as temples and sculptures

MESOPOTAMIA

The "land between the waters" in southwest Asia is part of the **Fertile Crescent**, which helped to encourage the earliest farming communities. Small-scale irrigation started in Mesopotamia around

6000 BCE. That caused an increase in the amount of food production, which led to an increase in population. By 3000 BCE, **Sumer** (as it came to be known) had a population of 100,000. Temples, public buildings, defensive walls, and irrigation systems were built by laborers recruited by government authorities. By 3000 BCE, its cities had kings with absolute authority, each ruling his own city-state.

These hereditary monarchs were at the top of the social order, followed closely by the priests and priestesses who were often younger relatives of the rulers. A noble class of warriors and judges advised the monarch. A fourth group was called the **free commoners**, who worked as farmers, builders, craftsmen, or professionals such as scribes. The **dependent clients**, a subgroup of commoners, owned no property and worked only on the estates of others. All commoners paid taxes with surplus food or labor. At the bottom of the social pyramid were the **slaves**, either prisoners of war or people serving punishment for debt crimes, who were agricultural laborers or domestic servants.

In Sumer, cities grew as they expanded irrigation systems, eventually developing into city-states. A city-state is a sovereign city (meaning it makes its own laws and is not ruled by anyone else) that has a hinterland or adjoining lands that support it with agricultural goods. Although they had a similar culture with regard to language, writing, and religion, each city-state had its own monarch and had its own special god or goddess that watched over it. Often warring over lands and goods, they built walls for defense. They also had distinctive step-shaped pyramids called ziggurats that were temples to the gods. Over time, these city-states were conquered and united into a single empire by many societies in succession—the Akkadians, Babylonians, Assyrians, and Persians, to name a few.

One of the most famous emperors of Mesopotamia was the Babylonian Hammurabi, who ruled from 1792 to 1750 BCE. Hammurabi used an organized central bureaucracy and regular taxation to aid in ruling his empire. He is most famous for his legal code of laws, which he promulgated on stone stele, or columns, throughout his empire; they were the first documented attempt in ancient history to connect crimes with specific punishments. Hammurabi's code of laws had three main principles. The first was the principle of retribution, whereby a crime was punished by a like sentence. If a person poked out another person's eye in a fight, that person's eye would be poked out as punishment. However, the second principle had to do with social standing. The lower in social standing you were, the more severe your punishment. A commoner poking out the eye of a noble in a fight would be put to death. A third principle was that government had a responsibility to its citizens. If your house was robbed and the thief was not caught, the local government would help reimburse you for your loss. Hammurabi's code was patriarchal—men were clearly the head of the household and had authority to sell their wives and children into slavery to pay off a debt. Women had rights of divorce and could own businesses, but it was clear that their first responsibility was to their husbands and homes.

The *Epic of Gilgamesh*, an epic poem from Mesopotamia, is one the earliest surviving works of literature. The story has been translated into many languages and has had a wide-ranging influence. Various tales and characters in the *Epic of Gilgamesh* can also be found in the Bible, such as the story of Noah and the Flood. It is also believed to have had a significant influence on the epic poems of Homer, which were written during the classical period in Greece.

EGYPT

The Nile River was truly a gift to Egypt. It gave Egypt the lifeblood of its civilizations. Around 5000 BCE, experimentation with agriculture began in this area. The people learned to plant crops such as barley and wheat after the floods had receded. They soon built dikes to protect the fields from the floods. By 4000 BCE, villages had developed irrigation systems.

Egypt also was protected by its geography. The Nile, of course, protected it from invasion, but so did the Red Sea, Mediterranean Sea, and Sahara Desert.

Ancient Egyptian society was ruled by pharaohs. It was under the leadership of these rulers that Egypt built some of the most beautiful and enduring architectural works of human history. The most famous are the pyramids of Giza, which were built as tombs for three successive pharaohs. The polytheistic Egyptians believed that the gods judged your life and that if found worthy, your spirit lived on in an afterlife. This led to the process of mummification and to elaborate tombs, like the pyramids, in whose walls the hieroglyphic accounts of the pharaoh's life were written.

The Egyptians excelled in making bronze weapons and were skilled in mathematics, medicine, and astronomy. The solar calendar of 365 days that we use today was first devised in ancient Egypt. Around 3100 BCE, the Egyptians developed their own written language made up of pictographs, or **hieroglyphics**.

For obvious reasons, the pharaoh was at the top of the social class structure, followed by priests, commoners, and slaves. Egypt had professional military forces and a bureaucracy of administrators and tax collectors. The way to get ahead in society was to be close to the pharaoh. Service to him meant higher status.

Unlike Mesopotamia, in Egypt women who were literate could often take on jobs as administrators, although with the exception of one female pharaoh, they did not assume the higher political positions.

Ancient Egyptian art attained a high level in painting and sculpture. Much that has survived comes from tombs of the pharaohs and therefore has an emphasis on life after death. These paintings and sculptures provide detailed depiction of gods, human beings, heroic battles, and nature, and were meant to provide comfort to the dead in the afterlife.

INDUS

The Indus is a civilization with much mystery even today. This urbanized civilization was discovered only in the early 20th century. It developed between 3000 BCE and 2500 BCE and had declined by 1500 BCE. Its language is still not understood, but we do know that its **polytheistic** religious belief system centered on a strong concern for fertility. Its entire area was approximately 500,000 square miles, larger than both Mesopotamia and Egypt.

Large Indus cities have been uncovered in recent years: The two largest ones have been named **Harappa** and **Mohenjo-Daro**. These walled cities, designed in a grid pattern, featured broad streets, marketplaces, temples, assembly halls, baths, and uniform housing. There were even rich and poor sections of town. The wealthiest people even had private bathrooms with showers and toilets that drained into city sewage systems.

Technologically and economically speaking, Indus had a lot going for it: it traded pottery, tools, and decorative items; it obtained gold, silver, and copper from Persia; and it obtained wool, leather, and olive oil from Mesopotamia. Metal tools of bronze and copper have been found, as well as jewelry made of precious stones. Cotton was cultivated in this area before 5000 BCE.

The writing system, however, has yet to be deciphered. It is still a mystery today. We do know that it used approximately 400 symbols to represent sounds and words. These symbols have been found on clay seals and copper tablets.

Sometime after 2000 BCE, the Indus civilization began to decline. A combination of environmental factors might have caused this, and by 1500 BCE, the civilization had collapsed.

ARYANS

The Aryans, a nomadic people of Indo-European origin, entered the Indian subcontinent through the Khyber Pass around 1700 BCE. They quickly dominated the inhabitants of the Indus valley, and established a racial mix in what is now **India**.

Few artifacts were left behind by the Aryans, so much about them is unknown. What we do know is from a collection of sacred hymns, songs, prayers, and rituals known as the **Vedas**. They reveal a hierarchical, male-dominated society. The Aryans were polytheistic with many gods connected to nature. The social structure had probably the largest impact on India; it developed gradually and became the basis for the **caste system**. People were divided into four **varnas** based on occupation and purity: brahmins (scholars and priests), ksatriyas (ruling and warrior class), vaisyas (merchants, farmers, craftsmen), and shudras (servants). The lower class of untouchables (outcastes) was incorporated into the system later. Aryans tried to prohibit intermarriage between the varnas, but this was difficult to enforce, and over the years a blending of Aryan and indigenous people took place.

SHANG AND ZHOU

The first river valley civilization in China developed along the **Huang He** or **Yellow River**. This river got its name from the light-colored **loess** soil that caused the river to appear yellow. Despite its fertile land, the river's devastating floods earned it the nickname "China's Sorrow." It was in this river valley where the earliest civilization in China developed, which was ruled by a dynasty. This dynasty is called the **Shang**, which ruled a northern territory from 1766 to 1122 BCE in what today is called China. Major archeological evidence used to prove the existence of the Shang dynasty is found in **"oracle bones."** Questions about—and predictions of—the future were written on these bones, so we have a type of written record. The development of written Chinese (pictograph) characters is traced back to the Shang. These pictures evolved into symbols, or ideographs. Additionally, the Shang developed **bronze metallurgy**, which aided in its rise as a military state.

The next and longer dynasty, the **Zhou** (1122 to 256 BCE), further cemented important Chinese cultural foundations. The most notable tradition was the concept of the **Mandate of Heaven**, meaning power to rule was granted from heaven. Since this power was divinely given, there was a direct connection between ruler and god. This power could be taken away, however, if justice and order were not maintained. Signs from the gods such as floods, earthquakes, and peasant rebellions were indications that the end was near for the dynasty.

Culturally and religiously, the Zhou placed great emphasis on the **veneration of ancestors**, and the family unit was the most important social structure. The belief was that if everyone honored their responsibilities toward the family, society would function smoothly. The Zhou had a strong elite ruling class, reinforced by hereditary aristocrats. A small class of free artisans and craftsmen, a large class of peasants, and slaves completed the social class structure. Additionally, during the Zhou period, **iron metallurgy** spread to China.

Even with all this structure, the Zhou lost control of the western half of the empire to other families as early as 771 BCE. Complete control was lost in the fifth century and was followed by the Warring States period, a time in which various noble families fought amongst each other for control of China. This period ended in 221 BCE with the rise of the Qin dynasty.

MESOAMERICA AND SOUTH AMERICA

In the Americas, agriculture developed around the same time as in our other civilizations, but the civilizations there did not develop in river valleys. Around 1500 BCE, the **Olmecs** settled in the coastal plain near the **Gulf of Mexico** along river banks. The periodic flooding left the land fertile for agriculture. The first important settlement was **San Lorenzo**, which was the religious, political, and economic center for the large population. Later, **La Venta** served as an important center, and with its abundant rainfall, there was no need to build an extensive irrigation system. Olmec artisans carved masks and human figurines out of jade, which they imported from a neighboring area. As in other societies, social status was often indicated by the type of clothing and ornaments a person wore. The more elaborate the dress and decoration, the higher the social class.

One of the great mysteries of the Olmecs is the **colossal heads** they built, which are six feet high and weigh between 16 to 18 tons each. It is believed that they are carvings of the leadership, but no one knows for sure. What we do know is that it took a lot of organization and labor to construct such things, especially since there were no draft animals to help with the work. The society was most likely authoritarian, in which the lower class performed the bidding of the upper class. The decline and fall of the Olmecs is also a bit of a mystery. Its ceremonial centers were destroyed and abandoned, but no one knows why.

In South America, urban centers developed in isolation from those in Mesoamerica, but at about the same time. Around 2500 BCE, cultivation of such crops as beans, peanuts, and potatoes was occurring in the **Andean heartland**. Around 1000 BCE, an important religious cult—the **Chavin**—gained influence and the society became more complex. Chavin de Huantar was the most important ceremonial center and had several large temple platforms. Artisans worked with ceramics, textiles, and gold. Societies in both Mesoamerica and South America constructed religious shrine centers. These early American civilizations would influence the civilizations and empires to develop later.

DEVELOPMENT AND SPREAD OF RELIGION

Since the earliest times, man has struggled with the unanswerable questions, "Why am I here?" "Who made me?" and "What happens after I die?" Religions developed around the world to address these questions.

Early civilizations were mostly polytheistic. Often, gods or goddesses were associated with nature, and sacrifices were made to these gods to ensure things such as good harvests. Over time, religions became more complex. Even after the emergence of codified religious beliefs, shamanism and animism continued to be important in many peoples' understanding of the forces of nature. In addition, ancestor veneration remained a part of religious belief in East Asia, Africa, and the Mediterranean world.

Around 600 BCE, major religions and philosophies emerged to address some new questions or concerns that the previous traditions may not have been sufficiently answering. Philosopher Karl Jaspers calls this time period the **Axial Age**. The axial represents the core ideas around which a society revolves. Great philosophers emerged during this period, with new answers to difficult questions. These "axial" ideas went on to make indelible marks on the civilizations in which they developed.

HINDUISM

The religion of Hinduism originated in India, but we cannot link a specific time or person to its creation. There was no "Mr. Hindu." It is a belief system that evolved over time. It actually refers to a wide variety of beliefs and practices that developed in South Asia. Hinduism is often described as not just a religion, but a way of life, because of the important impact it has on its followers.

At the most basic level, Hindus believe that they have a **dharma**, or duty, to perform in life. If all follow their dharma, the world works smoothly. Only when dharma is violated do things seem to be out of sync. This dharma is determined by birth and one's stage in life. If one follows his dharma, he will get good **karma**. It is the accumulation of this good karma (the sum of all good and bad deeds performed) that allows someone to move up in the level of **samsara** in the next life.

Hindus believe that they will be **reincarnated** (reborn) after death. The new position they assume in the next life will depend on how well they performed their dharma in the past life. The ultimate goal for Hindus is to end the cycle of reincarnation by finally reaching **moksha** or oneness with the universe. Hinduism is a polytheistic religion that believes in Brahma, the creator god, and his various incarnations including Vishnu, Shiva, and Devi. Bhatki is a popular practice in which followers have a personal devotion to a particular deity.

The social structure known as the **caste system** has had an enormous impact on the followers of Hinduism. The four varnas are the basis for the caste system. They are **Brahmins** (priests and scholars), **ksatriyas** (warriors and ruling class), **vaisyas** (farmers and businessmen), and **shudras** (servants). A fifth group at the bottom of society became known as the **untouchables**.

The caste system is based on the concepts of purity and pollution. This includes pure foods, sounds, and sights. Jobs are ranked because purity is associated with those who work with their minds, and pollution is associated with those who come in contact with polluted things such as sweat or human excrement. To ensure this purity, people should only marry members of their own caste.

Hinduism remains important in India and a few areas in Southeast Asia to which it spread. Some of the core ideas of Hinduism were reformed by Siddhartha Gautama into the religion of Buddhism, which later became a worldwide religion.

BUDDHISM

Siddhartha Gautama, who lived from approximately 563 BCE to 483 BCE, became an important axial-age thinker in India. He was raised as a prince in a small state near present-day Nepal. After living a sheltered life, he decided to leave the palace in search of answers to such questions as: "Why is there so much suffering in the world?" "Is there a way out of suffering?" After meditating under a bodhi tree, the prince reached enlightenment and became known as the **Buddha (enlightened one)**.

AP EXPERT TIP

The two epic poems the *Mahabharata*, with its important section called the *Baghavad Gita*, and the *Ramayana* are key elements of Hinduism. Other epic poems such as Homer's *Iliad* and *Odyssey*, and the *Sundiata* in Mali, played important roles in defining the culture of each of their societies. Knowing the role of literature in a society and being able to compare historical examples is a type of knowledge required by the AP exam.

The Buddha made a crucial decision that helped to transform his ideas from the thoughts of one man into a world religion: He decided to teach what he had learned to others. The Buddha taught that there were **four noble truths:**

1. All life is suffering.

2. Suffering is caused by desire.

3. There is a way out of suffering.

4. The way out of suffering is to follow the Eightfold Path.

The **Eightfold Path** includes right understanding, purpose, speech, conduct, livelihood, effort, awareness, and concentration. The idea was that if you want to stop suffering, you must stop **desiring**, and if you want to stop desiring, you must live in a righteous manner by following the Eightfold Path. The ultimate goal for Buddhists is to reach **nirvana**, which is the release from the cycles of reincarnation and the achievement of union with the universe.

Buddhism took the central ideas of Hinduism such as dharma, karma, and samsara, but then altered them significantly. According to Buddhism, people did not need the rituals of the Brahmins. Gods and goddesses are not necessary—everyone can seek enlightenment on his or her own, and no one is an outcast by birth (challenging the caste system, very important in India). There is, it espouses, complete equality among all believers.

Buddhism was a religion that "hit the road." The followers of the Buddha acted as **missionaries** spreading his message. These ideas particularly appealed to low-caste Hindus as well as women.

The Mauryan emperor **Asoka** actively encouraged the spread of Buddhism. Back in India, however, some Buddhist beliefs were absorbed into Hinduism, which remained the dominant religion. Buddhism spread throughout Asia, however, along the Silk Road, where it met with great success. It greatly influenced Central Asia, China, Japan, Korea, and Southeast Asia. As it spread, it would blend with the native ideas of the lands it encountered (syncretism). It was its flexibility and its message of universal acceptance that helped make Buddhism a major world religion.

AXIAL AGE IN CHINA

From the seventh century BCE to 221 BCE, no strong central government existed in China. This was a time of constant fighting and disorder, and is referred to as the **Era of Warring States**. It is within this time that three important philosophies emerged in China: **Confucianism, Daoism**, and **Legalism**. All attempted to end the fighting and restore order, but in different ways.

CONFUCIANISM

Confucius (551 to 479 BCE) was a philosopher who believed that his answers to the questions of why we are here and how we should live could bring an end to the existing warfare. The key to ending the chaos and to bringing back peace, he felt, was to find the right kind of leadership to rule China.

His two most important concepts were **ren** (appropriate feelings) and **li** (correct actions), which must be used together in order to have any effect. Additionally, **filial piety** (respect for one's parents) was a key concept.

Confucius taught that order would be achieved when people knew their proper roles and relationships to others. Rulers would rule by **moral example** and people would learn to behave properly through the example of those superior to them. According to Confucius, there are **five key relationships:**

1. Ruler to subject

2. Father to son

3. Husband to wife

4. Older brother to younger brother

5. Friend to friend

Confucianism became the most influential philosophy in China. During the Han dynasty, Confucian ideas were used (in addition to some Daoism and Legalism) to bring peace and order. These ideas left a permanent mark on China and were continually used by subsequent dynasties throughout China's history. These ideas also spread to Korea and Japan, where they became very influential.

DAOISM

Some claim that the Chinese sage **Laozi** founded the Daoist school of thought around the sixth century BCE, around the same time as Confucius; however, its ideas go back further in Chinese history. The **Tao te Ching** or **Dao te Ching**, a collection of Daoist wisdom, is attributed to Laozi. Daoist ideas represent a protest movement during the troubled times of the Era of Warring States.

The literal translation of the Dao is the **way**, the **way of nature**, or the **way of the cosmos**. According to Daoism, all life is interdependent, and human beings should exist in harmony with nature. Its advice is to relax and get in harmony with the Dao. In order to solve the problems of the day, Daoists taught the concept of **wu wei**, which means *act by not acting*. Do nothing and problems will solve themselves, like in nature. Be like water—soft and yielding—but at the same time, very naturally powerful.

Daoists believed it was useless to try to build institutions to govern men, because institutions (or anything that rewarded knowledge) were dangerous. Institutions lead to competition and, eventually, to fighting. The less government the better; the ideal state is a small, self-sufficient town. The ultimate goal should be to cultivate the virtues of patience, selflessness, and concern for all.

AP EXPERT TIP

Like many great religious leaders, Confucius did not write his knowledge down. Confucius's teachings were brought together by his disciples in a book called *The Analects*. Knowing the basic doctrines (books, poems, etc.) of the major religions is knowledge required by the AP exam.

You might wonder how a philosophy like this could bring an end to the Era of Warring States. In reality, it couldn't, but the idea of it was a rejection of some strict guidelines in society and a way to find an alternative way of life. In Chinese society, it provided a counterpoint to the proper behavior of Confucianism—it encouraged people to take time off, relax, and just let things happen. It allowed the Chinese to be Confucian at work and Daoist while not at work.

Daoism's attitude toward war was that it should be used only for defensive purposes. The Han followed this idea by stationing its troops along the Great Wall to maintain the safety of trade routes. Laozi gained many disciples in China, though some mixed his ideas with magic and attempted to search for immortality.

COMPARATIVE CLOSE-UP: SOCIAL HIERARCHY AND RELIGION

Religion	Social Hierarchy
Hinduism	Brahmins (scholars/priests)
	Ksatriyas (warrior/ruling class)
	Vaisyas (professional class—merchants, land owners, etc.)
	Shudras (servant class—laborers, servants, etc.)
	Untouchables (outcastes)
Confucianism	Peasants
	Merchants
	Warriors and others (such as theater performers)
	Scholar gentry

LEGALISM

The philosophy of Legalism was based on the principle that man was inherently evil and needed strict laws and punishment to behave properly. Additionally, a strong central government with an absolute leader would ensure a more stable society. Legalism was adopted by the first emperor of the Qin dynasty, Qin Shihuangdi, who created China's first centralized government and ended the Era of Warring States.

JUDAISM

The Hebrews were a nomadic people who migrated out of Mesopotamia sometime around 2000 BCE and settled in the area known as Palestine. By 1700 BCE, many Hebrews had migrated into Egypt. Some of them may have been employed as administrators and advisors, yet most, over time, were enslaved by the Egyptians. Sometime after 1300 BCE, Moses led the Hebrews out of Egypt in a flight that became known as the **Exodus**.

The Hebrews believed that they were protected by their own god **YHWH** (what may have been pronounced *Yahweh*, but was considered too holy a word to say aloud). They believed that they had a special relationship with this god. According to the Bible, the **Ten Commandments** were given to Moses by God, and at that time, it was revealed that the Hebrews were God's chosen people.

As a result, the Hebrews entered into a Covenant with God; they were forbidden from worshipping any other god and were obligated to follow the Ten Commandments. Some of these commandments included honoring your mother and father, not killing, and not committing adultery. The Hebrews believed that if they honored the Ten Commandments, YHWH would lead them to the promised land. Most important, the Hebrews (who became known as Jews) established a **monotheistic tradition**, which claims there is one creator (God) who made the world and all life.

The Hebrews returned to the "Promised Land" on the eastern shores of the Mediterranean, and the kingdom of **Israel** was established, led by a monarchy. The height of Israelite power came during the reigns of King David and his son Solomon around 1000 BCE. Later, the Assyrians invaded, destroyed the temple in Jerusalem, and scattered part of the population. The kingdom of Israel managed to keep its independence for a while, but when the Chaldeans defeated the Assyrians, they also conquered Israel, completely destroyed Jerusalem, and exiled the Israelites to Babylonia. This period in Jewish history is referred to as the Babylonian Captivity. However, when the Persians conquered the Chaldeans, they allowed the Israelites to return to Jerusalem. The temple was rebuilt, but the former kingdom of Israel was swallowed up by the Greek and Roman Empires after 330 BCE.

The Jews remained determined to preserve their culture. Uprisings against the Romans in 66 and 135 CE were suppressed with large military campaigns. Many Jews were killed and the temple was leveled. In 135 CE, the Romans drove the Jews out of their homeland, causing them to scatter. This scattering of the Jews is referred to as the **Diaspora**. Jews survived in scattered communities around the Mediterranean region, Persia, and Central Asia.

As a monotheistic religion, Judaism would go on to influence the development of Christianity and Islam.

ZOROASTRIANISM

Around 600 BCE, a Persian prophet named Zoroaster attempted to explain the wars, conquests, and famines that had plagued the Fertile Crescent since the rise of the first Sumerian city-states. He saw the Earth as a battleground between the forces of good and evil in which each person must participate. Zoroastrianism, like Judaism, was a monotheistic religion. According to Zoroaster, each person's actions battling for the forces of good would be judged at the end of time by the one god, Ahura

AP EXPERT TIP

You will see the Hebrews are also referred to as the Israelites and Jews. The terms are generally interchangeable up to the time of Jesus. In the Common Era, they are typically only referred to as the Jews.

Mazda. The influence of Zoroastrianism can be found in Judaism, Christianity, and Islam; for example, in the concept of Satan.

CHRISTIANITY

Jesus was born to Jewish parents about 4 BCE in the area know as **Judea** (today the country of Israel), which was part of the Roman Empire. At the time, there was tension between Rome and its Jewish subjects.

Jesus taught devotion to God and love for fellow human beings. He earned a reputation for wisdom and the power to perform miracles, *i.e.*, heal the sick. His message of the **Kingdom of God** alarmed Roman authorities, however, and to quell a potential rebellion, they had him executed on a cross in the early 30s CE.

Jesus had been concerned with the growing cosmopolitan nature of Jewish society and preached a simple message of love and compassion. These ideas appealed to the lower class, the urban population, and women. Men and women were considered spiritually equal before God. For many, this message gave them a sense of purpose. The faithful would experience **eternal life** in heaven with God.

The death of Jesus was just the beginning of this story. His followers believed that he rose from the dead and that he was the son of God. As such, they compiled a body of writings about his life and his messages; this became the **New Testament**.

The earliest followers of Jesus (Christians) were all Jews, but in the mid- first century CE, Paul began to spread Jesus' message to non-Jews (gentiles). He and other missionaries used the Roman roads and sea lanes to spread this new religion. However, Christians, much like the Jews, refused to honor the state cults or to worship the emperor as a god, and as a result, were often subject to campaigns of persecution.

Even so, the religion continued to spread throughout the empire until Emperor Constantine issued the **Edict of Milan** in 313 CE, making Christianity legal in the Roman Empire. Emperor Theodosius went on to make it the official religion of the empire.

Christianity also spread to Mesopotamia, Iran, and even parts of India. Over time, the Southwest Asian Christians and the Western (or Roman) Christians grew apart. Southwest Asian Christians followed a form of the religion called **Nestorian Christianity**. This form of Christianity continued to spread across the Silk Road into Central Asia, India, and China.

Another form of Christianity developed in Northern Africa and is called Coptic Christianity based on the Coptic language its followers use. Coptic Christian

AP EXPERT TIP

The terms *Old Testament*, *New Testament*, and *Gospels* are Christian. Although the Christian *Old Testament* contains much of the Jewish Bible, the *Tanakh*, the term *Old Testament* would refer to a Christian point of view.

kingdoms existed in Ethiopia since the sixth century, and the religion still thrives in Egypt and Ethiopia today.

COMPARATIVE CLOSE-UP: ROLE OF WOMEN IN RELIGION

Religion	Role of Women
Buddhism	Women could achieve nirvana. An alternative lifestyle was available for women as nuns in a monastery.
Christianity	Men and women were equal in the eyes of god. Women could go to heaven. Many early converts were women. Women could live in convents.
Confucianism	Men were superior to women. One of five key relationships is that of husband to wife.
Hinduism	Men were superior to women. Women were not allowed to read the sacred prayers, the Vedas. In order to reach moksha, one must be a male Brahmin.

CLASSICAL SOCIETIES

The political and cultural beginnings in the five classical societies of Persia, Greece, India, Rome, and China laid the foundations for future development. Classical Greek and Indian societies created the foundations for the development of future decentralized governments, while classical Roman and Chinese societies created the blueprint for later centralized states.

PERSIA

POLITICAL DEVELOPMENT

Ancient Persia was centered in present-day Iran. People first migrated to this area around 1000 BCE and established a number of small kingdoms. Around 550 BCE, the Persian king Cyrus began to conquer neighboring kingdoms. By 539 BCE, he controlled an empire that extended 2,000 miles from the Indus River to Anatolia (present-day Turkey). Cyrus's legacy is the method of his rule. Unlike most conquerors of this period, Cyrus honored local customs and religions of conquered peoples. He ended the Babylonian captivity of the Jews, allowing them to return to Jerusalem in 538 BCE to rebuild their city and temple.

The Persian emperor Darius, whose rule began in 522 BCE, is noted for his administrative genius. He divided the empire into 20 provinces, each of which closely resembled the homelands of the different peoples who lived in the empire. Each province was ruled by a **satrap**, who allowed the people under his jurisdiction to practice their own religion, speak their own language, and follow their own laws.

ECONOMIC DEVELOPMENT

Darius used other tools to maintain his empire, which also brought economic benefits. The Persians created an excellent road system that included the 1,677-mile **Royal Road**, which facilitated communication and trade within the empire. Darius also manufactured metal coins of standard value that were used throughout the empire. This network of roads and standardized coins facilitated trade.

GREECE

POLITICAL DEVELOPMENT

Greece's political identity revolved around the concept of the **polis** (city-state). Greece's geography of mountainous terrain helped in the development of this decentralized political structure. Different city-states took on different forms, and they emerged independently. A few functioned as monarchies, but most were based on some form of collaborative rule.

The two most famous city-states were **Sparta** and **Athens**. Sparta used military strength to impose order, while Athens used democratic principles to negotiate order. Athens's government was a direct democracy that relied on its small size and the intense participation of its citizens. Those citizens were free adult males. (This meant no women, foreigners, or slaves could be citizens.)

The Spartans, on the other hand, lived life with no luxuries, where distinction was earned through discipline and military talent. Boys began their rigorous military training at age seven, and girls received physical education to promote the birth of strong children.

Over time, population pressures led to the establishment of colonies along the Mediterranean Sea, yet a centralized state was not created. These colonies relied on their own resources and took their own course. They did, however, facilitate trade throughout the region.

Greek cities in Anatolia (modern-day Turkey) resented what they viewed as the oppressive rule of the Persian Empire and revolted. The revolt started the **Persian War** (500–470 BCE). Athenians, too, sent their own troops in support. In two separate wars a decade apart, the Persians attacked the Greek mainland. During the first war, the important victory at Marathon by the Athenians led to Athens's Golden Age. During the second war, the Athenian-led naval victory at Salamis and the Spartan-led army victory at Plataea stopped the Persian attempts to conquer the Greek city-states.

AP EXPERT TIP

The city-state form of government is common throughout history. Sumeri, Greece, the Maya civilization, Medieval Germany, East African Swahili, and arguably modern-day Singapore are all examples of city-states throughout history. Knowing the characteristics of this form of government and comparing historical examples are examples of the types of knowledge the AP exam may ask you to express.

The alliance of the Greeks against the Persians led to the formation of the **Delian League**, of which Athens served as the leader. However, this leadership soon caused resentment by other parts of the Greek world. The conflict came to a head during the **Peloponnesian War** (431–404 BCE). Sparta and Athens each led the two conflicting camps, and though Sparta was victorious, the internal conflict weakened Greece and left it vulnerable to domination by a stronger power. That stronger power came from Macedonia, a frontier state north of the Greek peninsula.

King Philip II (359–336 BCE) consolidated control of his kingdom and moved into Greece, and by 338 BCE, the region was under his control. His next goal was to conquer Persia, but that job would be left to his son, **Alexander**. Alexander, a skilled military commander and strategist, successfully conquered Persia by 330 BCE and went on to conquer most of the northwest regions of the Indian subcontinent. But his troops had had enough, and they refused to go any further. By 323 BCE, at the age of 33, Alexander the Great was dead. What he left behind was the creation of a **Hellenistic Empire and Era**. The empire was divided among three of his generals who were the namesakes for these areas: Antigonid (Greece and Macedonia), Ptolemaic (Egypt), and Seleucid (Persia).

ECONOMIC DEVELOPMENTS

The Greek world relied heavily on trade as the cornerstone of its economy. The Mediterranean Sea linked its communities through this trade and created a larger Greek community. During the Hellenistic Era, caravan trade flourished from Persia to the West, and sea lanes were widely traveled throughout the Mediterranean Sea, Persian Gulf, and Arabian Sea. This trade created a cosmopolitan culture.

SOCIAL STRUCTURE AND GENDER ROLES

Overall, Greece was a **patriarchal** society with fairly strict social divisions. Women were under the authority of their fathers, husbands, and then, sons. Most women owned no land and often wore veils in public. Their one public position could be that of a priestess of a religious cult. Literacy, however, was common among upper-class Greek women, and Spartan women took part in athletic competitions.

Slaves in Greek society were acquired because they had debt, were prisoners of war, or were traded. The treatment of slaves varied widely, depending of the needs and temperament of the owner.

CULTURE, ARTS, SCIENCE, AND TECHNOLOGY

Culturally, the Greeks stressed a central importance on human life and a growing appreciation of human beauty. This is seen through Greek religion, philosophy, art, architecture, literature, athletics, and science. **Polytheistic**, the Greeks believed that their gods were personifications of nature. Each city-state had its own patron god or goddess for whom rituals were performed.

One of the greatest legacies of classical Greek civilization is philosophy. The great philosopher **Socrates**, who posed questions and encouraged reflection, said, "The unexamined life is not worth living." His student **Plato** wrote *The Republic*, in which he described his ideal state ruled by a philosopher king. Plato's student **Aristotle** wrote on biology, physics, astronomy, politics, and ethics. Aristotle is considered the father of logic, and his system of deductive reasoning was an important element in the development of political systems, scientific advancements, and religion up to the modern era. In literature, the great epic poems attributed to Homer, the *Iliad* and the *Odyssey*, convey the value of the hero in Greek culture. In architecture, the Greeks built temples using pillars or columns, and they developed a realistic approach to human sculpture. The Olympic games were held regularly to demonstrate athletic excellence.

The Greeks also made great strides in anatomy, astronomy, and math, including the medical writings of Galen and the mathematics of Archimedes.

INDIA

POLITICAL DEVELOPMENT

Following the invasions of the Aryans, by the sixth century BCE India developed into **small regional kingdoms** that often fought each other. Though there were periods of centralized rule, the subcontinent remained **decentralized** through most of its early history.

One significant example of centralized rule was that of the **Mauryans**. In the 320s BCE, **Chandragupta Maurya** made his move to fill the power vacuum left after Alexander of Macedonia withdrew from the region. Maurya successfully dominated the area and set up a bureaucratic administrative system to rule his empire. His grandson, **Ashoka**, continued his grandfather's conquering ways until the bloody campaign to conquer Kalinga. This bloodbath convinced Ashoka to stop using a conquering approach and instead rule by moral example. He used his *Rock Edicts* (announcements carved into cliffs and in caves) to get his message out to people. During his reign, Ashoka set up a tightly organized bureaucracy that collected taxes and was made up of officials, accountants, and soldiers. He built roads, hospitals, and rest houses, which facilitated trade. After Ashoka's death, the Mauryan Empire declined and India returned to a land of large regional kingdoms, but order and stability was maintained with an increase in trade.

It was not until 320 CE that India would again be united under centralized rule. Chandra Gupta (no relation to the other one) established the **Gupta Empire** and conquered many of the regional kingdoms. The south, however, remained out of

AP EXPERT TIP

Ashoka converted to Buddhism and later used Buddhist monks to spread Buddhism across Central Asia and into Southeast Asia. Knowing causes and effects for the spread of religion is a type of knowledge commonly asked for on the AP World History exam.

his control. Instead of setting up an organized bureaucracy, the Guptas left the local government and administration in power. Under the Gupta, Hinduism emerged as the primary religion of Indian culture, while Buddhism mostly disappeared from the Indian subcontinent. Their rule continued until the invasion of the White Huns severely weakened the empire and India returned to regional rule.

ECONOMIC DEVELOPMENT

India's economy benefited from the expansion of agriculture and the increase in trade throughout the classical period. Ashoka encouraged agricultural development through irrigation and encouraged trade by building roads, wells, and inns along those roads. Agricultural surplus led to an increase in the number of towns; these towns maintained marketplaces and encouraged trade. Long-distance trade increased with China, Southeast Asia, and the Mediterranean basin. Overland trade via the **Silk Road** connected India with China through Central Asia. Ideas and technology, as well as goods, were spread along the Silk Road.

Indian sailors mastered the technique of riding the monsoon (seasonal) winds, and they sailed to Indonesia and Southeast Asia. Their goods, such as cotton and black pepper, made it all the way to Rome.

SOCIAL STRUCTURE AND GENDER ROLES

Like Greece, India developed into a **patriarchal** society with a strict social structure. Women were forbidden from reading the sacred prayers (the Vedas), and under Hindu law, they were legally minors and subject to the supervision of their fathers, husbands, and then sons.

In order to marry well, a woman's family needed a large dowry. Women were not allowed to inherit property, and a widow was not permitted to remarry. The social structure became dominated by the power of the Brahmins and the caste system. **Caste**—something that could not be changed—determined one's job, diet, and marriage. These restrictions were reinforced by the ruling class. As the Brahmins became more powerful, especially during the rule of the Guptas, caste distinctions grew more prominent.

CULTURE, ARTS, SCIENCE, TECHNOLOGY

During this period, India's culture thrived, including its advancements in the arts, math, and science. The Mauryan emperor Ashoka became a devout Buddhist around 260 BCE, after the battle at Kalinga, and changed the way he ruled his empire. He rewarded Buddhists with land and encouraged the spread of the religion by building monasteries and stupas (mound-like structures that contained Buddhist relics and that served as places of worship). He even sent out missionaries,

---

AP EXPERT TIP

Centralized rule means that the emperor rules directly through governors, military leaders, or scholars. Decentralized rule means that the emperor lets local rulers rule their own people although they must collect and pay taxes and/or tribute to the emperor. Centralized rule is often more stable and resistant to outside invaders.

who facilitated the spread of **Buddhism** to Central Asia, East Asia, and Southeast Asia. But through political support, **Hinduism** gradually eclipsed the influence of Buddhism. The Guptas gave land grants to Brahmins, supported education that promoted Hindu values, and built great temples in urban centers.

Unlike Greek art, Indian art during this time stressed symbolism rather than accurate representation. Math such as geometry and algebra and science flourished. The circumference of the Earth and the value of *pi* were calculated. Additionally, the concept of zero, the decimal system, and the number system we use today called Arabic numbers were developed.

CHINA

POLITICAL DEVELOPMENT

China's political development during this time period laid the foundation for what was to endure over 2,000 years. What kind of system can have that kind of lasting power?

It all started during a period referred to as the **Era of Warring States** (403–221 BCE). During this time of turmoil and warfare, three important philosophies emerged (the **Three Schools of Thought**) to address the problems of the day and attempt to end the fighting: Confucianism, Daoism, and Legalism. Legalism offered the firmest solution to China's problems, preaching a practical and ruthless approach to state rule. The foundation of a state's strength, it proposed, was in its agricultural production and its military, and strict laws and punishments were required to maintain order.

The first Chinese emperor thought these Legalist ideas might be the solution to China's problems. In 221 BCE, the first emperor, **Qin Shihuangdi**, ended the Era of Warring States and started China's tradition of centralized rule under the **Qin dynasty**. He created a centralized bureaucracy and divided the land into administrative provinces. For protection, he sponsored the building of defensive walls throughout the empire, which were the predecessor to China's **Great Wall**. Laws, currencies, weights, measures, and the Chinese script were standardized. As the emperor was not a fan of Confucianism, he had most of its books burned and had 460 scholars buried alive. His rule lasted only 14 years, but he established the precedent for centralized rule in China, which would last for 2,000 years. When the emperor died in 207 BCE, revolts broke out and a new dynasty—the Han—was established.

The **Han dynasty** (206 BCE–220 CE) was much longer than the Qin dynasty, and it also learned from the Qin's mistakes. The Han used what worked—such as

AP EXPERT TIP

Knowing the Chinese dynasties in correct order is essential for proper chronological understanding of much of world history. Memorizing the dynasties, their end and start dates, and key cultural and technological innovations will greatly assist you in both the multiple-choice and essay portions of the exam.

centralized rule and a strong bureaucracy—but lessened the Legalist hard edge of the rule. The most prominent Han emperor, **Wu Di** (141–87 BCE), built roads and canals, and established an imperial university with Confucianism as the basis for the curriculum. The university prepared students for the **civil service exams**, which became the entry test for government jobs. The Han emperors still exerted absolute control, but they used the Confucian ideas about their authority over the empire in the same way that a father has authority over his family and home. During the Han dynasty, a foreign policy of expansion was pursued, and North Vietnam, Korea, and Central Asia came under its control.

ECONOMIC DEVELOPMENT

China's economy was based on agriculture, and it flourished during this period with the increase in long-distance trade. Iron metallurgy was introduced, which led to an increase in agriculture. That, in turn, allowed for an increase in trade and an increase in the military strength of the empire. With the military expansion of the Han, overland trade could increase because peace and order were maintained.

It was during the Han dynasty that the trade route known as the **Silk Road** began to flourish. The route was a series of roads that allowed trade to connect the Han Empire with Central Asia, India, and the Roman Empire.

The Han also followed a **tributary system of trade**. Officially, the policy was that the Han did not need to trade with their inferior neighbors, so instead, they demanded tribute from neighboring groups. These neighboring groups would visit the court, bringing tribute, and the Chinese would give trade goods in return. In addition, the Han often sent gifts to nomad groups so as to prevent any possible invasion.

SOCIAL STRUCTURE AND GENDER ROLES

China, like the other classical civilizations, had a **patriarchal** society with a set social structure. A woman's most important role was to make a proper marriage that would strengthen the family's alliances. (Widowed women were, however, permitted to remarry.) Upper-class women were often tutored in writing, arts, and music, but overall, women were legally subordinate to their fathers and their husbands.

Socially, the highest class was that of the **scholar-gentry**. These landlord families were often the only ones able to take the civil service exam, because preparation was very expensive. Most Chinese were peasants who worked the land. Merchants, who gained great wealth during this period with the increase in trade, did not enjoy high social status because they did not produce anything, but rather lived off the labor of others.

CULTURE, ARTS, SCIENCE, TECHNOLOGY

In China, the family became the most important cultural and organizational unit in society. The **family** consisted both of its living members and its **ancestors**. Confucius's **filial piety**, respect or reverence for one's parents, was also very important. The family always provided for its own members.

Daoism's emphasis on being close to nature also had a lasting impact on China. This reverence for nature became a central value of the Han people. This was also a time of great invention and innovation. For many centuries, horses were not efficiently used as draft animals. The solution, developed in China by the fifth century CE, was to provide a collar around the neck and shoulders of the animal to distribute the weight. Collars of this kind reached Europe by the ninth century CE. This development enabled the horse to become the main draft animal of Eurasia for both plowing and hauling. Agriculture was also aided by the wheelbarrow, while watermills were created to grind grain. The sternpost rudder and compass aided sea travel. Possibly most important was the invention of **paper**, which increased the availability of the written word.

ROME

POLITICAL DEVELOPMENT

Rome's political history is one of change and evolution. In 509 BCE, the Roman nobility overthrew the Etruscan king, and what had been a monarchy became a **republic**—a government in which the people elect their representatives. The republic consisted of two consuls who were elected by an assembly that was dominated by the wealthy class, known as the **patricians**. The Senate, made up of patricians, advised these consuls.

This system of leadership created tension between the patricians and the common people, known as the **plebeians**. Eventually, the patricians granted the plebeians the right to elect tribunes, who had the right to veto. When a civil or military crisis occurred, a dictator was appointed for six months.

Things began to change as Rome expanded throughout the Italian peninsula and then the Mediterranean. It encountered a fierce competitor in the city of Carthage in North Africa, which had gained wealth through the thriving trade in the Mediterranean region. This economic competition led to the Punic Wars, which took place between 264 and 146 BCE. By the end of the conflict, Rome had sacked the city of Carthage, solidifying its domination of the Mediterranean. Rome was also expanding east, into the former empire of Alexander.

As Rome expanded, it transitioned from a republic to an **empire**. The wealth and power resulting from conquest led to a growth in problems, most notably, the unequal distribution of land and class tension. The wealthy had amassed large plantations using slave labor and the small farmers could not compete. Also, the growth of cities led to an increase in the urban lower class and an increase in poverty.

The Roman general **Julius Caesar** led the Roman army in its conquest of Gaul (present-day France), and in 46 BCE, he made himself dictator for life. He centralized military and political functions and initiated large-scale building projects, which gave jobs to the poor. But a group of senators feared Caesar was becoming a tyrant and assassinated him. His nephew, Octavian, took over, and in 27 BCE, was given the title Augustus. During his 45-year rule, Rome was a monarchy disguised as a republic. He centralized political and military power, but preserved the traditions of the republic. The continued expansion of the empire stimulated the growing economy, and cities emerged throughout. Economic prosperity, centralized power, and the strength of the Roman army resulted in stability throughout the empire, and the next two and a half centuries were called the **Pax Romana**, or Roman Peace.

Rome's system of law had begun in 450 BCE with the **Twelve Tables**, a series of laws that were organized into 12 sections and written down so they could be understood by all. As the empire spread, the laws went with it. Such laws as "a defendant is innocent until proven guilty" and "a defendant has the right to challenge his accuser before a judge" originated in Rome.

Height of the Roman Empire, 116 CE

AP EXPERT TIP

You should be able to compare various forms of labor throughout history; for example, which societies made extensive use of slaves (Greece and Rome) and which did not (India and China) and why.

ECONOMIC DEVELOPMENT

The key to the Roman Empire's economic success was its extensive system of **roads**. The 60,000 miles of roads linked the empire's 100 million people, linking all regions of the empire for trade and communication. This trade made the merchants very rich and created markets for the goods that the farmers produced, and as a result, the increase in tax revenue made the empire stronger. A **uniform currency** was used, and while **Latin** was the language of politics and the Romans, **Greek** was the *lingua franca* (common language) for trade throughout the Mediterranean.

All of this trade made the empire very interdependent. Cities grew and so did their populations. The cities had access to fresh water through the use of aqueducts, sewage, plumbing, and public baths.

SOCIAL STRUCTURE AND GENDER ROLES

Like other classical societies, Rome was **patriarchal**, where the eldest male, **paterfamilias**, ruled as father of the family. Roman law gave the paterfamilias authority to arrange marriage for the children and the right to sell them into slavery—or even execute them. Women's roles were in supervising domestic affairs; laws put strict limits on their inheritances, though this was inconsistently enforced. As the wealth of the empire increased, new classes emerged, and these new wealthy merchants and landowners built very large homes. On the other side, the poor were often unemployed. **Slaves**, one-third of the population by the second century CE, worked on large estates in the countryside or in the cities as domestic servants.

CULTURE, ARTS, SCIENCE, TECHNOLOGY

Much of Roman culture and achievements were inspired by the **Greek examples**. Romans were **polytheistic**, like the Greeks, and believed that the gods intervened directly in their lives. The empire tolerated the cultural practices of its subjects—if they paid their taxes, did not rebel, and revered the emperors and Roman gods. The Jews, strict monotheists, while scattered and generally accepted throughout the Roman Empire, were considered a problem in their homeland of Judea where rebellious groups often tried to overthrow Roman rule. After a series of bloody rebellions in the first and second centuries, the Jews were completely defeated by the Romans and forced out of the city of Jerusalem. This was the start of the Jewish Diaspora (or scattering) and of the rabbinical form of Judaism.

The **Christians**, originally a Jewish sect, were also seen as a threat to Roman rule and were often persecuted. However, the number of Christians continued to grow throughout the empire. By 313 CE, Emperor Constantine issued the **Edict of Milan**, which legalized Christianity in the empire. By 380 CE, Emperor Theodosius proclaimed Christianity as the empire's official religion.

Rome was also heavily influenced by the Greeks in art and architecture. Roman architecture took its inspiration from Greece, making its columns and arches more ornate. Improvements in engineering, including the invention of concrete, allowed the Romans to build stadiums, public baths, temples, aqueducts, and a system of roads.

ROLE OF TRADE IN CLASSICAL SOCIETIES

Long-distance trade expanded greatly during the classical period, allowing for the movement of goods and ideas. There were a few factors: the Han Empire secured the trade routes through Central Asia; the Mauryan Empire had declined in India, but regional states were able to provide the necessary stability and security; and the Romans kept the Mediterranean Sea safe for trade and travel. This stability and security allowed for long-distance trade to thrive.

SILK ROAD

The Silk Road trade originated during a diplomatic mission to Central Asia by nomads during the Han Empire. Though the diplomatic mission failed, the silk given as gifts was very popular, as were the horses that the diplomats brought from Central Asia. The trade route began in the east in Changan, went through Mongolia and Turkestan, and veered either north or south around the Taklamakan Desert. It branched southeast to India or through Central Asia and finally to the eastern end of the Roman Empire. New innovations such as yokes, special saddles, and horse stirrups helped Silk Road merchants move heavier loads across longer distances.

Almost never did one merchant make the entire journey. Instead, the caravan routes were traveled in stages, from one oasis town to the next. Buddhism became quite popular in such oasis towns as Samarkand, Kashgar, and Dunhuang, where merchants rested, sold their wares at market, and often built monasteries. Buddhism as well as Christianity and Hinduism were transformed as they moved along the Silk Road of the Classical age.

Goods That Traveled East to West	Goods That Traveled West to East
Silk	Glassware
Spices	Jewelry
Cotton	Bronze goods
Pearls	Wool and linen
Coral	Olive oil
Ivory	Gold and silver bullion

INDIAN OCEAN

The Indian Ocean is sometimes referred to as the sea lanes of the Silk Road. This ocean trade went from Guangzhou in southern China through the South China Sea, through the islands of Southeast Asia, India, the Arabian Sea, and the Persian Gulf. The principal players in the trade were Malay and Indian sailors. Religion and culture also spread across the seas. Some merchants spread Buddhism to Southeast Asia, while others promoted the Hindu cults of Shiva and Vishnu.

MEDITERRANEAN SEA

The Mediterranean Sea is often referred to as the **Roman Lake**, because the Roman Empire surrounded the sea. Sea trade flowed from Syria to Spain to North Africa. The Romans kept their lake safe and free from pirates, which allowed the trade to thrive and grow and transport goods from one part of the expansive empire to the other.

SPREAD OF DISEASE

During the second and third centuries CE, both the Han and Roman Empires suffered large-scale outbreaks of epidemic disease. From the trade and interaction that had taken place, the incidence of disease increased. Diseases such as smallpox, measles, and bubonic plague had a devastating effect on the population because people did not have the immunity or the medicine to combat them. In the second century in the Roman Empire, the population dropped by 25 percent, and it was even worse in the cities. The effects of these diseases caused great economic and social disruptions. Trade within the empires declined, and economies became more regionally focused.

MOVEMENT OF PEOPLES

BANTU MIGRATION

The migration of the Bantu people began around 2000 BCE, and by 1000 CE, the Bantu occupied most of sub-Saharan Africa. Resources were stretched to their limits as the population increased. As a result, groups of people began to leave the areas (in modern-day Nigeria) to set up new agricultural settlements; the process repeated itself slowly.

The Bantu people often intermarried with those they came in contact with, and these people often adopted the Bantu language and joined the Bantu society. Around 1000 BCE, the Bantus began to produce iron tools, which enabled them to clear more land and expand agriculture. This led to an increase in population and more migration. Around 500 CE, the cultivation of bananas—which had made their way to Africa via the Indian Ocean trade—enabled the Bantus to expand into heavily forested regions and to continue the migration process. All of this migrating led to an increase in the overall population of Africa—from 3.5 million in 400 BCE to 22 million in 1000 CE—and the spread of agriculture throughout much of Africa. Today there are over 500 distinct (though related) languages that can be traced back to the Bantus.

POLYNESIAN MIGRATION

Humans migrated to Australia around 60,000 years ago via watercraft that could travel what were then the low level seas. These people developed maritime technology and agricultural expertise and eventually established settlements in the islands of the Pacific Ocean. Beginning around 2000 BCE, the movements that settled the Polynesian islands commenced to islands such as Vanuatu, Fiji, Samoa, and later, Hawaii. Long-distance voyages were taken on double canoes with large triangular sails, which carried a platform between the two hulls for shelter.

Some scholars believe that the **settlement** was accidental by sailors being blown off course, while others believe it was a planned colonization. As the migration spread, so did the cultivation of new food crops such as yams, taros, breadfruit, and bananas, and the introduction of domesticated animals such as dogs, pigs, and chickens. The Polynesian islands developed into hierarchical chiefdoms in which leadership was passed down to the eldest son, and relatives served as the local aristocracy. Conflict between groups, as well as population pressure, often led to further migration to new areas. The cultures and languages of these widely dispersed islands often adapted and evolved differently.

FALL OF CLASSICAL EMPIRES

As the Foundations period drew to an end, the classical societies that helped to shape it were all suffering through periods of decline, for mostly similar reasons. The following chart outlines some of the reasons. The recovery from this decline shapes the beginning of our next chapter.

	Han	Western Rome	Gupta
Time of Fall	220 CE	476 CE	550 CE
Economic Reasons	Scholar officials were often exempt from taxes, and peasants often fled from tax collectors to these estates. As a result, a severe reduction in tax revenue financially crippled the empire. Long-distance trade did decrease, but the Chinese were quite self-sufficient and were not severely hurt by this.	The rich landowning class often resisted paying their taxes and when the tax collectors did approach, they were driven away by the landowners' private armies. Also the church land was not taxable. As the empire declined, so did the trade because of unsafe roads and because it relied on economic interdependence. The drop in tax revenue and inflation crippled Rome's economy.	The government had great difficulty raising enough taxes to pay the army to protect its borders.

Time of Fall	Han 220 CE	Western Rome 476 CE	Gupta 550 CE
Political Reasons	The government was unable to check the power of the large private estate owners. The emperor heavily relied on the advice of his court officials and was often misinformed for their personal gain.	The government had trouble finding bureaucrats who could enforce the laws. Power struggles for the throne plagued the empire. From 235 to 284 CE, 25 out of 26 emperors died a violent death. The division of the empire into two sections allowed the eastern portion to remain stronger, while the western portion weakened.	The regional powers of the Guptas allowed them to keep much of their administrative power. They eventually grew more powerful than the central government.
Social Reasons	The population increase led to smaller family plots and increased difficulty of the peasant class to pay taxes.	Diseases dramatically reduced the population, in particular the farming population.	
Role of Nomadic Invasions	The Xiongnu invaded, but only after the empire had already fallen. Nomadic invasions took place because the empire was no longer providing them with what they needed.	The Roman army could not defend against the movement of such nomadic groups as the Ostrogoths, Huns, and Visigoths. Rome was sacked by the Visigoths in 476 CE.	The government was too weak to defend against the nomadic invasions of the White Huns.

All the classical societies entered a period of recovery where they were all decentralized following their collapse, but the **western half of the Roman Empire (Western Europe) experienced the most severe collapse.** A few possible reasons:

- Rome was economically interdependent, and the decline in trade severely hurt the economy.

- Continual waves of nomadic invasions made recovery difficult.

- The spread of disease led to a decrease in population and a weakened empire.

THE ENVIRONMENT

Environmental problems, such as siltation, saltation, and deforestation, while less dramatic than the impact of diseases, were subtle factors in the collapse of many societies and empires.

As settled agriculture spread throughout Africa and Eurasia, extensive irrigation systems and slash-and-burn agriculture took a toll on the land. By 600 CE, people had been farming the same lands for thousands of years. Crops such as wheat and barley depleted the soil of nutrients and, in some areas, led to desertification. Irrigation systems left deposits of salt, which over thousands of years left lands sterile, a particular problem in more arid regions like Mesopotamia. Flood control and irrigation systems, like those used in China, built up the river bottoms and made the rivers flow faster. This exacerbated flooding problems, often making them worse than they had been historically. In addition, flood control systems tended to build up silt around the river's mouth, often filling in land and changing the river's course (Mesopotamia and China).

Another environmental challenge was deforestation. In an age when the only fuel available for fires and the main building material for structures such as homes was wood, forests around urban and agricultural areas became denuded of large trees. The loss of ground cover resulted in loss of topsoil, mudslides in hilly areas, and challenges to local economies as the need for wood forced urban areas to ship timber in from farther away. Although these challenges were often noted in ancient accounts, there was little that ancient and classical societies could do to avoid these problems.

Agricultural societies, to include pastoralists, also introduced new diseases into human civilizations. Agriculture upsets the soil and allows for more standing water, spreading the breeding ground for the anopheles mosquito, which spreads malaria. Close contact with domesticated animals such as cattle and pigs allowed for the spread of viruses such as measles and smallpox that plagued mankind until the modern era. Other diseases like bubonic plague spread as rats, a vector in the transmission of the bacteria causing the disease, became more common around human settlements.

REVIEW QUESTIONS

MULTIPLE-CHOICE QUESTIONS

Please note that these are content-specific review questions for this chapter, designed to help you perform well on the exam.

1. All of the following are developments for the period 8000 BCE to 600 CE EXCEPT

   (A) agriculture.

   (B) iron technology.

   (C) writing.

   (D) gunpowder technology.

2. The change to an agriculturally based economy as a result of the Neolithic Revolution

   (A) was gradual, as it took hundreds or thousands of years.

   (B) developed in one part of the world and spread from there.

   (C) was universally accepted throughout the world.

   (D) had little impact on the environment.

3. Which classical society was located in South Asia?

   (A) Roman

   (B) Han

   (C) Mauryan

   (D) Qin

4. The development of agriculture led to an increase in population because

   (A) farming was much less labor intensive than hunting and gathering.

   (B) the stable food source allowed for more permanent homes and larger families.

   (C) farming provided a healthier diet than hunting and gathering.

   (D) hunting and gathering was an extremely dangerous lifestyle.

5. Pastoral nomads are similar to settled farmers in that they both

   (A) grow crops.

   (B) domesticate animals.

   (C) settle into larger communities.

   (D) have job specialization.

6. The Neolithic Revolution influenced gender roles in that

   (A) men's and women's economic roles were deemed equal.

   (B) work outside of the home was more highly valued.

   (C) women no longer worked.

   (D) men played the only significant economic role.

7. Which of the following is NOT a characteristic of early civilizations?

   (A) Diverse people

   (B) Job specialization

   (C) Social stratification

   (D) Representative government

8. The phrases below describe what culture?

   • Used cuneiform as a writing system

   • Was organized into city-states

   • Used Hammurabi's Code as the system of law

   (A) Egypt

   (B) Indus

   (C) Mesopotamia

   (D) Shang

9. The Egyptians were to the Nile as the Chinese were to the

(A) Tigris.
(B) Euphrates.
(C) Huang He.
(D) Indus.

10. All of the early river valley civilizations were

(A) city-states.
(B) polytheistic.
(C) law givers.
(D) pastoralists.

11. The Chinese concept of Mandate of Heaven refers to

(A) the power granted to the ruler from divine sources.
(B) the belief that China was superior to the rest of the world.
(C) the emperor's obligation to give laws to his people.
(D) the never-ending power of the emperor.

12. The Indus civilization is still somewhat of a mystery to archaeologists because

(A) the Aryans destroyed all the remains of the civilization.
(B) its writing system has not been deciphered.
(C) the small size of the civilization makes it difficult to excavate.
(D) its isolation from the rest of the world limited trade and diffusion.

13. The period known as the "Era of Warring States" refers to

(A) the nomadic invasions that brought an end to the Roman Empire.
(B) the period of disorder in China before the establishment of the Qin dynasty.
(C) the transition from republic to empire in Rome.
(D) the revolt that ended the reign of the first emperor of China.

14. What ideas do Hinduism and Buddhism have in common?

(A) Universal salvation
(B) Reincarnation
(C) The caste system
(D) Monotheism

15. Which of the following religions both used missionaries to spread their message?

(A) Judaism and Christianity
(B) Confucianism and Daoism
(C) Buddhism and Daoism
(D) Christianity and Buddhism

16. Which of the following pairs did NOT influence the same geographic region?

(A) Confucius and Laozi
(B) Ashoka and Siddhartha Gautama
(C) Socrates and Alexander
(D) Wu Di and Chandra Gupta

17. The social hierarchies of both Hinduism and Confucianism demonstrate the value of

(A) peasants.
(B) landowners.
(C) government officials.
(D) scholars.

18. The Mauryan and Gupta Empires both demonstrated India's

    (A) long and consistent history of imperial rule.
    (B) political centralization overtaking regional kingdoms.
    (C) large influence of Islamic rule and culture.
    (D) history of rule by nomadic invaders.

19. Which statement most accurately compares the fall of the Han and Roman Empires?

    (A) Nomadic invasions were more of a problem in Han than in Rome.
    (B) Imperial authorities held more political power than regional authorities.
    (C) Leaders were assassinated in both empires.
    (D) Large landowners successfully avoided paying taxes.

20. Long-distance trade flourished in the classical societies because

    (A) many merchants could travel the entire length of the Silk Road.
    (B) the imperial powers kept trade routes safe and secure.
    (C) Chinese emissaries negotiated with Roman officials.
    (D) India remained centrally ruled throughout the period.

21. Which two religions gave women access to spiritual salvation?

    (A) Confucianism and Buddhism
    (B) Daoism and Confucianism
    (C) Buddhism and Christianity
    (D) Confucianism and Judaism

22. Both Greek and Chinese classical societies had a(n)

    (A) decentralized political structure.
    (B) fluid social structure.
    (C) unbroken dynastic cycle.
    (D) patriarchal family structure.

23. Which of the following is true of both the Qin and Han dynasties?

    (A) Confucianism was the philosophical basis of the government.
    (B) The merchant class was highly regarded.
    (C) The central government was strong.
    (D) Trade was discouraged.

24. Which of the following civilizations was characterized by government participation by its citizens?

    (A) China
    (B) India
    (C) Egypt
    (D) Rome

25. All of the following were factors in the Bantu migrations EXCEPT

    (A) population pressures.
    (B) use of iron tools.
    (C) spread of agriculture.
    (D) floods.

DOCUMENT-BASED QUESTION

This DBQ is a practice activity. The actual question on the exam may be longer.

Directions: The following question is based on the accompanying Documents 1 to 4. (The documents have been edited for the purpose of this exercise.)

This question is designed to test your ability to work with and understand historical documents. Write an essay that:

- Has a relevant thesis and supports that thesis with evidence from the documents.

- Uses all of the documents.

- Analyzes the documents by grouping them in as many appropriate ways as possible.

- Does not simply summarize the documents individually.

- Takes into account the sources of the documents and analyzes the authors' points of view.

- Explains the need for at least one additional type of document.

You may refer to relevant historical information not mentioned in the documents.

Based on the following documents, analyze and describe the traditional roles of women in ancient China. Identify an additional type of document and explain how it would help your analysis of the traditional roles of women in ancient China.

Historical Background: India's predominantly decentralized history of regional kingdoms was interrupted by the conquest of Babur and the establishment of the Mughal Empire, a Muslim-Turkish dynasty, which ruled from 1523 to the mid-1700s.

DOCUMENT 1

Source: Liu Hsiang (first century BCE), a renowned scholar, editor, and author, *Biographies of Admirable Women*, a writing about the mother of the great Confucian philosopher Mencius.

His mother answered, "A woman's duties are to cook the five grains, heat the wine, look after her parents-in-law, make clothes, and that is all! Therefore she cultivates the skills required in the women's quarters and has no ambition to manage affairs outside of her house. She must follow the 'three submissions.' When she is young, she must submit to her parents. After marriage, she must submit to her husband. When she is widowed, she must submit to her son."

DOCUMENT 2

Source: Ban Zhao (first century CE), China's foremost female scholar, imperial historian, poet, and tutor of an empress.

Womanly Qualifications

A woman (ought to) have four qualifications: (1) womanly virtue; (2) womanly words; (3) womanly bearing; and (4) womanly work. Now what is called womanly virtue need not be brilliant ability, exceptionally different from others. Womanly words need be neither clever in debate nor keen in conversation. Womanly appearance requires neither a pretty nor a perfect face and form. Womanly work need not be work done more skillfully than that of others.

To guard carefully her chastity; to control circumspectly her behavior; in every motion to exhibit modesty; and to model each act on the best usage, this is womanly virtue.

To choose her words with care; to avoid vulgar language; to speak at appropriate times; and not to weary others with much conversation, may be called the characteristics of womanly words.

To wash and scrub filth away; to keep clothes and ornaments fresh and clean; to wash the head and bathe the body regularly, and to keep the person free from disgraceful filth, may be called the characteristics of womanly bearing. With whole-hearted devotion to sew and to weave; to love not gossip and silly laughing; in cleanliness and order (to prepare) the wine and food for serving guests, may be called the characteristics of womanly work.

DOCUMENT 3

Source: Fu Xuan, 217–278 CE, a noted Chinese poet and philosopher of the Western Jin dynasty.

How sad it is to be a woman:
Nothing on earth is held so cheap.
Boys stand leaning at the door
Like Gods fallen out of Heaven.
Their hearts brave the Four Oceans,
The wind and dust of a thousand miles.
No one is glad when a girl is born:
By *her* the family sets no store.

When she grows up, she hides in her room
Afraid to look a man in the face.
No one cries when she leaves her home—
Sudden as clouds when the rain stops.
She bows and kneels countless times.
She must humble herself even to the servants.

DOCUMENT 4

Source: A Buddhist song. This text was found among the ancient Buddhist writing unearthed from the caves at Dunhuang.

At ten, like a flowering branch in the rain,
She is slender, delicate, and full of grace.
Her parents are themselves as young as the rising moon
And do not allow her past the red curtain without a reason.
At twenty, receiving the hairpin, she is a spring bud.
Her parents arrange her betrothal; the matter's well done.
A fragrant carriage comes at evening to carry her to her lord.
Like Hsiao-shih and his wife, at dawn they depart with the clouds.
At forty she is mistress of a prosperous house and makes plans.

Three sons and five daughters give her some trouble.
With her ch'in not far away, she toils always at her loom,
Her only fear that the sun will set too soon.
At fifty, afraid of her husband's dislike,
She strains to please him with every charm,
Trying to remember the many tricks she had learned since the age of sixteen.
No longer is she afraid of mothers- and sisters-in-law.
At sixty, face wrinkled and hair like silk thread,
She walks unsteadily and speaks little.
Distresses that her sons can find no brides.
Grieved that her daughters have departed for their husband's homes.

CONTINUITY AND CHANGE-OVER-TIME QUESTION

Directions: You are to answer the following question. You should spend five minutes organizing or outlining your essay. Write an essay that:

- Has a relevant thesis and supports that thesis with appropriate historical evidence.

- Addresses all parts of the question.

- Uses historical context to show continuity and change over time.

- Analyzes the process of continuity and change over time.

  Prompt: Describe and analyze the continuities and changes in ONE of the following religions or belief systems from the beginning of the religion or belief system up to 600 CE.

  - Hinduism: India

  - Confucianism: China

  - Christianity: Roman Empire

COMPARATIVE QUESTION

Directions: You are to answer the following question. You should spend five minutes organizing or outlining your essay. Write an essay that:

- Has a relevant thesis and supports that thesis with appropriate historical evidence.

- Addresses all parts of the question.

- Makes direct, relevant comparisons.

- Analyzes relevant reasons for similarities and differences.

Prompt: Analyze similarities and differences in the collapses of TWO of the following empires.

- Rome (200–600 CE)

- Han (50 BCE–220 CE)

- Gupta (300–550 CE)

ANSWERS AND EXPLANATIONS

MULTIPLE-CHOICE ANSWERS

1. D

The development of agriculture, iron, and writing all occurred in this period. However, the use of gunpowder technology did not begin until 600 to 1450, during the Song dynasty.

2. A

The Neolithic Revolution was a gradual event that probably started with experimentation with seeds. Farming is something that developed gradually, over a long period of time.

3. C

The Mauryan dynasty was located in India, which is in South Asia.

4. B

In hunting and gathering communities, populations remained low because of the scarcity of food and the need to move. The development of agriculture allowed these communities to develop permanent homes and have larger families.

5. B

Both pastoral nomads and settled farmers rely on the domestication of animals for their economic survival.

6. B

The development of farming led to a division of labor. Work that was conducted outside the home was deemed more valuable than work conducted inside the home.

7. D

Representative government was not a characteristic of early civilizations. Most of these civilizations were ruled by a small elite class.

8. C

Mesopotamia used cuneiform as a writing system; was organized into city-states; and used Hammurabi's Code as the system of law. (Hammurabi was an important ruler of the area.) Of the answer choices, this is the only culture that used cuneiform. Egypt used hieroglyphics.

9. C

Early Chinese civilization developed along the Yellow, or Huang He, River. The Tigris and Euphrates were in Mesopotamia. The Indus River is in India.

10. B

Though some of the early civilizations such as Mesopotamia were organized into city-states, others such as Egypt were organized into kingdoms. All of the civilizations were, however, polytheistic.

11. A

The Mandate of Heaven is the belief that the gods have granted power to the ruler, but that power can also be taken away. Certain signs indicate the loss of the mandate, such as floods, peasant revolts, and nomadic invasions.

12. B

Although the Indus civilization was discovered in the early 20th century, the writing system found on clay seals has yet to be deciphered.

13. B

The Era of Warring States was a period of hundreds of years when no one state could control China; instead, the smaller states battled each other for control.

14. B

The rebirth of the soul, or reincarnation, is an essential belief of both Hindus and Buddhists, who both believe that it takes many lives to accumulate the necessary amount of karma to be released from the cycle of rebirth.

15. D

Both Christianity and Buddhism are considered universal religions, meaning that they are open to all people. Universal religions are also often associated with a missionary component, which spreads the belief to new converts.

16. D

Wu Di was an emperor of the Han dynasty in China (East Asia). Chandra Gupta was the first ruler of the Mauryan Empire in India (South Asia).

17. D

In both Hinduism and Confucianism, scholars are highly regarded. The highest caste in Hinduism is the Brahmin class, which consists of priests and scholars. Confucius taught that learning separated the inferior man from the superior man.

18. B

Most of India's history is characterized by a decentralized government of regional kingdoms. Both the Mauryan and Gupta Empires were successfully able to centralize large parts of the Indian subcontinent.

19. D

Neither the Han nor the Roman Empire was able to collect sufficient tax revenues. In both cases, large landowners avoided paying taxes. In fact, they often protected peasants on their land who were attempting to escape the tax collectors.

20. B

If trade routes were safe and well maintained, long-distance trade flourished. Oftentimes, when imperial rule weakened, roads were not long maintained. Travel became unsafe, and trade would decline as a result.

21. C

Both Buddhism and Christianity preached that women and men had equal access to salvation, though their equality on Earth was not guaranteed.

22. D

Both Greek and Chinese classical societies were patriarchal: The man was considered the head of the household and the most respected member.

23. C

The Qin used a strict Legalist philosophy to rule, while the Han placed a strong emphasis on Confucianism. However, in order to keep their empires organized, both societies used a strong central government with a powerful emperor.

24. D

In the early days of Rome, the government was a republic, which meant that the citizens chose representatives to rule for them. Rome had a Senate, which passed laws and made decisions for its people, but as the city grew into an empire, the Senate lost most of its power to an all-powerful emperor.

25. D

The use of agriculture led to population pressure, which contributed to the Bantu migration. Also, the use of iron tools allowed for more land to be available for cultivation, which in turn caused population growth.

DOCUMENT-BASED QUESTION: SAMPLE RESPONSE

The traditional roles of women in China have been shaped by philosophical beliefs such as Confucianism. According to the documents, the traditional role of women has been inferior and subservient to men, but women were expected to conduct themselves with proper behavior and teach that behavior to their children. In the end, women held a special place in the family in which they would be respected and eventually worshipped as an ancestor.

In China's patriarchal society, a woman's traditional role was one of subservience. In the excerpt from *Biographies of Admirable Women* by Liu Hsiang, Mencius's mother describes the subservient role of women (Document 1). She is always in a place of submission, whether to her parents, husband, or son. Liu Hsiang's purpose is to use the mother of Mencius, a Confucian scholar, to reinforce and promote the idea of proper Confucian behavior in women. In the poem, written by Fu Xuan, women's lives are described as sad and cheap compared to men (Document 3). No one is glad when a girl is born, but everyone is elated when a boy is born. Unlike the birth of a boy, which is viewed as a wealth-gaining opportunity, the birth of a girl is seen as a burden to the family. This poem written by a noted Chinese poet and philosopher of the Western Jin dynasty expresses a generalized view of women and does not offer specific evidence to support these ideas, but the emotions of the poem communicate the author's pity for the plight of women. While Fu's point of view as a man writing about the lives of women gives this poem's message great weight, it would be helpful to know a Chinese woman's interpretation of the poem. Would a woman living in China during this time believe that her life was both sad and cheap? According to a Buddhist song, which expresses an ideal role of women, girls are protected at age 10 and rely on a proper marriage arranged by her parents, but as she grows up her role changes (Document 4). This ancient Buddhist writing was unearthed from the caves at Dunhuang. It would be helpful to know if lower-class and higher-class women in China shared the feeling of this song, in order to judge if women's roles varied according to class.

Like other members of Chinese society, women were expected to behave in a proper way and set an example for others to follow. The excerpt from *Biographies of Admirable Women* states that the woman is to know her place and focus on cooking, looking after her parents-in-law, and making clothes, and that she should have no outside ambition (Document 1). According to a Buddhist song, women were expected to serve as the mistress of the home and, as had been done for her, focus on arranging a proper marriage for her children (Document 4). As a dutiful wife, she must continue to please her husband throughout the marriage, though as the cycle of life continues, her children leave home and her role continues to change. According to Ban Zhao, China's foremost female scholar in the first century CE, a woman must have certain qualifications, which include virtue, words, bearing, and work (Document 2). A woman must exhibit modesty, avoid any use of vulgar language, and speak only during appropriate times. She should focus on her work at home and keep a clean and orderly home. This document, written by a female who served as the imperial historian, poet, and tutor of an empress, expresses an idealized view of women whose purpose was to communicate the proper and ideal behavior desired by women in Chinese society. Ban's point of view as a scholar may have led her to understate the hardships Chinese women endured in their traditional roles since she may not have wanted to "rock the boat" too much. It would be helpful to also see a firsthand account of a woman's life in the form of a diary entry, to see if it agreed with Ban Zhao's view of the role of women. Additionally, knowing the views of women outside of China would serve as a helpful comparison: One could judge if the role of women in China was characteristic of the time or more particular to traditional Chinese beliefs.

The examination of a poem, a Buddhist song, and the writing of an imperial female scholar clearly communicate the traditional role of women in Chinese society. In China's patriarchal society, women were subservient to men, were expected to follow the model of an ideal female, and were expected to run the workings of the household. Reinforced by philosophical beliefs such as Confucianism, these traditional roles for Chinese women shaped the lives of women throughout most of history.

The student earns the thesis point and 3 points for understanding all of the documents and using all of the documents to support the argument. The student earns 1 point for addressing point-of-view analysis twice and another point for supporting the requests for additional documents. Two groups are provided addressing women's roles as subservient (Documents 1, 3, and 4), and proper behavior (Documents 1, 4, and 2). Because the student made a second successful additional document request, an expanded core point is awarded, for a total of 8 points.

CONTINUITY AND CHANGE-OVER-TIME QUESTION: SAMPLE RESPONSE

Christianity had both a political and cultural impact on the Roman Empire from the birth of Christ to the fall of the empire because of its missionary thrust and its eventual political support. The religion also appealed to both the lower class and women throughout the period. Although Christianity was at first rejected by Roman authorities and the Christians were treated as scapegoats, it was eventually accepted by Roman authorities and gained a privileged status.

Around the turn of the millennium, the Roman Empire was culturally influenced by polytheistic beliefs. The emperor himself was to be worshipped as a god. Though the empire was culturally tolerant, the Jews, who were monotheistic, could not worship the Roman gods or the emperor. It was in this environment that Jesus was born. His message was one of forgiveness, love, and the promise of salvation for those who believed. The Roman authorities believed Jesus was a threat to their power, and he was sentenced to death. It was not until Jesus died, however, that his message began to spread widely. One follower, Paul, began to convert Jews as well as non-Jews to Christianity. This helped to make Christianity a universal religion. The Christians, a minority group, were often persecuted by Roman authorities and used as scapegoats, and as a result many became martyrs. It was this martyrdom that helped the religion to spread further. Christianity's message especially appealed to the lower class and women because of the promise of salvation for all who believe, not just wealthy men.

Christianity's fate drastically changed during the rule of the Roman emperor Constantine. The emperor's mother was a Christian and so he issued the Edict of Milan, making Christianity legal in the Roman Empire. This political acceptance transformed Christianity from a fringe, persecuted cultural and religious group to one that had the favor of the emperor himself. This political fortune of Christianity improved even more when Emperor Theodosius made Christianity the official religion of the Roman Empire. For those who wanted political acceptance, conversion to Christianity was the path to follow.

Additionally, with government support, missionaries could travel to all parts of the empire to spread the word. The Church became more organized and gained land from its government support. Some historians even argue that devotion to Christianity replaced devotion to Rome and the emperor, and may have contributed to the fall of the empire. Regardless, Christianity's political support allowed it to get organized, so much so that when the empire did fall, the Church replaced it as the centralizing force in the region.

Christianity and the Roman Empire started with a less-than-favorable relationship. Jesus, with his idea of the kingdom of God, was viewed as threatening to the Roman power. But his message of peace, forgiveness, and salvation remained powerful and was influential enough to attract many converts, despite the government persecution. The relationship, however, reversed toward the end of the Roman Empire, when Christianity received official government patronage. Christianity, like another universal religion—Buddhism—benefited from its missionary approach and most of all, the political patronage of the powers that be.

This essay's strong thesis statement at the end of the first paragraph earns its first point. Setting up background in the second paragraph, the student's clear topic sentences in the second and third paragraphs address continuity and change, respectively, earning both addressing points. The essay offers some evidence for both continuity and change but is vague on the details—for example, failing to cite specific years for Theodosius making it the official religion, and not citing specific historians in the third paragraph. Further, the writer is scant on the details of how Christianity "got organized" and in what specific way that the Church "gained land from government support." The last paragraph summarizes the continuity and change, and even alludes to Buddhism for global context, but, again, does so scantily. Thus, it does not earns two expanded core points for its evidence and its inclusion of analysis and global context for both continuity and change. The student would earn 6 total points for this essay.

COMPARATIVE QUESTION: SAMPLE RESPONSE

The great classical empires of Rome and Han dominated much of Eurasia for hundreds of years. Their strength and stability allowed for great advancement and trade to flourish. Similar economic and political factors led to the collapse of both empires, such as difficulty collecting taxes and government corruption. Yet the effects they saw from a decline in trade differed, as did their timing and involvement of nomadic invasions in their demise.

Both the Roman and Han Empires had great difficulty sustaining a strong tax collection system toward the end of their empires. In the Han Empire, scholar officials were often exempt from taxes, and peasants were subject to high taxes. As the empire was weakening, peasants often fled from the tax collectors to the estates of the scholar officials. The result was an unstable empire—financially unable to maintain its public works. Similarly in Rome, the rich landowning class often resisted paying their taxes. They were able to do this because of the private armies they had amassed to protect their land. Just like in the Han Empire, Roman peasants began to seek refuge from tax collectors on these estates. Additionally, Church land was not taxable, and toward the end of the empire, the Church had amassed a great deal of land and power. Rome's inability to collect sufficient taxes led to a decline in the maintenance of its famous system of roads. This, in turn, led to a decline in trade. Rome had become economically interdependent with various parts of its empire, and this decline in trade further weakened the empire. The Han Empire also had difficulty maintaining the safety and stability of its trade routes and roads. That, however, had less of an impact on the empire's fall because the Chinese economy was much more self-sufficient than that of Rome.

Politically, both governments had serious problems with corruption. In the Han Empire, the emperor began to rely on the advice of his court officials who often advised him in ways that promoted their own interests. Away in his palace, the emperor was quite isolated from his empire, and could not see for himself the poor advice he was being given. Throughout it all, though, the emperor did maintain his power. In Rome, being an emperor was a much more dangerous and short-lived job. From 235 to 284 CE, 25 of 26 emperors died a violent death. This constant change in leadership and the power struggles that ensued left the Roman government in disarray. Additionally, the empire had been divided into two sections: the eastern section remained strong, while the western section weakened significantly. In both empires, nomadic invasions damaged the political hold on the area. In the Han Empire, the Xiongnu invaded China, but only after the empire had already fallen. This occurred because the empire could no longer provide them with the goods they required. This set off a wave of nomadic migrations that would eventually make its way to the Roman Empire. As nomads continued to migrate, they put pressure on other nomadic groups to move, often into settled land. The Roman army had great difficulty defending itself against the movement of such groups as the Ostrogoths, Huns, and Visigoths. The great city of Rome was eventually sacked by the Visigoths in 476 CE, bringing an end to the western portion of the empire.

As the great empires came to an end, it became clear that the key to maintaining a great empire is the ability to collect sufficient taxes to pay for the services needed by the population. Without sufficient tax revenue, the Han and Roman Empires could not sufficiently maintain their empires, protect their people, or continue to trade.

This essay's strong thesis statement in the last two sentences of the first paragraph wins 1 point. Although the second and third paragraphs address in detail the similarities between the collapses of Han and Rome, the writer lacks detail on the significant differences in the collapse of both, earning only 1 of the addressing points. In addition, although the evidence is hefty in supporting the collapse of Rome, it supplies little illustration of the Han collapse and how that collapse was similar to/different from that of Rome. Thus, the writer earns only 1 evidence point . The last paragraph summarizes the similarities but totally fails to address any differences, earning it, again, only 1 point. The essay's final score is 4 points.

CHAPTER 4: 600 TO 1450 CE

IF YOU ONLY LEARN SIX THINGS IN THIS CHAPTER . . .

1. Like the Foundations period, this time period witnesses a tremendous growth in long-distance trade due to the improvements in technology. Trade through the Silk Road, the Indian Ocean, the trans-Saharan trade, and the Mediterranean Sea led to the spread of ideas, religions, and technology.

2. Major technological developments such as the compass, improved shipbuilding technology, and gunpowder shaped the development of the world.

3. The movement of people greatly altered our world. Nomadic groups such as the Turks, Mongols, and Vikings, for instance, interacted with settled people—often because of their technology—leading to further change and development.

4. Religions such as Islam, Christianity, and Buddhism preached the equality of all believers in the eyes of God. And though patriarchal values continued to dominate, the monastic life of Buddhism and Christianity offered an alternative path for women.

5. The spread of religion aided by the increase in trade often acted as a unifying force, though it sometimes caused conflict. Christianity and the Church served as the centralizing force in Western Europe, and throughout East Asia, the spread of Confucianism and Buddhism solidified a cultural identity. The new religion of Islam created a new cultural world known as Dar al-Islam, which transcended political boundaries.

6. The political structures of many areas adapted and changed to the new conditions of the world. Centralized empires like the Byzantine, Arab Caliphates, and the Tang and Song dynasties built on the successful models of the past, while decentralized areas (Western Europe and Japan) developed political organization that more effectively dealt with their unique issues. The movements of the Mongols altered much of Asia's political structure for a time, and the recovery from that Mongol period introduced political structures, which defined many areas for centuries to follow.

THE BIG PICTURE

1. Interactions between people and the environment

   In other words: **How does the environment shape human societies, and how do humans shape the environment?**

Major technological developments shaped the development of the world, including the compass, improved shipbuilding technology, and gunpowder. The movement of people including the Bantus, Turks, Mongols, and Vikings greatly altered our world. One of the worst epidemic diseases in history, the bubonic plague (or Black Death), spread during this period due to the movement of people and the increase in interaction.

2. Development and interaction of cultures

   In other words: **How do people express themselves, and what is the impact of ideas?**

The spread of religion during this time period often acted as a unifying force. For example, Christianity and the Church served as the centralizing force in Western Europe during most of this period. Also, the spread of Confucianism and Buddhism throughout East Asia solidified a cultural identity in those areas. The new religion of Islam created a new cultural world known as Dar al-Islam, which transcended political boundaries.

3. State-building, expansion, and conflict

   In other words: **How do people govern themselves?**

Following the fall of the classical empires, the political structures of many areas adapted and changed to the new conditions of the world. Centralized empires like the Byzantine, Arab Caliphates, and the Tang and Song dynasties built off the successful models of the past. Decentralized areas like Western Europe and Japan developed political organization that more effectively dealt with their unique issues. The movements of the Mongols altered much of Asia's political structure for a time. Finally, the recovery from the Mongol period introduced political structures that defined many areas for centuries to follow.

4. Creation, expansion, and interaction of economic systems

   In other words: **How do economic developments affect the world?**

This time period witnessed a tremendous growth in long-distance trade through the Silk Road, the Indian Ocean, trans-Saharan trade, and the Mediterranean Sea. During the period known as Pax Mongolia, when peace and order was established due to the vast Mongol Empire, trade and interaction were at their height.

5. Development and transformation of social structures

   In other words: **How do people identify themselves socially, and what roles do men and women have?**

Although most societies continued to reinforce their patriarchal nature and strict social structure, the spread of universal religions had some effects. Religions such as Islam, Christianity, and Buddhism preached the equality of all believers. The monastic life of both Buddhism and Christianity offered an alternative path for women.

WHY THIS PERIODIZATION?

This unit begins in 600 CE after the great classical civilizations of the Foundations period fell and the world seemed to be in a period of recovery. Both China and Europe went through periods of decentralization in their recovery. China eventually reunited as an imperial empire, but the Roman Empire never successfully reunited in Europe, and regional kingdoms developed there instead.

The new player on the scene was Islam. This new religion and identity had far-reaching consequences culturally, politically, economically, and intellectually throughout the period. Additionally, the world became more integrated than ever—thanks to the movement of nomads like the Turks and Mongols, the increase in long-distance trade, and the continual spread of religion. As the period came to a close in 1450 CE, the world shifted once again as Europeans looked outward and explored the world, with the help of "southern" technology and ideas.

POST-CLASSICAL POLITICAL DEVELOPMENTS

"NEW" EMPIRES

After the fall of the Han and Roman Empires, a form of political centralization eventually returned in part of the world: China, the former Eastern Roman Empire (now known as the Byzantine Empire), and a new player—the Islamic Caliphates.

TANG DYNASTY (618 TO 907 CE)

POLITICAL DEVELOPMENT

Following the fall of the Han dynasty, China returned to regional small kingdoms for the next 400 years. It was not until 581 CE that the Sui dynasty reunited China. This short-lived but influential dynasty used Buddhism and the Confucian civil service system to establish legitimacy. In addition, it started the construction of the Grand Canal and launched numerous military campaigns to expand the empire. Rebellions overthrew the empire in 618, but it had laid an important foundation for future dynasties.

The Tang dynasty that followed was more focused on scholars than on soldiers. It did, however, expand its territory beyond China proper to Tibet and Korea. It also completed the Grand Canal and offered support to Buddhism, Daoism, and Confucianism. The capital, Changan, was a major political center, to which foreign diplomats visited from the Byzantine and Arab worlds. Confucian beliefs were further incorporated into the Chinese government through the examination system.

In the middle of the eighth century, Tang power began to decline as higher taxation created tension within the population. Peasant rebellions led to more independent regional rule and to the abdication of the emperor. After this, there was a period of rule by regional warlords for the next 50 years.

ECONOMIC DEVELOPMENTS

The dynasty established military garrisons as far out as Kashgar, which allowed for the protection and security of **Silk Road** trade. An **equal field system** was established, in which all peasants were given land in return for tax in grain and corvée (unpaid labor), and at death they were to return it to the government. Even with this system, however, the Tang had difficulty breaking the power of the large landowners.

Changan was a major trading center and cosmopolitan city. The West Market there flourished with Indian, Iranian, Syrian, and Arab traders and their goods. By 640, its population reached two million, making it the largest city in the world at that time.

CULTURAL DEVELOPMENTS

Culturally, the Tang dynasty was heavily influenced by the spread of **Buddhism**. **Empress Wu**, originally the emperor's concubine, amassed her own personal power, and in 690 was given the title of Heavenly Empress. Concerned (or possibly obsessed) with any possible threat to her power, she had thousands of the emperor's concubines killed and had their sons banned from office. On a positive note, she started a school dedicated to Buddhist and Confucian scholarship. Her support for Buddhism, and in particular its art, increased the religion's influence throughout China.

Buddhism experienced a serious backlash toward the end of the dynasty. This "foreign religion" was attacked for the economic and political power it had obtained. From 841 to 845 CE, an **anti-Buddhist campaign** destroyed many monasteries and seriously weakened the religion's influence on China. In the wake of this backlash, Neo-Confucianism developed: Confucian scholars wanted a new form of Confucianism that would limit foreign influence. The result was an incorporation of Buddhist and Confucian ideas. Some ideas included individual self-improvement, the idea that human beings are good, and the goal to strive and perfect oneself.

Women's marriages during the Tang dynasty were arranged within their own social class, but upper-class women could own property, move about in public, and even remarry. If all other heirs had died, women could inherit property. Poetry flourished with such poets as **Li Bai** and **Du Fu**.

INFLUENCE

Neo-Confucianism moved to the forefront of Chinese philosophy and was also very influential in Japan and Korea. Neighboring peoples became tributary states that had to pay honor (usually in the form of the form of gold or agricultural products) to China. Delegations from the "outside," such as Japan or Siam (present-day Thailand), had to show great deference to the Chinese emperor and performed the kowtow—a prostrate bow during which one touches one's head to the ground multiple times—in the imperial presence. This furthered the Chinese self-perception of being superior to all foreigners.

SONG DYNASTY (960 TO 1279 CE)

POLITICAL DEVELOPMENT

By 960, the Song dynasty had reestablished centralized control over China. The civil service exam system retained great prominence during this period. It successfully checked the power of the landed aristocracy and developed alongside a powerful, moral elite. Upward mobility existed through the exam system, but it took place very rarely. The Song deemphasized a military approach to security and instead reestablished the **tribute system** with its nomad neighbors. This was a system of literally "paying off" the nomads with such gifts as bolts of silk to keep the peace.

The Song, however, experienced military and economic weakness. The scholar-controlled professional army was often ineffective, and too much paper money in circulation caused inflation. By 1126, they had lost the northern half of the empire to nomads. The Southern Song continued to flourish until 1274. However, military threats from the north continued, and finally the most powerful of all northern groups invaded in the 1200s, absorbing the Song dynasty into the new Mongol Empire.

ECONOMIC DEVELOPMENT

Historians often refer to the developments during the Song dynasty as an **economic revolution**. Rice production doubled due to the new fast-ripening rice from Champa. Internal trade from the

Yellow Sea and Grand Canal flourished due to the increased number of merchants and the growth in population, and the capital of Kaifeng became a **manufacturing center** with its production of cannons, movable type printing, water-powered mills, looms, and high-quality porcelain. China had more per capita production than any other country in the world. Minted copper coins were used as cash and eventually replaced with paper currency. Officials collected taxes in cash—not goods—and letters of credit (known as flying cash) were used by merchants.

The Southern Song established their capital at **Hangzhou**, and though this smaller area had less taxable land, commerce soared. With their cotton sails and **magnetic compasses**, the Song had the most powerful navy in the world, and eventually, the availability of more goods for sale. As a result, the dynasty's power shifted from the north to the south, and the Song became the leaders in Afro-Eurasian trade. Song goods traveled to Southeast Asia, India, Persia, and East Africa.

TANG AND SONG INNOVATIONS

- The first use of the compass to aid maritime navigation
- A water-powered clock, demonstrating facility in mechanical engineering
- The invention of gunpowder—first demonstrated during the late 1000s CE, the explosive combination of sulfur and saltpeter would alter weapons technology forever and lead to the first cannons, rockets, and incendiary bombs
- Philosophy—Neo-Confucian thought delved into the ancient texts and further codified traditional Chinese philosophy; it blended Confucianism with elements of Daoism and Buddhism
- Urbanization, with some cities exceeding one million inhabitants
- A printing press with movable type
- Stylized and symbolic landscape painting
- Paper money
- Letters of credit (flying cash)

CULTURAL DEVELOPMENTS

During the Song dynasty, women were entitled to keep their dowries and had access to new jobs such as merchants, but they also were the subject of a practice called **foot-binding**. The practice originated with the aristocratic class, copying the emperor's concubines or Turkish dancers at court, and was viewed as a sign of wealth and status. Girls as young as six or seven had their feet bound to create "lily-like" feet in order to secure a better marriage. The result was an increase in the restriction of freedom of women.

ISLAMIC CALIPHATES

ISLAM: THE RELIGION

Prior to the introduction of Islam, Arabs lived in separate, loyal tribal groups and were often involved in overland and maritime trade. Most people practiced an animist type of religion that involved the worship of idols.

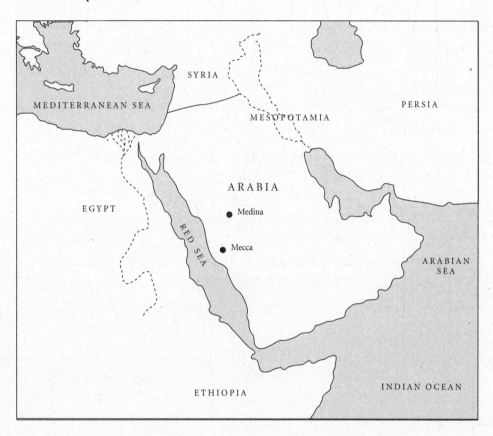

Arabia

Muhammad was born in 570 CE in Mecca and later married a merchant widow named Khadija. Together, they traveled on caravans and met Jews, Zoroastrians, and Christians. When Muhammad was 40, the angel Gabriel appeared to him as he was sleeping in a cave and revealed that he had been selected to receive divine inspiration. The message was that there was only one all-powerful and all-knowing God, **Allah**. Muhammad, who claimed to have no supernatural powers himself, was to be God's messenger.

Muhammad preached that all people were to submit to Allah and that everyone was equal in the eyes of Allah. All would face a final day of judgment; those who had submitted to God would go to heaven, and those who had not would go to hell. Muhammad's message was not met with enthusiasm in Mecca, and he fled to Medina in 622, a journey known as the hegira.

Muhammad's message was quite popular in Medina, where he was viewed as a prophet and a political leader. Further organizing his new religion, he taught that he was the last of a long line of prophets from the Jewish and Christian scriptures that included Abraham, Moses, David, and Jesus. In 630, he and his followers returned to **Mecca**, captured the city, and destroyed the idols.

After his death, Muhammad's revelations were written down by his followers in the **Quran**, which is believed to be the actual words of God as revealed to Muhammad. The word *Islam* means "submission" to God's will.

FIVE PILLARS OF ISLAM

Islam is based on five duties (called pillars) that define the faith. These are:

1. Statement of faith: There is no god but Allah, and Muhammad is his messenger.

2. Pray five times a day facing Mecca.

3. Give alms (charity) to the poor.

4. Fast during the holy month of Ramadan.

5. Make a pilgrimage, or hajj, to Mecca during one's lifetime, if able.

Islam is a **universal religion** that is open to everyone. It promises salvation to all who believe and follow the rules, which are easy to understand. Islam appealed to women because they had equal status to men before God, they could keep their dowries as wives, and there was a prohibition on female infanticide. Like Christianity, Islam appealed to the poor and powerless, and it gave the community a strong sense of brotherhood.

POLITICAL DEVELOPMENT

By the time of Muhammad's death, almost all of Arabia was under Islamic control. There was disagreement, however, over his successor. One group, the Shia, believed that the leader should be a descendant of Muhammad. The other group, the Sunni, preferred that it be the wisest member of the strongest tribe. Because none of Muhammad's sons survived into adulthood, direct hereditary succession was never an option. Therefore, Muhammad's father-in-law Abu Bakr was made the first caliph. Caliphs were both political and religious leaders. Moreover, the split between Shia and Sunni Muslims led to religious and political divisions in the Muslim world that endure to today.

After the first four caliphs, the **Umayyad clan** took control in 661 CE and transformed the caliphate into a hereditary monarchy, with its government centered in Damascus. They continued on to conquer Syria, Egypt, Persia, Byzantine territory in West Asia, North Africa, and Spain. Their military skills, the soldiers' commitment to Islam, and the promise of plunder helped them in these successful conquests. The Umayyad Caliphate set up a bureaucratic structure in which local administrators governed the conquered areas. All cultures were tolerated as long as they obeyed the rules of Islam, paid their taxes, and did not revolt. Arabic became the language of administration, business, law, and trade.

The **Abbasid clan** overthrew the Umayyad dynasty in 750 CE and moved the capital of the empire to Baghdad, making it one of the most important political and commercial centers of the world. At the time, Baghdad was the second largest city in the world next to Changan. The size of the Abbasid Empire made it difficult to control. Eventually, the remaining Umayyad prince settled in Spain and established a separate caliphate there. Berber tribesmen controlled much of the northern African coast, and the Mamluks revolted and gained control over Egypt from 1250 to 1517 CE. Thus, by the mid-ninth century, the Abbasid political authority had become mostly symbolic, and the caliphate was broken into smaller states. Despite this, the culture of the Muslim world (language, laws, religion, trade, etc.) created a common bond from Spain to many parts of Africa, the Middle East, Central and South Asia, and into the islands of Southeast Asia. The term Dar al-Islam, or "all under Islam," refers to these areas in which a Muslim traveler or trader found himself welcome regardless of where he came from.

ECONOMIC DEVELOPMENTS

Trade flourished throughout the caliphate and beyond, as Muslim merchants relied on a common set of rules. Improved irrigation led to great production of agriculture and an increase in tax revenues. Artisans flourished in the cities as they became centers for manufacturing pottery, fabrics, and rugs. Paper was imported from China, and soon, paper mills were set up. The vast Islamic empire also spread many types of agriculture, including sugarcane, citrus fruits, and coffee.

CULTURAL DEVELOPMENTS

Mosques, hospitals, schools, and orphanages were built throughout the empire. Intellectual developments such as algebra, the concept of longitude and latitude, and the study of Greek philosophers such as Aristotle, took place. **The House of Wisdom**, built in Baghdad in 830, sought out Greek and Persian texts and translated them into Arabic. Universities were established in Cordoba, Toledo, and Granada. In art and architecture, the use of images was forbidden (remember the idol worship), so instead, the use of geometric shapes and calligraphy were used in their works.

INFLUENCE

Even though the Caliphate declined and ended with the Mongol invasions, the influence of Islam continued to spread throughout the period. Islam spread to West Africa through Trans-Saharan trade, to East Africa and Southeast Asia through Indian Ocean trade, to Central Asia and China through the Silk Road, and to India through the migrations of the Turks. By the conclusion of this period, Dar al-Islam had developed into one of the most dominant influences throughout the Eastern Hemisphere.

BYZANTINE EMPIRE (FOURTH CENTURY TO 1453 CE)

POLITICAL DEVELOPMENT

The Byzantine Empire, a continuation of the **Eastern Roman Empire**, was the only survivor from the classical age. The Roman Empire had officially been divided into east and west in 375 CE, with the western half severely weakened because the east produced the majority of grain and controlled the major trade routes.

The most famous emperor, Justinian, who ruled from 527 to 565 CE, tried unsuccessfully to reconquer Western Rome. His laws, however, were a success. His Body of Civil Law (**Justinian's Code**) was based on the Roman Twelve Tables of Law. Justinian controlled both political and religious power in his empire, and he also replaced Latin with Greek as the official language of the empire.

The strong central government was a hereditary monarchy. It made law, had an efficient military, oversaw effective land distribution, and had a bureaucracy that answered to the emperor. The emperor was considered a friend and imitator of Christ, and as the head of the Church, appointed the patriarch. The empire was divided into themes—or military districts—and military generals were appointed to rule. Free peasants were given land for military service.

ECONOMIC DEVELOPMENTS

Its location on the Mediterranean Sea contributed to strong trade in the Byzantine Empire. Silk worms were smuggled out of China, which allowed a Byzantine silk industry to develop. Artisans produced glassware, linen, jewelry, gold, and silver.

CULTURAL DEVELOPMENTS

Most subjects spoke Greek, but it was not forced on people. In theory, there was social mobility through the bureaucracy, army, trade, or service to the Church, but in reality, mobility was rare. Constantinople (present-day Istanbul, Turkey) was the political, commercial, and intellectual center, with libraries containing Greek, Latin, Persian, and Hebrew texts.

The Byzantine and Roman Christian churches had been growing apart since the fall of Rome, and a disagreement over the worship of icons—images of saints—seemed to be the final straw. The Pope and the Patriarch excommunicated each other, and in 1054, the church officially split into the **Roman Catholic Church** and the **Eastern Orthodox Church**. This Eastern Orthodox form of Christianity later spread to the Slavic people and Russia.

DECENTRALIZED STATES

WESTERN EUROPE—EARLY MIDDLE AGES (AROUND 500 TO 1000 CE)

POLITICAL DEVELOPMENT

Compared to Byzantium, China, and the Islamic world, Western Europe was at this time considerably backward. Those other societies were able to build centralized governments supported by a bureaucracy, but Western Europe remained politically decentralized. The Franks came closest to reestablishing imperial control with the leadership of Clovis, and later, the Carolingian Empire of **Charlemagne**. Both leaders used the Roman Catholic Church to strengthen their legitimacy, but were unsuccessful in setting up a political structure that could outlast their rule.

Instead, Europe developed a **feudal system** in which land was given to vassals in exchange for military service and loyalty. This allowed various lords and vassals to gain and compete for power, but left the central authority quite weak. The one centralizing power in this period was the Church and its ruler, the Pope, and by the 13th century, the Church owned one-third of all the land in Europe.

ECONOMIC DEVELOPMENTS

The absence of a strong central authority led many peasants to seek protection on large estates. These peasants became **serfs**; they had the right to work a portion of the land and could pass that right onto their children, but they could not leave the land. They could keep a portion of what they grew, but the majority of their earnings went to the lord. In addition, they paid taxes for use of the lord's mill, were required to work on the lord's lands as well as provide labor in the off season, and had to provide gifts, like chickens, on holidays.

These estates became large walled **manors** that were economically self-sufficient. They maintained mills, bakeries, and breweries. They had their own private armies served by armor-clad knights. The introduction of the heavy plow led to an increase in agricultural production, but the surplus was not substantial enough to sustain cities and towns in the early Middle Ages.

During the Late Middle Ages and early modern period (13th to 17th century CE), European cities began to grow and increasingly trade among one another. As a result, trade organizations developed. One of the most important was the Hanseatic League, which was an alliance of trading cities and their merchant guilds that controlled trade along the coast of Northern Europe.

CULTURAL DEVELOPMENTS

Birth was the determining factor of one's social status. Noblewomen had more power and authority than peasant women and could inherit land if widowed or if without sons. Marriage was the key to political power, and marital alliances were crucial to a family's continued success. Christian nunneries were a way for women to escape their traditional duties, and some women could exercise leadership skills.

Beginning in the 12th century, the code of conduct called chivalry developed. It stressed honor, modesty, loyalty, and duty. As warfare decreased, it incorporated courtly romance and knight participation in tournaments to prove their skills. Chivalry, unlike its Japanese counterpart bushido, was never really effective at controlling the military men's behavior and was more of an ideal than an actual code of conduct.

Christianity was the principal source of religious, moral, and cultural authority throughout the period, and strong papal leadership contributed to this influence. Monasteries were the dominant feature in social and cultural life, and they often had large landholdings. Monks preserved classical knowledge by hand-copying great literature and philosophical works.

COMPARATIVE CLOSE-UP: POLITICAL AND SOCIAL INSTITUTIONS IN WESTERN AND EASTERN EUROPE

	Western Europe	Eastern Europe
Political Institutions	Local authority of lord of manor. Central authority was weak.	Absolute power of emperor as centralizing authority supported by bureaucracy.
Social Institutions	Church as social and cultural unifier. Pope is spiritual head and strong centralizing figure. Latin is the language of the Church.	Emperor and patriarch are co-heads of the Church. Greek is the language of the Church.

JAPAN (AROUND 600 TO 1000 CE)

POLITICAL DEVELOPMENT

Japan's geography as a group of islands led to the development of small, isolated, independent communities that were often self-sufficient. Clan members cooperated with each other much like a large, extended family. By the 600s, the Yamato clan gained religious and cultural influence on other clans and wanted to copy China's model of empire-building and create a strong, stable state. Its leaders began to call themselves **emperors of Japan**. They were unsuccessful in creating a centralized state, however, and Japan remained divided by its clans. The Fujiwara clan, which dominated between 710 and 785 CE, sent emissaries to China and modeled their capital, Nara, on Changan. They could not, however, successfully introduce a Chinese-style bureaucracy, and a strict hereditary hierarchy developed instead.

During the Kamakura Shogunate, the emperor and his court kept their capital in Kyoto, yet a military dictatorship existed, ruled by powerful landholding clans. A Japanese form of **feudalism** developed in which the **shogun**—supreme general—controlled the centralized military government and divided the land into regional units based on military power. The regional military leaders were the **daimyo**, and the warriors who fought for them were the **samurai**. Over the centuries, the samurai military class developed a strict warrior code called bushido.

The emperor remained in power throughout this period, but served only as a symbolic figurehead. Many shoguns were overthrown, but the emperor was not.

ECONOMIC DEVELOPMENT

Japan was a predominantly agrarian society with an artisan class of weavers, carpenters, and ironworkers. Local trade was regulated by clan leaders. Trade and manufacturing developed more in the Kamakura Period, which focused on markets in larger towns and foreign trade with Korea and China.

Most people were peasants who worked on land that was owned by a lord or by Buddhist monasteries. Though their freedom was limited, peasants could keep what was left of their harvest after paying their tax quota. Those unable to pay their taxes became landless laborers known as **genin**, and could be bought and sold with the land. As slaves, they performed jobs such as burying the dead or curing leather.

CULTURAL DEVELOPMENT

Japan adopted many foreign ideas, but remained culturally true to its own traditions. According to **Shinto**, the religion native to Japan, everything possessed a spirit, or kami. Natural forces and nature were awe-inspiring, and shrines were built to honor kami. The first ruler from the Yamato clan claimed descent from the supreme Shinto deity, the Sun Goddess.

Japan was also strongly influenced by Korea and China. It adopted Chinese technology, Chinese script, and Buddhism (though Japan developed its own version of Buddhism, which added a strong aesthetic dimension known as **Zen Buddhism**). During the Heian period (794 to 1185), contact with China was cut off, and concentration was focused on expressing Japanese cultural values.

In a lavish court lifestyle, women dominated literature. *The Tale of Genji,* for instance, was written by Lady Murasaki. Wives inherited land from their husbands and often owned land, and priestesses dominated religious life. Over time, however, women began to lose power and influence.

NOMADIC EMPIRES

VIKINGS (AROUND 800 TO 1100 CE)

The Vikings were a nomadic group who had settled in present-day Scandinavia (Denmark, Norway, and Sweden). In order to supplement their farm production, they conducted seasonal raids into Europe and ransacked towns. Using small and maneuverable boats, they raided and terrorized coastal communities in France, Scotland, Ireland, and England. The Vikings eventually evolved from plunderers into traders, and established communities in Scotland, northern France, and Eastern Europe.

These outstanding seafarers also traded actively throughout the North Sea and Baltic Sea. In the 800s, they colonized Iceland and Greenland, and around 1000, established a colony that lasted only a few decades in Newfoundland, modern Canada. The transplanted Viking settlements in France became known as Normans (or **Northmen**).

In 1066, a Norman lord named William from northern France invaded England with his army. He defeated the Saxons and established Norman power in what is now Britain. Over time, the Normans and Vikings were Christianized and absorbed into the larger European feudal order.

TURKS (AROUND 1000 TO 1450 CE)

The Turks, a pastoral nomadic group from the **central Asian steppes**, began to gradually migrate out of the steppes at the end of the first millennium. They were often hired by Muslim leaders as mercenaries, or hired soldiers. The **Seljuk Turks**, who had converted to Islam, invaded Abbasid territory and captured Baghdad in 1055. The caliph was left as the spiritual authority of the empire, but the Seljuk Sultan became the secular monarch. By 1071, they defeated the Byzantine Empire and took most of Anatolia (modern-day Turkey).

The **Afghan Turks** were nomads from Afghanistan and began a series of raids into India in the 10th century. They looted cities for gold and jewels and destroyed Hindu temples and then left. It wasn't until the 12th century that they invaded and then started to govern. This started the **Delhi Sultanate**, which ruled northern India from 1206 to 1526. These Turks introduced a strong Muslim presence in India.

MONGOLS (AROUND 1200 TO 1550 CE)

As the chapter began in 600 CE, it would have been difficult to predict that the Mongols, a pastoral nomadic group from the central Asian steppes, would create the world's largest empire. These nomadic herders' lives revolved around their sheep, goats, and yaks for food, clothing, and shelter, their camels for transportation, and their horses for mobility. This clan-based society was organized around bloodlines. The man born Temujin, later renamed **Genghis Khan**, successfully united the various Mongol tribes.

The Mongols' greatest strength was their **mobility**. In times of war, they had total male mobilization. Every male from 15 to 70 had to serve, and each was rewarded with captured goods. The military strategy was extremely effective. Often the Mongol armies would seem to retreat only to quickly turn around and resume the attack. They were also masters at psychological warfare. Genghis Khan is believed to have said, **"Submit and live. Resist and die."**

AP EXPERT TIP

Migrations are an important part of world history, even today. Knowing why peoples move (political, economic, cultural, or environmental reasons called push-pull factors) and the consequences of their movements are essential elements in understanding the development of human civilization during this time frame. You should be able to compare the causes and effects of the migrations of the Vikings, Turks, Mongols, Aztecs, and Arabs.

A sharp decline in the mean annual temperature may have caused less and shorter grass to grow, and may have forced the Mongols to trade or raid the settled societies. Once his troops were united, Genghis Khan led them into Central Asia, Tibet, Northern China, and Persia. In 1215, the Mongols attacked and destroyed present-day Beijing. The Mongol charge continued into Afghanistan and Persia, yet in 1227, the Great Khan died, and his empire was divided amongst his four sons.

CHINA: THE YUAN DYNASTY

In 1279, Genghis Khan's grandson, **Kublai Khan**, defeated the Southern Song dynasty, and for the first time, China was under foreign rule. Khan created a Chinese-style dynasty, taking the name Yuan, with a fixed and regular tax payment system and a strong central government. Foreigners, not Chinese, were employed in the bureaucracy, and the civil service exam was not used. The Chinese were subject to different laws and were consciously separated from the Mongols.

Connecting Beijing to Vienna (in present-day Austria) was a communication system using horse relays and 1,400 postal stations. In time, overland and maritime trade flourished, and though the Mongols were not directly involved in the trade, they welcomed merchants and foreigners. Merchants converted their foreign currency to paper money when they crossed into China.

THE MIDDLE EAST: THE ILKHANATES

In 1258, Kublai's brother, **Hulegu**, defeated the Abbasid Caliphate. The Mongols in the Middle East employed local bureaucrats in the government and converted to Islam by 1295. The local rulers were permitted to rule, as long as they delivered the tax revenue and maintained order. Though they did not support agriculture, they did facilitate trade, and Mongol culture often mixed with that of the conquered people.

As the Mongols continued west, they met with their first and only major defeat. The armies of the **Mamluks**, a slave dynasty in Egypt, defeated the Mongols in 1260 and stopped the movement of the Mongols in that region.

RUSSIA: THE GOLDEN HORDE

The Mongol ruler **Batu** conquered and ruled Russia but kept a large number of the local rulers intact. The taxes on the peasants were heavy, but they were collected by Russian bureaucrats. Trade was supported, and although these Mongols were Muslim and conversion was encouraged, missionaries were allowed to visit.

PAX MONGOLIA

At the peak of Mongolian power, with huge areas of Asia and Europe under one rule, there was a period called the **Mongol Peace**. For about a century, Mongol rule united two continents and allowed for relatively safe trade and contacts between very different cultures. It did so by eliminating tariffs.

During this period, the **Silk Road trade** reached its greatest height. Paper money—a Chinese innovation—was used in many parts of the empire. It was also common for the Mongols to convert to or adopt the local religions, or at least be religiously tolerant.

Mongolian Conquests

MONGOL DECLINE

In 1274 and 1281, the Mongols tried again to expand their empire—they invaded Japan. Typhoon winds destroyed their fleet both times, however. The Japanese believed these kamikaze, or "sacred winds," had protected them.

Despite great military accomplishment, the Mongol Empire lasted hardly three or four generations. While the Mongols were successful conquerors, they were poor administrators. Overspending led to inflation in different corners of the empire, and after the death of Kublai, leadership was weak and ineffectual. Rivalry among the successors of the great Khan further destabilized the empire, and the vast domain was divided among various generals. By 1350, most of the Mongols' huge territory had been reconquered by other armies.

IMPACT OF INTERACTION

WEST AFRICAN KINGDOMS

One area that was greatly affected by the increase in interaction throughout this period was the region of West Africa. The introduction of the domesticated camel allowed for an increased flow of trade across the Sahara Desert, and as a result, Muslim and North African merchants began to establish commercial relations with West Africa.

GHANA (AROUND 500 TO 1200 CE)

Ghana was a regional state around the 400s or 500s CE, and an increase in **trans-Saharan trade** led to its growth in power and influence. It became an important commercial site and a center for trade in gold from the south, which it controlled and taxed. In return, it received ivory, slaves, horses, cloth, and salt.

As Ghana's wealth and power increased, it built a large army funded by the tax on trade, which kept order and trade safe. In the 900s CE, the kings converted to **Islam**, which led to improved relations with Muslim merchants. Islam was not forced on the people, however, and traditional animistic beliefs continued to be important. Those who did engage in the trade often converted to Islam.

After 1000 CE, Ghana found itself under assault from northern Berbers and other tribal groups nearby. It was eventually absorbed by the West African kingdom of Mali.

MALI (1235 TO LATE 1400S CE)

During this period, the trans-Saharan trade in gold and salt continued to increase. Mali controlled and taxed all trade. The rulers honored Islam and provided protection and lodging for merchants. Conversion to Islam was encouraged on a voluntary basis. The ***Sundiata*** is an epic poem that tells how the first Mali emperor came to power. The poem, a fascinating combination of historical fact and magical story, was composed and recited by Mali griots—storytellers.

The most famous Mali emperor was **Mansa Musa**, who ruled from 1312 to 1337. A devout Muslim, Mansa Musa fulfilled one of the five pillars of faith and went on a pilgrimage, or hajj, to Mecca, unlike most Muslims. He brought thousands of soldiers, attendants, subjects, and slaves with him, as well as hundreds of camels carrying satchels of gold. He also built libraries, Islamic schools, and mosques throughout the kingdom.

Timbuktu was the political capital of Mali, and it was also a regional cultural center of Islamic scholarship and art for all of West Africa. This was the peak of Malian power and wealth. After 1350 CE, provinces began to assert their independence and break away from the empire.

CHRISTIANITY IN NORTH AND EAST AFRICA (BEGINNING IN THE FIRST CENTURY CE)

Many Africans in the northern part of the continent converted to Islam after 700 CE, yet there remained a significant Christian tradition in **Egypt** and **Ethiopia**. It is believed that Saint Mark preached to the East Africans during the Roman period. Ethiopia evolved into a kingdom with strong Christian traditions. It also developed a unique style of art and architecture. There is a strong monastic strain in both Ethiopian and Egyptian (**Coptic**) Christianity. With the coming of Islam, Christians were allowed to worship freely, and a unique linguistic and artistic expression of Christianity emerged.

East African City-States (around 900 to 1500 CE)

As the trans-Saharan trade was to West Africa, the **Indian Ocean trade** was to East Africa. Bantu people had settled on the coast, and Arabic merchants who traded along the East African coast interacted to create such East African city-states as **Mogadishu**, **Kilwa**, and **Sofala**. These states are often referred to as **Swahili city-states**, named for their language, which was a blend of Bantu and Arabic.

In the 900s, Islamic merchants traded gold, slaves, and ivory for pottery, glass, and textiles from Persia, India, and China. As trade increased, so did the wealth of the city-states. Much like Ghana and Mali, these powerful city-states were governed by kings, who converted to Islam, ruled as caliphs, and taxed and controlled the trade. They built stone mosques and public buildings, and the ruling elite dressed in silk from China.

In the 1200s, the kingdom of **Zimbabwe** created a magnificent stone complex known as Great Zimbabwe, which was a city of stone towers, palaces, and public buildings. The ruling elite and wealthy merchants of East Africa often converted to Islam, but did not completely give up their own religious and cultural traditions. For the rulers, Islam meant legitimacy and alliances.

Europe during the High Middle Ages (around 1000 to 1450 CE)

While the traditional feudal economy was based on agriculture in the countryside, a new pre-modern economy was evolving by the year 1100 CE. During the early medieval period, the old Roman towns shrank in size. Now, after centuries of decline, increased trade began to stimulate the growth of commercial cities in the heart of Europe. Most often located on riversides, these towns grew into marketplaces where goods could be sold. Some representative examples of these new urban centers included:

Bruges: Located in Flanders, Bruges was ideally located on a river system that connected the North Sea with Central Europe along the Rhine. Cross-channel trade brought raw wool from England, which was made into clothing to sell.

Hamburg: Part of a league of cities called the Hanseatic league, Hamburg was a major port on the North Sea. The league regulated taxes and created rules for fair trade among the member cities.

Florence: This central Italian city controlled the flow of goods up and down the peninsula. Called the Republic of Florence, this city-state became a center for banking and commerce by 1300 CE.

Service providers and craftspeople set up businesses in these towns, further stimulating growth. Among those providing services were barbers, blacksmiths, coopers (barrel makers), jewelers, leatherworkers (tanners), innkeepers, and wine/beer merchants. These cities began to plan their growth, regulate business, and collect taxes. Wealthy towns in Italy invested in new buildings and statuary for beautification.

CRUSADES (1095 TO 1204 CE)

The Crusades were a series of Christian holy wars conducted against infidels (non-believers). The most significant was a massive expedition led by the Roman Catholic Church to recapture Palestine (the land of Christian origins) from the Muslims. **Pope Urban II** launched the Crusades in 1095, when he called for Christian knights to take up arms and seize the Holy Land.

After the First Crusade, the Christians captured Edessa, Antioch, and Jerusalem, and carved up that territory into feudal states; however, the disorganized Muslim forces reorganized, and retook Jerusalem in 1187. The Fourth Crusade never made it to the Holy Land. The crusaders, supported by the merchants of Venice, conquered and sacked Constantinople, the capital of the Byzantine Empire. They held the city for over 50 years until it was retaken. This severely weakened the Byzantine Empire.

Though the quest for the Holy Land was a failure, it led to great economic developments in Europe; it encouraged **trade with Muslim merchants** and created an increase in European demand for Asian goods. As a result, Italian merchants from places like Venice and Genoa greatly profited, and Europe was reintroduced to the goods, technology, and culture of the outside world.

LONG-DISTANCE TRADE

The period 600 to 1450 witnessed a large increase in the volume of long-distance trade. Overland trade included luxury goods of high value, such as silk and precious stones. The sea lanes were used for bulkier commodities, such as steel, stone, coral, and building materials.

The **Silk Road** linked the Eurasian land mass through trade. **Trans-Saharan trade** connected West Africa to other parts of the Muslim world and beyond. The **Indian Ocean** linked China, Southeast Asia, India, Arabia, and East Africa through ocean trade. The **Mediterranean Sea** linked Europe with the goods from the Muslim world and Asia.

As a result of so much exchange, cities that strategically sat along the trade route grew substantially. Melaka, for instance, served as an important port city on the Indian Ocean. It maintained a safe environment for the markets, welcomed all merchants, and charged reasonable fees. As a result, it thrived in this interconnected world, along with cities like Hangzhou, Samarkand, Baghdad, Kilwa, Venice, and Timbuktu.

Foreign merchants set up their own communities, where they often influenced the culture along trade routes. For example, Muslim merchants in the Indian Ocean region, Chinese merchants in Southeast Asia, and Jewish merchants in the Mediterranean all had diaspora communities in these trade cities.

Cities also grew during this time period because of increased agricultural productivity, increased trade, and slightly warmer global temperatures.

AP EXPERT TIP

Note that spellings for geographic features and cities vary according to sources. For example, Melaka is also commonly spelled as Malacca, and Samarkand is often spelled as Samarqand. Use a dictionary to learn how to pronounce names and places correctly.

MISSIONARY CAMPAIGNS

BUDDHISM

From the start, Buddhism was a missionary religion. **Theravada** Buddhism, the stricter form of the religion, spread to Southeast Asia, while **Mahayana** Buddhism spread to Central and East Asia. The latter form focused more on meditation and rituals and included the worship of holy people, known as bodhisattvas. Also, it had a greater tolerance for prior cultural traditions.

Along the Silk Road, Buddhism traveled to **Central Asia** and adapted to polytheism. In **Tibet**, Buddhism became popular as it combined shamanism and the importance of rituals. In East Asia, monks, merchants, and missionaries adapted Buddhism to the political ideas of Confucianism by including ancestor-worship and a focus on family. They also mixed in Daoist ideas.

Particularly during chaotic times, Buddhism appealed to people as an avenue toward **personal salvation**. Chinese Buddhism spread to **Korea**, where it received royal support, and to **Japan**. In Japan, it was initially resisted by Shinto leaders, but eventually, **syncretism** (the fusion of differing systems of beliefs) occurred after Buddhism blended in the worship of Shinto divinities.

Because Buddhism lacked an organized Church, it was able to merge with the local ideas of the people. However, it did become vulnerable to more organized forces. In Central Asia, for instance, Islam eventually replaced Buddhism as the dominant religion. In China, the Tang dynasty turned against it in the ninth century.

CHRISTIANITY

Like Buddhism, Christianity became a missionary religion early on. When the Western Roman Empire was declining, Christian missionary efforts turned toward Northern Europe. The Western Church and the **Pope** sponsored missionary campaigns aimed at converting the Germanic people. The Eastern Orthodox Church also spread Christianity to Eastern Europe and Russia.

As was the case with Buddhism, syncretism aided the spread of Christianity. Pagan heroes or holy figures (the saints) were seen as mediators between God and his people. Polytheistic holidays such as winter solstice were incorporated by placing Christmas on the same day. In Asia, **Nestorian Christianity** spread to Mesopotamia and Persia, where Islamic conquerors allowed Christians to practice their religion. Merchants spread Nestorian Christianity as far as India, Central Asia, and China, but they received little or no support from these areas' rulers.

ISLAM

Islam spread through two main avenues: **military conquest** and **trade and missionary activity**. Through military conquest and political influence, the religion spread because of its **tolerance** for other beliefs (people were rarely forced to convert) and a special tax levied against non-Muslims.

Through trade and missionary activity, the religion spread because of its simple message of what to do and what not to do. Plus, lower-class individuals welcomed their inclusion as spiritual equals as well as Islam's emphasis on charity.

Islam also legitimized the role of merchants. The **Sufis** were the most active missionaries after 900 CE, spreading Islam to Southern Europe, sub-Saharan Africa, Central Asia, India, and Southeast Asia. In sub-Saharan Africa, merchants introduced Islam to the ruling class through trade, where syncretism occurred. The kings still held a divine position, and women continued to have a prominent place in society, as was the local custom. In East Africa, Islam arrived via the Indian Ocean, where it mixed Arabic and African languages to create Swahili. In India, Turks brought Islam in the 11th century when they formed the Delhi Sultanate and used Hindu stories with Muslim characters, attracting both warriors and low-caste Hindus.

AGRICULTURAL AND TECHNOLOGICAL DIFFUSION

The increase in global interaction through this time period led to the spread of agriculture and technology and great changes throughout the world.

Originated	Spread to	Caused
Magnetic compass from China	Europe via the Indian Ocean trade	Increase in maritime trade and exploration
Sugarcane from Southwest Asia	European Crusaders	Italian Mediterranean island plantations and an increase in slave labor
Gunpowder from China	Persia, the Middle East, and eventually Europe by the Mongols	Increase in gunpowder weapon technology

TRAVELERS: IBN BATTUTA, MARCO POLO, AND RABBAN SAUMA

The tremendous amount of long-distance interaction in this time period can be illustrated through the travels of three individuals: a Muslim scholar, an Italian merchant, and a Nestorian Christian priest. Each recorded his observations during his travels.

	Ibn Battuta 1304–1369	Marco Polo 1253–1324	Rabban Sauma 1225–1294
Background	Muslim scholar from Morocco	Italian merchant from Venice	Nestorian Christian priest from Mongol Empire in China
Places traveled	Throughout Dar al-Islam: West Africa, India, Southeast Asia	Over the Silk Road to the Mongol Empire in China. Traveled throughout the empire.	Began pilgrimage to Jerusalem in Beijing, but diverted when sent by Mongol Ilkhan of Persia to meet with kings of France and England and Pope to negotiate alliances against Muslims
Significance	Demonstrated the widespread influence of Islam. Found government positions as a qadi or judge throughout the lands he traveled.	Allowed by Kublai Khan to pursue mercantile and domestic missions throughout the empire. Influenced European interest in goods from the East.	Did not succeed in attracting the support of Christian Europe to the Mongol cause. Europeans never conquered the Middle East, but instead went around it to reach the Indian Ocean.

THE SPREAD OF DISEASE: PLAGUE (1340S TO LATE 1600S CE)

Along with the spread of religion, technology, and goods along the trade routes came disease. The **Black Plague** spread from the Yunnan region of southwest China. It spread by way of rodents: First, it infected the rodent, then the fleas living on the rodents spread the disease to humans. In the 1340s, Mongols, merchants, and travelers spread the disease even farther along the **trade routes** west of China. Oasis towns, trading cities of Central Asia, Black Sea ports, the Mediterranean Sea, and Western Europe were all affected.

Most victims of this devastating disease died in just a few days. As a result, population decreased significantly, causing great **labor shortages** (some scholars estimate that as many as 75 million, out of a world population of 450 million, died). In Western Europe, workers demanded higher wages and peasants rebelled, leading to a decrease in serfdom and a weakening of the feudal system. **Anti-Semitism** also increased, as Jews, used as scapegoats, were accused of poisoning the wells. Some Christians questioned their faith amid all of the death and seemingly senseless destruction.

RECOVERY AND RENAISSANCE IN ASIA AND EUROPE (BEGINNING AROUND 1400 CE)

CHINESE POLITICAL DEVELOPMENT

The Ming dynasty might be viewed as China's comeback dynasty after the rule of the Mongols. In 1368, the Mongol Yuan dynasty collapsed, after which Emperor Hongwu started the Ming dynasty. His first order of business was to eliminate all evidence that the Mongols had ever ruled China. The Confucian education system and **civil service exam** were reinstated, and central authority was tightened.

The Ming relied on mandarins, a class of powerful officials, to implement their policies on the local level. Laborers were conscripted to rebuild irrigation systems, and as a result, agricultural production increased. Though the Ming did not actively promote trade, private merchants traded manufactured porcelain, silk, and cotton. The dynasty lasted until 1644.

EUROPEAN POLITICAL DEVELOPMENT

By the 1400s, the regional states in Europe were developing into **strong, powerful monarchies.** They were now in a position to tax citizens directly and to maintain large standing armies. Italy, Milan, Venice, and Florence benefited greatly from the increase in trade, which led to an increase in tax revenues. That, in turn, led to an increase in strength and authority.

Kings in France and England began to successfully assert their authority over their feudal lords. In Spain, Fernando of Aragon and Isabel of Castile married and went on to unite Spain by reconquering the lands formerly controlled by Muslims. The **competition** among these states led to a refinement and improvement in weapons, ships, and technology, setting up these regional states for a more dominant position in the world.

CHINESE INTELLECTUAL DEVELOPMENTS

During the Ming dynasty, Chinese cultural traditions were strongly promoted, and **Neo-Confucian** schools were established and supported. Confucian values such as self-discipline, filial piety, and obedience to rulers were stressed. Projects were funded that emphasized Chinese cultural traditions, such as the **Yongle Encyclopedia**, which was the work of more than 2,000 scholars and the largest general encyclopedia of its time. It covered a wide array of subjects, including agriculture, art, astronomy, drama, geology, history, literature, medicine, natural sciences, religion, and technology. Popular culture thrived with the increase in printing. Novels such as *The Dream of the Red Chamber* and *Journey to the West* were extremely popular.

Jesuit missionaries such as Matteo Ricci arrived, introducing European science and technology. The Jesuit goal of converting the Chinese population to Christianity proved to be unsuccessful, however.

EUROPEAN INTELLECTUAL DEVELOPMENTS

The increase in interaction with and interest in the outside world sparked a major intellectual and artistic movement known as the **Renaissance**. Contact with the **Islamic world** reintroduced the ancient Greek and Roman texts that had been preserved and developed by Arabs. From the 1300s through the 1500s, painters, sculptors, and writers drew inspiration from the **Greek** and **Roman** classical past.

The study of these classical texts became known as the **studia humanitates**, which was usually translated as the "liberal arts." The philosophy behind the study of liberal arts was **humanism**. Humanism stressed human beings, their achievements, and their capabilities. While medieval scholars and artists focused their work on revealing God, humanist scholars and artists attempted to reveal human nature. In Italy, artists such as Leonardo da Vinci and Michelangelo used perspective to create realistic masterpieces. Famous noble families, such as the Medici family, had grown wealthy as merchants, since Italy was perfectly located for receiving goods from the Middle East and Asia. This lucrative trade with the Islamic and Byzantine cultures allowed wealthy Italians to become patrons of painters, sculptors, and scientists.

CHINESE EXPLORATION

After reestablishing authority over China, the Ming decided to refurbish the large Chinese navy and conduct a "comeback tour." From 1405 to 1433, seven massive naval expeditions were sponsored to reestablish Chinese presence in the Indian Ocean, impose imperial control over trade, and impress foreign people with Ming power.

The expeditions were led by the Muslim eunuch **Zheng He**. They involved over 300 ships with 28,000 troops, sailing to Southeast Asia, India, the Persian Gulf, Arabia, and East Africa, with Zheng dispensing and receiving gifts along the way. But in 1433, the voyages ended. Zheng's records were destroyed and the ships were allowed to rot. Pressure from Confucian officials convinced the emperor that the voyages were too expensive and offered nothing that China needed. Additionally, the age-old concern of a Mongol invasion from the North reappeared, and it was deemed more important to protect that northern border than to explore the seas.

EUROPEAN EXPLORATION

In the 1400s, the ideas of the Renaissance pushed some Europeans to look outward and explore. These explorations were not diplomatic, but instead focused on profits, the spread of Christianity, and the desire for adventure. The goods from the East—particularly spices—that Europeans desired were incredibly expensive because of the long overland journey they took to reach Europe.

But what if Europeans could find their own route to Asia by sea and cut out the Muslim middleman's profits? The **Portuguese** were the early leaders in exploration, under the leadership of

Prince Henry the Navigator. He set up schools in his native land and sponsored expeditions along the West African coast.

Competition heated up among European powers, and a race to dominate the seas began. This competition continued well into our next time period, with the European involvement in the Indian Ocean trade and the encounter with the Americas.

AMERICAN CIVILIZATIONS

MAYA (AROUND 300 TO 900 CE)

Borrowing from Olmec traditions, the Mayans developed a large domain and lived in scattered settlements on the Yucatán peninsula in southeastern Mexico. Archaeologists have discovered the following features of their regional culture:

- An agricultural economy
- Distinctive temple complexes and massive pyramids
- A ritualistic polytheism
- Urban areas with thousands of people
- Independent city-states, linked by trade
- A staple diet of maize (corn) and beans

AZTEC (AROUND 1400 TO 1521 CE)

Also known as the Mexica people, the Aztecs were the last great Mesoamerican culture before the arrival of the Europeans. Taking advantage of the Toltecs' decline, the Aztecs used their fighting skills to take control of the Lake Texcoco region. The Aztec culture was characterized by:

- A militant warrior tradition
- Rule by severe despots
- A priestly class to oversee rituals, including human sacrifice
- A ritualistic polytheistic religion with an extensive pantheon
- A large urban capital with 150,000 inhabitants
- An agricultural economy with cacao beans sometimes used as currency
- A decentralized network of city-states that paid tribute

INCA (AROUND 1400 TO 1540 CE)

In the Andean highlands of South America, clans developed a rich and complex culture, which led to the rise of an empire in the 1300s CE. These people—the Incas—conquered a large area and absorbed many groups in central-western South America. In 90 years, the Incan Empire grew into a stretch of land that covered over 3,000 miles from north to south. History remembers the Incas for:

- A centralized empire with its capital at Cuzco (in present-day Peru)

- An extensive, irrigated agricultural economy that adapted to the steep and rugged terrain of the Andes

- Large urban centers

- A polytheistic religion centered around worship of the sun

- A patriarchal society with few rights for women

- A privileged class of nobles, headed by a king, in which royal ancestors were revered and worshipped

- No written language, but a system of recordkeeping called **quipu** that used knotted strings to record such information as tax obligations, census records, and other numeric data

- Impressive achievements in building with cut stone

REVIEW QUESTIONS

MULTIPLE-CHOICE QUESTIONS

Please note that these are content-specific review questions for this chapter, designed to help you perform well on the exam.

1. The fall of the Tang dynasty in the middle of the eighth century was aided by

    (A) foreign interference.

    (B) Japanese invasions.

    (C) deflationary pressures on the economy.

    (D) peasant revolts.

2. Most Mesoamerican rulers tended to be both

    (A) benign and powerless.

    (B) liberal and generous.

    (C) scholarly and artistic.

    (D) despotic and severe.

3. In what order did these three monotheistic religions come into being?

    (A) Judaism, Christianity, Islam

    (B) Christianity, Islam, Judaism

    (C) Judaism, Islam, Christianity

    (D) Christianity, Judaism, Islam

4. Which of the following statements best describes the similarity between the impact of the Roman and Mongol empires?

    (A) They both brought all of Africa under one rule.

    (B) They both created an enduring peace.

    (C) They both led to the establishment of large navies.

    (D) They both established a common language.

5. Written evidence of the life of Muhammad is largely found in the

    (A) Old Testament.

    (B) Bible.

    (C) Quran.

    (D) Gospels.

6. The goal of the Christian Crusades was to

    (A) evangelize the Africans.

    (B) conquer Asia Minor.

    (C) increase papal territories.

    (D) retake the Holy Land from the Muslims.

7. The main unifying institution in medieval Europe was the

    (A) monarchy.

    (B) Roman Catholic Church.

    (C) artists' guilds.

    (D) University of Paris.

8. Islam was brought into India over time by the

    (A) Umayyads.

    (B) Ottomans.

    (C) Delhi Sultanate.

    (D) Sunni Caliphate.

9. The Mongolian Empire declined because of

   (A) religious differences with the native peoples.

   (B) administrative problems owing to the large territory involved.

   (C) feeble rulers after Genghis Khan.

   (D) Russian counterattacks.

10. Two religions that encouraged the monastic life were

    (A) Islam and Confucianism.

    (B) Taoism and Judaism.

    (C) Buddhism and Christianity.

    (D) Judaism and Islam.

11. Which of the following was NOT a part of Chinese culture adopted by the Japanese?

    (E) Confucian values

    (F) A system of writing

    (G) The bushido code

    (H) Buddhist theology

12. The Black Death was

    (A) spread along Euro-Asian trade routes.

    (B) confined to China and South Asia.

    (C) primarily deadly in Northern Europe.

    (D) purposely spread by the Mongols.

13. During the feudal period in Western Europe,

    (A) independent domains fought regularly with one another.

    (B) women were allowed to rule fiefs.

    (C) priests were allowed to marry.

    (D) the birthrate declined.

14. Organizations of merchants and craftspeople in European cities were called .

    (A) granges.

    (B) guilds.

    (C) ecclesia.

    (D) fiefdoms.

15. Japanese feudalism resulted in part because of

    (A) the emperor's ability to rule effectively.

    (B) the failure of the Heian to govern efficiently.

    (C) the overthrow of the shogun after 1200 CE.

    (D) the decline of the samurai class.

16. The basis of the Mayan economy was

    (A) crafts and manufacturing.

    (B) agriculture, which produced maize, beans, and cacao beans.

    (C) trade with the Pueblos to the north.

    (D) fishing and hunting.

17. Alliances between European feudal lords were often the result of

    (A) trade relations between the domains.

    (B) papal decree.

    (C) the need for a defense against the marauding Vikings.

    (D) the Black Death.

18. All of the following statements is true of the Tang dynasty EXCEPT

    (A) the capital city was the largest in the world.

    (B) the empire expanded its territory to Tibet and Korea.

    (C) the government discouraged trade and foreign influence.

    (D) Buddhists were persecuted toward the end of the empire.

19. Which of the following statements is true of the Turks and the Mongols?

    (A) Both conquered and ruled Japan.

    (B) Both were skilled administrators and bureaucrats.

    (C) Both had written languages based on Arabic.

    (D) Both were pastoral nomads originally from the Central Asian steppes.

20. Which of the following happened after the fall of the Mongol Empire?

    (A) The Byzantine Empire reunited the former Roman Empire.

    (B) Muhammad led his followers to Medina.

    (C) The Delhi Sultanate invaded and conquered India.

    (D) The Ming dynasty reunited China under Chinese rule.

21. Which of the following statements is true of the time period 600 to 1450 CE?

    (A) The Tang dynasty stabilized China after Mongol rule.

    (B) Long-distance trade flourished.

    (C) Western Europe dominated global political affairs.

    (D) The Turks expanded as far as sub-Saharan Africa.

22. The term *chivalry* in medieval Europe is most like

    (A) salvation.

    (B) samsara.

    (C) bushido.

    (D) samurai.

23. Which of the following statements accurately compares West and East Africa during the time period 600 to 1450 CE?

    (A) Trans-Saharan trade was for West Africa what Indian Ocean trade was for East Africa.

    (B) Christianity converted large parts of the population in both regions.

    (C) Both areas were ruled by centralizing governments controlled by an emperor.

    (D) The areas were isolated throughout this time period.

24. Melakka and Venice were important examples of

    (A) Silk Road oasis towns.

    (B) pilgrimage sites.

    (C) political capitals.

    (D) trading ports.

25. Which of the following regions had the greatest navigational technology during the time period 600 to 1450 CE?

    (A) West Africa

    (B) Japan

    (C) Western Europe

    (D) China

DOCUMENT-BASED QUESTION

This DBQ is a practice activity. The actual question on the exam may be longer.

Directions: The following question is based on the accompanying Documents 1 to 4. (The documents have been edited for the purpose of this exercise.)

This question is designed to test your ability to work with and understand historical documents. Write an essay that:

- Has a relevant thesis and supports that thesis with evidence from the documents.

- Uses all of the documents.

- Analyzes the documents by grouping them in as many appropriate ways as possible.

- Does not simply summarize the documents individually.

- Takes into account the sources of the documents and analyzes the authors' points of view.

- Explains the need for at least one additional type of document.

You may refer to relevant historical information not mentioned in the documents.

Based on the following documents, describe European motivations for the Crusades. Identify an additional type of document and explain how it would help your analysis of the European motivations for the Crusades.

Historical Background: The Crusades were a series of Christian holy wars conducted against infidels (non-believers), the most significant was a massive expedition led by the Roman Catholic Church to recapture Palestine (the land of Christian origins) from the Muslims. Even before the Crusades, Christian peoples in conflict with other migrating peoples of different faiths saw the call to war as not merely a defense of their lands and way of life but also as a means of preserving their faith. Questions as to whether fighting in a war was a means of exercising one's faith therefore led to promulgations by Church leaders.

DOCUMENT 1

Source: Pope Leo IV (847–855), Forgiveness of Sins for Those Who Die in Battle with the Heathen.

Given to the Frankish Army

Now we hope that none of you will be slain, but we wish you to know that the kingdom of heaven will be given as a reward to those who shall be killed in this war. For the Omnipotent knows that they lost their lives fighting for the truth of the faith, for the preservation of their country, and the defense of Christians. And therefore God will give them the reward which we have named.

DOCUMENT 2

Source: Pope John VIII, Indulgence for Fighting the Heathen, 878.

John VIII to the bishops in the realm of Louis II [the Stammerer]:

You have modestly expressed a desire to know whether those who have recently died in war, fighting in defense of the church of God and for the preservation of the Christian religion and of the state, or those who may in the future fall in the same cause, may obtain indulgence for their sins. We confidently reply that those who, out of love to the Christian religion, shall die in battle fighting bravely against pagans or unbelievers, shall receive eternal life. For the Lord has said through his prophet: "In whatever hour a sinner shall be converted, I will remember his sins no longer." By the intercession of St. Peter, who has the power of binding and loosing in heaven and on the earth, we absolve, as far as is permissible, all such and commend them by our prayers to the Lord.

DOCUMENT 3

Source: Pope Gregory VII, Call for a Crusade, 1074.

Gregory, bishop, servant of the servants of God, to all who are willing to defend the Christian faith, greeting and apostolic benediction:

We hereby inform you that the bearer of this letter, on his recent return from across the sea [from Palestine], came to Rome to visit us. He repeated what we had heard from many others, that a pagan race had overcome the Christians and with horrible cruelty had devastated everything almost to the walls of Constantinople, and were now governing the conquered lands with tyrannical violence, and that they had slain many thousands of Christians as if they were but sheep. If we love God and wish to be recognized as Christians, we should be filled with grief at the misfortune of this great empire [the Greek] and the murder of so many Christians. But simply to grieve is not our whole duty. The example of our Redeemer and the bond of fraternal love demand that we should lay down our lives to liberate them. "Because he has laid down his life for us: and we ought to lay down our lives for the brethren," [1 John 3:16]. Know, therefore, that we are trusting in the mercy of God and in the power of his might and that we are striving in all possible ways and making preparations to render aid to the Christian Empire [the Greek] as quickly as possible. Send messengers to us at once to inform us of what God may inspire you to do in this matter.

DOCUMENT 4

Source: Chronicle of Fulcher of Chartres, written between 1101 and 1128. Fulcher was present at Council of Clermont, where Pope Urban II issued his call for the First Crusade in 1095 and participated in the Crusades.

The Pope's Exhortation Concerning the Expedition to Jerusalem:

3. "For, as most of you have been told, the Turks, a race of Persians, who have penetrated within the boundaries of Romania even to the Mediterranean to that point which they call the Arm of Saint George, in occupying more and more of the lands of the Christians, have overcome them, already victims of seven battles, and have killed and captured them, have overthrown churches, and have laid waste God's kingdom. If you permit this supinely for very long, God's faithful ones will be still further subjected.

4. Concerning this affair, I, with suppliant prayer—not I but the Lord, exhort you, heralds of Christ, to persuade all of whatever class, both knights and footmen, both rich and poor, in numerous edicts, to strive to help expel that wicked race from our Christian lands before it is too late.

5. I speak to those present, I send word to those not here; moreover, Christ commands it. Remission of sins will be granted for those going thither, if they end a shackled life either on land or in crossing the sea, or in struggling against the heathen. I, being vested with that gift from God, grant this to those who go."

CONTINUITY AND CHANGE-OVER-TIME QUESTION

Directions: You are to answer the following question. You should spend five minutes organizing or outlining your essay. Write an essay that:

- Has a relevant thesis and supports that thesis with appropriate historical evidence.

- Addresses all parts of the question.

- Uses world historical context to show continuity and change over time.

- Analyzes the process of continuity and change over time.

  Prompt: Describe and analyze continuities and changes in the impact of nomads on ONE of the following areas from 600 to 1450.

- East Asia (China and/or Japan)

- Russia

- Middle East

COMPARATIVE QUESTION

Directions: You are to answer the following question. You should spend five minutes organizing or outlining your essay. Write an essay that:

- Has a relevant thesis and supports that thesis with appropriate historical evidence.

- Addresses all parts of the question.

- Makes direct, relevant comparisons.

- Analyzes relevant reasons for similarities and differences.

   Prompt: Discuss the similarities and differences in the political and social influence of TWO of the following religions from 600 to 1450.

- Christianity—Europe

- Islam—West Africa

- Buddhism—China

ANSWERS AND EXPLANATIONS

MULTIPLE-CHOICE ANSWERS

1. D

In times of famine or if taxes were too high, the peasants would rise up, sometimes leading to the overthrow of the government. Tang power declined as higher taxes led to peasant rebellions and the abdication of the emperor. The Japanese did not have the military might to intrude in China until after the 1920s and the end of Chinese imperial history.

2. D

Mesoamerican kings were very powerful and ruled with an iron hand. The punishments they meted out were often cruel and painful. Human sacrifice was common within the context of religious practices.

3. A

Judaism emerged first in the deserts of Mesopotamia around 2000 BCE. Christianity was a sect within Judaism that broke away in the first century CE. Islam came into being in the mid-600s CE in Arabia.

4. B

The Roman Empire led to the Pax Romana, and the Mongolian Empire led to the Pax Mongolia. These empire-created periods of peace enabled trade to flourish within their realms. Neither empire brought all of Africa under its rule, established a large navy, or a common language.

5. C

Historical evidence about the life of Muhammad is mostly found in the scriptures that he himself dictated. These make up the Holy Book of Islam called the *Quran* (Koran). Both the Old Testament and the Gospels were written long before Muhammad lived.

6. D

Pope Urban II urged Christian soldiers to liberate the Holy Land from the Muslims in 1095. He offered an indulgence, or pardoning of sins, for all who answered this call to arms. Urban urged solidarity with the Byzantine Empire and sought Christian control over the holy sites, such as Jerusalem.

7. B

With the fragmentation of political power after the collapse of the Roman Empire, the Christian Church became the most important institution in Europe. It supported many of the universities where priests were often professors. Artists' guilds were local organizations in some urban areas.

8. C

The Muslims gradually conquered the subcontinent and established the Delhi Sultanate by 1200 CE. Also called the "slave" dynasty in its early period, this sultanate was a succession of Muslim rulers who ruled northern India from the 13th century. The Ottoman Empire did not extend as far east as India.

9. B

The Mongol Empire was vast and did not long survive the death of Kublai Khan. Though they were able military conquerors, the Mongols were challenged as administrators of so large an empire. The Russians were conquered by the Mongols and were ruled by them for many years.

10. C

Both Buddhism and Christianity developed strong monastic traditions. Living a devotional life separate from the rest of the world has continued to have appeal for the faithful. Monasteries are not a feature of Judaic or Islamic traditions.

11. C

The bushido, or "way of the warrior," is a uniquely Japanese tradition that defined samurai culture. This elite warrior caste developed over many centuries in feudal Japan. China was the origin of many other aspects of Japanese culture such as the ideographs used in writing and strong Confucian values within the family and society.

12. A

Believed to have originated in China in the 1330s, the plague, or Black Death, came to Europe aboard trading ships. It is estimated to have killed 25 million people throughout Europe and was weaker in the northern climes where the fleas that spread it could not survive the cold.

13. A

Warfare was a constant feature of the feudal period in Europe. Local lords often fought with nearby rivals for territory. Although women were involved in political marriages where large land was transferred, they were not rulers. Priests were expected to be celibate and not to marry, according to the traditions of the Roman Catholic Church.

14. B

Guilds were early associations to which artisans and craftspeople could belong in medieval Europe. They existed partly to encourage public service, but also to act as a kind of fraternity for their members. Granges were farmer associations in 19th century-America, and ecclesia has to do with the Church.

15. B

The collapse of Heian rule in Japan encouraged a descent into decentralized warfare after 1179 CE. The warrior class had evolved into many small armies, and feudal domains began to define the political order in Japan. The emperor continued to be marginalized in the imperial capital of Kyoto.

16. B

The growth of maize and beans was the mainstay of the Mayan economy, and these products were also the staples in their diet. Fish was not a common feature of their everyday diet. As a pre-industrial society, there was no manufacture of goods in great quantity in the Mayan Empire.

17. C

Feudal lords that might otherwise have fought one another found common cause when Norsemen, or Vikings, attacked from the North. Lords in Scotland, England, and France were very afraid of the quick and brutal Viking raids from 800 CE. The Black Death caused a net drop in the population and birthrate of Europe in the 14th century.

18. C

The Tang dynasty supported long-distance trade, and the Silk Road trade flourished during its reign. Foreigners were welcome, particularly in the enormous capital city of Changan, which was known for its quarters of foreign merchants.

19. D

Although the Mongols attempted to conquer Japan, they were unsuccessful. Neither the Turks nor the Mongols were skilled administrators, and they often used local people to help them rule. They did not base their written languages on Arabic, but both were originally from the Central Asian steppes.

20. D

After the Mongols' rule ended, the Ming dynasty established Chinese rule in China. The Byzantine Empire never successfully reunited the Roman Empire. Muhammad led followers to Medina, and the Delhi Sultanate conquered India before the Mongol Empire was established.

21. B

Due to trade routes such as the Silk Road, Indian Ocean, trans-Saharan, and Mediterranean Sea, long-distance trade flourished during this period. The Tang dynasty ruled before the Mongols. Western Europe was decentralized and did not dominate global political affairs. The Turks never made it as far as sub-Saharan Africa.

22. C

The Japanese term bushido refers to the samurai code of conduct. The European term *chivalry* refers to the code of conduct for knights.

23. A

Trans-Saharan trade and Indian Ocean trade were the lifeblood of West Africa and East Africa, respectively. Christianity influenced parts of the population in East Africa. West Africa was controlled by a centralizing emperor, but East Africa was organized into city-states. The areas were not isolated, but interacted extensively.

24. D

Melakka was an important trading port in Southeast Asia on the Indian Ocean. Venice was an important trading port in Italy on the Mediterranean Sea.

25. D

The Chinese were the dominant force in navigational technology during this period, with inventions such as the compass and sternpost rudder, and later with the Ming fleet that sailed the Indian Ocean under the leadership of Zheng He.

DOCUMENT-BASED QUESTION: SAMPLE RESPONSE

From 600 to 1450, the Catholic Church held great power over the Western European world. Kings at the time were relatively weak and the Pope was the centralizing figure in the region. As the Islamic world grew stronger and more powerful, the Catholic Church took note. In an attempt to combat the Muslim threat, the Church called for a series of Crusades. The goal of these Crusades was to push back the Muslims and protect fellow Christians. The motivations given to recruit willing participants in these efforts were primarily religious and political.

Since the Catholic Church held the power to decide who could receive salvation, a major religious motivation for participation in the Crusades was the promise of eternal life. Pope Leo IV, with the purpose of motivating the troops, gave a message to the Frankish army in the ninth century that promised heaven as the reward for anyone who was killed in the fighting (Document 1). Since the Franks, according to the Pope, were fighting for the truth of the faith and aiding the defense of Christians, God would look out for them in the afterlife. Later in the ninth century, Pope John VIII gave a message to his bishops, again with the purpose of motivating and encouraging participation in the fight (Document 2). It promised indulgence for the sins of those who fought for the Christian religion and state. It would be helpful to know if the bishops receiving the Pope's letter were convinced of the validity of this mission and more important, if the soldiers who received the promise of salvation were truly motivated by this reason or other more economic reasons, such as the opportunity to obtain their own land. Lastly, Pope Urban II, according to the Fulcher of Chartres, told his audience at the Council of Clermont, in 1095, that Christ commanded the Crusades, and that those who participated would have their sins forgiven (Document 4). Pope Urban, also, with an intent to stir up hatred for the Muslims, told his audience that the Muslims had already killed and captured Christians, and had destroyed God's churches. Because Pope Urban had a vested interest in stirring up anti-Muslim sentiment, the reliability of his statements regarding the killing of Christians at the hands of Muslims can be called into question.

In addition to the religious motivation to fight in the Crusades, the Church used political incentives to draw in participants. In his letter, Pope John VIII explicitly linked Christianity and the state, giving the mission a political, as well as religious, purpose (Document 2). By doing this, the Pope made the state an instrument of the Church. Almost 200 years later in 1074 CE, Pope Gregory VII called for his own Crusade (Document 3). His purpose was to equate the Muslims with an almost subhuman race that was threatening Christian civilization. He was trying to appeal to Western European Christians to defend their fellow Christians in the Byzantine Empire, thus creating a religious and political bond between the two. However, because he was appealing to the emotions of European Christians and his power would have been increased as a result of a successful Crusade, the reliability of Pope Gregory VII's description of the "tyrannical violence" of the Muslims can be disputed. Because the call from Pope Urban II in 1095 initiated the Crusades to recapture the Holy land in Palestine, it would be helpful to know how Pope Gregory's message was received and why the mass movement did not begin after his call for a Crusade. Additionally, did the average Christian in Western Europe feel an allegiance to Byzantine Christians because of their common faith, or were there other motivations to get involved?

After Pope Urban's call for a Crusade in 1095, much of the next 200 years involved a movement by the Catholic Church and Christian kingdoms to reconquer the Holy Land. The Church used both religious motivation (the promise of salvation) and political motivation (the reconquering of land) to stir up involvement. Additionally, the economic motive of potential wealth drove many crusaders into the movement.

The essay earns the point for thesis, and 3 points for understanding and using the documents. The essay contains two additional document requests and earns 1 point; however, it has only one point-of-view analysis that works and so does not earn that point.

The essay has two document groups that earn it the grouping point. The first concerns religious motivations (Documents 1, 2, and 4), while the second examines political motivations (2, 3, and 4). The essay gets a score of 6. If the first POV analysis had worked, then the document would be an 8 due to the outside historical information the author included on possible economic motivations.

CONTINUITY AND CHANGE-OVER-TIME QUESTION: SAMPLE RESPONSE

Between the years 600 and 1450, China went from being a Chinese state to part of a larger empire controlled by foreign conquerors as a result of Mongol conquest. However, throughout the period, a Chinese sense of cultural identity remained. The political implications of Mongol conquest meant that China would become a unified kingdom governed by the rulers of the majority of Asia. The economic implications meant that long-distance trade would be able to flourish in areas such as the Silk Road.

Mongol conquest of China meant, essentially, the creation of the Yuan dynasty. The reason for the Chinese name in an empire controlled by nomads stemmed from the Chinese cultural identity, and the need to appease the Chinese people with a false sense that foreign invaders were ruling in a traditional Chinese way. The most obvious example of the refusal of the Mongols to govern the Middle Kingdom as it had been during the previous dynasties was the abolition of the civil service exam. The reasoning behind this was that Mongols were illiterate and unfamiliar with Confucian ethics, thereby making it impossible for them to hold political office if the exam system remained in place. However, a perfect example of the Mongol desire to give the illusion of Chinese rule was the maintaining of the Chinese bureaucracy, with the emperor at the top. Of course, the major change in the Yuan dynasty from the previous dynasties was the fact that Mongols rather than Chinese held political offices.

Mongol conquest of China, along with most other regions in Asia, meant a flourishing, secure trade network. With Mongol control of essentially the entire Silk Road, overland trade was able to expand. The issuing of what were effectively passports by the Mongols all but ensured that merchants would not be harmed while traveling on overland trade routes. This, in turn, built the Chinese economy to a respectable state. This prosperity and relative safety encouraged travel to and from China in the Yuan dynasty, as seen with the famous Marco Polo. This economic stability even discouraged immediate uprising in China, as the Mongols ruled through the Yuan dynasty for a considerable time. Chinese cultural identity regained its full empowerment with the replacement of the Yuan by the Ming dynasty. This shows the continuity of Chinese identity throughout this period. In spite of economic and political stability, the Chinese carried their cultural identity throughout Mongol rule so that the Ming would feel it necessary to regain the glory and authority commanded by the Middle Kingdom with the Ming voyages.

Between 600 and 1450, China went from being a Chinese state to part of a larger empire controlled by foreign conquerors, as a result of the Mongol conquest. However, a sense of Chinese cultural identity remained throughout the time period. The implications of Mongol conquest, on a global scale, meant stability and prosperity for most of Asia

.—Written by Michael Knowles, Fox Lane High School, Bedford, New York

Not only does this writer's thesis in the first paragraph earns its first point for directly addressing the prompt, but the closing paragraph also ties up the essay neatly by summarizing the prompt with a confident finality. The topic sentences of the second and third paragraphs indicate that the writer intends to address political and economic aspects of continuity and change, earning both addressing points. Furthermore, the ample evidence delivers on the promise of the topic sentences, gaining two points. However, the essay lacks any analysis of global context/impact, missing its writer a point in this area. Final point total is 8.

COMPARATIVE QUESTION: SAMPLE RESPONSE

Both Christianity in Europe and Buddhism in China were used by political authorities to establish legitimacy from 600 to 1450, and they both offered universal salvation. In Europe, Christianity became the dominant religious force, while in China, Buddhism was important, though it did not replace other philosophies or religions as the dominant belief.

Politically, both Christianity and Buddhism thrived due to official patronage. In Europe, following the fall of the Western Roman Empire, the Christian Church became the only centralizing force in the region. The Pope grew to be the most powerful religious and political figure. Kings, who were relatively weak at this time, owed allegiance to the Pope as the supreme power. Christianity served as a vehicle for leaders to unite their people under a common belief. German kings, like Clovis, converted to Christianity and their subjects soon followed. The religion and its Pope were even powerful enough to compel kings and knights to fight on behalf of the faith against the perceived infidels the Muslims. Buddhism also benefited from political patronage, but its hold over all of China was not very powerful. It became more popular in China during the unstable times after the Han Empire fell. So similarly to Christianity, Buddhism offered some solace in a time of disorder. During the Sui and later Tang dynasties, emperors used a connection with the religion to establish their own legitimacy. Empress Wu, in particular, favored Buddhism and had many schools and monasteries established. But toward the end of the Tang dynasty, Buddhism suffered persecution during anti-Buddhist campaigns. The "foreign" religion was blamed for many of China's problems and attacked for much of its wealth. Although Buddhism remained influential in China's culture, it did not take on the dominant all-consuming characteristic of Christianity in Europe.

Socially, Christianity and Buddhism had many similar effects. Both religions offered a form of universal salvation. Christianity promises all who believe a place in heaven after this life. This afterlife was not determined by gender, social, or economic status, but by faith. As a result, Christianity attracted large numbers of the poor, as well as women. Similarly, Buddhism preached that all could (after many lives) achieve nirvana, or a release from reincarnation and suffering. This idea appealed to many women. Additionally, in both religions, life as a nun in a convent offered an alternative life to women who did not want to follow the traditional path.

Christianity and Buddhism both thrived and spread from 600 to 1450. Political patronage helped both the religions and the rulers who used them to help establish legitimacy. Socially, both religions opened up a chance for salvation or escape to those who always felt disenfranchised.

Although the thesis relates the similarities of Christianity and Buddhism, it doesn't explicitly address where the two diverge, losing it the critical point here. The second paragraph's topic sentence and its evidence treat the similarities and differences, granting it a point for evidence and another for direct, relevant comparisons. However, the third paragraph fails to address specifically any differences and provides little evidence and analysis, earning it only 1 point. The closing paragraph is little more than a restatement of points already made. Final point total is 4.

CHAPTER 5: 1450 TO 1750 CE

IF YOU ONLY LEARN SIX THINGS IN THIS CHAPTER . . .

1. As a result of the search for a faster way to the trade routes of the Indian Ocean, the Americas are included in the global trade network, and the process of true globalization begins. This encounter sets off the Columbian Exchange of goods, disease, and cultures, which spreads throughout the world.

2. Improvements in and the spread of shipping technologies and gunpowder weapons allow European countries to begin to exercise a more prominent role in world affairs.

3. Native American people die by the millions due to their exposure to previously unknown European diseases. African people are forcibly transported across the Atlantic Ocean to fill the need for forced labor on plantations.

4. New social structures emerge like those in the Americas based on race. While few women exert power publicly, women of the harem in the Ottoman Empire wield considerable power behind the scenes.

5. In Europe, the Renaissance and Reformation challenge previously accepted beliefs and the power of the Roman Catholic Church. In others parts of the world such as China, reaffirmation of more traditional beliefs is viewed as the key to stability.

6. European empires such as Spain and Portugal stretch their power overseas to conquer and control the newly encountered Americas. At the same time, dominant land-based empires such as the Ottoman, Mughal, and Qing grow powerful.

THE BIG PICTURE

1. Interactions between people and the environment

   In other words: **How does the environment shape human societies, and how do humans shape the environment?**

Improvements in and the spread of shipping technologies and gunpowder weapons allowed European countries to begin their dominance of the world. Native American people died by the millions due to their exposure to previously unknown European diseases, and in Africa, people were forcibly transported across the Atlantic Ocean to fill the need for labor on plantations. The introduction of European agriculture and settlement patterns in the Americas led to deforestation and soil depletion.

2. Development and interaction of cultures

   In other words: **How do people express themselves, and what is the impact of ideas?**

In Europe, the Renaissance and Reformation challenged previously accepted beliefs and the power of the Roman Catholic Church. In others parts of the world, like China, reaffirmation of more traditional beliefs was viewed as the key to stability.

3. State-building, expansion, and conflict

   In other words: **How do people govern themselves?**

The predominant form of political organization remained the empire. European empires, like those of Spain and Portugal, stretched their power overseas to conquer and control the newly encountered Americas. At the same time, dominant land-based empires such as the Ottoman, Mughal, and Qing grew powerful.

4. Creation, expansion, and interaction of economic systems

   In other words: **How do economic developments affect the world?**

During this period, the world becomes truly global. For the first time, the Americas are included in the global trade network and the process of true globalization begins. Trade is extended throughout all parts of the world. The European nations gain access to Asian trade routes and attempt to control them. The Columbian Exchange of goods, disease, and cultures spreads throughout the world.

5. Development and transformation of social structures

   In other words: **How do people identify themselves socially, and what roles do men and women have?**

In the Americas, a new social structure emerges based on race. Those with pure European blood are considered the highest socially and politically, and those with indigenous or African blood are considered the lowest. Women of the harem in the Ottoman Empire wield considerable power behind the scenes.

WHY THIS PERIODIZATION?

The most significant change that occurs in this time period is the inclusion of the Americas in the global trade network. With this inclusion, a truly global economy develops. As Europeans are getting ready to reach out and explore the world around them, the previous world power, China, is more focused on internal stability. This shift allows Europe to rise as a dominant world power.

The empires of the day needed to decide the degree to which they should interact with the outside world. While European kingdoms embraced outside interaction and conquest, many other empires were more insular and focused on preservation and stability.

IMPACT OF INTERACTION—THE DEVELOPMENT OF A GLOBAL ECONOMY

EUROPEAN EXPLORATION

As discussed in the last chapter, the Ming dynasty had extensively explored the Indian Ocean from 1405 to 1433, but under pressure from conservative forces, decided to halt the voyages and destroy their ships. The Indian Ocean continued to be a thriving trade route, however, with non-European participants such as **Muslims**, **Indians**, **Malays**, and others. So when the European powers entered Indian Ocean trade, they were not so much creating this vibrant trade route as inserting themselves into an existing one. But by doing so, the world shifted from a primarily Asian-centered economy to a global economy.

As Europe emerged out of its more isolated period, the desire to explore came with it. The major motivations for this exploration included the search for resources and new trade routes to Asian markets, and the desire to spread Christianity. The Asian goods that Europe received, such as **pepper**, **ginger**, **cloves**, and **nutmeg**, were very expensive. Europeans wanted to gain direct access to these trade items and cut out the middleman. Additionally, **the Ottoman conquest of Constantinople in 1453** defeated the last vestiges of the Byzantine Empire, solidifying Muslim influence in the region and making it less friendly to European traders. The acquisition of technology from China and the Muslim world helped the Europeans expand their seagoing capabilities with such things as the sternpost rudder, triangular lateen sails, a magnetic compass, and the astrolabe. The early leader in exploration was Portugal, which established sugar plantations on islands in the Atlantic off the coast of Africa, but many other expeditions would follow. The Portuguese were aided in their explorations by developing the caravel (a small, highly maneuverable sailing ship). Caravels were widely used by the Portuguese for ocean voyages during the age of European discovery.

Columbus's First Voyage

Explorer	Year	Accomplishment
Bartolomeu Dias (Portugal)	1488	Rounded Cape of Good Hope at the tip of Africa and entered the Indian Ocean
Christopher Columbus (Spain)	1492	Sailed west to reach Asia and instead reached the Bahamas. Sailed around Caribbean, but thought he had reached island just off the coast of Asia
Vasco da Gama (Spain)	1497	Reached Calicut in India by rounding Africa
Ferdinand Magellan (Spain)	1519–1522	Sailed around South America to the Philippine Islands (where he was killed); his men sailed back through the Indian Ocean and were the first to circumnavigate the globe

TRADING-POST EMPIRES

The initial goal of European powers in exploring the Indian Ocean was not to conquer, but rather to control the lucrative trade. They wanted to force merchant ships to trade in fortified trading sites and to pay duties for the privilege. By the mid-1500s, Portugal had 50 trading posts from West Africa to East Asia, but by the late 1500s, its power began to decline. The small country with its small population could not sustain the large seaborne empire.

The English and the Dutch quickly took Portugal's place as the dominant powers with their faster, cheaper, and more powerful ships. Additionally, they used **joint stock companies**, in which investors, rather than the crown, funded the expeditions.

Trading Posts

COLUMBIAN EXCHANGE

The inclusion of the Americas in the global trade network set off the global diffusion of plants, food, crops, animals, humans, and diseases known as the Columbian Exchange. The most devastating effect of this diffusion was the spread of **smallpox** to the Americas, to which the native people had no immunity. The Aztec Empire lost 95 percent of its population within a century and in this weakened state was controlled by its Spanish conquerors. Between 1500 and 1800, 100 million people died from the spread of disease to the Americas. Smallpox and other diseases were brought to the Americas by human carriers as well as by the rats and mosquitoes that Europeans unknowingly brought with them.

The **diffusion of food crops and animals** also revolutionized life around the world, leading to an increase in the nutritional value of diets and a population increase worldwide.

Europe to the Americas	Americas to Africa, Asia, and Europe
Wheat	Maize
Sugarcane	Potatoes
Cotton	Beans
Horses	Tomatoes
Cattle	Pepper
Pigs	Peanuts
Sheep	Avocadoes
Goats	Pineapples
Chickens	Tobacco

MERCANTILISM: THE ROLE AND IMPACT OF SILVER

Silver, the most abundant American precious metal, was responsible for stimulating a truly global trade network. The two areas rich in silver were Mexico and the Potosí mines in the Andes, which employed large numbers of indigenous labor (usually forced). Driven in part by China's desire for silver as a medium of exchange, this mining industry powered the Spanish economy and stimulated the world economy. However, the principal driving force behind the Spanish drive for silver in particular, and of the creation of an empire in general, was the economic theory of mercantilism that held sway in Europe at the time. Mercantilism is economic nationalism for the purpose of building a wealthy and powerful state. **Adam Smith** coined the term "mercantile system" to describe the system in which nation-states enrich themselves by restraining imports and encouraging exports. The goal of mercantilist policies was to achieve a favorable balance of trade that would bring gold and silver into the country and also to maintain domestic employment. The most important economic rationale for mercantilism in the 16th century was the growth of a nation's power relative to competitive nation-states. Viewed in terms of mercantilist theory, the Spanish colonization of the Americas makes a great deal of sense. Silver was used to trade for silk and porcelain in Asia, and it financed Spain's powerful army and bureaucracy; in order for the Spanish to purchase Chinese goods at that time, they needed to use American silver.

ROLE AND IMPACT OF SUGAR

Another influential product of this time period was sugar. The cultivation and production of sugar was a complex, requiring land, labor, buildings, animals, capital, and technical skills. It required both intensive labor (for planting and harvesting the cane) and specialized skills (for the sugar-making process). Because smallpox had wiped out so many native peoples in the Americas, enslaved Africans became the main labor force. These slaves invariably worked under very harsh conditions—mistreatment, extreme heat, and poor nutrition—leading to significant disease and death.

These sugar plantations were, in many aspects, proto-factories in that they were financed and organized to create a single product in a complex manufacturing process that took place in one area and resembled the way in which the future manufacturing processes of the Industrial Revolution would look. Certainly the lessons learned from the sugar plantations would be learned by generations of European businessmen and eventually translated into the textile industry, thus kicking off the Industrial Revolution of the 19th century.

STATE-BUILDING

OTTOMAN EMPIRE (EARLY 1300S TO 1923)

The Ottoman Empire got its start as a band of seminomadic Turks who migrated to northwest Anatolia in the 13th century, but through their military might, transformed into a major political power. As the Mongols' power declined in the Middle East, the Ottomans replaced them as the dominant influence.

Military might and gunpowder weapons drove the Ottomans to power. An elite fighting force of slave troops made of Christian boys (called **janissaries**) led the military powerhouse. In 1453, the Ottomans captured Constantinople and ended the long life of the Byzantine Empire. Under the leadership of sultans such as Mehmed and Suleyman, a tightly centralized absolute monarchy ruled the land. Additionally, Islamic religious scholars and legal experts served administrative functions. As the empire became more wealthy, though, the sultans grew more distant and removed themselves from the running of the government. The vizier headed the bureaucracy and often had more control and power than the sultan. Political succession was also a serious problem as succeeding sultans would often have all their brothers executed to eliminate any challenge to their authority.

In the capital city Istanbul, formerly Constantinople, the cathedral Hagia Sophia was converted to a grand mosque. This thriving city also had aqueducts, a flourishing marketplace, rest houses, religious schools, and hospitals. A large merchant and artisan class conducted business, but commercial exchanges and handicraft production were closely regulated by the government.

The sultan's harem, or private domain, was an influential element in Ottoman politics and society. His concubines and female relatives resided in the harem, and were accorded status when they had sons. Members of the harem—who were very close to the sultan and wielded a lot of political power—were often of slave origin and were non-Muslim, as the enslavement of Muslims was forbidden. They were trained and educated in reading, the Quran, sewing, and music.

The sultan's mother was given the title **queen mother**, and she served as an advisor to the throne. She administered the imperial household and engaged in diplomatic relations.

The empire reached its peak in the mid-1600s but became too large to maintain. The effectiveness of the administration declined and was plagued by corruption. The successors to the throne often lived sheltered lives and were unequipped to rule. Finally, as European military and naval technology outpaced theirs, the Ottomans were ill-equipped to effectively compete.

Expansion of the Ottoman Empire

MUGHAL INDIA (1523 TO MID-1700S)

India's history of predominantly decentralized regional kingdoms was interrupted during this time by the conquest of Babur and the establishment of the Mughal Empire. Babur, a descendant of Turkic nomads, began his conquest of India in 1526, and his grandson **Akbar** continued in this vein for the rule of India.

Akbar, a strong military commander, was also interested in uniting his empire. Akbar created a religion called the Divine Faith in which he combined elements of Islam and Hinduism. The purpose of the religion was to promote religious unity, although it also legitimized the ruler as head of state and head of religion. He patronized the arts and was very interested in religious discussion. He initiated a policy of cooperation with Hindu rulers and the Hindu population by encouraging intermarriage, he **abolished the jizya** (non-Muslim tax), and he promoted Hindus to high-ranking government jobs. His descendants, Jahangir and Shah Jahan, were also **great patrons of the arts**. Painting workshops were expanded, leading to the creation of thousands of exquisite miniatures. Mughal architecture often blended Persian and Hindu traditions by using Islamic domes, arches, and minarets, along with Hindu ornamentation. The most famous example of Mughal architecture is the **Taj Mahal**, which Emperor Shah Jahan built as a tomb for his late wife.

Taj Mahal

Aurangzeb, Shah Jahan's son, seized the throne with a neglectful and corrupt bureaucracy and pushed to extend Muslim control to the whole of India. He also sought to rid India of all Hindu influences (bringing back the non-Muslim tax) and to purify India's Islam. His many wars drained the treasury, and peasant uprisings and revolts by both Muslim and Hindu princes weakened the empire.

Additionally, India had become a major overseas destination for European traders who demanded cotton. With a weakened empire, those traders were able to increase their influence.

SONGHAY (1464 TO 1591)

In the 1400s, the West African state of Songhay emerged to take power over the weakened Mali Empire. Its leader, Sunni Ali, consolidated his empire by appointing governors to oversee the provinces, building a large army, and creating an imperial navy to patrol the Niger River. The lucrative **trans-Saharan trade** flowed through the city of Gao, which brought salt, textiles, and metal in exchange for gold and slaves.

All Songhay emperors were **Muslims** who supported mosques, schools, and the Islamic university at **Timbuktu**. Still, even though Islam served as the cultural foundation of the empire and a key element in establishing cooperation with Muslim merchants, traditional religious beliefs were not abandoned.

Just as the Europeans were making inroads into Africa, the Songhay Empire began to lose control of its many subject peoples. The empire went into decline and was defeated by the Moroccans in 1591.

KONGO (AROUND 1300S TO 1600S)

In the 14th century, the Kongo emerged as a **centralized state** along the west coast of central Africa. In this organized state, a powerful king ruled, and officials oversaw military, judicial, and financial affairs. In 1482, a small **Portuguese** fleet arrived and initiated **commercial relations**, and within a few years the Portuguese had developed a close political and diplomatic relationship with the king. They provided him military force, which supported both of their interests. The kings also converted to **Christianity** in an effort to improve commercial and diplomatic relations. King Affonso I was a devout Roman Catholic and attempted to convert all of his subjects to Christianity.

The relationship between Portugal and Kongo seemed like one in which the participants were equal. The interaction brought wealth and foreign recognition to Kongo, but it eventually led to its decline. The Portuguese brought textiles, weapons, and craftsmen there, and they wanted gold, silver, and ivory. They especially wanted slaves, though, and in exchange for weapons, they began **slave raids** with the cooperation of local leaders. These dealings undermined the king's authority, however, and Kongo was defeated in war with the Portuguese in 1665. Thereafter, the kingdom never recovered its former power.

SPANISH AND PORTUGUESE OVERSEAS EXPANSION/EMPIRE (1500S TO EARLY 1800S)

Although Spanish conquistadors led the way in the conquest of the Americas, the Spanish crown was not far behind. The two major areas of the empire—New Spain (Mexico) and New Castile (Peru)—were each governed by a **viceroy**, who was responsible to the Spanish king. In 1494, the Treaty of Tordesillas, which was really a decree made by Pope Alexander VI and not a treaty between nations, divided the Americas in half: The Spanish controlled the west, and the Portuguese controlled the east.

This system was one in which Native Americans worked under brutal conditions. Anyone who resisted this coerced labor was hunted down and killed. Harsh treatment, starvation, and disease resulted in a huge decline in the population. Bartolome de las Casas, a conquistador turned priest, spoke out against the encomienda system and the treatment of Native Americans. His report to the Spanish crown resulted in passage of the New Laws of the Indies in 1542, which forbade the enslavement of Native Americans. This led to the establishment of the **repartimiento system**, under which Native Americans were supposed to receive a fair wage for their limited labor duty. However, these laws were not enforced and many Native Americans ended up in debt servitude. By 1530, the dramatic decline in the Native American population led Spain to solve the resulting labor shortage by importing enslaved Africans.

This led to the creation of the Atlantic slave trade or the **Atlantic system**. By 1650, nearly 300,000 enslaved Africans were forced to labor on **plantations** and in gold and silver mines. Enslaved Africans were part of a transatlantic trading network known as the **triangular trade**.

The triangular trade was comprised of a network of trade routes that connected the Americas (including the West Indies) with Europe and Africa. The network carried a variety of traded goods, and in keeping with mercantilist economic theory, operated mostly to the benefit of European powers.

Along with its goal of increasing its wealth through the creation of an empire, Spain desired to gain souls for Christianity. As a result, along with conquistadors came missionaries. They built mission churches to convert Native Americans, many of whom adopted Christianity but blended it with their own religious traditions. For the most part, however, these Spanish missionaries forcibly imposed European culture over Native American culture.

The social result of the conquest of this new empire was a multicultural and ethnically mixed population. The majority of the early migrants were men. The **peninsulares**, the highest social class, came directly from the Iberian peninsula, and their descendants were the **Creoles**. The mix of Europeans and Native Americans were the **mestizos**, and the mix of Europeans and Africans were the **mulattoes**. At the bottom of the social order were the Native Americans, Africans, and the mixed class of **zambos**.

QING DYNASTY (1644 TO 1911)

By the 1640s, the Ming dynasty had declined and been taken over by a peasant army. However, the Manchu, a community of hunters, fisherman, and farmers from the lands to the northeast of China, soon ousted them and took over as the Qing dynasty . Thus, China came under the rule of foreigners for the second time. The Manchus established and expanded their rule through military conquest. Like Chinggis Khan, who reorganized the Mongol army to lessen the importance of tribal allegiances, the Manchu leader Nurhaci created a large army consisting of units called **banners**, which were organized on a social basis. Each banner was comprised of a set of military companies, but included the families and slaves of the soldiers. Banners were led by a hereditary captain, many of whom came from Nurhaci's own lineage. When the Manchu army defeated new groups, they were incorporated to several banners to decrease their potential for causing problems.

The Manchu had made a conscious effort to mimic Chinese culture generations before this and, unlike the Mongols, bolstered many aspects of Chinese government to include using the Confucian civil service exam system. Like the Mongols, however, the Manchu wanted to preserve their own ethnic and cultural identity, so they forbade intermarriage between Manchu and Han Chinese, forbade Chinese from traveling to Manchuria and from learning their language, and forced Chinese men to wear their hair in a braid called a queue as a sign of submission.

The Qing dynasty created a multiethnic empire that was larger than any earlier Chinese dynasty. They expanded into Taiwan in 1683, Mongolia in 1696, and Tibet in the 1720s. By this time, the expanding Qing and Russian empires were nearing each other, which resulted in Manchu and Russian leaders approving a treaty that defined borders and regulated trade. The final area to be annexed was Chinese Turkestan in the 1750s. The Manchus ruled Tibet and Turkestan relatively lightly. Local religious leaders were allowed to remain in place and men were not forced to wear the queue.

RUSSIAN EMPIRE (1480 TO 1917)

After hundreds of years under Mongol tributary rule, Russia emerged as an empire of it own merit. The Mongols had forced the Russian princes to submit to their rule and to give them tribute and slaves. The princes collected the khan's taxes and suppressed popular uprisings, gaining power in the process. Eventually, the Muscovite princes were able to defeat their rivals for power. Ivan III, a grand prince of Moscow, stopped paying tribute to the Mongols and in 1480, began building an empire for himself. He established a strong central government ruled by an absolute monarch, the **czar**, who was also the head of the **Russian Orthodox Church**. The czar thus also received his authority from God. After a reign of terror by Ivan the Terrible, the **Romanov family** came to power in 1613, and it ruled Russia for the next 300 years.

Peter the Great, who reigned from 1682 to 1725, was fascinated with **Western technology** and instituted a policy of forced and rapid modernization. He established industries based on the most advanced science and technology. He was not interested in representative government, though, and instead reformed the military with professional soldiers and began to construct a navy. He required every nobleman to serve in the army or civil service for life. Needing skilled technicians and experts, he established schools to turn them out. Peter also created an interlocking military-civilian bureaucracy that had 14 ranks and functioned as a meritocracy, with some people from non-noble origins rising to positions of great authority. His obsession with "everything Western" is best symbolized by his insistence that all Russian men wear Western clothes and shave their beards, and by his construction of the capital city, **St. Petersburg**, his window to the West.

JAPAN: TOKUGAWA SHOGUNATE (1600 TO 1867)

After a period of civil war and disorder that began in 1467 over succession to the shogunate and devolved into power struggles among various **daimyos** (warlords), Tokugawa Ieyasu established the Tokugawa Shogunate in 1600. He wanted to stabilize the region and prevent civil war. He did this by increasing his control over the daimyos, insisting that they spend every other year at the **capital**, **Edo (now Tokyo)**, where he could keep an eye on them.

Relationships with the outside world were also **closely controlled**. Japanese were forbidden from going abroad and from constructing large ships. Europeans were expelled from Japan and foreign merchants were not allowed to trade in Japanese ports (the only exception was a small number of Chinese and Dutch ships). Despite all these restrictions, the Japanese **economy grew**, as agricultural production increased and the population grew. In these more peaceful times, the samurai became government administrators.

Christianity had made some important inroads in Japan by 1580, with 150,000 Japanese Christian converts, but the government ended these missions and went as far as torturing and executing the missionaries who did not leave. The **Dutch merchants** continued to be the principal source of information about Europe, keeping the Japanese up-to-date with important scientific and technological developments.

SYSTEMS OF FORCED LABOR

ATLANTIC SLAVE TRADE

The forced migration of over 15 million Africans to the New World is one of the most significant outcomes of both the Age of Exploration and the Columbian Exchange that followed. Slavery existed in Africa since ancient times: Tribes would often take prisoners from neighboring tribes and enslave them. African law did not recognize private property, so land did not equal wealth. Control over human labor was what equaled wealth. The spread of Islam also established new trade routes across the northern part of the continent that took African slaves to the Middle East.

By the time Europeans ventured into sub-Saharan Africa, the slave traffic had been well-established for 500 years. The Portuguese explored the west coast of Africa in the 1500s, establishing trade relations with various tribes, and after they secured a piece of the New World in Brazil, brought slaves from Africa for their newly established **plantations**. The slave trade had become **trans-oceanic**, and profits from it encouraged other Europeans to enter the business.

By the mid-1600s, competing stations and fleets brought thousands of slaves monthly across the ocean. This ocean journey, known as the **Middle Passage**, consisted of a four- to six-week trip below-deck in cramped quarters. The death toll en route was considerable, with as many as half the enslaved Africans on any one ship dying from disease or brutal mistreatment during the journey. For most African slaves, the end destinations were either Brazil or the sugar plantations in the Caribbean. The **triangular trade** that developed sent European manufactured goods (firearms, in particular) to Africa in exchange for slaves, slaves to the Caribbean and American mainland, and American products back to Europe.

As more slaves were brought to the coast, African kingdoms reoriented their economies to trade with the Europeans. Some African societies benefited economically from the trade, but several experienced severe population loss and a change in male-female ratios. Also, many slaves were traded for guns, and the addition of firearms led to an increase in political conflict in Africa.

Plantation societies were located in the most tropical regions of the Americas, cultivating **cash crops** such as sugar, tobacco, cotton, or coffee. The goal and purpose of the plantation was to gain as much profit as possible from the export of these cash crops.

Though many of the enslaved Africans were Christianized by the Europeans, they retained parts of their language and culture. A unique cultural synthesis occurred, as African music, dress, and mannerisms mixed with Spanish and indigenous cultures in the Americas. Indeed, the Atlantic slave trade and the institution of slavery had an enormous impact on the economies of the Portuguese and Spanish colonies of South America as well as on the Dutch, French, and British colonies of the Caribbean and North America. The labor of enslaved Africans produced huge profits in the extraction of gold and silver as well as in the production of cash crops such as sugar, cotton, rice, and tobacco. Moreover, enslaved Africans assumed positions as skilled laborers, supervisors, and administrators and worked as domestic servants.

ENCOMIENDA SYSTEM

The early Spanish settlers in the Caribbean needed to recruit a great deal of labor. In fact, the encomienda system gave them the **right to demand labor** in the mines and fields of native peoples. The laborers were worked hard and punished severely.

Cortez and Pizarro brought this system to the American mainland. On the **haciendas** (large estates), natives were often abused; as a result, Spanish officials replaced the encomienda system with the repartimiento system. This system compelled native communities **to supply labor** for Spanish mines and farms, but it limited their work time and it compensated them with wages. Many communities, however, were required to send groups of laborers to work on state projects. In Peru, for instance, the labor system called **mita** mobilized thousands of natives to work in the silver mines. They were paid wages, but there were also many abuses. The mita system had disastrous impacts on the Native American populations of Peru, as it drained them of able-bodied workers at a time when their communities were experiencing huge population losses due to epidemics of Old-World diseases. It also led to Native Americans fleeing their communities to avoid being compelled into service. With fewer workers able to work the fields, agricultural production decreased leading to famine and malnutrition. The demise of these systems led to the establishment of the Atlantic slave trade and slavery in the Americas.

RUSSIAN SERFDOM

After the Mongol rule of Russia, many free peasants fell into **great debt** and were forced to become serfs on large estates. The Russian government encouraged this process beginning in the 1500s because it was a way to satisfy the nobility and to **regulate the peasants** at the same time. As new territories were added to the empire, serfdom extended along with it.

In 1649, an act proclaimed that serfs were born into their status and could not escape it. Serfs could be bought and sold, gambled away, and punished by their masters. Whole villages could be sold to supply manufacturing labor, but serfs were not literally slaves. Serfs who were illiterate and poor had to pay high taxes and owed extensive labor service to their landlords in the form of agriculture, mining, or manufacturing.

CULTURAL AND INTELLECTUAL CHANGES

EUROPEAN RENAISSANCE (BEGINNING IN THE 1400S)

Changes and tensions in the early 15th century CE led to new ways of thinking about the nature of humanity and the world. The changes took place slowly, starting on the Italian peninsula. The Crusades had brought southern Europe into contact with Arab culture, and this stimulated an interest in other cultures and trade. Scholars were uncovering long-forgotten **Roman and Greek** written works that had been preserved and studied by Islamic scholars and that subsequently fired the minds of intellectuals in southern Europe. This intellectual reorientation became known as the Renaissance, or rebirth. The **rebirth** referred to the reappearance of ancient approaches to understanding the world.

HALLMARKS OF THE RENAISSANCE

- A new view of man as a creative and rational being
- A rediscovery of ancient Greco–Roman knowledge
- Unparalleled accomplishments in literature, music, and art
- A celebration of the human individual

Renaissance Italy was a patchwork of feudal domains—lands belonging to the Roman Catholic Church, kingdoms, and city-states. Famous noble families such as the Medicis had grown wealthy as merchants, since Italy was perfectly located for receiving goods from the Middle East and Asia. This lucrative trade with the **Islamic** and **Byzantine cultures** allowed wealthy Italians to become patrons of painters, sculptors, and scientists. The period was also a celebration of the Roman past; classical architecture and engineering were reexamined and relearned.

A new human ideal was created as the concept of a multifaceted **Renaissance man** emerged. Perhaps the best example of such a learned and talented individual was **Leonardo da Vinci**: As an artist, scientist, musician, architect, and engineer, he combined the talents of many men into one person. He made realistic sketches of models in his studio, going as far as to dissect corpses to learn how bones and muscles worked. Today, Leonardo's paintings are noted for their realism. *The Last Supper*, a painting whose subject matter is overtly religious (it depicts Christ and his apostles on the night before the crucifixion) is also a masterpiece of perspective, which is one of the innovations Renaissance artists are noted for.

Perhaps the single-most important development of the Renaissance was the **printing revolution**. In 1456, **Johann Gutenberg** of Germany printed the first complete edition of the Bible using the first printing press in the West (the Chinese had been using movable type for centuries). This printing revolution brought enormous changes to Europe. Printed books were less expensive and easier to read than copied manuscripts. The increase in the availability of books led to a rapid rise in literacy. European readers gained access to a wide range of knowledge on subjects including medicine, law, mathematics, and philosophy. Along with helping to spread classical knowledge and Renaissance ideas, these new printing presses also helped fuel the religious turmoil that Europe experienced during the 1500s.

PROTESTANT REFORMATION (BEGINNING IN THE 1500S)

Just as the Renaissance inspired an era of exploration, it also created an atmosphere that encouraged debate and criticism of the existing order. The most powerful institution of the day was the Catholic Church, headquartered in Rome. It had held great power over kings and peasants alike for centuries, and had grown large, wealthy, and corrupt. Practices such as selling forgiveness and salvation began to offend even those in the priesthood.

A movement to reform the Church grew out of these concerns. In 1517, in the German domain of Wittenburg, an obscure priest named **Martin Luther** posted a list of issues that he believed the Church should address. The main issues raised by those that would reform the Church were:

- Divisions within the papacy, in which more than one pope claimed authority
- Religious traditions and rituals that were not derived from the Scriptures (such as purgatory, pilgrimages, and worship of the saints)
- Corrupt practices such as the sale of indulgences (forgiveness) and religious relics
- Church finances and income
- Lack of piety in the priesthood

Martin Luther and his fellow reformer's views unleashed a storm of controversy that eventually split the Catholic Church. It also divided Europe between those loyal to the pope in Rome and those who broke away to form other churches. Luther was excommunicated from the Church but was protected by sympathetic German princes. The German lands were divided in hundreds of small kingdoms, nominally ruled over by the Holy Roman Emperor, in this case Charles V of Spain, a staunch Catholic. Many of the Northern German princes resented having to support both an "emperor" who was not German and the Church. Siding with Luther for both religious and political reasons, these princes were called Protestants. The German area became divided into two armed camps, Catholics and Protestants. The resulting conflict devastated the German lands, but ended in a treaty (the **Peace of Augsburg**, 1555) that enabled each prince to decide which religion—Catholic or Lutheran—would be the religion of his land. As a result, most states in northern Germany chose Lutheranism, while the south stayed largely Catholic.

The Protestant movement spread from central Europe to the Netherlands, Switzerland, France, and Denmark. The English King Henry VII, once a staunch supporter of the Catholic Church, fell away from the Church after a dispute with the pope, and with the help of his Parliament created a new Church of England, of which the English monarch was the head.

ENLIGHTENMENT (BEGINNING IN THE 1700S)

The Enlightenment is known for its outpouring of **intellectual** and **philosophical thought**. It began in the 1600s when two English political thinkers who had lived through the horrors of the English Civil War came to strikingly different conclusions about human nature and the proper form of government. **Thomas Hobbes** believed that people are naturally selfish and wicked and therefore a strong government, particularly an **absolute monarchy**, was needed to keep order. **John Locke**, on the other hand, thought people were basically good and capable of reason, and therefore he favored some form of **self-government**. According to Locke, people are born free and possess certain **natural rights** (life, liberty, and property), and a government's purpose is to protect those rights. If government fails at this job, Locke reasoned, the people had the right to overthrow it. This notion would later inspire revolutions in Europe and the Americas. Intellectual revolutionaries in their own right, Enlightenment thinkers were reformists who put forth ideas such as the following:

John Locke (England)	Voltaire (France)	Montesquieu (France)
Thought all men are born with natural rights and should be free	Said freedom of speech should be permitted	Urged tolerance and a government segmented into parts that shared power

OUTCOMES OF THE PROTESTANT REFORMATIONS

- A redrawing of the religious map of Europe, with mostly Protestants in the north and Catholics in the south
- A decline in the power of the Roman Catholic Church
- Further power struggles between the citizenry and monarchs; in England, when radical Protestants took over the Parliament, civil war erupted and the king was arrested and later publicly beheaded
- A series of wars that would pit Catholics and Protestants against each other for the next 200 years

This new emphasis on free thought led to the **questioning of traditional authority**. Both the Church and the monarchy were being challenged, and the political radicalism of the Enlightenment would cause great anxiety in the courts of Europe. Though it started in England, the Enlightenment was centered in Paris, where it reached its peak in the mid-1700s. There, people called **philosophes** gathered to discuss politics and ideas. The philosophes believed that reason (which along with **nature**, **happiness**, **progress**, **and liberty** constituted the philosophes' core beliefs) could be applied to all aspects of life.

As a result of the Roman Catholic mission to China, Jesuits brought back **Chinese knowledge to Europe**. The Confucian civil service exams influenced European rulers, and the rational morality of Confucianism appealed to Enlightenment philosophers.

SCIENTIFIC REVOLUTION

The emergence of modern science, along with Enlightenment ideals, has had a tremendous impact on the development of the modern world and the modern mentality. Prior to 1500, scholars mostly relied on Greek or Roman texts or the Bible to answer questions about the natural world. Participants in the Scientific Revolution challenged these ideas by carefully and methodically observing nature.

The Scientific Revolution began as scientists used observation to challenge accepted notions about the structure and composition of the universe. The Polish cleric and astronomer Nicolaus Copernicus paved the way in the 1543 when he put forth his **heliocentric** theory of the universe, which contradicted Church teachings of an Earth-centered universe. Building on this revolutionary finding, as well as the work of others, the Italian scientist **Galileo Galilei** constructed his own telescope in 1609 and used it to develop new theories about the universe. His findings angered both Catholic and Protestant leaders because they challenged the teachings and authority of the Christian Churches. Indeed, Galileo was put on trial before the **Inquisition** and forced to read a signed confession in which he stated these new ideas were false.

The revolution in scientific thinking that Galileo and other astronomers began eventually developed into a new approach to science called the **scientific method**. This is a logical method for developing and testing ideas using observation and experimentation. Use of the scientific method led to significant advances in the fields of biology, medicine, and chemistry as well as to the later development of the social sciences in the late 19th century.

THE ENVIRONMENT

During this time frame, human societies continued their mastery over their environment. Perhaps the most significant event was the discovery of the Americas and the resultant Columbian Exchange of biologicals between the New and Old Worlds. New foods like the potato, which was introduced to Europe from the Americas, had a huge impact on food production and population increases. In the Americas, entire landscapes were stripped to build plantations that grew mostly cash crops like sugarcane and coffee. As previously noted, this led to a degradation of the topsoil and loss of vegetative cover that encouraged flooding and mudslides. The raising of cattle and pigs led to dramatic changes in the landscape as forests were cut for the former, while the latter, with vast feral populations, may have been responsible for the transmission of diseases in the North American regions initially explored by the Spanish. The introduction of horses to the Americas had a significant impact on some Native Americans as they left their farms to become nomads, following and hunting the plains' roaming buffalo herds. Of course the most dramatic exchange was that of diseases. Smallpox, measles, and other diseases to which the natives of the Americas had no immunity devastated their populations; some estimates are as high as 90 percent mortality rates. The loss of natives played a direct role in their inability to fend off European advancement and also led to the importation of enslaved Africans to work on plantations.

Climatically, the Little Ice Age, a several-hundred-year period of cooling and warming trends in the Earth's temperature, had dramatic impacts on human society. Although no one is in agreement on the exact timings, the period generally lasted from about the late 15th century to the mid-18th century. As temperatures fell, growing seasons shortened and some types of crops, particularly grains in the north, failed completely. The freezing of rivers and harbors often had dramatic results on warfare, allowing armies to cross what were normally barriers to their movement. At the same time, the harsh conditions took a toll on living conditions in the field, often depleting an army's strength before it could be effective.

A glimmer of awareness of the need to manage natural resources can be seen in the Tokugawa Shogunate's laws to restrict timbering operations and plant new trees when old ones were cut, and in Louis XIV's forestry program to manage France's timber resources. Although these programs were mainly economically motivated, the idea that a nation's resources should be managed by the state would play an important role in the development of future environmental management programs.

REVIEW QUESTIONS

MULTIPLE-CHOICE QUESTIONS

Please note that these are content-specific review questions for this chapter, designed to help you perform well on the exam.

1. The Manchu Qing dynasty adopted many Chinese customs from the Ming dynasty such as

   (A) granting higher status to the merchant class.

   (B) the examination system for choosing government officials.

   (C) wearing elaborate hairpieces at festivals.

   (D) refusing to eat pork.

2. An ideal Renaissance man is one who

   (A) is knowledgeable in many fields and proficient in the arts.

   (B) paints like Leonardo.

   (C) knows the arts of war.

   (D) is a patron of the guilds.

3. Central to the thinking of 17th-century scientists in Europe was

   (A) a focus on the Christian belief in original sin.

   (B) a mechanistic view of the human body and the world at large.

   (C) a defense of Ptolemy's geocentric theory.

   (D) a belief in the expanding universe.

4. The late Mughals created discontent among their people by

   (A) easing the tax burdens of the wealthy.

   (B) forfeiting territory to the Marathas.

   (C) discriminating against Hindus and promoting Islamic law.

   (D) allowing too much autonomy in the provinces.

5. Merchants were at the bottom of the Confucian social hierarchy because

   (A) they had too much power in the imperial court.

   (B) they did not produce anything.

   (C) artisans were jealous of their wealth.

   (D) the emperors were often indebted to them for loans.

6. The Aztec and Inca civilizations were unable to defend themselves against the aggression and weaponry of the

   (A) Portuguese military.

   (B) Spanish conquistadores.

   (C) Dutch mariners.

   (D) English diplomats.

7. After 1603, the Tokugawa Shogunate disallowed

   (A) merchant families from trading outside their home domain.

   (B) any Japanese from traveling outside the home islands.

   (C) the daimyo from collecting taxes.

   (D) the making of sake in the rural domains.

8. Renaissance interest in the Greek and Roman texts was due in large part to

(A) the reintroduction of these texts from the Muslim world.

(B) the discovery of these texts during the voyages to the New World.

(C) the rejection of outside influence and focus on values of the Middle Ages.

(D) encouragement by the Roman Catholic authorities to reexamine the past.

9. The African slave trade delivered the majority of slaves to

(A) New France.

(B) the Caribbean islands and Brazil.

(C) British America.

(D) Mexico.

10. Renaissance paintings were characterized by all the following EXCEPT

(A) use of perspective.

(B) large frescoes on walls.

(C) realism.

(D) epic romantic scenes from nature.

11. In the late Middle Ages, one of the causes of the decline of papal authority was

(A) a long famine in Central Europe.

(B) the decline of the monastic orders.

(C) Islamic conquering of Europe.

(D) the massive mortality rate during the Black Death.

12. Enlightenment philosophy was a threat to European monarchies because it

(A) supported the authority of the pope.

(B) supported state-run education.

(C) suggested the idea of individual liberty and rights.

(D) pushed for the overthrow of the capitalist system.

13. The Qing rulers of China segregated themselves from their subjects by doing all of the following EXCEPT

(A) forcing Chinese men to wear their hair in a long braid.

(B) forbidding Chinese to travel to Manchuria.

(C) disallowing marriage between Manchu and Chinese.

(D) abandoning the traditional examination system to choose government officials.

14. Magellan's voyage around the world in 1519 resulted in

(A) the further spreading of Protestantism.

(B) Spanish claims in the Pacific.

(C) a visit to the Forbidden City.

(D) a knighthood for Magellan upon his return.

15. All of the following were effects of the global trade of silver EXCEPT

(A) the strengthening of the world economy.

(B) the increase in outside interest in the Americas.

(C) the increase of the power of the Spanish.

(D) the bypassing of China in global trade.

16. All of the following were important features of Peter the Great's efforts to westernize Russia EXCEPT

(A) modernizing the army and navy.

(B) instituting a parliamentary-style government.

(C) encouraging Western-style dress.

(D) traveling abroad to study technology.

17. Which of the following rulers was the most religiously tolerant?

    (A) Louis XIV of France

    (B) Henry VIII of England

    (C) Akbar the Great of the Mughals

    (D) Shah Abbas of the Safavids

18. A significant effect of the Columbian Exchange was that

    (A) European power slowly declined.

    (B) American diseases spread to Europe.

    (C) world population declined.

    (D) American foods were introduced to European diets.

19. Which of the following statements accurately reflects a major difference between slavery in the Americas and Russian serfdom?

    (A) Russian serfs were the local peasant population, while slaves in the Americas were brought by force from Africa.

    (B) Slaves in the Americas performed primarily agricultural work, while serfs in Russia did not.

    (C) Serfdom was a permanent institution, while slavery in the Americas was temporary.

    (D) Serfs were bound to their owner, while slaves were bound to the land.

20. Sugar and tobacco are important examples of

    (A) African crops.

    (B) cash crops.

    (C) cooler climate crops.

    (D) Asian crops.

21. Which of the following is true of both Spanish and Portuguese colonies in the Americas from 1450 to 1750?

    (A) They both outlawed slave labor by 1750.

    (B) Little to no intermarriage occurred with the indigenous populations.

    (C) As the plantation system grew, so did the use of slave labor.

    (D) The Catholic Church was not successful in converting natives in the regions.

22. After Columbus's encounter with the Americas,

    (A) the Ming dynasty stopped its voyages.

    (B) the Byzantine Empire was conquered by the Ottoman Empire.

    (C) slavery was introduced to Africa.

    (D) the Native American population drastically declined.

23. The statements below refer to which empire?

    • Originally were seminomadic Turks

    • Had an elite fighting force of slave troops made of Christian boys

    • Islamic religious scholars served administrative functions

    (A) Mughal Empire

    (B) Ottoman Empire

    (C) Songhay Empire

    (D) Qing Empire

24. What distinguishes the time period 1450 to 1750 from earlier time periods?

 (A) Inclusion of the Americas in global trade

 (B) The introduction of the institution of slavery

 (C) The first use of ships in Indian Ocean trade

 (D) The removal of China from any involvement in world trade

25. The Manchus and the Mongols were both

 (A) defeated by the Ottomans.

 (B) involved in the Atlantic Ocean trade.

 (C) rulers of Japan.

 (D) outsiders who conquered China.

DOCUMENT-BASED QUESTION

This DBQ is a practice activity. The actual question on the exam may be longer.

Directions: The following question is based on the accompanying Documents 1 to 4. (The documents have been edited for the purpose of this exercise.)

This question is designed to test your ability to work with and understand historical documents. Write an essay that:

- Has a relevant thesis and supports that thesis with evidence from the documents.

- Uses all or all but one of the documents.

- Analyzes the documents by grouping them in as many appropriate ways as possible

- Does not simply summarize the documents individually.

- Takes into account the sources of the documents and analyzes the authors' points of view.

- Explains the need for at least one additional type of document.

You may refer to relevant historical information not mentioned in the documents.

Based on the following documents, analyze the effects of Mughal rule on India. Identify an additional type of document and explain how it would help your analysis of the effects of Mughal rule on India.

DOCUMENT 1

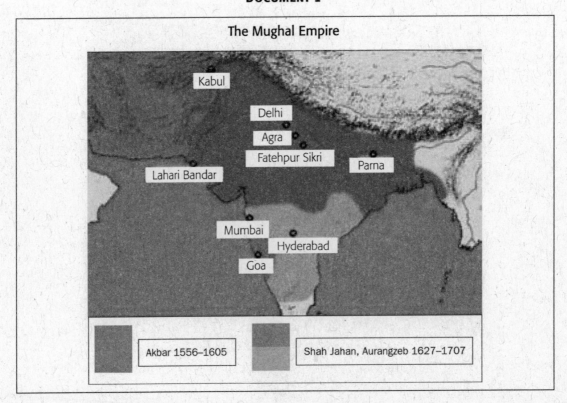

DOCUMENT 2

Source: The Great Moghul Jahangir, Letter to James I, King of England, 1617 AD.

I have given my general command to all the kingdoms and ports of my dominions to receive all the merchants of the English nation as the subjects of my friend; that in what place so ever they choose to live, they may have free liberty without any restraint; and at what port so ever they shall arrive, that neither Portugal nor any other shall dare to molest their quiet; and in what city so ever they shall have residence, I have commanded all my governors and captains to give them freedom answerable to their own desires; to sell, buy, and to transport into their country at their pleasure.

For confirmation of our love and friendship, I desire your Majesty to command your merchants to bring in their ships of all sorts of rarities and rich goods fit for my palace; and that you be pleased to send me your royal letters by every opportunity, that I may rejoice in your health and prosperous affairs; that our friendship may be interchanged and eternal.

The God of heaven give you and us increase of honor.

DOCUMENT 3

Source: François Bernier, a French physician who visited India and Bengal between 1656 and 1668, An Account of India and the Great Moghul, 1655.

Shah Jahan has left and communicated his name to the strangers that now govern Indostan, the country of the Indians; though those that are employed in public charges and offices, and even those that are listed in the militia, be not all of the race of the Mughal, but strangers and nations gathered out of all countries, most of them Persians, some Arabians, and some Turks. For, to be esteemed a Mogul it is enough to be a stranger, white of face, and a Mohammedan; in distinction as well to the Indians, who are brown and pagans.

In this same extent of country there are sundry nations which the Mughal is not full master of, most of them still retaining their particular sovereigns and lords that neither obey him nor pay him tribute but from constraint; many that do little, some that do nothing at all, and some also that receive tribute from him.

Of the like sort are more than a hundred rajahs, or considerable heathen sovereigns, dispersed through the whole empire, some near to, others remote from, Agra and Delhi.

The Mughal is obliged to keep these rajahs in his service for sundry reasons: the first, because the militia of the rajahs is very good and because there are rajahs any one of whom can bring into the field above twenty-five thousand men; the second, the better to bridle the other rajahs and to reduce them to reason, when they cantonize, or when they refuse to pay tribute, or when, out of fear or other cause, they will not leave their country to serve in the army when the Mughal requires it; the third, the better to nourish jealousies and keenness among them.

DOCUMENT 4

Source: Baktha'war Khan, early 1680s, an advisor to Aurangzeb [Mughal emperor 1658–1707], excerpts from his history of the world.

In consideration of their rank and merit, he (Aurangzeb) shows much honor and respect to the saints and learned men, and through his cordial and liberal exertions, the sublime doctrines of our pure religion have obtained such prevalence throughout the wide territories of Hindustan as they never had in the reign of any former king.

Hindu writers have been entirely excluded from holding public offices, and all the worshipping places of the infidels (Hindus) and the great temples of these infamous people have been thrown down and destroyed in a manner which excites astonishment at the successful completion of so difficult a task.

CONTINUITY AND CHANGE-OVER-TIME QUESTION

Directions: Answer the following question. You should spend five minutes organizing or outlining your essay. Write an essay that:

- Has a relevant thesis and supports that thesis with appropriate historical evidence.

- Addresses all parts of the question.

- Uses world historical context to show continuity and change over time.

- Analyzes the process of continuity and change over time.

   Prompt: Choose ONE of the following regions and analyze the continuities and changes in its involvement in trade from 600 to 1750.

   - China

   - Sub-Saharan Africa

   - South Asia

   - Middle East

COMPARATIVE QUESTION

Directions: Answer the following question. You should spend five minutes organizing or outlining your essay. Write an essay that:

- Has a relevant thesis and supports that thesis with appropriate historical evidence.

- Addresses all parts of the question.

- Makes direct, relevant comparisons.

- Analyzes relevant reasons for similarities and differences.

Prompt: Analyze the similarities and differences in the interaction with Western Europe of TWO of the following regions during the era 1450 to 1750.

- Russia

- Ottoman Empire

- Tokugawa Japan

- Latin America

ANSWERS AND EXPLANATIONS

MULTIPLE-CHOICE ANSWERS

1. B

The Qings adopted many Neo-Confucian customs, such as the civil service system of choosing able men for government service. Merchants were looked down upon in the Confucian social hierarchy. Chinese men had to wear a distinctive braid of hair down their backs. Pork is a standard part of the Chinese diet.

2. A

In celebrating the individual, Renaissance ideals suggested that an educated person should be versed in many disciplines. Men were taught how to be literate, socially adept, and well-spoken. They were expected to be knowledgeable in music, science, and military affairs. Though the guilds existed during this time period, patronizing them was not a mark of learning or accomplishment.

3. B

Part of the post-Renaissance view of the world involved looking into systems that one could observe; if the human heart is a pump, then the body is a kind of machine. Our Earth was part of a "system" of other planets. The geocentric theory was already discredited by this time. The Church had great influence in the 17th century, but scientists were not limited by orthodox beliefs such as original sin.

4. C

The later Mughal rulers became increasingly orthodox in their Muslim faith and discriminated against the Hindu majority. This helped bring about their downfall, as rival Hindu kingdoms ate away at their territories. The Mughals overlapped with the arrival of the Europeans, but they did not make treaties with them. Taxation upon the wealthy was not a cause of instability as the Mughal reign declined.

5. B

Merchants were not part of the scholar elite in traditional China and they were not valued. They were seen as nonproductive members of society. They had no influence in the imperial court. Artisans had a higher status because they made things of value for the population, unlike the merchants who bought and sold goods.

6. B

After initial successes by Spanish explorers, the crown sent out military adventurers in search of riches. These conquistadores were the first white men to encounter the Aztec and Inca peoples. Accompanying them were missionary priests, not diplomats. Likewise, the Dutch explored the eastern coast of North America and South Africa. The Portuguese were given dominion over Brazil in eastern South America, so they did not have contact with the Aztecs or Incas, who were located in other regions of the Americas.

7. B

After 1603, Tokugawa Ieyasu disallowed any Japanese from traveling beyond the home islands. This edict held sway for over two centuries, though there were some who defied the law and sailed to other lands. Very limited trade was allowed with the Dutch, and the daimyo certainly needed to continue collecting taxes from the peasantry. Merchants tended to work in their own provinces, but as the Tokugawa era progressed, more widespread commerce developed. Sake was never prohibited in Japanese history.

8. A

The Islamic world had preserved, developed, and studied the ancient texts of the Greeks and the Romans. The increase in trade in Europe after the Crusades led to the reintroduction of these texts after they had been translated into Arabic.

9. B

As the New World economy evolved, the slave trade expanded to meet its demands. The Spanish and Portuguese set up large plantations in Central and South America to grow sugar and other products. Most of these plantations were in Brazil and the islands of the Caribbean. The slaves came primarily from the Gold Coast of Africa, and relatively few were sent to British America to work the farms there. Very few slaves were transported to New France on the St. Lawrence seaway, as the commerce there focused on the fur business. The Spanish were involved in the slave trade, but only a small percentage of slaves were used in Mexico, since large plantations were not common.

10. D

Epic scenes of nature were common during the Romantic period in the 19th century—not during the Renaissance. Painters during the Renaissance pioneered the use of perspective and light when creating their works. Raphael's wall frescoes are some of the most famous works of Renaissance art. A new lifelike realism was also a hallmark of the period's art.

11. D

The huge mortality rate of the Black Death in medieval times had a great impact on Europe. One effect was a spiritual malaise that caused disenchantment with the Church and its leaders. The prayers to save loved ones from the scourge often went unanswered, and this produced a crisis of faith. There was no famine in Europe of any significance, and the monastic orders were a tiny part of the greater population. The Popes used the Crusades against Islam as a means to rally support for the Church.

12. C

Enlightenment philosophy produced work that both supported and challenged the kings and dynasties of the day. Voltaire and Rousseau suggested that humans have innate dignity and should enjoy the right to freedom and happiness. These thoughts framed the political revolutions in America, France,

and many other locales later on. Philosophers of the time period were anticlerical, and by extension critical of the Church and its influence. The Church-run schools were also criticized by the philosophers as they advocated a national system of education that would not be influenced by the Catholics. Enlightenment emphasis on rights would later influence the abolition movement, but this was not connected to monarchy.

13. D

The Qing separated themselves from the Chinese in terms of dress and mandated hairstyles and by limiting travel within the empire. However, they did borrow the Confucian tradition of using the classic examinations to select promising young scholars for civil service. Manchu and Chinese were not allowed to marry each other.

14. B

Sailing west for the Spanish, Magellan beat the other European nations to the Pacific. On that voyage, he was able to claim Guam and the Philippines before he was killed by the natives. One boat survived, however, and returned to Spain to record the new claims. Guam and Manila became new outposts for Spain until the 19th century. This furthered the spread of Catholicism as the empires of Europe grew around the world. Magellan was killed in the Philippines and did not land in northern China. Del Cano was the one to continue the voyage after Magellan's death, and it was he who was honored back in Spain. The voyages of both Columbus and Magellan established Spain as the new maritime power in Western Europe. As the riches flowed in from the New World in the form of gold and silver, Spain became a major consumer of goods from the rest of Europe.

15. D

China was the integral player in the silver trade, since it was the demand for silver in China and the demand for Chinese goods that drove the trade. As a result of the silver trade, the world economy strengthened, interest in America's silver mines increased, and Spain gained wealth and power.

16.　B

Peter the Great was interested in westernizing and modernizing Russia, but he was not interested in liberalizing the government. He wanted to modernize the army, navy, dress, technology, and trade, but he also wanted to maintain absolute power.

17.　C

Akbar the Great, the Mughal emperor, was a Muslim but was religiously tolerant of Hindus in his empire that ruled India. He abolished the non-Muslim tax and gave Hindus positions in the government. The other three rulers listed were known for being religiously intolerant.

18.　D

American foods such as potatoes, corn, and tomatoes were introduced to European diets and influenced the cultural traditions of that area. European power increased, not declined, during this period. European diseases such as smallpox spread to the Americas, not the other way around. World population increased overall, not declined, because of the healthier diets.

19.　A

Serfdom in Russia developed as a way to control the peasant population and satisfy the noble class. Slaves in the Americas were imported from Africa through the Atlantic slave trade. Both serfs and slaves performed agricultural work such as working on plantations. Both institutions were permanent: serfs were bound to the land, while slaves were bound to their owner.

20.　B

Both sugar and tobacco were cash crops that were grown in the Americas and Caribbean on large plantations. The growth of products like these led to an increase in demand for African slave labor, and in turn, the slave trade.

21.　C

In both colonies, the plantation system grew throughout the period, and with that came the demand for slave labor. Slave labor was not outlawed until the next period. Intermarriage with indigenous people did occur and created a class of mestizos. The Catholic Church was powerful and influential in both areas.

22.　D

Due to the introduction of diseases such as smallpox, the Native American populations drastically declined. Their lack of immunity to these diseases led to devastating consequences. The Ming voyages were halted 60 years before Columbus set sail. The Byzantine Empire was conquered by the Ottomans in 1453. Slavery had been an institution in Africa.

23.　B

The Ottoman Empire was founded by a group that was originally seminomadic Turks who settled in Anatolia, the elite force of slave troops was known as janissaries, and the Islamic scholars served as administrators in the empire.

24.　A

The European encounter with the Americas in 1492 set the stage for truly global trade. Slavery had been an institution throughout history. Ships had been used in Indian Ocean trade for centuries. China remained involved in world trade, in particular the silver trade.

25.　D

Both the Manchus, who established the Qing dynasty, and the Mongols, who established the Yuan dynasty, were outsiders who conquered and ruled China.

DOCUMENT-BASED QUESTION: SAMPLE RESPONSE

During most of the time period 1450 to 1750, the subcontinent of India was ruled by the Mughal dynasty. While the Mughals conquered almost the entire subcontinent, they ruled with the cooperation of the local princes. This cooperation was later extended to the European merchants who came to trade along the Indian Ocean. However, unlike the control and cooperation established with the local Indian princes over whom the Mughal always had the upper hand, they allowed the European traders too much independence, which eventually led to their ability to control the area. Additionally, the exclusion and persecution of the majority of the Hindu population led to the decline in the empire.

As seen in the map, the Mughals, who were Turkish nomads, successfully conquered and dominated most of the Indian subcontinent (Document 1). The domination of the Indian subcontinent by a centralizing power had happened only a few times in history before. However, this domination would not have been possible without the help and cooperation of the local Indian princes, or rajahs. According to the account written by François Bernier, a French physician writing during his travels to India, the Mughals had conquered a large and wealthy empire but they allowed some local rulers to remain in power (Document 3). This outsider view expresses the idea that wealthy rajahs thrived in this period and that the Mughals kept them in power for particular reasons, such as the fact that they could use their own strong militias to defend the empire. Also, the relationship of the rajahs with the empire often prevented them from allying together against the Mughals; instead it often pitted one against another. It would be helpful to have evidence from the perspective of both the rajahs themselves and the Mughal emperors to determine if their interpretation of the relationship would concur with that of François Bernier.

It appears that the Mughals tried to establish a similar relationship with the European traders who entered Indian ports in hopes of profiting from the lucrative Indian Ocean trade. The emperor Jahangir wrote a letter to King James I of England in 1617 expressing his wishes to fully cooperate with the English (Document 2). The tone of this letter seems almost overly accommodating, especially coming from the emperor of the Mughals. The emperor, in his letter, promises to receive the English as friends and give them full liberty in their port of choice. The purpose seems to be to encourage trade with the English, which could economically benefit the Mughals. However, the tone of this letter seems to give the English the upper hand in the relationship, rather than the Mughals. It would be helpful to have evidence of King James's response to Jahangir's letter, to see if the English king respected Mughal authority or disregarded it. Later, in the Mughal Empire under the rule of Aurangzeb, the impact was also negative. In an effort to praise the efforts of his ruler, Baktha'war Khan, an advisor to the emperor, describes the emperor's efforts to eliminate the Hindu influence in the kingdom (Document 4). Aurangzeb ordered the Hindu temples destroyed in order to promote what he believed to be the one true religion, Islam. This persecution led to discontent in a majority Hindu Empire and weakened the Mughal ruler.

Although Baktha'war Khan's point of view as an advisor to Aurangzeb gives his account of discrimination against Hindus weight, he may have been motivated to portray Aurangzeb in a negative light because of personal issues between the two Mughals. Therefore, it would be helpful to get a firsthand account from a Hindu who lived during the rule of Aurangzeb to elevate the degree to which Hindus felt persecuted.

As the Mughal Empire declined, European influence increased in the area and religious division returned. The empire that had conquered almost the entire subcontinent of India and had succeeded in dealing with the decentralized nature of India (through cooperation yet control of the local rajahs) seemed to weaken under the influence of the European traders. It lost control of its economic affairs and divided itself along religious lines.

This essay earns the thesis point and 1 point for understanding the meaning of all of the documents. It gets only 1 point for using the documents because information from the historical background is used instead of evidence from Document 1. The essay has one successful POV analysis for Document 2, but lacks a second POV analysis that would have earned it this point. It includes a successful additional document request at the end of the third paragraph and earns that point.

The essay has two sections. One concerns the political effects of Mughal rule (Documents 1 and 3); the second group of documents focuses on the economic and cultural effects of Mughal rule (Documents 2 and 4).

This essay earns a total of 5 points.

CONTINUITY AND CHANGE-OVER-TIME QUESTION: SAMPLE RESPONSE

Between 600 and 1750, China was continuously an integral player in the expanding global trade network. However, it simultaneously regressed from being the enthusiastic leader in an expansive world economy to playing more of a supporting role. This transition was partly self-imposed as its self-views and worldview shifted, though the incorporation of the Americas by Europe into the global economy also caused a decline in China's centrality (even geographic) and dominance. However, while China may have grown more detached from the trade network, it was too strong and influential to ever disassociate completely.

The beginning of these thousand years in history was strong for China. The Tang dynasty was established around the year 600 and it prospered agriculturally (three-field system), politically (civil service examinations), and technologically. These factors combined created a strong, stable China based on a Confucian traditional foundation, allowing for a strong economy to arise. Between 600 and 1450, China was truly the world leader in trade. It increased its presence in and then came to dominate the Indian Ocean and the South China Sea, building connections with the Middle East and Southeast Asia, respectively. This maritime advancement was made possible by new naval technologies developed under the Tang and Song dynasties, such as the magnetic compass and improved ships. Gunpowder, another technological improvement, would make its way through the trade network to the Middle East and aid the later establishment of Islamic Empires, and to Europeans who used firearms to help conquer the Americas. Another change which took place during this earlier period was industrialization increase. Especially under Song rule, new port cities were built where Arab and Persian merchants became somewhat assimilated into Chinese society. Larger cities and more expansive trade cycles necessitated the development of new economic systems in China, and paper money, banking, and a "flying cash" system all were established. Also, trade increase leads inevitably to interaction increase, and new religions, such as Buddhism, integrated themselves into Chinese culture. Buddhism blended with the consistently prominent Confucianism to create a new special type of Confucianism known as Neo-Confucianism, which had profound political consequences. Throughout this period China continued using the Silk Road as a means of relations with the Mediterranean world and Chinese luxury items such as porcelain and silk were in high demand. Closer to the end of this period, the Yuan dynasty (Mongol rule) was replaced by the Chinese Ming's, who radically altered China's position as the most dominant global trader.

From around 1450 to 1750, China separated itself from the global market significantly. The beginning of this movement was marked by the closing of many ports and the destruction of ships and travel records by the Ming (though the following Qing dynasty similarly regulated trade). These actions were very consequential, for China lost its dominance in Indian Ocean and Pacific trade, allowing Arabs, Persians, and Europeans to grow politically and economically stronger. China self-imposed this isolation because it feared foreign influence after being under Mongol control, and also because it was ethnocentric and found little value in foreign goods. This attitude, along with the decrease in technological development (Chinese Confucianism, still prominent, favored government stability over technological innovation), greatly reduced China's previous enthusiastic trade participation and allowed a rising Europe to dominate the world with their age of colonization. Still, China remained consistently important to global trade, greatly due to the desire for Chinese luxury goods. Europeans extracted silver (the new global commodity) from the Americas and used it to pay for Chinese products. Japan paid China with silver as well. While the Chinese were exporting porcelain, silk, and spices as before, they did not import many products, but rather used silver as their currency. The Chinese consumption of silver (which eventually led to severe dependency-based economic problems) kept them an active member of global trade, for they were too great and influential a country to ever completely detach. However, China lost its desire to steer the world economy, and in doing so handed the reins over to Europe.

China was always important to global trade during the years 600 to 1750, though its dominance and desire to incorporate foreign ideas and products decreased. These years in world history are best defined by the establishment of a truly global economy, especially with the inclusion of the Americas. China's regression in trade impacted not only their society, but also European society. China closed the door to the Western world (though remained connected), and allowed Europe to rise to become the most influential and powerful area in the global economy and the world.

—Written by Gabi Tortorello, Fox Lane High School, Bedford, New York

COMPARATIVE QUESTION: SAMPLE RESPONSE

From 1450 to 1750, Western European interaction with the outside world reached new heights. Due to improvements in navigational technology, Western European countries began to explore the outside world. While Russian leaders embraced Western ideas and technology in hopes of strengthening their own empire, Japanese leaders rejected Western influence because they viewed it as a threat to stability. However, despite their radically different approaches in interacting with the West, both countries improved economically during this time period.

Economically, while Russia encouraged trade and interaction with the West, Japan rejected it. Czars like Peter the Great believed that Russia had fallen drastically behind the advancements of the West and was determined to have Russia catch up. After traveling to Western Europe, Peter brought back advisers to help him remold Russia in a more Western image. He encouraged use of Western shipping technology to modernize his navy and increased trading relationships with Western Europe. However, as serfdom was declining in Western Europe, it was extended in Russia in an effort to control the peasant population and satisfy the noble class. On the other hand, in Japan, after some initial dealings with European traders, the Tokugawa Shogunate closed its ports. Trade was not permitted with Europe, nor was outside travel. The Shogun viewed Western influence as a destabilizing force that could damage Japanese society. The one exception was the trade that was established with Dutch traders. This selective trade allowed the Japanese to stay abreast of developments in Europe while controlling outside interaction. Despite this external trade cut-off, internal trade flourished throughout Japan in this period and the Japanese economy improved.

Culturally, Russian leadership wanted to imitate Western culture and style. Peter the Great insisted that nobles no longer wear traditional Russian robes, but instead wear Western European-style clothes. Peter even insisted that Russian men shave their beards. For those who resisted, Peter was known to rip off the beard himself. Also, the seclusion of women was ended, and men and women were encouraged to socialize openly in public. In Japan, Christian missionaries had, at first, converted some native people. The Tokugawa Shogunate, however, expelled the missionaries and executed those who would not leave.

Again, this Western influence was seen as a destabilizing force and something that would weaken Japan.

During this age of interaction, Japan and Russia took radically different paths. Russia, with some success, tried to actively copy Western economic and cultural developments, while Japan rejected them. Both countries had the goal of strengthening their homelands, but used different methods to achieve that aim.

CHAPTER 6: 1750 TO 1900 CE

IF YOU ONLY LEARN SIX THINGS IN THIS CHAPTER . . .

1. Industrialization led the world to become truly interdependent. Industrialized nations in search of raw materials and new markets often imperialized areas to advance their economic interests.

2. Populations grew and many people migrated to cities in search of work in factories. Free-wage laborers were more desirable than forced labor in this new market-driven economy. As a result, slaves and serfs were emancipated.

3. Women gained some economic opportunities in the factories but were paid considerably less than their male counterparts. These new economic opportunities and Enlightenment ideals pushed women to fight for political rights, as well.

4. The working class emerged as a force for change. Through organization into unions, these workers were able to advocate for improved working conditions, which were dangerous and oppressive.

5. Western culture strongly influenced many Asian and African areas through colonization. At the same time, Asian and African culture and art strongly influenced European intellectuals and artists. Enlightenment ideals such as equality, freedom of speech, and freedom of religion became very influential in many parts of the world, yet in other parts, traditional religious organization maintained power and influence.

6. The ideas of the Enlightenment said that the government was responsible to its people, inspiring revolutions and independence movements and pushing some governments to experiment with democratic values. This democracy, however, proved to extend to a limited class of people. "The nation" and nationalism became the new concepts of identity in the 19th century and would soon spread to many parts of the world.

THE BIG PICTURE

1. Interactions between people and the environment

   In other words: **How does the environment shape human societies, and how do humans shape the environment?**

New technologies quickened the pace of life. As population grew, many migrated to the cities in search of opportunities in the factories. Free wage laborers were more desirable than forced labor in this new market-driven economy and as a result, slaves and serfs were emancipated.

2. Development and interaction of cultures

   In other words: **How do people express themselves, and what is the impact of ideas?**

As the world interacted more than ever, so did the cultures of the world. Western culture strongly influenced many Asian and African areas through colonization, and Asian and African culture and art were extremely influential on European intellectuals and artists. Enlightenment ideals such as equality, freedom of speech, and freedom of religion became very influential in many parts of the world. At the same time, traditional religious organizations maintained power and influence in other parts of the world.

3. State-building, expansion, and conflict

   In other words: **How do people govern themselves?**

The ideas of the Enlightenment said that the government was responsible to its people. This idea inspired revolutions and independence movements throughout the period. Governments experimented with democratic values, but this democracy was extended to a limited class of people. Older land-based empires struggled with change and the adaptation to the new age. The nation became the new concept of identity in the 19th century and would soon spread worldwide.

4. Creation, expansion, and interaction of economic systems

   In other words: **How do economic developments affect the world?**

With the development of industrialization, the world became truly interdependent. The industrialized nations in search of raw materials and new markets often imperialized areas to protect economic interests.

5. Development and transformation of social structures

   In other words: **How do people identify themselves socially, and what roles do men and women have?**

Industrialization changed almost everything. The way people worked, lived, traveled, related to their families, communicated, and identified themselves changed for many people. At the same time, many traditional forces resisted change. Religious influence and patriarchal gender structures remained in many parts of the world.

The middle class and an industrial working class emerged as both economic and political forces. The middle class often led the political revolutions of the period and benefited in the new industrial age. Women gained some economic opportunities in factories, but they were paid considerably less than their male counterparts. These new economic opportunities and Enlightenment ideals pushed women to fight for political rights. The working class also emerged as a force for change: Through organization into unions, it was able to advocate for change in working conditions.

WHY THIS PERIODIZATION?

This time period can be summarized into five key words: revolution, nationalism, industrialization, imperialism, and emancipation. The revolutions and independence movements inspired by the Enlightenment had worldwide effects, redefining the relationship between the government and the governed. The concept of the nation shaped how people defined their identity, and it became the dominant political force.

Industrialization changed the way people worked and lived. More powerful, industrialized nations reached out to dominate Asian and African areas economically and politically to advance their own interests. Slaves and serfs were emancipated in this new wage- and market-driven world, and women fought for their own emancipation.

REVOLUTIONS AND INDEPENDENCE MOVEMENTS

NORTH AMERICA

From 1756 to 1763, France and Great Britain fought a war that is known as the Seven Years' War. While the war broke out in Europe, it quickly spread to North America where the French and their Native American allies fought the British and their colonist allies, and to India where both fought with Indian allies. The war proved to be a disaster for the French who lost in all three places, losing their Canadian territories in North America and their trading region in India. Because it was fought on three continents, the Seven Years' War can be called the first global war.

Britain's Empire in America seemed secure after its victory over France in 1763, but the cost of the war had been high. Dealing with this debt started a chain of events that led to deteriorating relations between the crown in London and its subjects in North America. The British government thought that the American colonists should pay for a portion of the costs of the war since it was fought in part to protect the colonist's interests. Therefore, Parliament enacted a series of laws aimed at raising tax revenues from the colonists, even though they were not represented in Parliament.

The American colonists argued that they could govern their own affairs with the famous quote, "no taxation without representation." In 1774, the Continental Congress organized and coordinated colonial resistance, and in 1775, British troops and American militia clashed at Lexington, Massachusetts. On July 4, 1776, the **Declaration of Independence**—inspired by Enlightenment ideas—justified independence. It listed a long list of abuses by the British king amid a declaration that **all men were created equal**. Though the British enjoyed many advantages, such as the strong government, navy, army, and loyalists, the war was fought from a great distance, and the colonists had the support of other European states.

By 1781, the American Revolution ended and the British surrendered to George Washington. In 1783, the Peace of Paris formally recognized American independence. The colonies created a federal republic with 13 states and a written constitution that guaranteed freedom of speech and religion.

In reality, however, there was no legal and political equality. Only men of property enjoyed full rights, and the landless men, women, slaves, and indigenous people did not have access to this new freedom. Yet this was an important step in the development of a government responsible to its people.

FRANCE

Unlike the Americans who wanted the right to self-govern, the French revolutionaries in France wanted to replace the "old order" with completely new political, social, and cultural structures. The causes of this discontent included large war debts, a large tax burden on the peasants, and the increasing gap between the rich and poor. The king was forced to call the Estates General in hopes of addressing the war debts by increasing tax on the nobility.

The three estates consisted of:

Estate	Who	Numbers	% of Population	% of Land Ownership	Taxes Paid
1st Estate	Roman Catholic Clergy	100,000	<1% of pop	10% of land	no taxes
2nd Estate	Nobility	400,000	2% of pop	20% of land	no taxes
3rd Estate	Peasants, townsfolk	24 million	98% of pop	70% of land	extensive taxes

The Third Estate was further differentiated by three subdivisions. Peasants and serfs made up the bulk of the Third Estate but had no voice in government and still lived under very feudal conditions, including extensive taxation in the form of labor service to the nobles. The townsfolk, workers in the cities, worked for small wages and were mostly concerned with getting enough bread to feed their families. Finally, the merchants, bankers, and other businessmen made up a class called the bourgeoisie. The bourgeoisie were the wealthiest class in France and were the leaders of the Third Estate. The bourgeoisie, despite their wealth, were still considered commoners by the nobility; the bourgeoisie wanted to see social as well as political equality in France. The Estates General convened in May 1789, but a dispute over voting created a deadlock. Traditionally, each estate met and voted separately, with the result being that the First and

Second estates always outvoted the Third Estate two to one. This time, the Third Estate wanted all the estates to meet as one and votes to be counted per head. After weeks of wrangling, the Third Estate, claiming to represent the interests of all French people, declared themselves the National Assembly. Spurred on by the peasants storming the Bastille, the National Assembly began making governmental reforms. These included ending the privileged status of nobles and issuing the **Declaration of the Rights of Man and of the Citizen**, which, like the Declaration of Independence, reflected Enlightenment political ideals. In 1791, the Assembly produced a new constitution that replaced the absolute monarchy with a limited monarchy. However, these reforms were not enough for French radicals, who, backed by Paris crowds, took control of the Assembly.

The Committee for Public Safety, led by Maximilien Robespierre, now governed France and instigated a "Reign of Terror," executing many aristocrats. Eventually, the revolution turned on the very radicals that started it, and it thrust France into war with the powers of Europe. The kingdoms of Austria, Britain, and Russia combined in a coalition that was meant to defeat France and undo the revolution.

The creation of a large revolutionary army to defend France helped catapult **Napoleon Bonaparte** to power. He named himself First Consul, then Consul for Life, and finally Emperor. In 1804, Napoleon issued his moderate Civil Code, which affirmed the political and legal equality of all adult men, established a merit-based society, and protected private property. However, it also limited free speech and allowed censorship of the newspapers.

Napoleon and his army defeated many of the powers of Europe and took control of much of the continent. The Napoleonic era lasted from 1803 to 1814, as warfare ranged from Europe to North Africa and the Middle East. At times, France found itself faced with multiple enemies. Taking on Russia in 1812 proved fatal, however, as the army did not survive the winter campaign. The victors met at the **Congress of Vienna** in 1815 to restore the French monarchy and protect the old regimes. Attempted revolutions (most notably in 1830 and 1848) continued to shake the old monarchies throughout the 1800s.

HAITI

The island of Hispaniola in the Caribbean was a major center of **sugar production**. The Spanish controlled the east (Santo Domingo), and the French controlled the west (Saint Domingue), one of the richest of all the European colonies. Saint Domingue's population consisted of 40,000 white French settlers, 30,000 gens de couleur (free people of color), and 500,000 black slaves, most born in Africa. These slaves worked under brutal conditions, and the mortality rate was very high. There was also a large community of escaped slaves, known as maroons.

The French colonial government had sent 800 gens de couleur to fight in the American Revolution, and they returned with ideas of reforming their own society. When the French Revolution broke out in 1789, the white settlers sought the right to govern themselves, but opposed extending political and legal equality to the gens de couleur. This led to civil war between these two groups.

While these two groups were in conflict, a **slave revolt** occurred in August of 1791. As a result, the whites, gens de couleurs, and slaves battled each other. French troops—and later, British and Spanish troops—invaded the island in hopes of gaining control. The slaves, however, were led by Toussaint Louverture, who built a strong and disciplined army, and by 1797, controlled most of Saint Domingue.

In 1801, a constitution was written that granted equality and citizenship to all, and in 1803, independence was declared. By 1804, Haiti was the **second independent republic in the Western Hemisphere**, and the first republic that abolished slavery. Great economic difficulty followed independence, however. Many nations such as the United States refused to recognize or conduct trade with Haiti because of slave emancipation, and a new nation of small farmers was not as productive as the former large-scale plantation economy.

Slave resistance in other plantation societies, such as Brazil, established self-sufficient communities of former slaves known as maroon societies.

Latin America

In Latin America, the colonies controlled by the Spanish and Portuguese were comprised of a governing class of 30,000 peninsulares, 3.5 million Creoles, and 10 million less-privileged classes including black slaves, indigenous people, and those of mixed racial backgrounds. The Creoles were a wealthy class from the plantation economy and trade, but they had grievances about the administrative control and economic regulations of the colonies. They did not seek social reform, but rather sought to displace the powerful peninsulares. A crucial document in the history of Latin American independence movements is the **Jamaica Letter** written by the Creole leader Simón Bolívar. This letter was written in response to a request that Bolívar express his views on the independence movement in Venezuela and the form of government under which the country should operate. Like the Declaration of Independence and the Declaration of the Rights of Man and of the Citizen, the Jamaica letter is firmly rooted in Enlightenment political ideals.

Napoleon's invasion of Spain and Portugal in 1807 weakened the authority of those countries in the colonies, and by 1810, revolts were occurring in Argentina, Venezuela, and Mexico. In Mexico, a peasant rebellion was led by Father Miguel de Hildalgo, but conservative Creole forces gained control of the movement. Simón Bolívar led the revolts in South America and by 1824 deposed the Spanish armies. His goal was to achieve a United States of Latin America, but it did not last. The Portuguese royal family had fled to Brazil when Napoleon invaded that nation in 1807. When the king returned in 1821, he left his son, Pedro, to rule as regent. Pedro agreed to the demands of Creoles and declared Brazil independent.

As a result of these independence movements, the Creoles became the dominant class, and many of the peninsulares returned to Europe. The society remained quite stratified and slavery continued. The wealth and power of the Roman Catholic Church remained and the lower classes continued to be repressed.

NATIONALISM AND THE NATION-STATE

Europe was also seeing major shifts in political power at this time. Britain had made itself the model of an imperial power with a strong military and commercial base. Older powers—such as Russia and Austria—showed their age as their autocratic traditions created increasing tension within their large empires.

During the 19th century, people came to identify themselves as part of a community called a **nation**. The forces that drew these people together were their common language, customs, cultural traditions, values, historical experiences, and, sometimes, religion.

UNIFICATION OF ITALY AND GERMANY

The spirit of nationalism was rising in two regions where small domains left over from the Middle Ages were still in place. On the Italian peninsula, the Roman Catholic Church still had great influence and discouraged the growth of Italian nationalism. The pope himself personally held large estates in central Italy. Under the leadership of Garibaldi in the south, young men pushed for an Italian nation, fighting a military campaign to unite the people behind this idea. In the north, **Count Camillo di Cavour**, the prime minister to King Victor Emmanuel II of Sardinia, aligned with France and expelled Austria from northern Italy. In 1870, the nation of Italy was proclaimed, and the king of Sardinia was chosen as its sovereign.

Farther north, the kingdom of Prussia was becoming more powerful after the defeat of Napoleon. The chancellor of Prussia, **Otto von Bismarck**, had a vision of a united Germany and so engineered a series of wars with Denmark and Austria to consolidate the territory needed for a nation. The final stroke was to maneuver France to declare war on Prussia and to use that as a pretext for gathering all the German domains together to fight as one. The war was a resounding victory for Prussia, and Bismarck proclaimed the birth of the German nation. He did this in the French palace at Versailles, humiliating France by taking territory on the French-German border.

The birth of a unified Germany would cause a noticeable shift in the balance of power in Europe. France was in decline, and Germany would now begin to rival Great Britain as an industrial producer and leader in technology. Prussia was proud of its army, and German military tactics were becoming well-known around the world. The military traditions of old Prussia would now flex their muscles, as Germany looked to be a new world power.

The new German nation was in many ways deeply conservative in its politics. Bismarck, however, supported a series of reforms that established state pensions and public health insurance plans that used the government to protect the social welfare of the masses.

ZIONISM

One problem with the formation of nations was the issue of **minority** groups. Often, a minority group living within a nation did not fit the nation's identity. One such group was the Jews. The Jews did not have their own territory, but rather lived as a minority in other nations. As **anti-Semitism** (hostility or prejudice toward Jews or Judaism) rose in the 19th century, so did the Zionist movement. This movement sought to establish a Jewish state in Palestine. A Jewish reporter, Theodor Herzl, launched the Zionist movement in 1897.

LATIN AMERICA

By the 1830s, most of Latin America was made up of independent nations. The leaders of these independence movements had hoped to create representative governments with freedom of commerce and protection of private property. They often feared, however, that the mass population was unprepared for self-rule. **Early constitutions** were written to create order and representation, but voting restrictions regarding property and literacy were instituted. Some early leaders, like Simón Bolívar, dreamed of a unified Latin America, but regional rivalries and economic competition prevented that from occurring.

These new nations faced many problems, such as economies that had been disrupted by many years of warfare and by large armies loyal to regional commanders (**caudillos**) instead of the new national government. Most leaders agreed that the governments should be republics, but disagreed on what kind. That is, should it be a strong central government or a regional state-based government?

Additionally, the role of the **Catholic Church** remained strong. Few questioned its doctrines, but many wanted to limit its role in civil life. In Mexico, for example, politics was a struggle between conservatives and liberals, and instability and financial difficulty made it a target for **foreign intervention** by the United States and Europe.

INDUSTRIALIZATION

The rise of modern industry was a direct outcome of the scientific activity and invention of the 1600s. Water power was being harnessed to create mechanical energy, which would run more efficient mills. A machine that pumped water out of mines was patented in 1769. It ran on coal that heated water, and the steam pressure was used to push a piston. The steam engine would be the foundation of a new mechanical age in which cars, trains, boats, and factories would all be piston-driven.

The consequences of this revolution would impact human labor, consumption, family structure, and much more. Major economic and social changes that occurred in industrialized nations were:

Before Industrialization	After Industrialization
Agricultural/rural economy	Capitalist/urban economy
Family-farm economy	Wage-earning economy
Asian-based manufacturing	Factory-based manufacturing
Rural-based population	Urban population

FACTORS OF INDUSTRIALIZATION

- An increase in agricultural production
- Technical knowledge and invention
- A large population to serve as a workforce
- Possession of natural resources like coal and iron ore
- Investment capital (money) to build factories
- A stable and capitalist-minded government
- A stable government that provides protections for private property
- Sea ports, rivers, and canals

PRECONDITIONS FOR INDUSTRIALIZATION

Why was England the first to make the technological leap into a modern economy? Several factors encouraged industrialization, and England possessed all of them in the early 1700s. England's location on the Atlantic gave it access to raw materials from around the globe as well as access to markets for its manufactured goods. It had a wealth of natural resources, including coal and iron ore. It had a large labor pool that was no longer needed for agricultural production. Britain was also blessed with many navigable rivers that enabled factories to be located in a variety of places. It also had access to capital from a business class that had grown wealthy through commerce, especially from the Atlantic slave trade.

Poorer nations often have plenty of people, but they struggle to come up with investment capital and a stable government to help along industrialization. France and the United States were close behind Great Britain in developing industrial capability. The United States and Germany both surpassed Britain in terms of steel production by 1900, while other nations such as Russia lagged behind.

AN AGRICULTURAL REVOLUTION

Strangely, the Industrial Revolution was, in part, made possible by advances in agriculture in Western Europe. The Dutch began this process by erecting earthen walls to reclaim land from the sea and using fertilizer from livestock to renew soil nutrients. In the 1700s, British farmers began experimenting with crop rotation, and Jethro Tull invented a mechanical seed drill that sped up the planting process. Farmers began to share their knowledge and techniques through farm journals.

TECHNOLOGY

New sources of energy and new materials allowed manufacturers to change how things were produced. During the 1700s, people began to harness new sources of energy such as coal, which was used to develop the steam engine that was a key power source of the Industrial Revolution. Coal was also vital in the production of iron, which was used to construct machinery and steam engines. New methods for producing iron resulted in a better product produced at lower costs. Iron was a vital material during the Industrial Revolution, especially after the world began to build railroads.

A "second industrial revolution" in steel, chemicals, and electricity transformed society in the late 19th century. New types of production and the general expansion of knowledge led to new fields of sciences such as engineering and medicine.

FINANCIAL INSTITUTIONS

New financial systems also developed to support the new industrial production. More complex corporate structures, stock markets, and insurance enabled businessmen to raise the capital they needed to begin or expand production as well as to protect their investments from loss. Large businesses often had a global reach. Transnational corporations such as the United Fruit Company had operations that affected lives in North, Central, and South America. The ideals of laissez-faire capitalism that Adam Smith had proposed became the inspiration for these changes.

IMPACT ON GENDER, FAMILY, AND SOCIAL STRUCTURES

Industrialization greatly impacted gender roles and families. It also radically altered the traditional social structures of the day. Slavery declined, because slaves could not consume industrial products as did free-wage laborers. The family, which had been a self-sufficient economic unit, moved that economic production outside the home. Working-class women and children entered the workforce as cheap factory laborers.

A sharp distinction was now being made between family life and work life. Men's status increased because industrial work and the wage were considered more important than domestic work. Middle-class values became distinct from those of the industrial working class. Middle-class women generally did not work outside the home, but instead were pressured to conform to the new models of behavior often referred to as the **"cult of domesticity."**

THE FACTORY SYSTEM

The Industrial Revolution led to the establishment of the **factory system** in which factories employed large amounts of workers and power-driven machines to mass-produce goods. In the late 1800s, manufacturers sought to increase productivity and profits by designing products with **interchangeable parts**, identical components that could be used in place of one another. This processed simplified assembly, but it also made a lot of factory work tedious and repetitive.

GLOBAL EFFECTS OF INDUSTRIALIZATION

As a result of industrialization, a new **global division of labor** emerged. Industrial societies needed raw materials from other lands and a large demand for materials such as raw cotton from India and Egypt, and rubber from Brazil and the Congo. Latin America, sub-Saharan Africa, South Asia, and Southeast Asia became dependent on exporting cash crop products to the industrialized nations, but established little or no industrialization themselves. Most of the profits from these cash crops went abroad, and wealth was concentrated in the hands of the few.

The **dependency theory** attempts to explain the uneven result of development. Instead of underdevelopment being a result of failed modernization, it claims that underdevelopment and development are part of the same process because the development of some areas is achieved at the expense of others. One example of this would be the development of a cash crop economy in Africa, which reinforced Africans' dependency on European manufactured goods.

ADVANCES IN TRANSPORTATION AND COMMUNICATION

During both the first and second Industrial Revolutions, technology transformed transportation and communication. During the first Industrial Revolution, the development of the steam engine led to creation of steamships and steam-powered locomotives, which rapidly sped up transportation. The creation of canals enabled heavy loads to be transported long distances and linked previously separate waterways. During the second Industrial Revolution, the development of the internal combustion engine transformed how machines operated and began the rise of oil as a global commodity. During this period, the development of the telegraph and later that of the telephone revolutionized the speed at which businesses and people could communicate with each other.

REACTIONS TO INDUSTRIALIZATION

SOCIALISM

As the 19th century progressed, the ideas of tolerance and egalitarianism from the Enlightenment inspired many political movements. Some were revolutionary, while others were liberal or reformist. As the Industrial Revolution redefined both society and the economy, other tensions arose.

The appalling conditions that workers experienced in the 1800s inspired **anticapitalist reform** and revolutionary movements. Under the broad title of *socialism*, these movements critiqued the money economy and suggested instead a utopian alternative—an economy that was run by the workers. The utopians sought to create self-sufficient communities in which property was owned in common and work was shared. One of the most prominent socialist thinkers was **Karl Marx**, who advocated the **overthrow of the moneyed classes**, to be followed by a "workers' state." Socialist movements ranged from revolutionary to liberal.

UNIONISM

Less radical was the union movement, which advocated the organization of workers so that they could negotiate with their employers for **better wages** and **working conditions**. This led to extreme tensions and considerable bloodshed: Factories fought to stop workers from banding together, and workers fought to remain unified. As a left-wing movement, unionism was often accused of being socialistic. The lines became blurred, as some workers became radicalized and adopted violence as a tactic.

LIBERALISM

The most mainstream response to industrialization was the rise of **liberalism**, which resulted from the rapid growth of the middle class. With philosophical roots in the Enlightenment, liberals wanted written constitutions based on separation of powers. They were opposed to monarchies and proponents of "natural rights." Having greatly benefited from the new capitalist, industrial economy, liberals were staunch supporters of the laissez-faire economics espoused by Adam Smith among others.

REFORM AND REACTION

The traditional empires of the Ottomans, Russia, China, and Japan all had to deal with similar issues during this period. They had to decide **how much they wanted to reform** in the new industrial world. How much should they change their societies? They all tried to change with the times, but with varying degrees of success. In each case, conservative forces came to resist the attempts at reforms.

OTTOMAN EMPIRE

By the 1700s, the armies of the Ottoman Empire had fallen behind those of Europe, in both strength and technology. And as the empire's military weakened, its vulnerability increased. The central government was becoming less effective, while the provinces were becoming increasingly independent—often controlling their own private armies.

In addition to losing control of territory, the Ottomans also experienced a decrease in trade. They were circumvented as Europe began to trade directly with India and China. Also, much trade shifted to the Atlantic Ocean, in which the Ottomans had no involvement. European products flowed into the empire, and it began to depend heavily on foreign loans. Europeans were even given **capitulations** (special rights and privileges), such as being subject to only their own laws, not those of the Ottomans. All of this was a great blow to the empire's ego.

The empire did attempt to reform itself beginning with the rule of Mahmud II. Mahmud organized a more effective army and a system of secondary education and built new roads, telegraph lines, and a postal service. These reforms continued into the **Tanzimat era** (1839–1879), when the government used the French legal system as a guide to reform its own laws. Additionally, public trials and equality were instituted before the laws for Muslims and those from other religious groups.

These reforms were met with much opposition, particularly from religious conservatives and the Ottoman bureaucracy. The **Young Turks**, a group of exiled Ottoman subjects, pushed for universal suffrage, equality before the law, and the emancipation of women. In 1908, they led a coup that overthrew the sultan and set up a "puppet" sultan that they controlled. Though the Ottoman Empire had attempted to reform and change with the times, it was left weak and vulnerable by the end of the 19th century.

RUSSIA

Much like the Ottoman Empire, the Russian Empire was autocratic, multiethnic, multilingual, and multicultural. The ruling czars were supported by both the Russian Orthodox Church and the noble class, which owned most of the land. The peasants were the majority of the population, and the institution of serfdom served as a guarantee of social stability. But unlike the Ottomans who were losing territory, the Russian Empire had **vastly expanded**—east to Manchuria, south into the Caucasus and Central Asia, and southwest to the Mediterranean. Its military power and strength was not up to par with that of Europe, however, as demonstrated in its defeat in the **Crimean War**.

The military defeat of the Crimean War highlighted the weakness of Russia's military and economy as compared to Europe's, pushing the government to modernize. A first step was the **emancipation of the serfs** by Czar Alexander II in 1861. He also created district assemblies (**zemstvos**) in 1864, in which all classes had elected representatives, but were subordinate to czarist authority.

The government also encouraged industrialization. Policies designed to stimulate economic development were issued, such as the construction of the **Trans-Siberian Railroad** and the remodeling of the state bank. This relatively fast-paced, government-sponsored industrialization led to many peasant rebellions and industrial worker strikes. The government limited the maximum workday to 11.5 hours in 1897 as a response, though it also prohibited trade unions and outlawed strikes.

The anti-government protest increased through the involvement of the university students and intellectuals known as the **intelligentsia**. The more these groups were repressed by the government, the more radical they became. A member of the revolutionary "People's Will" group, which was organized in 1879 and employed terrorism in their attempt to overthrow Russia's czarist autocracy, assassinated Czar Alexander II in 1881, bringing an end to government reform. The new czars used repression—not reform—to control the people. Czar Nicholas II, in an attempt to deflect attention from the growing opposition, focused on expansion through the **Russo–Japanese War** in 1904, but the Russians suffered an embarrassing defeat.

In January 1905, a group of workers marched to the czar's Winter Palace to petition and were killed by government troops. The **Bloody Sunday** massacre set off anger and rebellion across the empire, which as a whole was known as the Revolution of 1905. The government made concessions by creating a legislative body called the Duma, but in reality, not much changed in Russia.

CHINA

Europeans trying to trade with China found themselves at a disadvantage. With its vast population and resources, China was self-sufficient and, along with its superior attitude toward foreigners, required nothing that the Europeans produced. Europeans, Britain in particular, desired trade with China to acquire silks, lacquerware, and tea, which was rapidly becoming the national drink of England. British merchants paid in silver bullion for Chinese goods. The amount of bullion a nation or company had determined its wealth and its strength (mercantilism). This drain of silver from England led its merchants to find something the Chinese wanted other than bullion. They found it in opium, an addictive narcotic made from the poppy plant. Despite the emperor's making the opium trade illegal, British merchants smuggled it into China, where Chinese merchants were only too happy to buy it for silver, which the British merchants turned around and used to buy Chinese goods, making a profit on both ends. This reversed the silver drain from Britain to China where the number of opium addicts was growing tremendously, causing labor problems.

The Chinese, like the Ottomans and Russians, had to deal with their own issues of reform and reaction in the 19th century. The Qing had grown more and more ineffective as rulers of China. New food crops brought about a rapid population increase. During the Qing dynasty, it is estimated that the Chinese population quadrupled to 420,000,000. This increase created great strains on the nation, and famines were increasingly common. A series of wars and rebellions further weakened the dynasty in the 1800s.

Aggressive British traders began to import opium from India into China, and a customs dispute in Guangzhou led to the first **Opium War** in 1839. This resulted in two humiliating defeats for China and a series of **unequal treaties** that gave Britain and other European nations commercial entry into China.

Rebellions such as the **Taiping Rebellion** placed further stress on China. An obscure scholar named **Hong Xiuquan**, who believed he was the brother of Jesus Christ, founded an offshoot of Christianity. A social reform movement grew from this in the 1850s, which the government began to suppress. Hong established the Taiping Tianguo (Heavenly Kingdom), and his followers created an army that, within two years of fighting, controlled a large territory in central China.

Internal disputes within the Taipings finally helped the Qing dynasty defeat them, but it was a desperate 10-year struggle that exhausted the imperial treasury. The death toll is estimated in the millions, making it the bloodiest civil war in human history.

The government did attempt reforms so it could change with the times. With government-sponsored grants in the 1860s and 1870s, local leaders promoted military and economic reform in China using the slogan, "Chinese learning at the base, Western learning for use." These leaders built modern shipyards, railroads, and weapon industries, and they founded academies for the study of science. It was a great foundation and beginning, but the **Self-Strengthening Movement** only brought minimal change. It also experienced resistance from the imperial government.

The last major reform effort was known as the **Hundred Days of Reform**. This ambitious movement reinterpreted Confucian thought to justify radical changes to the system, with the intent to remake China into a powerful modern industrial society. The Emperor Guangzu instituted a program to change China into a constitutional monarchy, guarantee civil liberties, and encourage foreign influence. These proposed changes were strongly resisted by the imperial household. Particularly upset was the Empress Dowager Cixi, who cancelled the reforms and imprisoned the emperor. With that, China's chance for a reformed society ended.

Another rebellion further complicated issues in China. In 1900, the anti-foreign **Boxer Rebellion** sought to rid China of foreigners and foreign influence. Empress Cixi threw her support behind the movement, hoping to end all foreign influence. A multinational force from countries such as the United States, Russia, and Japan, however, handily defeated the Boxers and forced China to pay an indemnity for the damages.

Amidst all of these rebellions and attempts at reform, a revolutionary movement was slowly emerging in China. It was composed of young men and women who had traveled outside Asia—who had seen the new liberalism and modernization of the West and hoped to import it to China. Cells were organized in Guangzhou and overseas in Tokyo and Honolulu, where plots to overthrow the Qing were made.

Under the leadership of **Sun Yixian** (Sun Yat Sen), the revolutionaries attempted many unsuccessful uprisings, but it wasn't until 1911 that the Qing were forced to abdicate. With the dynasty in considerable chaos, the **modern Republic of China** was proclaimed. Sun dreamed of a progressive and democratic China based on his **Three Principles of the People**, but his dream would be shattered by a civil war and the subsequent rise of Communist China in the mid-20th century.

SUN YIXIAN'S THREE PRINCIPLES OF THE PEOPLE

1. Nationalism: Self-determination of the Chinese people; freedom from foreign influence (pertaining to both Manchu rule and European encroachment)
2. Democracy: Self-rule with a constitutional government
3. Socialism: "The People's Livelihood," which combined a desire to modernize with a desire to institute land reform in China

JAPAN—THE MEIJI RESTORATION

Japan made the most radical reforms and changes in its response to the challenges of reform and reaction and emerged from this period as a world power. Even as it continued to selectively isolate itself from the rest of world, it was changing from a feudal to a commercial economy.

The Japanese knew of China's humiliation at the hands of the British in the mid-1800s. After the California Gold Rush of 1849, the United States became more interested in Pacific commerce, sending a mission to conclude a trade agreement with Japan. It arrived in Edo (Tokyo) Bay in 1853 with a modern fleet of armed steamships. For the Japanese, who had restricted its trade from much of the world for over two centuries, this was an awe-inspiring sight. They told the Americans to leave, but this caused tense debate within the shogunate and the samurai class.

Two clans in the south—Satsuma and Choshu—supported a new policy to **"revere the emperor and repel the barbarians."** This was a veiled critique of the shogun in Edo, as they perceived his inability to ward off the Western "barbarians" as embarrassing. This was their chance to restore the emperor in Kyoto to prominence.

A younger generation of reform-minded samurai from domains distant from Edo made bold plans to undermine the bakufu. These "men of spirit" banded together to overthrow the shogun and to advance the idea that Japan needed to modernize. They armed themselves with guns from the West, and a civil war broke out in 1866. When the antigovernment forces showed their superiority of outside technology, the momentum began to shift in favor of the rebels.

The overthrow of the Tokugawa regime was complete in 1868, when the victorious reformers pronounced that they had restored the emperor to his throne. They named him **Meiji**, or **Enlightened One**. The nation rallied around the 16-year-old emperor, and plans were made to move the imperial "presence" to the renamed capital of Tokyo (Eastern Capital). This great transition in Japanese history has been called both a **revolution** and a **restoration**. Historians debate about which term to use because the Japanese did not overthrow the old order and replace it with something new. Rather, they reached into their past and used an older model to transform their nation.

The rapidity of the industrialization and modernization of Japan became a marvel to the observing world. Within the first generation of the Meiji period, Japan had built a **modern infrastructure** and **military**, had defeated the Chinese and Russians in war, and had begun building an empire in the Pacific that European powers had to take note of. This was a clear sign that industrialization was achievable by non-Europeans and that new power shifts were in the wind.

COMPARATIVE CLOSE-UP: REFORM AND REACTION IN THE 19TH CENTURY

	Political	Economic	Social
Ottoman Empire	Institute French legal system (equality before the law, public trials) but it is met with considerable opposition. Empire collapses after World War I.	As trade shifts to the Atlantic Ocean, becomes heavily reliant on European loans.	Young Turks push for universal suffrage and emancipation of women.
Russia	Zemstvos (local assemblies) is created. Duma established after Revolution of 1905, but is subject to whim of czar. Czar overthrown in 1917.	Government sponsors industrialization projects such as the Trans-Siberian Railroad.	Emancipated the serfs in 1861. Students and intelligentsia spread ideas of change in the countryside.
China	Hundred Days of Reform attempts to create constitutional monarchy, but halted by Empress Cixi. Rebellions like the Taiping and Boxer weaken the empire. Dynasty overthrown in 1911.	After loss in Opium War, European powers gain economic concessions under the Unequal Treaties and divide China into spheres of influence.	Peasant-led Taiping Rebellion attempts to create a more egalitarian society, but is eventually defeated.
Japan	Tokugawa Shogunate is overthrown and the emperor is restored to power. A legislative body, the Diet, is formed.	Government sponsors massive industrialization and trade. Japan rises to economic prominence.	The old feudal order is disrupted. Samurai class loses power, but some transition to roles in industrial leadership. New industrial working class develops.

IMPERIALISM AND ITS IMPACT

The European (and later United States and Japanese) drive to imperialize had three major motives: economic, political, and cultural. Economically, the overseas colonies served as **sources of raw materials and markets for manufactured goods**. Politically, these colonies were strategic sites with harbors and supply stations for commercial ventures and naval ships. The key was to gain the advantage before one's rival did. It also focused public attention on the quest of imperialist ventures and stirred up feelings of nationalism at home.

The cultural motivation and justification for imperialism arose in part from the concept of **Social Darwinism**, which attempted to apply the principles of Darwinian evolution to societies and politics. According to proponents of this theory, societies either prospered or failed because, as is the case in nature, only the strong survive and are able to dominate the weak. Therefore, Western European and American societies must be better than those in Asia and Africa and therefore had the right to impose their economic and political will on them.

Culturally, **missionaries** hoped to convert the Asian and African people to Christianity. While many missionaries served as protectors of native peoples, some saw their mission as one of bringing civilization to the uncivilized.

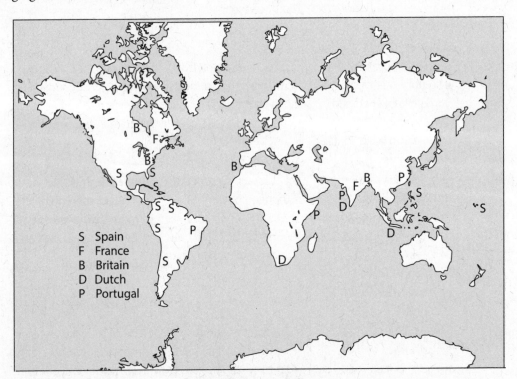

European Imperialism

INDIA

England's involvement in India began strictly as a business venture. The **British East India Company** enjoyed a monopoly on English trade with India, and it soon took advantage of the Mughal Empire's weakness. Expanding its trading posts, it began a campaign to the British government to outright conquer and protect its interests. It enforced its rule with a small British army and Indian troops, known as **sepoys**. In 1857, the sepoys **mutinied** after they received rifles with cartridges greased in animal fat (cow fat was offensive to Hindus and pig fat was offensive to Muslims). The sepoys killed British officers, escalating the conflict into a large-scale rebellion.

By May 1858, the British government had crushed the rebellion and restored its authority. It went on to impose direct imperial rule on India with a viceroy who served as the representative of British authority.

Under British rule, forests were cleared; tea, coffee, and opium began to be cultivated; and railroads, telegraphs, canals, harbors, and irrigation systems were built. English-style schools were set up for Indian elites and Indian customs such as sati (a religious funeral practice among some Indian communities in which a recently widowed woman would immolate herself on her husband's funeral pyre) were suppressed. British imperialism had a profound effect on the decline of the Indian textile industry, because British merchants desired Indian cotton, which would be shipped to England, made into textiles, and then sold in India.

British rule in India helped to create a sense of Indian national identity. The elites who had been educated in British universities were inspired by Enlightenment values and began to criticize the British colonial regime. They called for political and social reform. As such, with British approval, the **Indian National Congress** was founded (1885) as a forum for educated Indians to communicate their views on public affairs to colonial officials. By the end of the 19th century, the Congress sought self-rule and joined forces with the **All-Indian Muslim League**. In 1909, wealthy Indians were given the right to vote, but by that time, the push for reform had become a mass movement.

AFRICA

With the exception of coastal colonies and trading posts, Europeans had little presence in Africa in the early part of this time period, but the scramble for Africa would change all that. From 1875 to 1900, almost the entire continent was carved up by European nations (Ethiopia and Liberia were the only two African nations to retain their independence) spurred on by the quest to exploit African resources and outmaneuver their rivals.

In 1885, **King Leopold II of Belgium** established the Congo Free State. He called it a free-trade zone, but in reality it was his personal colony with rubber plantations supported by forced labor. The labor conditions were brutal; male rubber tappers were often driven to death, making this one of the most heinous forced labor systems the world has ever known. The British gained influence in Egypt in 1882, when they occupied the area to protect their financial interests and the **Suez Canal**. As European competition heated up, the potential for conflict seemed imminent. In response to this rising tension, German Chancellor Otto von Bismarck called the **Berlin Conference**. Delegates (none of which were African) were invited to establish the ground rules for the colonization of Africa. It was decided that any European state could establish an African colony after notifying the others.

European colonies in Africa had three main types of rule: **direct rule**, **indirect rule**, and **settler rule**. The French, Belgians, Germans, and Portuguese used direct rule to govern their African colonies. They had centralized administrations, usually in urban centers that stressed policies of assimilation. This meant that the colonialists had the intention of "civilizing" African societies so they would be more like Europe. The British mostly used indirect rule to govern their colonies. This system used indigenous African rulers within the colonial administration, although they often had a subordinate role. Settler rule refers to the type of colonialism in which European settlers imposed direct rule on their colonies. Settler colonies differed from other African colonies in that many immigrants from Europe settled in these colonies. These settlers were not like missionaries or European colonial officials. They were more like early European immigrants to the United States and Canada, who planned to make the colonies their permanent home.

JAPAN

Because Japan was so greatly strengthened by the government-sponsored industrialization, it, too, was able to enter the imperialism game. In 1876, the Japanese bought modern warships from the British and went on to defeat Korea easily. In fact, Japan forced Korea to sign unequal treaties, much like those to which Japan itself had been subjected earlier.

The **Sino-Japanese War** (1894) was sparked by a rebellion in Korea. Japan quickly defeated the Chinese fleet and Korea became a dependency of Japan. China also ceded Taiwan, the Pescadores Islands, and the Liaodong peninsula, and was forced to sign unequal treaties. Japan also defeated Russia in the **Russo-Japanese War** (1904) over territory in Manchuria and Korea, solidifying itself as a world player.

LEGACIES OF IMPERIALISM

Many economic and social changes occurred throughout the world as a result of imperialism. For one, manufacturers were transformed into suppliers of raw materials and consumers of imported goods. In India, for instance, the cultivation of cotton became solely used for export to England, and inexpensive English textiles were then imported. India, once the world's leading manufacturer of cotton, became a consumer of British textiles.

Migration increased as well. Europeans migrated to the United States, Canada, Argentina, Australia, and South Africa in search of cheap land and better economic opportunities. These Europeans often served as a new labor force in industrializing areas. Most traveled as free agents, though some were indentured servants.

Migrants from Asia and Africa, on the other hand, were most often **indentured servants** and went to tropical lands in the Americas, the Caribbean, Africa, and Oceania. With the decrease in slavery, planters still needed laborers to work on their plantations. Since most of the migrant laborers were men, gender roles in the home societies shifted as women took on roles that men had done previously. Indentured servants were offered free passage, food, shelter, clothing, and some compensation, in return for five to seven years of work. As a result, large communities from around the world migrated to new lands, bringing their culture and traditions.

Despite their success at creating supportive ethnic enclaves when they were allowed to immigrate, migrants were often subjected to regulations aimed at blocking their entry into a new nation. For example, the Chinese Exclusion Act was passed by the United States Congress in 1882. This act placed a 10-year moratorium on Chinese immigration. The rationale for this discriminatory law was that Chinese migrants posed a threat to the social order.

The theory of **scientific racism** developed during this period of imperialism to explain differences in race. These theorists assumed that humans consisted of several distinct racial groups and that the European racial groups were intellectually and morally superior. These ideas were often used as justification for the treatment of colonial peoples. In addition, **Social Darwinists** adapted Darwin's evolutionary idea of "survival of the fittest" to explain the development of human societies. These ideas were used to justify the invariably unequal and often brutal mistreatment of non-whites by European imperialists and colonizers.

EMANCIPATION

SLAVERY

Many 19th-century liberals in Europe and North America supported the abolition of slavery, as the Enlightenment ideas of liberty and equality seemed to openly conflict with that institution. Additionally, frequent slave revolts in the 1700s and 1800s were making slavery an expensive and dangerous business. Economically, it became **less profitable**, as protection from the revolts required an expensive military force. Also, even in more peaceful times, slaves generally worked only as hard as they had to in order to avoid punishment, because they had no incentives to do otherwise. Wage laborers can be given incentive either by promising them higher wages for greater productivity or by threatening them with loss of employment if they fail to meet or exceed production quotas.

As the price of sugar decreased, the profitability of sugar decreased, but the price for slaves increased. Many plantation owners shifted their investments to manufacturing, where wage labor was more profitable. In turn, those laborers would buy the manufactured goods. Though a secret slave trade continued through much of the century, the slave trade ended first in Great Britain in 1807, and then in the United States in 1808. (Here, however, the importation of slaves ended, though not the institution of slavery itself.) The emancipation of the slaves came later, though that took much longer: British colonies in 1833, French colonies in 1848, the United States in 1865, and Brazil in 1888.

Freedom, however, did not bring equality. In the states of the southern United States, for example, property requirements, literacy tests, and poll taxes were required to prevent freed slaves from voting, and many individuals were forced to continue with low-paying jobs.

The ending of the slave trade from Africa and the eventual emancipation of slavery in the Americas led to an increase in indentured servitude to replace the slaves. Indentured servants signed a contract giving them transportation to the land where they would work, room and board, and a small wage in return for five to seven years of labor. In the mid to late 19th century, these indentured servants came from Asian nations like India, Ceylon (now called Sri Lanka), the Philippines, China, and Indonesia. This migration led to distinct cultural changes in many Latin American and Caribbean nations such as the establishment of a variety of ethnic enclaves.

SERFDOM

The key to social change and reform in Russia was the emancipation of the serfs. Opposition to serfdom had been growing since the 1700s. While some opposed it on moral grounds, most saw it as an **obstacle to the economic development** in Russia, as well as a source of instability because of potential peasant revolt.

In 1861, Czar Alexander II abolished serfdom, and the government compensated landowners for the loss of land and serfs. The serfs gained their freedom and their labor obligations were gradually cancelled. They won very few political rights and had to pay a redemption tax for most of the land they received.

Few serfs prospered and most were desperately poor. Their emancipation led to very little increase in agricultural production, since peasants continued to use traditional methods of farming. It did, however, create a large urban labor force for the newly industrialized empire.

CHANGING ROLES OF WOMEN

Generally speaking, Enlightenment thinkers were fairly conservative in their view of women's roles in society. In an effort to challenge these accepted beliefs, Mary Wollstonecraft wrote *A Vindication of the Rights of Women*, which argued that women should possess the same rights granted to men (education, for one).

In Britain, Canada, and the United States, a reform and pro-democratic women's movement became active in the 19th century. Women began to push for the right to vote in democratic elections. These powerful feminist movements sought legal and economic gains for women, along with access to professions, education, and the right to vote. In 1848, an assembly of 300 women met in **Seneca Falls, New York**, demanding political rights, equality in marriage, and employment.

Some feminists, however, were wary of granting women the right to vote, fearing they were too conservative and religious and would thus vote accordingly. The movement continued, however, and Norway became the first country to grant women the right to vote (1910). Several others followed after World War I, including Great Britain (1918) and the United States (1920).

CULTURAL INFLUENCES

AFRICAN AND ASIAN INFLUENCES ON EUROPEAN ART

During this time of seemingly Western cultural dominance, European artists took note of the artistic styles of both Africa and Asia. They admired the dramatic, spare style of traditional West African sculpture, wood, and metalwork, as well as the use of color and stylized forms of design in Japan. Based on those Japanese influences, the Impressionists focused on simple themes in nature, feeling that this type of art liberated them from the rules of classical painting. A new movement of modern art was soon launched, free of traditional constraints.

CULTURAL POLICIES OF MEIJI JAPAN

As Japan was opening up to the industrialization of the West, it was also heavily influenced by the culture of the West. Japanese literature was affected by European models, and writers experimented with Western verse. Architects and artists created large buildings of steel, with Greek columns like those seen in the West.

Many Japanese also copied Western fashion and hairstyles. Amidst all of these influences, however, Japan also continued to preserve its own values.

LEISURE AND CONSUMPTION

The industrial age brought higher wages and fewer work hours. These changes gave people new opportunities. The middle class increased, leading to a new focus on the concept of leisure. The field of advertising communicated to the people the sense of needing things. The bicycle, for instance, became the "must-have item" of the 1880s. Popular newspapers, theaters, and professional sports all became popular in this new era of leisure and consumption.

THE ENVIRONMENT

The Industrial Revolution had significant and long-lasting impacts on the environment. Air and water pollution affected the health of people living in the rapidly growing urban areas, as well as an increase in noise pollution. Entire landscapes were destroyed as humans cut down timber for railroad ties, stripped hills and mountains for ores, and denuded areas of vegetative cover for farming. This increase in deforestation exacerbated desertification in some areas and flooding and mudslides in others. Mechanical methods of hunting made fishing and whaling more effective with the result that many areas were significantly depleted even by the early 20th century; many whale species were in danger of becoming extinct, until the discovery of petroleum products made whale oil less valuable. Improved firearms made hunting easier, often with disastrous results as animals like the bison of the North American plains were hunted almost to extinction. The invention of dynamite in 1867 opened the way to more effective removing of earth and stone, particularly for mines and tunnels.

Improvements in medicine and better diets coming from more food production led to a dramatic rise in population as well as to an increase in the average life expectancy. Global population in 1750 was 790 million. By 1900, the population had almost doubled. Urbanization increased even faster than population growth because new methods of transportation (most notably railroads and steamships) led to increases in both internal migration within a country and external migration. Cities were some of the most dramatic examples of human changes to the environment during this period.

It was also during this era, however, that concern for the environment, beyond the need to conserve for a nation's resources, first began to assert itself. Many nations formed forestry services, initially based on the French and then the American model. National parks and nature preserves were created to keep areas from being developed. Western curiosity and scientific observations began to note the interconnectedness of nature to include man's impact. Scientific methods in medicine and chemistry began to find and then develop cures and preventative measures like sanitation systems, use of soaps and disinfectants, and vaccinations for many of the diseases that had plagued mankind throughout the centuries.

REVIEW QUESTIONS

MULTIPLE-CHOICE QUESTIONS

Please note that these are content-specific review questions for this chapter, designed to help you perform well on the exam.

1. A major factor in the expansion of industrialization was the development of

    (A) socialism.

    (B) feudalism.

    (C) land grants.

    (D) railroads.

2. In the 18th century, France and England fought over territory in

    (A) Asia and Central America.

    (B) Africa and the Balkans.

    (C) Asia and the Caribbean.

    (D) North America and Asia.

3. The Berlin conference of 1885 was able to

    (A) partition China so that Germany benefited.

    (B) deal with economic problems in Asia.

    (C) resolve issues of European rivalry in Africa.

    (D) bring all of Africa under European control.

4. All of the following are factors stimulating industrialization EXCEPT

    (A) an organized union movement.

    (B) an ample population to serve as a workforce.

    (C) investment capital.

    (D) access to natural resources.

5. The American and French Revolutions were both caused in part by

    (A) food shortages owing to poor harvests.

    (B) problems of royal succession.

    (C) high taxation that bred discontent.

    (D) lack of social mobility in the peasant class.

6. Which of the following statements is true regarding the growth of nationalism in the 19th century?

    (A) War and conflict were often used as vehicles to unite the people.

    (B) The transition to nationhood was usually smooth with little internal conflict.

    (C) Only European nations experienced a growth in nationalism.

    (D) European imperialism prevented the rise of nationalism in Asia.

7. The American desire for a trade relationship with Japan in 1853 led to

    (A) the overthrow of the shogun and the modernization of the country.

    (B) increased tensions between China and Korea.

    (C) greater Russian influence in Manchuria.

    (D) the colonization of Taiwan.

8. All of the following are catalysts for political revolution EXCEPT

   (A) excessive taxation.

   (B) a large gap between rich and poor.

   (C) a powerful feminist movement.

   (D) a corrupt and uncaring regime.

9. In the 18th century, MOST revolutionary leaders tended to be members of the

   (A) slave class.

   (B) working class.

   (C) Catholic clergy.

   (D) educated middle class.

10. The 17th- and 18th-century slave trade had the greatest impact on which part of Africa?

    (A) East Africa

    (B) West Africa

    (C) Sub-Saharan Africa

    (D) South Africa

11. Which of the following statements best describes the significance of Social Darwinism?

    (A) It was a significant breakthrough in revolutionary theory.

    (B) It led to an increase in urbanization throughout much of Europe.

    (C) It influenced the development of the factory model of production.

    (D) It was used as a justification for the inferior treatment of colonial people.

12. The first republic to grant equality to all its citizens in the Western Hemisphere was

    (A) the United States.

    (B) Bolivia.

    (C) Haiti.

    (D) Jamaica.

13. The early leaders in Indian nationalism came primarily from which class?

    (A) Western educated elites

    (B) Labor leaders

    (C) Landed peasants

    (D) The aristocracy

14. All of the following are effects of the Haitian Revolution EXCEPT

    (A) the plantation economy continued to flourish.

    (B) slaves were freed.

    (C) the United States refused to recognize Haiti's independence.

    (D) other independence movements followed.

15. Japan's industrialization was greatly helped by

    (A) large mineral deposits in Hokkaido.

    (B) a growing support for democracy.

    (C) a centralized pro-business government.

    (D) the partnership with China.

16. The transportation revolution that accompanied the first Industrial Revolution was stimulated by

    (A) war in Turkey.

    (B) the crash of 1892.

    (C) political revolutions in the Americas.

    (D) canals.

17. Which of the following African regions was able to defeat European powers in the 19th century?

    (A) Liberia

    (B) Ethiopia

    (C) Egypt

    (D) Morocco

18. In which rebellion in India in the mid-1800s did natives challenge British power?

    (A) Zulu
    (B) Taiping
    (C) Boxer
    (D) Sepoy

19. Which of the following is NOT a characteristic of capitalism?

    (A) Private ownership of property
    (B) Upward social mobility
    (C) The dynamics of supply and demand
    (D) Government ownership of industry

20. Independence movements in South America in the early 19th century took advantage of

    (A) the inflationary policies instituted by Spain.
    (B) Spain's involvement in the Napoleonic Wars.
    (C) the American victory over Spain in Cuba.
    (D) the silver trade in Asia.

21. The following statements refer to which of the following entities?

    • Abolished serfdom in 1861

    • Government-sponsored industrialization

    • Humiliating loss in Crimean War

    (A) China
    (B) England
    (C) Russia
    (D) Ottoman Empire

22. Revolutionary activists seeking to overthrow the Qing dynasty in the 19th century tended to be

    (A) disaffected Mandarins.
    (B) court eunuchs.
    (C) disgruntled peasants.
    (D) young, educated men who had traveled abroad.

23. Liberalism should be viewed as political ideology that

    (A) supported the transition to an industrial, capitalist economy.
    (B) is the ideological predecessor to socialism.
    (C) developed in response to European colonialism.
    (D) grew out of the labor movement.

24. China was able to avoid imperial control in the early 20th century because

    (A) Britain and the United States were opposed to outright colonization.
    (B) Europe was more concerned with the rise of Japan.
    (C) China was too far away from Europe.
    (D) Russia agreed to stay out of Asia.

25. The following statements refer to which of the following entities?

    • Unequal trading agreements with Western Europeans

    • Anti-Western uprising in 1900

    • Self-strengthening movement was met with imperial opposition

    (A) Japan
    (B) India
    (C) China
    (D) Ottoman Empire

DOCUMENT-BASED QUESTION

This DBQ is a practice activity. The actual question on the exam may be longer.

Directions: The following question is based on the accompanying Documents 1 to 4. (The documents have been edited for the purpose of this exercise.)

This question is designed to test your ability to work with and understand historical documents. Write an essay that:

- Has a relevant thesis and supports that thesis with evidence from the documents.

- Uses all or all but one of the documents.

- Analyzes the documents by grouping them in as many appropriate ways as possible.

- Does not simply summarize the documents individually.

- Takes into account the sources of the documents and analyzes the authors' points of view.

- Explains the need for at least one additional type of document.

You may refer to relevant historical information not mentioned in the documents.

> Using the documents, analyze issues involved with independence and nation building in Latin America. Identify an additional document and explain how it would help you analyze independence and nation building in Latin America.

> **Historical Background:** After nearly 300 years of colonization and enmeshment in the trade triumvirate of sugar/tobacco/slaves among the Americas, Africa, and Europe, Latin America saw the blossoming of independence from European rule. Many times, however, its nascent attempts at democracy were compromised by the Monroe Doctrine and the growing influence of the United States in the hemisphere.

DOCUMENT 1

Source: Simón de Bolívar, leader of independence movements in South America: Message to the Congress of Angostura, Venezuela, 1819:

We are not Europeans; we are not Indians; we are but a mixed species of aborigines and Spaniards. Americans by birth and Europeans by law, we find ourselves engaged in a dual conflict: we are disputing with the natives for titles of ownership, and at the same time we are struggling to maintain ourselves in the country that gave us birth against the opposition of the invaders.

. . . Nothing in our fundamental laws would have to be altered were we to adopt a legislative power similar to that held by the British Parliament. Like the North Americans, we have divided national representation into two chambers: that of Representatives and the Senate. If the Senate were hereditary rather than elective, it would, in my opinion, be the basis, the tie, the very soul of our republic. In political storms this body would arrest the thunderbolts of the government and would repel any violent popular reaction.

DOCUMENT 2

Source: *Plan of Iguala* issued on the eve of declaring independence from Spain. Mexican elites intended it to act as a compromise between Mexico's divided classes on February 24, 1821:

ART. 1. The Mexican nation is independent of the Spanish nation, and of every other, even on its own Continent.

ART. 2. Its religion shall be Catholic, which all its inhabitants profess.

ART. 3. They shall be all united, without any distinction between Americans and Europeans.

ART. 4. The government shall be a constitutional monarchy.

ART. 11. The distinction of castes is abolished, which was made by the Spanish law, excluding them from the rights of citizenship. All the inhabitants of the country are citizens, and equal, and the door of advancement is open to virtue and merit.

DOCUMENT 3

Source: Memoirs of Peru's José Rufino Echenique, a successful caudillo (military leader), 1840s:

I had left my hacienda and come to Lima to buy some mules that I had heard were on sale near the port. Passing the street which runs in front of the Palace of Government, I met my friend Colonel Ros, who told me of Hercelles's defeat. He also said that Hercelles himself had been captured and was presently being brought as prisoner to Lima, but that an order had been issued to execute him before arriving . . . .

As soon as I got home, steadfast in my purpose, I sent for a well-known war-captain named Contreras who was extremely loyal to me. I told him to gather 25 men of absolute trustworthiness, to arm them, to lead them out the road to Chancay, to ambush the party that was bringing Hercelles prisoner, and to rescue him. He agreed but, as he gathered the men and arms, the news arrived that Hercelles had been executed immediately upon receipt of the order to that effect. Not only that, his head had been cut off and sent to the place where he began the revolution, to be displayed as an example and a warning. Lazo, the Minister of Government, gave that order, and it was the last straw for me. I determined to move against the government at the first opportunity.

DOCUMENT 4

Source: Francisco Bilbao (1823–1865), a Chilean liberal, critical of the government, from *America in Danger*, 1862:

The conquest of power is the supreme goal. This leads to the immoral doctrine that "the end justifies the means . . ." But since there are constitutional provisions that guarantee everyone his rights, and I cannot violate them, I invoke the system of "preserving the form." If the constitution declares: "Thought is free," I add: "within the limits established by law"—and since the law referred to is not the constitutional provision but one that was issued afterwards . . . The election is free, it is said: but what if I control the election returns? What if I, the established power, name the inspector of the election returns, if the law permits one to vote 20 times a day in the same election? What if I dominate the elections and frighten my opponents away with impunity? What happens then? Why, the government party is perpetuated in office, and the popular will is flouted and swindled. But "the form has been preserved," and long live free elections!

We have behind us a half-century of independence from Spain. How many years of true liberty have any of the new nations enjoyed? That is difficult to say; it is easier to reckon the years of anarchy and despotism that they have endured.

CONTINUITY AND CHANGE-OVER-TIME QUESTION

Directions: You are to answer the following question. You should spend five minutes organizing or outlining your essay. Write an essay that:

- Has a relevant thesis and supports that thesis with appropriate historical evidence.

- Addresses all parts of the question.

- Uses world historical context to show continuities and changes over time.

- Analyzes the process of continuity and change over time.

Prompt: Describe the continuities and changes in the effects of the process of industrialism in ONE of the following civilizations from 1750 to 1900.

- China

- Japan

- Russia

- Ottoman Empire

COMPARATIVE QUESTION

Directions: You are to answer the following question. You should spend five minutes organizing or outlining your essay. Write an essay that:

- Has a relevant thesis and supports that thesis with appropriate historical evidence.

- Addresses all parts of the question.

- Makes direct, relevant comparisons.

- Analyzes relevant reasons for similarities and differences.

  Prompt: Analyze similarities and differences in approaches to social and political reform and resistance to reform for TWO of the following civilizations for the 19th century.

  - China

  - Japan

  - Ottoman Empire

  - Russia

ANSWERS AND EXPLANATIONS

MULTIPLE-CHOICE ANSWERS

1. D
The introduction of the railroad allowed industrialization to become a world event. The movement of goods and people became a standard feature of an industrialized nation, and the use of railroads increased a nation's ability to industrialize. The development of socialism was a result of industrialization. Feudalism predates industrialization. Land grants may have aided some factory owners, but did not contribute to industrialization becoming a more global event.

2. D
The Seven Years' War was the first truly global conflict, pitting various European powers against each other. The two major rivals—France and Britain—fought over territories in Asia and the Americas. Britain won, and India and Canada were securely in the British Empire. Britain and France had no imperial interest in the Balkans.

3. C
The 1880s were a time of aggressive empire-building by rival European nations. Germany invited other nations to Berlin so that territorial issues in Africa could be resolved. Except for Ethiopia and Liberia, all of Africa was colonized by the Europeans. China was able to play the powers off of one another, avoiding partition and colonization.

4. A
Three of the four main stimulants of industrialization are listed in answer choices (B) through (D). Nations need a large (preferably low-wage-earning) workforce, money for investment, and natural resources. In the 1800s, England had all of these in the form of surplus farmworkers, coal, and the best banking system extant. A labor movement can inhibit business growth if a nation is crippled with strikes or slowdowns.

5. C
The merchants in Boston and the peasants in Lille were both opposed to the taxes they paid in the 18th century. The Boston Tea Party and the storming of the Bastille both came about in part because of tax revolts. There were no peasants in America at this time.

6. A
Nationalist leaders often used war and conflict to unite their people. Bismarck in Germany and Cavour in Italy engaged in war with neighboring areas. Internal conflict was quite prevalent on the path to the nation-state. The growth of nationalism was felt beyond the borders of Europe, such as in Latin America. In some ways, European imperialism contributed to the rise of nationalism in Asia, as in the case of Indian nationalism stemming from the British rule.

7. A
The Tokugawa Shogunate was coming under increasing attack from critical daimyo when the Americans arrived in 1853. The insistence of the United States in making a trade agreement led to the movement to oust the bakufu and restore the emperor. Taiwan was still a part of the Qing Empire at this point.

8. C
Many revolutions, from France to China to Cuba, took place because a largely poor majority was being oppressed by a wealthy elite. Feminism, which has to do with equality between the sexes, is not a factor in political revolution, although it is a dynamic in social revolution.

9. D
Education seems to be the common background of revolutionaries, whether from the 18th century or after. Men such as John Adams and Danton were well-schooled, and most belonged to the middle

class. While the working class was often oppressed, it did not have the skills to organize and express revolutionary thinking.

10. B

The slave trade evolved partly from the profits to be had and the supply of human beings available. The Portuguese were some of the first to establish relationships with West African tribes that delivered captured peoples for transport to the New World. Sub-Saharan Africa encompasses the continent south of the Sahara desert. There was slave trading in this region, but not as much as in the north and west. East Africa was the farthest from the Atlantic, so few slaves were shipped from there across the continent.

11. D

Social Darwinists used Charles Darwin's theory of evolution and survival of the fittest to justify the inferior treatment of colonial people. According to the theory, the non-Europeans were "less-evolved" or "less fit" to rule themselves and needed the guidance of the "more fit" Europeans.

12. C

The only republic to outlaw slavery and grant freedom to all of its citizens was the former French colony of Saint Domingue, which was renamed Haiti.

13. A

Asian leaders in the various independence movements were all educated professionals, for example, members of the Indian National Congress. Most had received their educations in Europe. Studying law in England could expose them to Western liberalism. They also met whites who were sympathetic to their cause.

14. A

The plantation economy was hurt by the revolution in Haiti because the newly freed slaves wanted their own smaller plots of land and did not want to work on plantations like when they were slaves.

Haiti's economy had been flourishing because of sugar plantations, but without slave labor, it steadily declined.

15. C

A newly constituted government after 1867 was involved in many aspects of the modernization of Japan. Loans were given to help new companies get started, and close ties were forged between big business and the government. This new government was a very limited form of democracy, and there were no natural resources to speak of under Japan's control.

16. D

Canals were needed for the Industrial Revolution, which was creating huge amounts of heavy products that had to be moved. Roads simply could not handle such weights, and the vehicles needed to move this produce did not exist. Canals were the answer to moving heavy objects large distances.

17. B

Ethiopia defeated the Italians in the battle of Dugali in 1887. This thwarted Italian designs on Ethiopia as the Europeans sought to gain colonies in Africa. Liberia was an American-sponsored haven for slaves who wanted to return to Africa. Egypt was dominated at different times by France and Britain. Parts of Morocco were absorbed into the Spanish and French Empires.

18. D

The Sepoy uprising was a rebellion against British rule in northern India. The sepoys were Indians serving in the British army. After it was put down, the British were more vigilant about their colonial subjects serving in their military. The Zulus had attacked the British in rural South Africa. The Boxer Rebellion was against all foreigners in China in 1900.

19. D

Government ownership of property or industry is usually a feature of socialism. Today, most governments combine elements of both capitalism and socialism, as private property is allowed. Capitalism has safeguarded the ownership of private property. Property, whether in the form of money, valuable commodities, or other equity, is what defines wealth in the modern capitalistic world. The opportunity for advancement or upward mobility has been the motivation for many who want to better their socioeconomic status in a monetary-based system. In a capitalistic, market-based economy, the prices of goods are often determined by the laws of supply and demand. The more scarce and desirable the product, the higher its cost. Likewise, overproduction leads to falling prices.

20. B
When Napoleon took control of Spain in the early 1800s, advocates of independence in South America were encouraged to push for their freedom. The Spanish were defeated by the United States in the Spanish American War in the late 19th century (1898). The silver trade in Asia did not directly contribute to the independence movements in South America.

21. C
The statement refers to Russia, which abolished serfdom in 1861, and was involved in government-sponsored industrialization, but whose military inferiority was highlighted during its loss to superior European powers during the Crimean War.

22. D
Revolutionary activists in China tended to be educated and had some foreign contacts. Sun Yixian traveled widely, studied Western government, and dreamed of transforming China into a modern nation. Mandarins had the most to lose in a reformed China and did support the revolutionaries. Court eunuchs had only their influence in court as a power base and would not tend to join a liberal movement. Peasants were mostly illiterate and did not have access to revolutionary propaganda. This was especially true in the countryside, which was quite isolated from urban political unrest. Guangzhou, in the south, was the focus of much revolutionary activity from the 1890s forward.

23. A
Liberalism is a political ideology that developed during the Industrial Revolution as a result of the growth of the middle class, who benefitted from and supported the transition to an industrial, capitalist economy.

24. A
There was considerable competition for Chinese commercial advantages by foreign nations from the mid-19th century. This led to much tension amongst the great powers of the day. By 1900, the United States and Britain sponsored the idea of the "open door," whereby all nations would be able to trade with China equally. This was done in the hope of easing international problems in Asia and also to limit Russian and German aspirations in China. Japan was a rising power, but also an imperialistic party in China. As an ally of Britain and a new military power, it tended to take a reactive stance in China. During the Boxer Rebellion, Japan joined with the other European powers in relieving the legations in Beijing. China was very accessible by sea and also overland via Russia. Russia was very involved in establishing a sphere of interest in Manchuria in northeast China.

25. C
The three statements refer to China during the Qing dynasty. After their defeat in the Opium Wars, China was forced to sign unequal treaties with Britain and other European powers that gave them exclusive trading in sections of China. The anti-Western uprising, known as the Boxer Rebellion, was aimed at ridding China of foreign devils, but was ultimately unsuccessful and put down by European powers. Chinese intellectuals pursued a self-strengthening movement to improve China intellectually and technologically, but imperial forces, in particular the Empress Dowager, opposed the movement and suppressed it.

DOCUMENT-BASED QUESTION: SAMPLE RESPONSE

The Spanish colonies of Latin America struggled for their independence from the crown in the early 19th century. The Creoles often led these movements, seeking more economic and political freedom. The issues of the independence movements and nation-building in Latin America included their mix of Spanish and indigenous heritages and their struggles to uphold the constitution guidelines they set for themselves while keeping the nation united.

Latin American nations struggled to create a national identity and unite the diverse social and cultural groups in their lands. Simón Bolívar, a leader of the independence movements, wrote in his message to the Congress of Angostura in 1819 that the Latin Americans are a unique group (Document 1). They are not solely Europeans and they are not solely Indians, but rather, a mix of the two. This mix is something unique upon which a national identity could be built. Bolívar's point of view was that of an independence leader and a Creole attempted to inspire and motivate the congress he addressed. The Plan de Iguala, written by Mexican elites on the eve of declaring independence, attempts to address the racial divide (Document 2). The provision calls for "all united, without any distinction between Americans and Europeans" and any distinction of castes was to be abolished. The inclusion of these provisions points out the problem that existed between the European, mixed, and native populations. This document attempted to bring the groups together by creating a united front against Spain. It would be helpful to find out if these provisions were also included in the constitution and if they were carried out. Politically, Latin American nations struggled to create a stable government that united and had the allegiance of its people. Bolívar states that Latin America should not build its republic like North America, but rather like the English parliamentary system. Unlike North America, he advocated the creation of a hereditary senate to watch over the people.

Fifty years later, Chilean liberal Francisco Bilbao commented on what became Bolívar's vision for a republican Latin America (Document 4). Bilbao criticizes that although the constitution guarantees freedom and rights, in practice, these things are ignored. Instead, freedom is limited by the law; elections may be free, but they are extremely corrupt, and a hypocritical system has developed. Instead of upholding the ideals of a free constitutional republic, in many ways, Latin American independent countries replicated the colonial system they sought to oppose. Bilbao states that instead of 50 years of liberty since independence, Latin American countries, in particular Chile, have endured 50 years of anarchy and despotism. These two points of view come from educated members of society heavily involved in governmental affairs. It would help to have evidence from the lower class to confirm that this mistreatment is occurring. Also, a document of the actual constitutions of these new nations would be helpful to analyze what rights are supposed to be upheld. To further complicate matters, the memoir of Peru's José Rufino Echenique points out the role of the caudillos (Document 3). These regional military leaders often commanded more allegiance than the federal governments. In his memoir, Echenique describes how he was able to gather a force quickly to defend a friend against the government and when this friend was executed, Echenique was ready to move against the government. As a personal memoir, this account may exaggerate Echenique's willingness to risk life and limb for his friend, but it does demonstrate the extreme loyalty the caudillos were able to garner from the people.

The Latin American independence movements were often fought in the name of freedom and new opportunities, but unfortunately, these freedoms were often violated. The Creole class who led the movement often replaced the peninsular class it overthrew, and retained the same privileges as their former oppressors. Socially, mistreatment of non-Europeans continued to be an issue, and politically, forming a stable government with a strong allegiance from the people remained a challenge.

The essay earns the thesis point, 1 point for understanding the meaning of the documents and 2 points for using all of the documents as evidence to support the argument. The essay includes two successful additional document requests and earns that point, and also earns the point for POV analysis, although the first one, for Document 1, is not as strong as the second one, for Document 3. The essay appropriately groups the documents in two, with one group addressing issues of social diversity and unity (Documents 1 and 2), and the second addressing issues of political unity (Documents 3 and 4). The essay earns all 7 of the basic core points. It might be awarded an expanded core point for the second additional document request; however, because that was a less significant request, the expanded core point would not automatically be awarded. Final score 7/8.

CONTINUITY AND CHANGE-OVER-TIME QUESTION: SAMPLE RESPONSE

The process known as industrialization revolutionized the world starting in the 18th century. Beginning in England, industrialization spread throughout the world, although not necessarily evenly, and left no area untouched. Japan was revolutionized by industrialization. At the beginning of that time period, Japan was a relatively isolated country with little involvement in world trade. The opening of Japan, followed by the Meiji Restoration, radically altered the country as it became both an industrial and imperialist power. Yet through all the change, Japan still held on to important elements of its unique culture.

As the time period begins in 1750, Japan was ruled by the Tokugawa Shogunate, a feudal government that closely controlled the country's interaction with the outside world. However, Commodore Matthew Perry from the United States entered Japan's ports with gunpowder weapons and insisted that they change their trade policy in 1853. This encounter resulted in Japan being forced to sign a series of unequal treaties. This interaction led to the overthrow of the Shogun and the return of the emperor to power, known as the Meiji Restoration.

With the government under the centralized control of the emperor, major changes occurred. Japan initiated a government-sponsored industrialization, which included the building of railroads and factories. Unlike China, which had European-built and owned factories and railroads, these were Japanese-owned and controlled. Japan also industrialized its military with the latest weapons and fighting techniques. With the backing of industrial strength, Japan began to reach out and dominate its neighbors. Japan's newly industrialized military was able to defeat Korea, China, and Russia in the early 20th century. These defeats served as a wake-up call to the outside world of all the changes that were occurring in Japan. Culturally, Japan was also adopting some Western traditions such as fashion, art, and writing styles. Through all these changes, Japan was able to hold on to its unique cultural identity and values, such as the importance of the group over the individual. This dedication to family, nation, and emperor helped propel Japan to prominence as a world power.

Industrialization brought radical changes to Japan from 1750 to 1900. A feudal, isolated kingdom in 1750, Japan became a burgeoning world power by 1900. Government-sponsored industrialization followed by imperial conquests helped Japan become a defeater of Western powers, instead of being defeated by Western powers.

The second paragraph recounts the history of how Japan was opened to trade, but it does little to analyze in detail the conditions under which this happened and the immediately resulting reactions/consequences in terms of industrialization. What does it mean to the status of Japan's industrial output in 1750 that it was insulated, didn't trade without the outside world, and was forced to sign unequal treaties. Further, it does not address what this opening meant to the world beyond the efforts of the U.S. to open it to trade. 0 points in that paragraph. In its first third, the third paragraph does a solid job of addressing the industrialization's effects on Japan but it swiftly runs off-topic by discussing Japan's military prowess and its adopting of Western culture. How did these result from industrialization? How might they have led to further industrialization. 1 point for evidence and analysis. The closing paragraph merely summarizes the points already weakly made in the previous paragraphs. Final point total is 2.

COMPARATIVE QUESTION: SAMPLE RESPONSE

During the 19th century, many nations were faced with the need to react to changes in the industrializing world and make necessary reforms to deal with these changes. Russia and China both attempted to reform their countries, and both faced internal resistance to a complete modern change. Russia's government pushed for economic change in the form of government-sponsored industrialization, but resisted most political changes and instead retained an absolute monarchy. China had some successful attempts at reform and change, but internal rebellions and imperial resistance to change prevented real reform from taking place. As a result, by the end of the 19th century, both dynasties were on the verge of revolution.

Economically, Russia was more successful at reform than China. The Russian serfs were emancipated in 1861, in the hopes of creating an urban working class to work the developing industrial factories. Under the leadership of finance minister Serge Witte, the government pushed hard to industrialize Russia by sponsoring such projects as the Trans-Siberian Railroad. Unfortunately, Russia was very far behind the West and much of the government pushing led to civil unrest. In China, the defeat to the British in the Opium Wars forced the Qing dynasty to sign a series of unequal treaties with European powers, allowing them to establish exclusive trading rights in China. As a result, the factories and railroads built in China were built and controlled by foreigners.

Politically, both Russia and China were resistant to long-lasting change. In Russia, the czar did free the serfs and allowed for the creation of zemstvos, or local assemblies, but any real attempt at curtailing his own power was avoided. After Czar Alexander II was assassinated, the czars who followed were more oppressive and more resistant to political change. This came to a head during Bloody Sunday in 1905, when a group visited the czar's winter palace to present a petition, but was met with gunfire. The Revolution of 1905 followed, after the czar permitted the creation of a duma, or parliament, but the czar would dismiss this body if he did not approve of its decisions. China also struggled with political change because of imperial resistance. Additionally, internal rebellions such as the Taiping Rebellion disrupted the country and highlighted the growing dissatisfaction with the Qing dynasty. The government attempted reforms during the Self-Strengthening movement, but much of these reforms were not carried out. During the 100 Days of Reform, the emperor suggested the creation of a constitutional monarchy, but he was soon deposed by the Empress Dowager and his dreams of reform were never fulfilled. In 1900, a group called the Boxers rebelled against the foreign control in China. The Empress Dowager gave the group her support, hoping they could remove the foreign influence, but the Qing dynasty was proven politically impotent when foreign powers had to put down the rebellion. By 1911, the last Chinese dynasty was overthrown.

The 19th century presented the world with many new economic and political changes. Those countries that successfully reformed and reacted, both politically and economically, survived and became powerful in the 20th century. Those who could not reform and react, like Russia and China, lost control of their empires politically and economically, and were overthrown.

This essay lacks a thesis statement that summarizes the similarities and differences between China and Russia. Instead, the entire first paragraph is an attempt to answer the prompt. Yet, it treats only their similarities. Thus, it misses the full points it could get. Although the second and third paragraphs address Russia's and China's attempts at reform and resistance, they, like the thesis paragraph fail to adequately address the similarities and differences, earning them only 1 point. In addition, the evidence is biased toward the actual instances of reform and resistance, with little to illustrate how Russia and China are similar/different. Last, although the writer mentions European powers, he does so without specifically addressing the global context/impact of Russia's/China's attempts at reform and resistance, thus missing the global context points. Final point total is 4.

CHAPTER 7: 1900 CE TO PRESENT

IF YOU ONLY LEARN SIX THINGS IN THIS CHAPTER . . .

1. Due to improvements in health care and the decrease of the death rate, the world population went from 1 billion people in 1900 to over 6 billion. The movement of people has also increased throughout the world, with many in search of better economic opportunities. Some refugees, too, are being forced to leave their homelands.

2. Traditional social structures have been challenged as a result of movements that have attempted to empower the working class, such as the introduction of communist governments in various parts of the world.

3. Women gained the right to vote in many parts of the world and access to new economic opportunities and education. The development of the birth control pill empowered women by allowing them to control their own reproductive systems.

4. The world became more and more integrated through technology, cultures blended, and some came to dominate. At the same time, religious fundamentalism has developed in some regions, possibly to combat this Western-dominated global culture.

5. The rise in the nation-state and nationalism has led to the adoption of political systems from totalitarianism to democracy. At the same time, the rise of a more globally connected world may blur the lines of the nation-state.

6. The world wars demonstrated the influence of technology on warfare, but also indicated the decline of Europe as the global power. Colonial areas asserted themselves and fought for independence, but were later faced with a new global conflict called the Cold War. Since the end of the Cold War, nations have made attempts at both economic and political reforms, and international and multinational organizations have made attempts to establish a new world order.

THE BIG PICTURE

1. Interactions between people and the environment

   In other words: **How does the environment shape human societies, and how do humans shape the environment?**

One of the most significant changes in the 20th century was the growth from 1 billion people worldwide in 1900 to over 6 billion. The increase in technology and health care has led to longer lives and a higher rate of infant survival throughout the world. Movement of people has also increased throughout the world, with many individuals seeking better economic opportunities in new areas. Additionally, some refugees are forced to leave their homelands.

Though health care has improved tremendously, epidemic diseases such as AIDS and malaria have continued to plague the world, particularly in developing countries with the least access to new medicines. The development of nuclear weapons changed the nature of war. During the Cold War, the major goal was to stop the other side from dominating. Now that more nations have access to weapons of mass destruction, diplomatic issues are more tenuous than ever.

2. Development and interaction of cultures

   In other words: **How do people express themselves, and what is the impact of ideas?**

Has our world developed a global culture? As the world becomes more and more integrated through technology, cultures blend and some come to dominate. Religious fundamentalism has developed in some parts of the world, partially to combat this Western-dominated global culture. Intellectually, the developments of the 20th century boggle the mind. From the airplane to the atom bomb, the discoveries in math, science, and technology have revolutionized how we live and communicate.

3. State-building, expansion, and conflict

   In other words: **How do people govern themselves?**

If in the 19th century the nation-state had its start, in the 21st century the nation-state seems to have taken over the world. There seems to be no area that is not a nation-state. This rise in the nation-state and nationalism has led to the use of a variety of political systems from totalitarianism to democracy. At the same time, the rise of a more globally connected world may blur the lines of the nation-state. As regional trade organizations such as the European Union develop and become more interconnected and religious fundamentalism grows, are nation-states losing their political hold?

4. Creation, expansion, and interaction of economic systems

In other words: **How do economic developments affect the world?**

It can be said that much of the change that occurs in this century had its beginning in the 19th century. The industrialization and increase in communication that began in the 19th century continued to grow and spread at a tremendous rate in the 20th century. The late 20th century saw the rise of an increasingly global economy and the rise in power of multinational corporations, which led to economic development in many parts of the world.

5. Development and transformation of social structures

In other words: **How do people identify themselves socially, and what roles do men and women have?**

The introduction of communist governments in various parts of the world challenged traditional social structure models, attempting to empower the working class. Unfortunately, new elite party classes often emerged, which went on to replace the older ruling class. Women gained both the right to vote in many parts of the world as well as access to new economic opportunities and education. The development of the birth control pill empowered women by allowing them to control their own reproductive systems.

WHY THIS PERIODIZATION?

The 20th century witnessed change occurring at a rate that had never been seen before in world history. The cataclysms of two world wars affected almost all aspects of human life in the first half of the century. The rise and fall of communist regimes, together with the decolonization movements of the second half of the century, also transformed the global political landscape. The world became more interdependent as economic, technological, and cultural globalization tied peoples together tighter than ever before.

GLOBAL CONFLICT

WORLD WAR I

LONGER-TERM CAUSES OF WWI

- **Alliances:** The alliance system had led to many open and secret agreements between nations. Most of these were defensive plans that would protect a nation in the event it was attacked. Germany, Austria, and Italy all had agreements to this effect. Likewise, France and Russia were allied if Germany were to attack either one.

- **Imperialism:** Tensions stemmed from imperialism and the competition for foreign colonies, as in Africa.

- **Militarism:** The arms race between the major powers—especially Germany and Britain—that were maintaining increasingly large fleets also led to a hope that these new tools of war would be used in the future. Military leaders were anxious to fight sooner than later, and civilians were also increasingly casualties of the fighting. Civilian fatalities in wartime climbed from 5 percent at the turn of the century, to 15 percent during World War I.

- **Nationalism:** After the successful creation of Italy and Germany by 1870, other ethnic groups hoped for nations of their own. This rising tide of nationalism was growing stronger among such peoples as the Poles, Bosnians, Czechs, and Yugoslavs. Pan-Germanism came into direct conflict with Pan-Slavism. An eagerness to redraw the map of Europe was mounting, and this was usually done through conquest and war.

The war actually began in the following way: During a tour of the southern Balkan provinces, the heir to the Austrian throne and his wife were assassinated in their car. The assassin was a Serbian Slav nationalist. Austria accused Serbia of supporting Yugoslav (southern Slavic) nationalism, and it declared war. Russia sided with Serbia, while Germany pledged support for Austria. When Germany declared war on Russia, France joined Russia. Great Britain was the last major European power to join, when Germany violated Belgium's neutrality on its way to attack France.

World War I was a new kind of war, particularly because of recent improvements in military weaponry. The use of machine guns and gas led to a significant increase in casualties. The war became defensive as **trenches** were built and defended. The heroic notion of war was gone.

Civilians, too, were involved in the war effort, as women entered the workforce. This **total war** involved the entire nation. Governments controlled industry, and they used propaganda to reinforce the evilness of the enemy.

The Treaty of Versailles: The leading Allied powers—Italy, Great Britain, France, and the United States—were labeled the "Big Four." They called a conference near Paris at the Palace of Versailles to settle the issues stemming from the war. In the end, France would not allow the generous peace that Wilson had envisioned. Instead, the treaty laid down harsh terms to which Germany had to agree. The map of Europe was redrawn, but nations such as Italy were still not satisfied with the results. Other nations such as Poland, Czechoslovakia, Hungary, and Yugoslavia were all created in 1919 by the peace settlement.

President Woodrow Wilson entered the Versailles meetings with his plan, called the **Fourteen Points**. In it, he called for self-determination of nationalities, peace without victory, disarmament, fair treatment of colonial peoples, and the establishment of the **League of Nations**, a multinational organization aimed at maintaining world peace. Most of his ideas were rejected at the meeting, though the League of Nations was created. Ironically, when Wilson brought the treaty back to the United States, Congress opposed it and the United States did not join the new league. The League of Nations was established in Geneva, Switzerland, in 1921, but it struggled to keep the peace and control its members when tensions arose.

IMPACT OF THE WAR ON THE ALLIES

- Though victorious, **Britain** was profoundly affected by the Great War. It had lost a significant percentage of its youth, and its economy was strained. After the war, debts were considerable and the once-proud empire took on a tired look. Britain's great empire became more and more of a burden, and native movements for independence in Africa and Asia were underway.

- **France** was devastated by the war. Whole sections of the nation were destroyed, and the nation had also suffered many casualties. War widows and amputees were in evidence in every city.

- **Italy** was one of the Allied leadership nations and had been promised large pieces of the Austrian Empire when the Allies won. It received some, but not all it had hoped for. Postwar politicians were able to capitalize on this situation, and Italy continued to press for more territory along the Adriatic coast.

- The **United States** was elevated to true world-power status by the war but was not really interested in playing that role. Conservatives won the White House in 1920, and the United States largely retreated from European affairs.

IMPACT OF THE WAR ON THE CENTRAL POWERS

- Germany was economically, politically, and socially wrecked. It had lost millions of men in the fighting, and now, by the terms of the Versailles treaty, was forced to pay huge amounts of reparations to the Allies. In addition, it lost all of its overseas empire, along with provinces on both eastern and western borders. The Kaiser abdicated and fled Germany, leaving a political vacuum. With the monarchy gone, a new government was assembled in Weimar in 1919. A weak democratic Germany with a president and chancellor was created.

- The Middle East: The Ottoman Empire collapsed in 1918. Turkey declared itself a republic and under the leadership of Ataturk, who instituted a program of modernization and westernization. Arab nationalism rose, in part inspired by Wilson's call for national self-determination, and disappointment in the terms of the peace treaty. In exchange for their help against the Central Powers, Arabs had been promised independence. Instead, their land was carved into French and British mandates. A center of tension was the British mandate of Palestine where Arab nationalists competed with Zionists for control of the land, land they had both been vaguely promised by the Allies.

OTHER MAJOR PLAYERS

- **Russia** was in shambles as the revolution gave way to civil war after 1918. Russia was not a party to the Versailles treaty because it withdrew from the war and signed a treaty with Germany in 1917. For two years, the forces of the left—led by the Bolsheviks (Reds) and the supporters of the czar (Whites)—fought to control Russia. It took two years of bitter fighting and the deaths of as many as a million Russians for the Reds to claim victory and declare the birth of the Union of Soviet Socialist Republics. The Bolsheviks shot the czar and his family to ensure the monarchy would be finished in Russia.

- **Japan** had fought on the Allied side during the war and hoped to add to its empire. It did not get what it wanted at Versailles, and a postwar economic downturn led to hard times for this country. Japan entered the war late and hoped for support as a large nation aspiring to democracy.

- **China:** When Japan gained some concessions in China through the treaty, there were riots in Beijing to protest. This led to a surge of nationalism in China and to a cultural and intellectual movement known as the May Fourth Movement. This movement marked an upsurge of Chinese nationalism and a shift toward a more populist political base rather than the rule of intellectual elites.

- **India** fought on the side of the British in World War I and had been promised self-government after the war. When the fighting ended, little change occurred. This led to a surge in Indian nationalism under the leadership of Mohandas Gandhi, and to the eventual independence of India in 1947.

GLOBAL DEPRESSION

The economy of the United States was crucial to the health of world markets. Europe had already seen an outflow of capital as the bull market in American stocks drew money to itself. When the market collapsed in October 1929, the reaction was felt around the world. American and foreign investors lost billions of dollars in the first week. The Depression led the United States government to take a more active role in the economy, a role that went largely unquestioned until the rise of American conservatism that began in the 1980s during the presidency of Ronald Reagan.

The impact was especially severe in Europe, which had depended on American loans to recover from World War I. The wave of bank failures in the United States had a ripple effect in London, Berlin, Tokyo, and other financial capitals. The bond market also shrank, and many investors were caught off guard as they tried to cover huge losses. This resulted in dramatic increases in bank failures and personal bankruptcies. Global unemployment rose to double-digit levels. In addition, the United States passed the highest tariff (a tax on imports) in its history, further blocking international trade.

CAUSES OF GLOBAL DEPRESSION

- Overdependence on American loans and buying
- Increase in tariffs and protectionism
- Industrial and farming surpluses leading to deflation
- Poor banking management

The great hardships of the Depression led to political instability and a rise in political extremism in many nations. Communists on the left criticized the obvious failings of capitalism, while fascists on the right sought to protect private enterprise and promote their nations. Japan, Italy, and Germany looked to dictatorial rule in an effort to pull themselves out of their economic hardships.

In the 1930s in Japan, the military replaced civilian politicians in the highest posts of government. Lacking natural resources, Japan needed an empire to provide crucial minerals for its own industrial needs. It had already gained Taiwan and Korea, but it now fixed its eye on Northeast China. **Japan's invasion of Manchuria** in 1931 led to diplomatic protests in the League of Nations, but the Japanese kept their new territory and soon walked out of the League. Similarly, **Italy invaded Ethiopia** in 1935.

RISE OF FASCIST AND TOTALITARIAN STATES

ITALY

The triumph of Marxist revolution in Russia after 1921 had great impact on world political thinking in the 1920s. Fear about a spread of communism to other nations that had been destabilized by the war led to new political movements in Europe. Groups of reactionary men started to organize in various European nations, but it was in Italy that the first expression of anticommunism emerged. A small group of men led by **Benito Mussolini** marched on Rome in 1922, demanding that they be allowed to form a government. The king gave in to this demand, and Italy was soon dominated by Mussolini and his fascists. Mussolini became the prototypical modern dictator as he accumulated more and more power.

FASCISM AS AN IDEOLOGY

- Opposition to communism as a threat to tradition and private property
- Ultranationalism and glorification of the state
- Militarism and glorification of war as the ultimate expression of power
- Alliances with big business and destruction of labor unions
- Rejection of liberalism and democracy, which were seen as weak and ineffective

SOVIET UNION

At the same time that Mussolini was consolidating his power in Italy, there was a transfer of power in Moscow. Lenin, the architect of the Bolshevik Revolution, died of a stroke seven years after the revolution. The power struggle within the Bolshevik party led to the rise of **Joseph Stalin**, who took control in 1927.

Stalin's ruthless elimination of all his rivals allowed him to take complete power in Russia by the 1930s. His leadership became associated with Soviet communism, but it is also referred to as Stalinism.

STALINISM AS PRACTICED

- Centralized control of the economy through the use of **Five-Year Plans**
- World leadership of the international communist movement
- Forced collectivization of all farming
- Promotion of atheism and forcing organized religion underground

GERMANY

The establishment of the Soviet state in Russia led to political backlashes in many other countries. After the war, Germany rebuilt its government as a parliamentary democracy. Burdened with war debts and rampant inflation, the new government tried to reestablish Germany's place in the international community. With the coming of the Depression, many feared that Germany would experience its own revolution and become the next communist state.

One of the political parties that developed in postwar Germany was the National Socialist German Workers' Party (the Nazi Party). Its charismatic leader **Adolf Hitler** spoke out against communism and used the anti-Semitic racism of his day to suggest that communism was really a global conspiracy organized by Jewish people and that Germany's economic problems could be blamed on the nation's Jewish population. Hitler also preached ultranationalism and the promise of a greater Germany, much as Mussolini had done in Italy. In 1933, he was appointed chancellor through the success of aggressive anticommunist propaganda. He became dictator, or führer, within a few years by eliminating most of his political opponents. He reorganized the government by insinuating the Nazi party into many areas of national life.

Stalin, Hitler, and Mussolini represented a new form of political leadership in the modern context. These 20th-century dictatorships defined the modern totalitarian regime. Whether in Berlin or Moscow, the following features were apparent:

TOTALITARIAN REGIMES

- A single leader with almost unquestioned authority
- A single party in charge of all government
- Creation of a police state to terrorize and control the populace
- Aggressive elimination of all opposition groups

THE LEAGUE OF NATIONS

The Treaty of Versailles had called for and organized a **League of Nations**, an organization made up of mostly European nations but also Ethiopia, Japan, Siam, and many Latin American nations. The United States, which reverted to an isolationist foreign policy after WWI, never joined. The League was never successful on a large scale with its primary purpose, that of stopping international conflict. Dominated by Britain and France, neither of whom wanted to go to war after the First World War, the League failed to act after the Japanese invasion of Manchuria, the Italian invasion of Ethiopia, and the Spanish Civil War. This inaction emboldened Hitler, who began his own expansion of German territory within Europe unopposed. The policy of **appeasement** (giving in to a bully in a vain attempt to hope the bullying will stop) culminated in the 1939 Munich Agreement in which Britain and France handed Hitler the Sudetenland, a largely German-speaking area in northern Czechoslovakia, with the understanding that Hitler would not take any other territory in that nation. He invaded and took the rest of the country in the spring of that year. Despite its many failings, the League had some successes, notably with combating malaria and other diseases in Europe, stopping labor abuses, controlling the distribution of opium products, and lessening the slave trade in Africa and Asia.

THE SPANISH CIVIL WAR

In the 1930s, Spain was a conflicted country, barely industrialized, with a growing urban population and a largely semi-feudalistic countryside controlled by rich families who were allied with the Roman Catholic Church. In 1932, the king abdicated and a republic was created. The first republican government was very liberal and attempted to introduce many reforms such as universal, non-religious education, equality for women, land reforms, etc. After an even more liberal government was elected in 1936, officers in the army, led by General Francisco Franco, revolted and began a civil war that lasted for four years. During the war, the fascist-leaning Franco asked for and received aid in the form of troops and equipment from both Italy and Germany. Hitler, in particular, saw the war as a way of testing new military equipment and practicing new tactics, tactics that would become the famous blitzkrieg of the German land and air forces during World War II. One such attack, on the town of Guernica, was a deliberate attack on a nonmilitary target to test the German air force, killed hundreds of civilians who previously had not taken part in the civil war. In response to this slaughter of innocent civilians, the painter **Pablo Picasso** produced one of the 20th century's most famous artistic works, *Guernica*. This work stands as a continual reminder of the tragedies of war and the suffering it inflicts upon individuals, particularly innocent civilians. Although the Republican government repeatedly asked for help from the League of Nations, it only received limited help from the Soviet Union and from international volunteers (to include many Americans) who formed brigades to help them fight. Franco defeated the Republican forces in 1939 and ruled the country with an iron hand until his death in 1975.

WORLD WAR II

Many of the unresolved issues at the end of the Great War were instrumental in causing the second—and far more devastating—world war. Tensions in both Europe and Asia were building throughout the 1930s, and both continents saw extensive fighting. As in the years before 1914, there were tense matchups between nations, which would eventually lead to war breaking out.

Historians debate when the Second World War began. While many point to the **German invasion of Poland in 1939**, the war in Asia had been going on since the Japanese **invasion of China in 1937**. Events in Europe affected the Asian conflict, especially when Germany overran France in 1940. This allowed Japan to take French Indochina, which had rubber and tin that the Japanese needed for their military machine. The Japanese attack on Pearl Harbor resulted in the United States abandoning its post–World War I isolationism and entering this new global conflict, a development that would alter its course and outcome.

From 1938 to 1942, the expansionism of both Japan and Germany was impressive. The Germans first succeeded in taking control of most of Eastern and Northern Europe with few casualties. After the fall of France, only Britain was left to fight the German army and air force, which bombed England aggressively in anticipation of an invasion. But the Royal Air Force managed to defend the skies over England, and Hitler turned his attention to his proclaimed enemy, the Soviet Union. A key year was 1941, as Germany launched a surprise invasion against the U.S.S.R., and Japan attacked the U.S. Navy in Hawaii. Both attacks were very well planned, catching the Russians and Americans completely off guard.

ORIGINS OF THE COLD WAR

There was no peace conference at the end of World War II. The Allies demanded unconditional surrender, and the Axis nations were in ruins from bombing raids. Their defeat had been total, and both Japan and Germany were occupied by the Allied armies. Within the framework of the occupation, the Allies held war trials to hold the Japanese and Germans accountable for the worst war in human history. Top generals and government officials were charged and convicted, and some were executed for crimes against humanity. This set a new precedent in international law, as making war would now be punishable in international courts. The toll of the war was staggering. Some estimates of the dead exceed 60 million, and millions more were brutalized and wounded in the greatest example of total war in human history. The fighting ranged from Africa to Asia to Europe to Australia. The two nations that emerged from the conflict in the best position to influence the postwar world order were the United States and the Soviet Union. These two superpowers would go on to engage in a "cold" war that largely shaped the political course of the second half of the 20th century.

By mid-1942, Japan controlled most of the western Pacific Ocean from New Guinea to the Aleutians, and Germany controlled most of Europe and parts of North Africa. But the Germans were turned back at Stalingrad, and the Japanese lost a large naval battle to the United States near Midway Island in June of 1942. From that point on, the industrial capacities of the United States and the U.S.S.R. were able to out-produce both of their enemies, and the Axis powers were put on the defensive.

The occupation of nations by Germany and Japan was a brutal exercise in militarist oppression and even extermination. Millions were killed in both Asia and Europe, as camps were set up to detain and even murder political enemies. China and Poland were the scenes of wholesale slaughter. The death toll in Europe alone is estimated at 20 million, as communists, labor leaders, Jews, homosexuals, the mentally disabled, and Gypsies were shot or gassed to death in specially designed chambers. In particular, Hitler targeted the Jews, blaming them for all of Germany's problems. Six million of Europe's 9.5 million Jews were killed in the Nazis' **Holocaust**. Millions of Chinese were also killed before the war ended, as the Japanese pushed across the continent.

New technologies were born during the war as both sides sought to outdo each other. The Germans and British developed radar to detect each other's planes. Sonar was invented to locate unseen submarines. Rockets were used in war for the first time—most notably by the Germans— as they delivered high explosives to Britain. But the most awesome weapon of all was the **nuclear bomb** that America developed and used to finish the war against the Japanese in the Pacific. Two bombs were dropped, on Hiroshima and Nagasaki, killing over 150,000 people and forcing the final capitulation of Japan in August 1945.

OUTCOMES OF WWII

The outcomes of World War II can be summed up as a **United States-Soviet ascendancy:**

- World War II only had two "winners" in that many of the victorious Allied powers were devastated in the fighting (especially France and China). Britain was crippled economically and was already losing control of parts of its empire. The greatest postwar status fell to the United States, which had entered the war late but had built up a gigantic military and industrial response to the Axis. Possession of the A-bomb meant that the United States was now alone at the pinnacle of power. It had suffered smaller losses in terms of men killed and, except for the attack on Hawaii in 1941, none of its territory was damaged.

- On the other side of the world, the Soviet Union had faced annihilation and survived to emerge as a great military power. Its losses had been almost 27 million, which was immensely traumatizing. Whole tracts of land had been decimated. Once victorious, the U.S.S.R. participated in the founding of the United Nations, a successor to the League of Nations that was established after the war and participated in the War Crimes Tribunal, and established its hegemony in Eastern Europe.

Much of the responsibility for settling postwar problems fell on the **United Nations** (UN), headquartered in New York City. Led by the five Allied victors of the war (United States, U.S.S.R., Great Britain, France, and the Republic of China), the UN established relief agencies and peacekeeping mechanisms. The task of postwar recovery—especially in war-torn Asia and Europe—was immense. As the leading superpower and wealthiest nation, the United States took on many of the costs for postwar rehabilitation.

The UN is a confederation that nations join voluntarily. The **General Assembly** is a forum for discussing world problems and their solutions. It cannot pass laws, but it can raise issues and suggest resolutions. Shortly after its founding, the UN was busy settling disputes in the Middle East and helping the many refugees left by World War II. To keep the peace, the UN has three responses to military aggression:

- Diplomatic protest and pressure brought to bear on the belligerent nation

- Economic sanctions used to pressure the aggressor nation

- Collective military action by member states to defend the nation(s) being attacked

CIVILIANS AT WAR

Although civilians have always been affected by war, World War II saw the first deliberate targeting of civilians as a strategy to defeat the opposing side. From the Spanish Civil War to the Japanese "Rape of Nanjing" to the Nazi Holocaust of the Jews to Allied firebombing of first German then Japanese cities, civilians became direct targets in the war. This culminated in the dropping of both atomic bombs to end the war in the Pacific. New types of media to include radio and cinema extended governments' ability to propagandize the war. From this point forward, no conflict, no matter how small, has excluded civilians from being targets. Terrorism, the deliberate use of violence or threat of violence for political purposes designed to influence a population's attitude, would become the norm for many political and non-political actors on the global stage.

THE COLD WAR (1945–1989)

Within a year of the end of the war, there were already tensions between the former Allies. Working together to occupy Germany and to help found the United Nations, the United States and the U.S.S.R. found more and more points of contention. The Soviet Union sought to control the nations on its western frontier, partly as a promoter of communism, but also to create a buffer to protect itself from future invasions. The United States protested, as this was in violation of wartime agreements.

Eventually, a de facto division took place, which divided Europe into a **capitalist West** and a **communist East**. In the middle of it all stood the divided former capital of Germany. Berlin had British, Russian, French, and American troops stationed in close proximity to one another. War almost erupted in 1948 when the Russians sealed off the city, denying the others access, but they finally relented.

FEATURES OF COMPETITION BETWEEN THE US AND U.S.S.R.

- **Technological:** The race to build bigger and more destructive weaponry intensified after the U.S.S.R. tested its first nuclear bomb in 1949. The thermonuclear bomb (H-bomb) followed in the 1950s. Space technology created new competition when the U.S.S.R. launched the first satellite in 1957. After this, there was a "space race," and then a "moon race," with both nations hoping to be the first to launch people into space. Moon landings by the United States in 1969 and Soviet space stations of the 1970s were some of the byproducts of this competition.

- **Geopolitical:** Both superpowers vied for influence across the globe, especially in the developing nations of Asia and Africa. Wars in Korea, Vietnam, India, Afghanistan, and Angola were fought with weapons provided by the Americans and Soviets.

- **Ideological:** Capitalism and communism were presented to the world as the two choices available for political organization. At least four nations were divided by this Cold War dichotomy in the 1950s.

The following year, the U.S.S.R. exploded its own nuclear device, and the rivalry with the United States turned to outright animosity and competition. This rivalry continued for four decades, as the United States and the U.S.S.R. competed for political influence throughout the world. It all came to an end when the Soviet Union collapsed in 1991.

The **Cold War** produced military alliances, such as the North Atlantic Treaty Organization (NATO) and the Warsaw Pact, which divided much of the world into anti-Communist and Communist camps. Proxy wars between the two sides took place in Latin America, Africa, and Asia.

By the mid-1950s, relations between the Soviet Union and the People's Republic of China began to deteriorate as they differed in their interpretation of Marxism. China encouraged a movement of **non-aligned nations** made up of developing countries. India and Indonesia were two prominent nations in this group. A famous meeting in Indonesia in 1955 gathered these nations together and China cultivated the many national leaders present. China hoped to connect with the developing world and use this to counteract Soviet Russian diplomacy. Chinese aid flowed to African and Asian nations as a part of this ideological outreach.

The United States took advantage of the Sino-Soviet split and normalized relations with China in the 1970s. The Cold War took on more of a tri-polar feel, as China had its own nuclear weapons and space program by the 1970s. The James Bond film series glamorized and promoted the conflicts associated with the Cold War. In these films, Bond invariably and dramatically saved the United States and the world from a variety of Cold War villains.

INDEPENDENCE AND NATIONALIST MOVEMENTS

Throughout the 20th century, independence movements and nationalism rose in many parts of the world. They were often set off as an opposing response to a colonial power or a competitive nationalist group.

INDIA

India's nationalist movement was led by the British-educated members of the **Indian National Congress**. The Government of India Act of 1919 transferred power over some domestic issues over to the Congress, but as political independence seemed to be on the rise, British repression rose alongside it. In 1919, the government cracked down on freedom of the press and assembly, and at Amritsar, a British general ordered troops to fire on a protest rally. In the eyes of India, British colonial rule had lost its legitimacy.

Under the leadership of **Mohandas Gandhi**, the Indian nationalist movement grew. Gandhi focused on the peasant roots and spiritual traditions of India and created a mass movement. His methods of **ahimsa**, nonviolence in the face of an attack, and **civil disobedience** against unjust laws effectively challenged British authority. Gandhi was unsuccessful, however, in allying with Muslim leadership, and a movement to create a separate Muslim state gained strength.

The British suspended the movement toward home rule during World War II, but after the war, it was difficult for them to maintain their empire. On August 15, 1947, independence was granted to India. However, when independence was granted, a long-standing issue emerged about the fate of the Muslim minority in a newly independent Hindu-dominated India. The leader of the Muslim League, Muhammad Ali Jinnah, insisted that Muslims have their own state. Violence between Hindus and Muslims persuaded the British to partition the subcontinent, which led to the creation of Hindu India and Muslim Pakistan. This division led to a mass migration of Muslim and Hindu refugees and terrible violence. Gandhi was devastated by the division of India and was later assassinated by a Hindu extremist.

SUB-SAHARAN AFRICA

By 1914, almost all of Africa had been carved up by European powers. Economically, it had been transformed into a **monoculture** of cash crops and mines of precious metals such as gold and diamonds, but the ownership of these plantations and mines was exclusively in the hands of Europeans. As in India, the post-World War II independence movements in Africa were often led by a small minority of Africans who had received a European education. Labor organizations, social clubs, literary circles, and youth movements all became vehicles for protest. A transnational Pan-African movement sought unity beyond national boundaries.

The process of independence itself varied widely across Africa. The Gold Coast, later **Ghana**, was the first to achieve its independence in 1957. Led by the U.S.-educated **Kwame Nkrumah**, strikes and protests were used to remove the British from power. **Kenya**, on the other hand, had a sizable European population that blocked independence. This led to an armed revolt and eventually independence in 1963.

The independence of the Belgian Congo was not planned at all. The Belgian government departed the **Congo** suddenly in 1959, leaving behind a country beset by chaos and civil war.

The **political borders** created by the European colonial powers led to nations that were comprised of unrelated ethnic groups who had a history of conflict that began long before the war and that often became rivals competing for power. This led to ethnic tension in many areas of Africa, including Nigeria with the Biafra secessionist movement and **Rwanda**, where conflict between the majority Hutus and minority Tutsis (formally favored by colonial powers) led to a 100-day genocide, resulting in the deaths of almost one million Tutsis in 1994.

In **South Africa**, the path to independence was very different. The Union of South Africa was formed in 1910 from former British colonies, but the majority black population was granted no rights. Instead, a series of restrictive laws was enacted with the goal of controlling the black population and maintaining the separate societies of black and white. This system was known as **apartheid**.

Under apartheid, 87 percent of the territory was designated for white citizens, and the remaining area was for black citizens. But under the leadership of the African National Congress (ANC), an organized resistance was formed. The government combated this resistance with repressive measures such as extensive jail times for opponents. International opposition against South Africa, like the United Nations economic sanctions and international boycotts, brought global attention to the problem.

Finally, in 1989, the National Party began to take apart the apartheid system. **Nelson Mandela** was released from jail after 26 years and the ANC was legalized. In 1994, elections for all people were held, and Mandela became the first freely elected president of South Africa.

ZIONISM AND PALESTINIAN NATIONALISM

Following World War I, the British held a **mandate** (a system in which a nation administers a territory on behalf of the League of Nations) in Palestine, but made conflicting promises to the Palestinian Arabs and the Jews. In the **Balfour Declaration of 1917**, the British government committed to support the creation of a homeland for Jews in Palestine and allowed Jews to migrate to Palestine during the mandate period. The Arab Palestinians saw the British rule and Jewish settlement as forms of imperial control, however.

Jewish migration to Palestine increased as Nazi persecution increased during World War II. By the end of the war, the Pan-Arabism movement opposed the creation of a Jewish state, and the Holocaust increased the Jewish commitment to the creation of a homeland. By 1947, the British gave up the mandate and turned the land over to the United Nations, which had plans to divide the area into two states. A civil war ensued and Jewish victories led to the creation of the Jewish state of **Israel** on May 14, 1948.

Continued fighting has plagued this region, including the Six Day War in 1967. The **Palestinian Liberation Organization (PLO)** was created and is dedicated to reclaiming the land and establishing a Palestinian state.

VIOLENCE AGAINST CIVILIANS

During the 20th century, movements that used violence against civilians developed in many parts of the world. The Provisional Irish Republican Army (IRA) is a paramilitary organization whose aim is to free Northern Ireland from British rule. It was formed in 1969 as a result of a split in the Irish Republican Army over how to respond to British colonialism. Al-Qaeda is a global militant Islamist organization founded by Osama bin Laden in the late 1980s. Al-Qaeda has attacked both civilian and military targets in various countries, including the September 11 attacks in the United States, the 1998 U.S. embassy bombings in Tanzania and Kenya, and the 2002 Bali bombings.

VIETNAM

The French colonial rule of Southeast Asia also had to deal with rising nationalism. Both France and her colonies were occupied by the Axis powers during the war. A group of Vietnamese nationalists under the leadership of **Ho Chi Minh** first fought the Japanese during the war, and then began a guerrilla campaign against the returning French. Ho Chi Minh was a Marxist who also admired the American revolutionary Thomas Jefferson. He hoped that the United States would support his movement, but the growing tensions between the United States and the U.S.S.R. worked against him.

The French-Indochina War lasted a gruesome nine years before the defeat at Dien Bien Phu forced France to admit it could not keep hold of its Asian possessions. A conference in Geneva in 1954 created four zones out of the former French Indochina: North and South Vietnam, Laos, and Cambodia.

After the French departure, Vietnam became a cold war sideshow: The United States gave aid to the south, while Beijing and Moscow supported the communists in the north. This evolved into a large-scale American war after 1965, as the United States tried to protect South Vietnam from communist encroachment. The costly effort failed, ending in a negotiated peace and communist victory in 1975.

REVOLUTIONS

RUSSIA

By 1914, Russia was far behind Western Europe economically and technologically. It lacked the capital to sufficiently build its own industry; was in debt to foreign investors; and was agriculturally unproductive. Losses in the Russo-Japanese War pointed out Russia's technological backwardness. After the Revolution of 1905, the czar conceded and allowed a legislative body (the **Duma**) to be assembled, but it was often dismissed if not in agreement with the czar. During World War I, Russian casualties numbered over two million, and that led to more tension throughout the country. Among other things, worker strikes began.

The disorder and chaos during **March of 1917** allowed the Duma to force the czar to abdicate the throne and put the provisional government in power. The government decided to stay in the war, and the food shortages, revolts, and continued strikes led to more disorder. **Vladimir Lenin**, the leader of the Bolsheviks, promised the people **"Peace, Land, Bread"**—exactly what they wanted and needed.

In November of 1917, Lenin's party seized power; in March of 1918, it signed the Treaty of Brest-Litovok with Germany, ending Russia's part in the war. For the next few years, a civil war raged throughout Russia between the Reds (communists) and the Whites (loyalists).

The **Bolshevik government** took control of the land, banks, and industries and used the Cheka, the secret police, to keep an eye on its people. However, the aftermath of World War I and civil war had caused famine throughout the Soviet Union, and so Lenin decided to take a more moderate course of action.

The **New Economic Policy** (NEP) instituted in 1921 allowed peasants to sell their products, but the government still controlled banking, trade, and heavy industry. Lenin died in 1924, and after a power struggle, **Joseph Stalin** came to power. Stalin instituted his **Five-Year Plans** with the goals of increasing industrial and agricultural productivity. Individual farms became collectivized (those who refused collectivization were killed, numbering over 14.5 million), and agricultural productivity declined, leading to great hardship. Industrial productivity increased a few years later, however, when Western Europe and the United States were hurting from the Great Depression. The Russian people experienced tremendous oppression during Stalin's **Great Purges** of the 1930s. Thousands were tried and executed and millions were imprisoned.

CHINA

China was on the winning side of both world wars, but few nations suffered more from World War II. Technically, the Nationalist (Guomindang) government had been ruling China since the **Revolution of 1911**, but in reality, the country was fragmented into a series of warlord-dominated zones. **Sun Yixian** (Sun Yat-sen), the father of modern China, died in 1924 and a young army officer named **Jiang Jieshi** (Chiang Kai Shek) inherited leadership of the struggling Republic of China.

After 1921, a new dynamic in the nation was exhibited by the stirrings of a **Chinese Communist Party** (CCP). Jiang tried to work with the communists until he turned on them in 1927, driving them underground. The CCP leadership and membership was harassed and hunted down throughout the 1930s until they retreated to the north and reorganized. The Japanese attacks in 1931 and 1937 rallied all of China to the defense of the nation. When Japan invaded, Chinese nationalists and communists alike tried to cooperate in their fight against the Japanese, but there was little trust.

After Japan surrendered in 1945, the United States tried to encourage a coalition government, but negotiations broke down and civil war resumed. For three years, the Chinese Communist Party (CCP) and the Nationalist Guomindang (GMD) fought each other. The communists prevailed in 1949, and their leader **Mao Zedong** proclaimed the birth of the People's Republic of China (PRC) from Beijing as the nationalists fled to Taiwan to regroup.

MAO'S INITIAL CHANGES TO CHINA

Economic	• All businesses were nationalized.
	• Land was distributed to peasants.
	• Peasants were urged to pool their land and work more efficiently on cooperative farms.
Political	• A one-party totalitarian state was established.
	• Communist party became supreme.
	• Government attacked crime and corruption.
Social	• Peasants were encouraged to "speak bitterness" against landlords (10,000 landlords were killed as a result).
	• Communist ideology replaced Confucian beliefs.
	• Schools were opened with emphasis on political education.
	• Health care workers were sent to remote areas.
	• Women won equality (but little opportunity in government and were paid less than men).
	• The extended family was weakened.

In order to increase agricultural and industrial production, Mao came up with and instituted a personalized plan (as Stalin had done) in the late 1950s. In the **Great Leap Forward**, all life was to be collective—family houses were torn down, and commune life replaced family life. Backyard steel furnaces were set up, which used scrap metal to make iron and steel.

The Great Leap Forward proved to be a great failure. Initial production statistics had been grossly inflated, and the backyard furnaces did not turn out iron of acceptable quality. The bad weather of the 1950s and 1960s and declining food production led to the deaths of at least 16 million Chinese.

As a result, some modifications were made to moderate the system. Mao's second major initiative was the **Cultural Revolution** of the 1960s. In an effort to re-revolutionize China, a group of university students known as the Red Guards rampaged cities, ordered the destruction of temples, and closed schools. The military was eventually needed to suppress the anarchy created by the Red Guards. As a result of this attempt to rid China of "bourgeois" or non-revolutionary tendencies, the country lost an entire generation of educated people.

COMPARATIVE CLOSE-UP: THE ROLE OF WOMEN DURING THE RUSSIAN AND CHINESE REVOLUTIONS

Russia	China
• Women served in the Red Army.	• A new marriage law forbade arranged marriage (was met with resistance).
• 65% of factory workers were women.	• Women worked alongside men in factories.
• The government ordered equal pay (though it was not enforced).	• State-run nurseries were set up to care for children.
• Maternity leave with full pay was established.	• Party leadership remained male.
• Women entered professions.	• Efforts were made to end foot-binding.

MEXICO

In the late 19th and beginning of the 20th centuries, Mexico was ruled by the dictatorship of **Porfirio Díaz**. Under this rule, 95 percent of the people owned no land, and foreign investors owned 20–25 percent of the land.

Very little had changed after Mexico achieved its independence from Spain in 1821 and the **Mexican Revolution** began. In 1910, the people rose up against Díaz under the leadership of Francisco Madero. Many of the leaders, who were mestizos, wanted to break the control of the Creole elite. Leaders such as Pancho Villa and Emiliano Zapata advocated land reform. Power changed hands continually throughout the civil war, as leaders were assassinated or overthrown. Eventually, conservative forces won out and Venustiano Carranza became president in 1916. He convened an assembly to write the **Constitution of 1917**.

The Constitution promised land reform, imposed restrictions on foreign economic control, set minimum salaries and maximum hours for workers, granted workers the right to unionize and strike, and placed restrictions on Church-ownership of property and control over education. In 1929, the National Revolutionary Party (later named the **Party of Institutionalized Revolution (PRI)**) was established in response to the political unrest that followed the assassination of president-elect Álvaro Obregón a year earlier. The PRI dominated politics for the remainder of the century, instituting land redistribution and standing up to foreign companies.

IRAN

The **Shah Reza**, who ruled Iran from 1953 to 1979, was heavily influenced by the West and pushed to modernize and westernize his country. He was oppressive, using secret police to monitor his people. Opposition to the shah's rule came from three camps: **the religious ulama**, who felt that traditional religion was being suppressed; **students and intellectuals**, who felt deprived of freedom; and **farmers and urban workers**, who were hurt by inflation and unemployment.

In 1979, demonstrations led by the religious leader **Ayatollah Khomeini** forced the Shah into exile. Under Khomeini's rule, the sharia (Islamic law) became the law of the land. Women, for instance, were required to return to traditional Islamic clothing and were also placed under legal restrictions. Some women saw this return to tradition as a stand against Western culture and imperialism.

CUBA

From 1939 to 1959, Cuba was ruled by the dictatorship of **Batista**, under which a small percentage of people were very wealthy and the masses of peasants were quite poor. **Fidel Castro** organized a guerrilla movement which initially failed, but eventually captured power in 1959. Though he had promised to hold elections, Castro did not do so, and at first, even denied that he was a communist. When he established close ties with the U.S.S.R., the United States viewed him as a threat.

In 1961, Castro announced his communist plans for Cuba: collectivized farms, centralized control of the economy, and free education and medical services. Tensions with the United States continued when a group of Cuban exiles in 1961, supported by the United States, attempted a failed invasion, known as the **Bay of Pigs**.

In 1962, a standoff known as the **Cuban Missile Crisis** occurred when Soviet missiles were discovered in Cuba. The United States and the Soviet Union compromised, and a third world war was avoided.

POLITICAL REFORM AND ECONOMIC CHANGES

Toward the second half of the 20th century, many countries experienced economic and political changes. These changes would set them on their future courses.

CHINA

After Mao died in 1976, **Deng Xiaoping** came to power and instituted a new program of economic modernization. The **Four Modernizations** included the following: industry, agriculture, technology, and national defense. Foreign investment was encouraged, and thousands of students were sent abroad to study.

As a result of these capitalist reforms, the economy boomed. Deng, however, was criticized for leaving out any democratic reforms. Criticism of the past was acceptable, as long as it didn't directly involve criticism of Marxist ideology. In May of 1989, massive student demonstrations occurred in **Tiananmen Square**. Students called for democratic reforms, but instead were met with troops and tanks sent to crush the rebellion. The Chinese government reinforced the ideas that party leadership and political stability were the keys to China's success.

INDIA

After independence from the British was achieved, India adopted under the leadership of Nehru a parliamentary political system based on that of Britain. The state took ownership of major industries, resources, transportation, and utilities, but local and retail businesses and farmland remained private.

Unlike Gandhi, Nehru advocated industrialization. India's foreign policy was one of **non-alignment** during the polarized Cold War. Tension continued with Muslim Pakistan when war broke out over the disputed land of **Kashmir**. Nehru's daughter, **Indira Gandhi**, later became prime minister and was extremely concerned about the growing population problem. As a result, she adopted a policy of forced sterilization that was extremely unpopular. Also, militant Sikhs in the Punjab demanded autonomy, and Gandhi ordered the rebels attacked. She was later assassinated by her Sikh bodyguard in 1984.

SOVIET UNION/RUSSIA

After the death of Stalin, **Khrushchev** came to power in 1953 and initiated a de-Stalinization movement that criticized Stalin's faults and encouraged more freedom of expression. From 1964 to 1982, **Brezhnev** maintained power and retreated from de-Stalinization. He instead took a restrictive policy toward dissidents and free expression. During this period, industrial growth declined; the primary problem was the absence of economic incentives and a system of production quotas.

When **Gorbachev** came to power in 1985, he introduced his policy of **perestroika** (restructuring), which marked the beginning of a market economy with limited free enterprise and some private property. His policy of **glasnost** (openness) encouraged a discussion of the strengths and weaknesses of the Soviet system. The formation of other parties and two-candidate elections were also introduced.

The Soviet Union, however, had major problems with its multiethnic population, and tensions rose along with the development of nationalist movements. The republics soon opted for independence, and the U.S.S.R. came to an end, as did the Cold War.

In December of 1991, Gorbachev resigned and Boris Yeltsin came to power. As the new ruler of Russia, Yeltsin pushed for economic reform, fighting economic inequality and corruption. Russia continues to struggle with major problems of corruption and an unstable economy. Perhaps the changes were too great and too fast.

EASTERN EUROPE

The Soviet Union dominated their satellite states in Eastern Europe following World War II, installing communist leaders and closely monitoring their progress. However, the economic hardships and lack of political liberties led to growing discontent.

In 1956, a student-led protest in Hungary expressed this discontent, but the powerful Soviet army was sent in to crush the movement. In the late 1960s in Czechoslovakia, a movement (known as the **Prague Spring**) began in the hopes of creating a form of socialism with more freedom of speech and economic freedom. This movement was short-lived, however, after Soviet troops invaded with the intention of crushing it.

Throughout the communist-controlled period, Eastern European nations did experience a rise in education and an increase in the urban working class. The former "privileged class" was removed and replaced by a new privileged class—members of the Communist Party.

As the U.S.S.R. was declining in the 1980s, liberation movements spread throughout the area. An independent labor movement, *Solidarity*, led by **Lech Walesa** fought for change in Poland. Czechoslovakia split into the Czech Republic and Slovakia in 1994. In East Germany, mass demonstrations in the summer and fall of 1989 led to the opening of the border with West Germany, the tearing down of the **Berlin Wall**, and the eventual reunification of Germany.

Now that Soviet domination was removed, Eastern European countries moved to join **NATO** (North Atlantic Treaty Organization) and the **EU** (European Union). Beginning in 1990, ethnic conflict developed in Yugoslavia, and under the Serbian leadership of Slobodan Milosevic, a policy of "ethnic cleansing" via genocide, in Bosnia and Kosovo was instituted. In 2000, Milosevic was ousted from power and was tried for war crimes at the **International War Crimes Tribunal**. Milosevic died in 2006.

JAPAN

For the five years following World War II, Japan was governed by an Allied administration that instituted a constitution, land reforms, and an education system. The goal was to make Japan **economically strong** so it could serve as a defense against communism in East Asia. The Japanese and United States formed a defensive alliance that allowed Japan to spend almost no money on its own defense—less than 1 percent of its gross domestic product.

Without having to pay for its own defense, Japan was able to focus on its economy. It soon experienced tremendous growth through the development of an **export economy**, with a large focus on technology. In recent years, however, Japan has suffered economic difficulties, with long-lasting economic stagnation that began in the 1990s and still continues today. Culturally, it has become a more individualistic society, but it retains an emphasis on the importance of a strong work ethic.

DEMOGRAPHIC AND ENVIRONMENTAL ISSUES

The human population of the world has grown tremendously in the past century and a half, topping over six billion people just before the 21st century. Improved life expectancy rates through the use of vaccines, sophisticated sewage systems, new medicines, and education contributed to this rise. Technological advances in agriculture, such as chemical fertilizers and high-producing seeds, transformed farming in much of the world. This Green Revolution produced more food for the growing population of the world. Birth rates in the industrialized West, where the nuclear family is the norm, dropped significantly, while birth rates in Asia and Africa increased dramatically through much of the 20th century. China and India both have populations over a billion, despite the one-child policy in China and birth control programs in India.

Although medical advances (such as antibiotics, vaccines, and new surgical techniques) increased the life span of people in wealthier countries, diseases associated with poverty (such as malaria, tuberculosis, and cholera) persisted. New epidemic diseases also flourished in the increasingly interconnected 20th-century world, such as the influenza pandemic of 1918 and AIDS. In addition, longer lives and changing lifestyles led to increases in diseases such as diabetes, heart disease, and certain kinds of cancer.

Though migration has been a theme throughout world history, it has increased throughout the past century both internally (when people move from rural to urban areas or when they flee urban areas due to civil strife) and externally (when people migrate long distances and across borders, often in search of better economic conditions). Push-pull factors include a lack of resources, job opportunities, political, religious, and ethnic persecution, as well as population pressures. One result has been rapid urbanization in many parts of the world, which brings a whole new set of challenges: slums, unemployment, and underemployment for some recent migrants.

Often, external migrations followed the connections created by previous imperialism. Communities of Algerians and Vietnamese, for example, have settled in Paris. Pakistanis and Jamaicans have settled in London. The increased interactions among different groups of people have resulted in new cultural identities as well as exclusionary reactions, such as anti-immigration movements.

This huge population growth, combined with industrialization, contributed to significant environmental problems that include the overuse of natural resources and a loss of animal species. Many oceanic fish species are significantly depleted to the point where governments have to prohibit commercial fishing. Unique flora and fauna species disappear with the destruction of tropical forests for slash-and-burn agriculture and timber operations. Smog pollutes many city areas, which can cause lung diseases and result in death. Water pollution denies the use of fresh water for many, particularly in third world nations. The damming of rivers often interrupts aquatic species' life cycles, and in some cases so much water is drained off of rivers and lakes for irrigation projects that they fail to reach their natural delta. Deforestation is as much a problem now as it has ever been in the past. The increased use of petroleum and heavy metals like mercury contribute to the pollution of land, air, and sea alike. The increased human population has also led to dramatic increases in the amount of trash produced by industrialized societies. Non-degradable and often toxic trash byproducts of modern societies end up in landfills or are transported to third world countries to be salvaged, but still leave mountains of trash.

Many scientists have theorized that global warming may be a consequence of the use of fossil fuels and the release of other pollutants.

However, this past century has also seen an increase in positive attitudes toward our environment. Environmentalism, a movement to protect and wisely use our natural resources, spawned in the late 19th century, is stronger than ever. Organizations like Greenpeace, the Sierra Club, and the World Wildlife Fund work to protect the environment through both direct action and in lobbying governments. Most national governments now have agencies designed to monitor industrial use of resources and their waste products. The use of local, regional, and national parks and wildlife refuges tries to keep natural areas intact for the enjoyment of future generations. International organizations track pollution and overuse of resources and provide aid to governments and communities. One of the biggest challenges facing the near future is that many nations who want to raise their standards of living through industrialization want to do so rapidly and end up having the same environmental issues that the Western countries like England and the United States did in the 19th and 20th centuries, as well as contributing to global environmental issues such as global warming.

TECHNOLOGICAL AND SCIENTIFIC ADVANCES

During the 20th century, new methods of communication (such as radio, television, and the Internet) and transportation (automobiles and airplanes) eliminated the problems associated with geographic distance. Major advances in energy technology such as the use of oil and nuclear power, increased industrial productivity, but came with considerable environmental costs. New scientific theories such as Einstein's **theory of relativity**, led to significant advances in human understanding.

SOCIETAL CHANGES

CHANGING GENDER ROLES

In 1914, there were few opportunities for women in most professions. The 19th century had seen a few pioneering women become doctors, but most females were relegated to child-rearing, nursing, or teaching. The fight for female suffrage in the West saw its first successes in New Zealand, Australia, and Finland. Militant activists in Great Britain and the United States won the right to vote after 1920. Fashion and popular culture helped create a new image of the modern woman—free from some of the constraints of traditional gender roles.

Social and economic parity was a much longer fight. Both world wars gave women more and more power in terms of wage-earning, but the demands of the workplace and the home continued to be a challenge for the modern woman. The postwar **feminist movement** publicized the issues of child care and equal pay for equal work in the 1970s. Politics, law, and medicine have become more open to women in the last half of the 20th century. Successful female heads of government in Israel, Great Britain, and the Philippines demonstrated that politics was no longer an all-male domain.

The sexual revolution of the sixties and seventies further defined male and female roles. Key issues such as access to **birth control** were advanced, giving women more control over their own lives. Greater earning power in the workplace also meant more independence. The institution of marriage was challenged, and some women opted to remain unattached or even to have children by themselves. Given the magnitude of these recent social changes, the impacts are still being felt and processed.

In parts of the developing world, changes to gender roles have varied. Some socialist and communist societies instituted important legal reforms for women, such as the 1950 marriage law in China which granted free choice of partners. In reality, many traditional beliefs still exist in China and other areas. The large population problem in China led to the establishment of the **one-child policy**, and as a result some 250 million births have been prevented, saving China from a population increase it would have had trouble accommodating. Despite having had powerful female heads of state, such as Indira Gandhi in India and Benazir Bhuto in Pakistan, **literacy rates** for women in South Asia are still far below those of men. In the 1980s, only 25 percent of the female population of India was literate.

New Forms of Spirituality

In the late 20th century, new forms of spirituality developed, while other believers emphasized particular ideas within existing religions and applied them to modern-day problems. The new form of spirituality commonly referred to as **New Age religions** draw inspiration from both Eastern and Western traditions and combine them with influences from self-help psychology. **Liberation theology** developed within the Catholic Church in the 1950s and 1960s as a response to poverty in Latin America. It interprets the teachings of Jesus Christ as being a vehicle for liberation from unjust conditions.

Globalization

Regional and International Organizations

The late 20th century brought about new patterns of economic and political organization that transcended national borders. **OPEC**, the Organization of Petroleum Exporting Countries, organized in 1960 in an effort to raise the price of oil through cooperation. The World Trade

Organization (**WTO**) formed from the General Agreement of Tariffs and Trade (**GATT**) in 1995 to promote unrestricted global trade.

Regional organizations have also formed to protect more local interests. **ASEAN**, the Association of Southeast Asian Nations, formed in 1967 to accelerate economic progress and promote political stability. The **EU**, European Union, formed from the European Community in 1993, in an effort to strengthen European economic trade relations and distance itself from the influence of the United States. **NAFTA**, North American Free Trade Agreement, involves the United States, Canada, and Mexico, working to remove trade barriers between these countries. Finally, nongovernmental organizations (**NGOs**) such as the Red Cross and Greenpeace work to tackle problems that reach beyond national boundaries and governments.

Human rights values have also attracted more attention from international organizations. In 1948, the newly formed United Nations issued a **Universal Declaration of Human Rights**. The rights of women have also received greater attention from the UN and other international organizations. The Nobel Peace Prize has often been awarded to those who have struggled to expand human rights, such as Aung San Suu Kyi of Burma (1991) and Liu Xiaobo of China (2010).

The anti-globalization movement is critical of the spread of corporate capitalism and the expansion of free trade. Movement participants share an opposition to the power of large, multinational corporations, which was gained through free trade agreements. These corporations are seen as trying to maximize profit at the expense of safe working conditions, fair pay for workers, and the health of the environment.

INTERNATIONALIZATION OF CULTURE

As the world becomes more and more connected, cultural lines have become blurred. Some refer to this as **cultural imperialism**. As Western companies and entertainment (in particular movies and music) spread worldwide, Western cultural ideas spread along with them. American companies like McDonald's, Coca-Cola, and Kentucky Fried Chicken can be found in most parts of the world today. With the spread of these products and ideas, some believe a consumer culture has developed, focusing on materialism and the promotion of **cultural conformity**. Viewed in a more positive light, globalization has enabled cultural diffusion to take place. A good example of this phenomenon is **Bollywood** (Indian cinema), a form of entertainment whose popularity spread through global media.

The rise of the use of the English language is also an indication of a developing global culture. Transmitted through the Internet, movies, and music, the use of the English language has spread worldwide. Yet even with the prevalence of a Western-oriented consumer culture, traditional forces remain strong in many parts of the world. Islamic fundamentalism, for instance, is a traditional force that very much reacts against Western culture, and the two ideals often clash.

Sports have become more internationalized, with the Olympics and the World Cup Soccer competitions enjoying popularity in all regions of the world. Global influences in music and film, such as the international popularity of reggae and American-style action movies, are another sign of the globalization of the 21st century.

MEGA-TRENDS

Since World War II and throughout the Cold War, the world saw certain mega-trends.

GLOBAL MEGA-TRENDS

- Rapid population growth: (world population in 1945: 2,350,000,000; in 2000: 6,100,000,000)
- Globalization in the form of multinational businesses such as Phillips, Bechtel, Microsoft, Ford Motors, and Sony
- Access to information through electronic/satellite transfer by phone, fax, and email
- Nationalism and the proliferation of nation-states
- Religious fundamentalism in many different varieties
- The rise of export economies

REVIEW QUESTIONS

MULTIPLE-CHOICE QUESTIONS

Please note that these are content-specific review questions for this chapter, designed to help you perform well on the exam.

1. All of the following are long-term causes of World War I (1914–1918) EXCEPT

   (A) the rise of nationalism.

   (B) competition for colonies.

   (C) naval weapons buildup.

   (D) economic recession.

2. All of the following are characteristic of fascism EXCEPT

   (A) ultranationalistic propaganda.

   (B) expansion and glorification of the military.

   (C) emphasis on sacrifice for the nation-state.

   (D) collectivization of farms.

3. American President Woodrow Wilson's postwar aims in World War I were summed up in the

   (A) Potsdam Declaration.

   (B) Treaty of Versailles.

   (C) Treaty of Brest-Litovsk.

   (D) Fourteen Points.

4. The failure of the League of Nations to keep the peace was largely due to

   (A) the aggressive leadership of the United States.

   (B) the fear of communism after 1917.

   (C) the hedonism of the 1920s.

   (D) vacillating leadership and lack of multilateral military resolve.

5. Free-trade associations created after World War II included

   (A) OPEC and NATO.

   (B) the EU and NAFTA.

   (C) APEC and the Warsaw Pact.

   (D) G-7 and UNESCO.

6. One of the major causes of the Global Depression in 1930 was

   (A) trade tensions that resulted in high protective tariffs.

   (B) the continued strength of the stock market.

   (C) underproduction of agricultural goods.

   (D) the rise of totalitarian regimes in Europe.

7. The purpose of the United Nations is to ensure world peace based on

   (A) the European alliance.

   (B) collective security.

   (C) political ideology.

   (D) military alliances.

8. Nations most affected by the Great Depression were those that

   (A) lowered their taxes.

   (B) were dependent on global trade.

   (C) had centralized banking systems.

   (D) had the smallest territory.

9. India was partitioned as it gained independence in 1947 because

    (A) the British could not agree on the political boundaries.

    (B) Muslims had their own desire for a state on the subcontinent.

    (C) Gandhi supported the idea.

    (D) Jinnah was assassinated shortly afterward.

10. The function of the World Trade Organization (WTO) is to

    (A) encourage protectionism.

    (B) buy and sell commodities.

    (C) oversee and manage world trade.

    (D) report to the United Nations about labor issues worldwide.

11. Internal migration is defined as the

    (A) importation of cheaper labor by industrialized nations.

    (B) creation of shanty towns in rural areas.

    (C) movement of people from rural to urban areas.

    (D) flight of refugees for political reasons.

12. Nations in the Balkans and Africa have both suffered because

    (A) nationalism did not take root.

    (B) political boundaries were drawn without regard for ethnic or tribal groups.

    (C) of pan-Slavic and pan-African solidarity.

    (D) of the indifference of the United Nations.

13. Black South Africans struggled against white minority rule prior to 1990 by supporting the

    (A) UN efforts to raise living standards.

    (B) African National Congress (ANC).

    (C) local township councils.

    (D) movement to desegregate the universities.

14. The main reason the United States increased its military support for South Vietnam in the 1960s was because

    (A) the U.S.S.R. was threatening Berlin.

    (B) the French told it to do so.

    (C) it had been an ally during World War II.

    (D) communism seemed to be expanding in the region.

15. Following the Revolution of 1979, Iran became

    (A) closely allied with the United States.

    (B) an Islamic theocracy.

    (C) ruled by the Sunni majority.

    (D) increasingly supportive of women's rights.

16. Mao Zedong departed from orthodox Marxism by gathering support from

    (A) urban workers.

    (B) the merchant class.

    (C) rural peasants.

    (D) the military class.

17. Indian nationalists hoped to achieve which of the following goals as a result of helping Great Britain during World War I?

    (A) Territorial expansion

    (B) British citizenship

    (C) Expansion of industrialization

    (D) Greater self-government

18. The major goal of the Zionist movement was to

    (A) rebuild a homeland for Jews in Palestine.

    (B) expel the British from India.

    (C) seek revenge on the German people.

    (D) be recognized by the United States.

19. Which of the following did Lenin and the Bolsheviks emphasize the LEAST during the Russian Revolution of 1917?

    (A) Withdrawal from World War I
    (B) Redistribution of land
    (C) Abolition of religion
    (D) Redistribution of wealth

20. All of the following were policies of communist China EXCEPT

    (A) to weaken family ties.
    (B) to discourage Confucian traditions.
    (C) to purge counterrevolutionaries.
    (A) to encourage workers to strike.

21. Which of the following is true of both the Mexican and Iranian Revolutions?

    (A) They were driven by a desire for a return to religious traditions.
    (B) Civil war between opposing groups resulted.
    (C) Foreign control and influence were lessened.
    (D) A democratic constitution was written.

22. Biodiversity and global warming are both important examples of

    (A) persecution of indigenous people.
    (B) improved weaponry.
    (C) military dictatorships.
    (D) environmental problems.

23. The independence movements in both India and Africa were led by the

    (A) peasants.
    (B) educated elite.
    (C) communists.
    (D) military.

24. All of the following are actions Castro took following the Cuban Revolution EXCEPT

    (A) collectivizing farms.
    (B) centralizing control of the economy.
    (C) seeking alliances with the Soviet Union.
    (D) instituting a nationwide election.

25. Which of the following conclusions is best supported by the graph below?

World Population Growth, 1750–2150

Source: United Nations, World Population Prospects, The 1998 Revision; and estimates by the Population Reference Bureau

(A) More-developed countries have had difficulty controlling their populations.

(B) Less-developed countries have become more politically influential due to population growth.

(C) World population will more than double between 1970 and 2150.

(D) Population growth in less-developed countries is caused by economic prosperity.

DOCUMENT-BASED QUESTION

This DBQ is a practice activity. The actual question on the exam may be longer.

Directions: The following question is based on the accompanying Documents 1 to 4. (Some of the documents have been edited for the purpose of this exercise.)

This question is designed to test your ability to work with and understand historical documents. Write an essay that:

- Has a relevant thesis and supports that thesis with evidence from the documents.

- Uses all or all but one of the documents.

- Analyzes the documents by grouping them in as many appropriate ways as possible.

- Does not simply summarize the documents individually.

- Takes into account the sources of the documents and analyzes the authors' points of view.

- Explains the need for at least one additional type of document.

You may refer to relevant historical information not mentioned in the documents.

Based on the following documents, analyze the effect of women's issues on population growth in developing nations. Identify an additional type of document and explain how it would help your analysis of the effects of women's issues on population growth in developing countries.

Historical Background: In the wake of the close of the Cold War and the rise of globalism, the fortunes of women and previously neglected populations gain marked new attention. Those countries and regions experiencing educational and self-sustaining initiatives see a corresponding rise in opportunities for women in the workplace, education, and entrepreneurship. Those areas, also, that experience an increase in economic stimulation and prosperity also see a drop in birthrate, as families require fewer children to maintain an industrial/technological economic base versus a solely agricultural one.

DOCUMENT 1

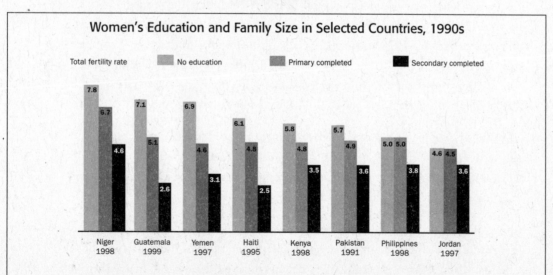

Women's Education and Family Size in Selected Countries, 1990s

Total fertility rate | No education | Primary completed | Secondary completed

Country	No education	Primary completed	Secondary completed
Niger 1998	7.8	6.7	4.6
Guatemala 1999	7.1	5.1	2.6
Yemen 1997	6.9	4.6	3.1
Haiti 1995	6.1	4.8	2.5
Kenya 1998	5.8	4.8	3.5
Pakistan 1991	5.7	4.9	3.6
Philippines 1998	5.0	5.0	3.8
Jordan 1997	4.6	4.5	3.6

Source: Population Reference Bureau, a nonprofit agency based in Washington, DC, that reports data collected by demographic and health surveys.

DOCUMENT 2

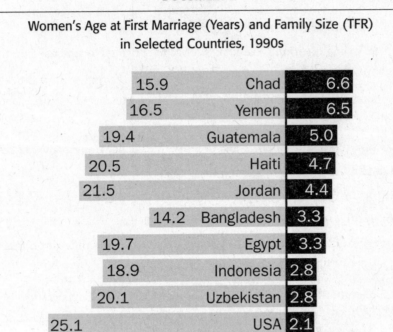

Women's Age at First Marriage (Years) and Family Size (TFR) in Selected Countries, 1990s

Average age as first marriage	Country	Total fertility rat
15.9	Chad	6.6
16.5	Yemen	6.5
19.4	Guatemala	5.0
20.5	Haiti	4.7
21.5	Jordan	4.4
14.2	Bangladesh	3.3
19.7	Egypt	3.3
18.9	Indonesia	2.8
20.1	Uzbekistan	2.8
25.1	USA	2.1

Source: Population Reference Bureau, based on reports from the World Population Data Sheet.

DOCUMENT 3

Source: Population Reference Bureau, article "An Example from India," which accompanied educational materials on women and population policy.

Kerala is primarily rural and agricultural, as is most of India. The residents have low incomes. Yet in the early 1990s, women in Kerala were bearing about two children, on average. Between 1970 and 1992, Kerala's TFR dropped from 4.1 to 2 children per woman, the largest decline of any Indian state. By the end of the 1990s, the total fertility rate was down to about 1.8 children per woman. The infant mortality rate is also low, 14 deaths of infants under age 1 per 1,000 live births in a given year.

Why are the women in Kerala different? One obvious difference is their higher educational level. While most Indian women cannot read and write, 85 percent of women in Kerala are literate. The state government has assigned a high priority to ensuring that all residents have access to education.

In traditional Keralese culture, women can inherit land and wield some political power—a sharp contrast with other parts of India. And, while in most of India girls are considered a drain on family finances because their parents must pay a dowry to marry them off, Keralese women bring their families a brideprice. In Kerala, girls are considered an asset.

DOCUMENT 4

Demographic and Socioeconomic Indicators in India and the United States, Late 1990s

	United States	India	Kerala
Total fertility rate	2.1	3.2	1.8
Infant mortality rate	7	68	14
Life expectancy (male)	74	60	71
Female literacy	99	57	85
Contraceptive relevance (all methods)	76	48.2	63.7

Sources: Population Reference Bureau, based on reports from the Registrar General of India and the International Institute for Population Science.

CONTINUITY AND CHANGE-OVER-TIME QUESTION

Directions: You are to answer the following question. You should spend five minutes organizing or outlining your essay. Write an essay that:

- Has a relevant thesis and supports that thesis with appropriate historical evidence.

- Addresses all parts of the question.

- Uses world historical context to show continuities and changes over time.

- Analyzes the process of continuity change over time.

Prompt: Analyze the continuities and changes in gender roles from 1900 to the present in ONE of the following regions.

- Latin America

- Russia

- South Asia

- China

COMPARATIVE QUESTION

Directions: You are to answer the following question. You should spend five minutes organizing or outlining your essay. Write an essay that:

- Has a relevant thesis and supports that thesis with appropriate historical evidence.

- Addresses all parts of the question.

- Makes direct, relevant comparisons.

- Analyzes relevant reasons for similarities and differences.

Prompt: Analyze the similarities and differences between World War I and World War II, using ONE of the following points of comparison.

- Causes of conflict

- Effects on civilians

- Effects on colonial areas

- The global effects of the war

ANSWERS AND EXPLANATIONS

MULTIPLE-CHOICE ANSWERS

1.   D

Recession was not a factor in the tensions leading up to the Great War. Competition for empires and national rivalries between Germany and Britain were more important factors: The rise of nationalism had helped create a unified Germany after 1870. As a rising power, Germany wanted to rival Great Britain, and its aggressive military buildup threatened the existing balance of power in Europe. Imperialistic rivalries also created tension between Britain and France.

2.   D

Collectivization of farms was not of interest to fascists. Big business leaders tend to support fascist regimes because fascism promises to protect them from communism, and it also deals with labor organizations. Fascist regimes return the favor with strict controls on workers and other benefits for business owners. One facet of the business-regime relationship is the prohibition of all labor unions. This, in addition to military contracts, binds industry to the government. Fascist regimes exalt the nation above all else, and individual choice is discouraged. Young men are groomed for the military, and service to the state is the desired goal for all.

3.   D

Within one year of entering the Great War, the United States promoted a list of war aims called the Fourteen Points. It was an idealistic postwar view that envisioned diplomacy replacing military might. Few of the points were realized, but many were used again after World War II to establish a more lasting postwar peace. The Potsdam Declaration was made late in World War II by the Allies. The Treaty of Brest-Litovsk was made between Germany and Russia, after the Russian Revolution.

4.   D

Without the membership of either the United States or Russia, the League of Nations was without strong leadership. The United States did not ratify the Treaty of Versailles, nor did it join the League of Nations. It was left to Britain and France to provide leadership to the League in Geneva, but they often could not agree on common issues. The establishment of the U.S.S.R. as a communist regime after 1917 was a big change, but even the Soviets joined the League after a time and tried to fit into the constellation of European powers.

5.   B

The European Union and the North American Free Trade Agreement were created to assist in the free trade of goods between nations. These trading blocs sought to stimulate business and to lead to consumer benefits, such as lower prices. NATO is not a trade association but rather a military alliance formed in 1949 to thwart communist expansion in Western Europe. APEC is a loose association of the countries in the Asia Pacific region; it hosts economic conferences every year. The G-7 was formed recently to allow major economic powers to share information on global problems.

6.   A

Trade competition between nations led to a decline in international business in the late 1920s. Many nations such as the United States established trade limits and barriers in the form of tariffs to protect domestic manufacturers. It was the overproduction of agricultural goods that hurt farmers in the 1920s. The farming industry was in economic distress years before the equity market collapsed in New York. The rise of dictators in Europe took place both before and after the onset of the Global Depression. Certainly in Germany, the National Socialists (Nazis) were able to use the economic hard times to their advantage and gain support from the middle and lower classes.

7. B

One of the principles of developing both the League of Nations (after World War I) and the UN (after World War II) was the idea that peace-loving nations need to band together in times of crisis. This failed in the 1930s, and the peace collapsed. In 1950 and 1990, the UN applied collective security to the respective crises in Korea and Kuwait. The UN mandate to keep the peace is global and not limited to the situation in Europe. Political debate does take place in the General Assembly, but no one political ideology is supposed to dominate. In 1950 and 1990, the UN had to gather troops to counter aggression in Korea and Iraq.

8. B

Industrial nations were hardest hit by the global Depression of the 1930s. Britain and the United States were particularly hard hit, along with Japan and Germany. Taxation was not a central cause of the Depression in the 1930s. Government revenues did plummet after the Depression struck, though, as the tax base shrank. Private banks, not governmental financial institutions, were the most vulnerable to failure during the Depression if they were over-invested in the collapsing equity markets.

9. B

During the British years of control over the Indian subcontinent, there were many different domains. When Gandhi urged the British to quit India and give it home rule, he envisioned a large secular democracy. Muslims finally broke with him and demanded a separate Islamic nation. The partition of British India created an independent India and a divided Pakistan in the east and west. Britain had tried vainly to avoid partition, but finally announced it would leave India at a pre-announced time. This was a de facto recognition that British India would not remain in one piece politically. Gandhi campaigned tirelessly against partition and went on public fasts to protest against the need for a separate Muslim state. It was he, and not Jinnah (leader of the Muslim separatist movement), who was assassinated shortly after independence.

10. C

The WTO is an adjunct part of the UN system and tries to oversee global trade. It has come under attack as a proponent of globalization, which some see as threatening jobs and displacing workers. The WTO is part of the public sector and it does engage in buying and selling. The International Labor Organization (ILO) reports to the UN on labor issues. The WTO is a proponent of free trade and works against protectionist sentiments around the world.

11. C

The last two centuries have seen great movement of people from rural farmland to urban areas, where there are more jobs. This internal migration is one of the great trends in world history since the Industrial Revolution. Migrant workers who come from other countries would be an example of external migration. Shanty towns are a form of temporary, crude housing, usually associated with urban areas. Refugees fleeing to other countries would not be an internal phenomena. Internal migration describes the physical movement of groups of people from one location to another.

12. B

Within the context of imperialism, empires have included many different ethnic groups and tribes. Taking ethnicity and tribalism into account has bedeviled politicians, as the world map has been redrawn many times through history. Africa was poorly segmented by the Europeans in the 1880s, and the Hapsburgs held many minorities within its empire until 1919. Nationalism did cause considerable problems in the Balkans as ethnic groups fought to establish their own countries, such as Croatia and Slovenia. Pan-Slavic solidarity did not stand the test of time as subgroups caused the disintegration of Yugoslavia after 1990. Ethnic and tribal tensions in Africa and the Balkans predate the founding of the UN and cannot be blamed on that international body.

13. B

The fight for the rights of black Africans in South Africa was led by the African National Congress, or ANC. Its leaders were imprisoned and tortured during the white minority control of the government until 1992. Efforts by the outside world were largely thwarted by the white minority regime in South Africa until the end of apartheid. Blacks and their townships had no political power in white South Africa. Desegregation of the universities was not a major goal of blacks during apartheid.

14. D

The Domino Theory was the fear that communism would continue to expand in Asia if its growth could not be halted. After the revolution in China in 1949 and the partition of Vietnam in 1954, communism seemed to threaten all of Southeast Asia. When the French left in the 1950s, the United States took more of an active role in trying to control the region. Cold War tensions in Berlin were not directly connected to the situation in Southeast Asia. After losing Indochina in 1954, France was in no position to tell the United States what to do in Southeast Asia. The French Indochina War (from 1946) was funded largely by the United States. South Vietnam had not been a country during World War II. It was created in the multilateral settlement in 1954 at Geneva.

15. B

The overthrow of the Shah in Iran was led by Shiite clerics, some of whom had been in exile. After the revolution, the mullahs took control and instituted Islamic rule within the nation. Iran is mostly Shiite, and women's rights were not championed in the 1979 revolution. The 1979 Iranian revolution was largely anti-American and resulted in the taking of the U.S. embassy by a local mob.

16. C

Orthodox Marxist thought predicted that urban workers would revolt against their capitalistic masters, and the world socialist revolution would begin in the cities. Mao Zedong adapted Marxist thought to the plight of the peasants in the countryside, and they were the vehicles by which Marxism was successful in overthrowing the Nationalists in 1949. The merchant class tended to support the Nationalists during the post–World War II revolution in China. The cadre of professional soldiers in China at this time was too small to constitute a class.

17. D

Through organizations such as the Indian National Congress, Indian nationalists had been fighting for greater self-government and believed from the British that their participation in the war would lead to that. India did not, however, achieve its independence until after World War II (in 1947).

18. A

The Zionist movement was created in the 19th century with the goal of creating a homeland for Jews in Palestine. This movement was furthered by the Balfour Declaration issued in 1917, giving British support to the Jewish homeland. This allowed for increased Jewish migration after the Holocaust and to the eventual UN recognition of the state of Israel in 1948.

19. C

Lenin's famous slogan "Peace, Land, Bread" laid out his vision for Russia. Peace meant the desire to end Russia's involvement in World War I. Land meant a more equitable distribution of land to the peasant and working classes. Bread meant an end to the starvation and economic hardships of the Russian people. Though Lenin and the Bolsheviks later took power away from the Russian Orthodox Church, this was not something they emphasized to win the support of the Russian people.

20. D

After the communist victory in 1949, Mao's goals were to create an egalitarian society based on the power of the peasants. He did so by tying people to the state rather than to their families; by pointing out the backwardness of Confucian thought; by collectivizing agriculture; and by ridding society of the "bad" elements, such as those considered to be counterrevolutionary. Through all these changes, it was important to maintain order, and therefore, the communist party would not encourage any worker strikes.

21. C

In Mexico, foreign companies owned much of the land and were reaping much of the profit. After the revolution, the new government made a strong effort to lessen foreign control of the economy. In Iran, the shah's government was seen as controlled by the West; after the revolution, an Islamic theocracy ruled, attempting to eliminate Western influence from the country.

22. D

Biodiversity has become threatened in the recent past because of the destruction of natural habits for many species and the depletion of natural resources. The Earth's temperature has been rising as well (called global warming). These are major environmental problems facing the world today.

23. B

In both India and Africa, leaders emerged who had been educated in Europe and the United States.

They used their experience and knowledge to return home and fight for the freedom of their own people. In India, Gandhi was a British-educated lawyer, and Kwame Nkrumah received his education in the United States.

24. D

Although Castro had promised elections prior to the revolution, this was never carried out. To this day, Castro himself maintains power. True to a communist philosophy, however, he did collectivize farms and centralize control of the economy. His alliance with the Soviet Union caused much tension and conflict with the United States.

25. C

According to the chart, world population in 1970 was approximately 5 billion people. By 2150, it will exceed 10 billion. More-developed countries had leveled off their population growths. It is unclear from the chart how much political influence less-developed countries will have due to population growth. Population growth is not necessarily caused by economic prosperity, since the less-developed nations have the greatest amount of growth.

DOCUMENT-BASED QUESTION: SAMPLE RESPONSE

The developing countries around the world are experiencing the largest population growth even though they may seem the least equipped to deal with such a large population. According to the documents presented, there is a direct correlation between the education and marriage age of females and the number of children they conceive. In countries where women are educated and valued as important members of the society, birthrates are lower and population growth is more under control.

When women are educated and marry older, they have fewer children. According to the graph of women's education and family size in selected countries in the 1990s, the more education a woman receives, the less likely she is to have a large family (Document 1). For example, women in Niger with no education have an average of 7.8 children, while women with a completed secondary education have only an average of 4.6 children. As women become more educated, they seem to be more aware of the strain a large family can be. The purpose of this graph it to promote education of women as a means of reducing family size in developing countries, and therefore only select countries have been included in the graph.

Likewise, according to the graph of women's age at first marriage, those women who wait longer to get married will have a smaller family (Document 2). In Chad, for example, the average age at first marriage for women is 15.9 and the total fertility rate is 6.6. On the other hand, in the United States, the average age at first marriage is 25.1 and the total fertility rate is 2.1. This indicates that older women may be more in control of the family-planning decisions or are simply older and therefore cannot have as many children as a woman who is married in her teens.

Finally, the example from the Indian state of Kerala attempts to point out that when a culture values women, it empowers them, and it is those empowered women who can control family size (Document 3). In Kerala, women bear only two children on average (Document 4). This low birthrate can be explained by the fact that 85 percent of the female population is literate, and the state government funds their education. Also, women can inherit land, have some political power, and are not considered a drain on their family financially because they bring their families a brideprice when they get married. The purpose of this document is to prove that when women are valued in society, they can effect change in that society. It would be helpful to have some testimonial evidence from women themselves to see if they see the link between education, marriage age, and the size of families. It would be important to examine the reasons women may still feel pressure to have large families in developing countries.

As the world population continues to increase, these documents suggest that the best way to deal with the problem of population growth is to empower women. When women can make some of their own choices, they will effect change. When women are educated, they will have fewer children, and population issues can be brought under control.

The essay earns 1 point for thesis and 2 points for using documents as evidence to support the argument of the essay. The essay addresses all four documents and demonstrates understanding of the meaning three of them (Documents 1, 2, and 3). The essay uses evidence from Document 4 as if it is an extension of Document 3, when in fact it presents a set of data from three different locations. Despite that, because the essay includes Document 4, the point for understanding is awarded. While there is no attempt at POV analysis, the additional document request is especially strong.

The essay has two sections. One addresses the effects of education and marriage age (Documents 1 and 2) and the second addresses the Indian state of Kerala (Documents 3 and 4). The first only works because the second paragraph of the essay has a topic sentence that addresses both documents in such a way as to show understanding of Document 2. Document two is not explicitly addressed until the third paragraph, separate from the discussion of document 1.

Final Score: 6

CONTINUED AND CHANGE-OVER-TIME QUESTION: SAMPLE RESPONSE

Throughout most of Chinese history, the traditions of Confucianism have long influenced gender roles. However, the victory of the communists after the Chinese Civil War altered the roles of gender for the remainder of the 20th century. According to Mao, women held up half the sky and should be treated as such. The introduction of communism gave women new opportunities, both politically and socially. However, for many the traditional role for women as wife and mother remains, as well as the preference of having boys in the family.

After the communists won the civil war in 1949, many of the changes they implemented began to affect gender roles. The communists banned the practice of foot-binding, which was a symbol of women's ornamental and subservient role in Chinese society. In the new communist society everyone was needed to work, and the traditional idea of a women being confined and not working did not suit this new society. Also, in the factories, women and men were expected to work side by side. Mao also passed a new marriage law, which forbade arranged marriages. Instead, women could choose their marriage partner. This law was met with much resistance, and even today many marriages in China are still arranged by one's parents.

While the women were working, the state-run nurseries watched over their children. Politically, though women could join the party, the party leadership remained mostly male. Later, during the rule of Deng Xiaoping, a one-child policy was initiated to slow down China's overwhelming population growth. Parents still preferred to have a boy, and this can be seen in reported cases of female infanticide and the large number of female babies in orphanages.

Even though women were expected to work and to carry out traditional household responsibilities at the same time, the changes initiated during the Mao years did bring them new opportunities. Economic and political participation broadened their experience and altered the traditional Confucian gender roles of China.

The first paragraph loses its thesis point because it effectively addresses only the second half of the century. True to form, the second paragraph picks up in 1949, leaving the gender roles of women in the first half of the century unrecounted (except for what we can infer from the changes made by the communists). The last part of the paragraph wanders, discussing arranged marriages and mentioning that, though forbidden by Mao, they are still arranged today. Why? With no analysis and little hard evidence, this essay might so far barely win 1 point. The third paragraph continues the wandering off the second paragraph, offering only general references and no information on time periods or years to provide a context, earning no points. The essay recounts the history of how Japan was opened to trade, but it does little to analyze in detail the conditions under which this happened and the immediately resulting reactions/consequences in terms of industrialization. What does it mean to the status of Japan's industrial output in 1750 that it was insulated, didn't trade without the outside world, and was forced to sign unequal treaties. Further, it does not address what this opening meant to the world beyond the efforts of the U.S. to open it to trade. 0 points in that paragraph. The closing paragraph merely summarizes the points already weakly made in the previous paragraphs. Final point total is 1.

COMPARATIVE QUESTION: SAMPLE RESPONSE

The First and Second World Wars were both the result of the accumulation of conflict that began in the 19th century. Nationalism, alliance systems, and acts of aggression all contributed to the start of these global conflicts. While WWI was more a result of growing tension and competition, WWII was caused by direct aggression.

Both wars were induced, at least partly, by the swelling of nationalist pride that began in the 19th century and endured into the 20th century. The assassination of Franz Ferdinand and the conflict between Serbia and Austria-Hungary, for example, was a result of Serbian nationalism and was fueled by a longing for self-determination, another idea that took root and spread during this time. World War II was also begun by nationalism, especially that of the Germans. It was this German nationalism and desire for self-determination that fueled Hitler's campaigns to take over Europe. Both wars were sparked by the upset of the delicate balance of power in Europe. In WWI, tensions between the big powers of the time—Germany, Britain, Russia, and France—upset this balance. Likewise, the balance was tipped once again when Hitler's campaign began and the German "Reich" began to expand at the expense of the sovereignty of the other powers of Europe.

While WWI began with a conflict between small countries, which then branched out through the tangled alliances of Europe to other, larger countries, WWII began with the big powers. WWI can be traced back to the rivalry between Austria-Hungary and Serbia. Over time, large powers such as Russia and Germany stepped in to defend their allies, and this enraged even more countries. The inception of WWI was therefore like a "ripple effect"— beginning quite small, and then expanding.

WWII was quite the opposite, beginning with the brutal campaigns and expansion of military powers Germany and Japan. If WWI began with a ripple, WWII began with an explosion. Large European powers got involved in WWI because they wanted to protect their allies, not because of direct acts of aggression against them. WWII was marked by such overt acts of aggression as the bombing of Pearl Harbor, the invasion of Poland, and the Rape of Nanking. While WWI began largely because of tension among countries that had been caused by competition for foreign markets and colonies, WWII was begun largely by fascist expansionism and Germany's desire to avenge its humiliating loss in World War I. Hitler's attacks on Europe and the transformation of Germany into a dictatorship was made possible because the German people were vulnerable and scarred by the previous war.

These wars can be considered one continual conflict that was not properly resolved in the interim between the two. The nationalism, alliances, and aggression that led to both wars point out that their roots were quite similar. The lesson learned is that the resolution of conflicts or lack thereof have shaped the way we make peace today.

The first paragraph gets straight to the point: it is the thesis statement and succinctly addresses the similarities and differences between the two World Wars. It earns its thesis point. The second, third, and fourth paragraphs wander and lose cohesion, however, with the second paragraph dwelling on the similarities of the two wars' conflicted beginnings, the third paragraph attempting to treat differences but dwelling mostly on World War II, and the fourth paragraph again addressing differences in a scattershot fashion. Though the writer does treat similarities and differences, the bewildering way in which it is done gains it only one of its addressing points. The writer's wandering also leads to a lack of focus when it comes to evidence and sustained analysis. The essay supplies much more evidence and analysis to World War II, while making passing references to World War I, with little evidence to back up those assertions. Therefore, the essay gets only 1 evidence point. Last, the concluding paragraph brings up the idea of the two being one continuous war, which mitigates against the writer's erstwhile attempts to highlight differences. Final point total is 3.

Part Four

PRACTICE TESTS

HOW TO TAKE THE PRACTICE TESTS

This section of this book contains four full-length practice tests. Taking a practice test gives you an idea of what it's like to sit through a full AP World History exam. You will find out which areas you're strong in, and where additional review may be required. Any mistakes you make now are ones you won't make on the actual exam, as long as you take the time to learn where you went wrong.

The four tests here are all full-length. They include 70 multiple-choice questions and three free-response (essay) questions. You will have 55 minutes for the multiple-choice section, a 10-minute reading period, and 120 minutes to answer the free-response questions.

Before taking a test, find a quiet place where you can work uninterrupted for three hours, and bring blank lined paper for your essays (you will get 16 pages for all three essays on the real exam). Time yourself according to the time limit at the beginning of each section. It's okay to take a short break between sections, but for the most accurate results, you should approximate real test-like conditions as much as possible. Use the 10-minute reading period to plan your answers for the free-response questions, but don't begin writing your responses until the 10 minutes are up.

Remember to pace yourself. Train yourself to be aware of the time you are spending on each problem. Take note of the general types of questions you encounter, as well as what strategies work best for them.

When you are done, read the detailed answer explanations that follow. These will help you identify areas that could use additional review. But don't only focus on the questions you got wrong. For those you got right, too, you can benefit from reading the answer explanation. You might learn something you didn't already know.

Before writing the free-response questions, you may want to review the material on essay writing found in chapter 2. Each essay has a different purpose and a different set of strategies for answering the question.

The sample free-response answers that follow the answers and explanations to the multiple-choice questions are intended to help you understand how an informed student might approach the question.

Good luck!

HOW TO COMPUTE YOUR SCORE

SCORING THE MULTIPLE-CHOICE QUESTIONS

There are 70 questions on this section. To compute your score, calculate the number of questions you got right, then multiply that number by 0.8571. This is your weighted score.

SCORING THE FREE-RESPONSE QUESTIONS

The readers will have specific points that they will be looking for in each essay (called a rubric). The general rubrics for each of the three free-response essays can be found in chapter 2. Although you will not be able to accurately score your own essays, you can get a better idea of how to apply the scoring system to your own writing by reviewing the rubrics for each essay. Readers use the rubric as the guide for assigning points. Each free-response question is worth a a total of 9 points, and each point is awarded based on the answers that you provide. Each piece of information that they are able to check off in your essay is a point toward a better score.

Try scoring your own essays using the sample rubrics provided. Then multiply each score by 2.2222. Add those three scores together to get your weighted Section II score.

Add your weighted scores for Sections I and II together to get your composite score (round to the nearest whole number).

AP SCORE CONVERSION CHART

Composite Score Range	AP Score
81–120	5
70–80	4
55–69	3
42–54	2
0–41	1

For more information on the way that the College Board computes AP scores, refer to chapter 1.

Practice Test 1 Answer Grid

1. Ⓐ Ⓑ Ⓒ Ⓓ
2. Ⓐ Ⓑ Ⓒ Ⓓ
3. Ⓐ Ⓑ Ⓒ Ⓓ
4. Ⓐ Ⓑ Ⓒ Ⓓ
5. Ⓐ Ⓑ Ⓒ Ⓓ
6. Ⓐ Ⓑ Ⓒ Ⓓ
7. Ⓐ Ⓑ Ⓒ Ⓓ
8. Ⓐ Ⓑ Ⓒ Ⓓ
9. Ⓐ Ⓑ Ⓒ Ⓓ
10. Ⓐ Ⓑ Ⓒ Ⓓ
11. Ⓐ Ⓑ Ⓒ Ⓓ
12. Ⓐ Ⓑ Ⓒ Ⓓ
13. Ⓐ Ⓑ Ⓒ Ⓓ
14. Ⓐ Ⓑ Ⓒ Ⓓ
15. Ⓐ Ⓑ Ⓒ Ⓓ
16. Ⓐ Ⓑ Ⓒ Ⓓ
17. Ⓐ Ⓑ Ⓒ Ⓓ
18. Ⓐ Ⓑ Ⓒ Ⓓ

19. Ⓐ Ⓑ Ⓒ Ⓓ
20. Ⓐ Ⓑ Ⓒ Ⓓ
21. Ⓐ Ⓑ Ⓒ Ⓓ
22. Ⓐ Ⓑ Ⓒ Ⓓ
23. Ⓐ Ⓑ Ⓒ Ⓓ
24. Ⓐ Ⓑ Ⓒ Ⓓ
25. Ⓐ Ⓑ Ⓒ Ⓓ
26. Ⓐ Ⓑ Ⓒ Ⓓ
27. Ⓐ Ⓑ Ⓒ Ⓓ
28. Ⓐ Ⓑ Ⓒ Ⓓ
29. Ⓐ Ⓑ Ⓒ Ⓓ
30. Ⓐ Ⓑ Ⓒ Ⓓ
31. Ⓐ Ⓑ Ⓒ Ⓓ
32. Ⓐ Ⓑ Ⓒ Ⓓ
33. Ⓐ Ⓑ Ⓒ Ⓓ
34. Ⓐ Ⓑ Ⓒ Ⓓ
35. Ⓐ Ⓑ Ⓒ Ⓓ
36. Ⓐ Ⓑ Ⓒ Ⓓ

37. Ⓐ Ⓑ Ⓒ Ⓓ
38. Ⓐ Ⓑ Ⓒ Ⓓ
39. Ⓐ Ⓑ Ⓒ Ⓓ
40. Ⓐ Ⓑ Ⓒ Ⓓ
41. Ⓐ Ⓑ Ⓒ Ⓓ
42. Ⓐ Ⓑ Ⓒ Ⓓ
43. Ⓐ Ⓑ Ⓒ Ⓓ
44. Ⓐ Ⓑ Ⓒ Ⓓ
45. Ⓐ Ⓑ Ⓒ Ⓓ
46. Ⓐ Ⓑ Ⓒ Ⓓ
47. Ⓐ Ⓑ Ⓒ Ⓓ
48. Ⓐ Ⓑ Ⓒ Ⓓ
49. Ⓐ Ⓑ Ⓒ Ⓓ
50. Ⓐ Ⓑ Ⓒ Ⓓ
51. Ⓐ Ⓑ Ⓒ Ⓓ
52. Ⓐ Ⓑ Ⓒ Ⓓ
53. Ⓐ Ⓑ Ⓒ Ⓓ
54. Ⓐ Ⓑ Ⓒ Ⓓ

55. Ⓐ Ⓑ Ⓒ Ⓓ
56. Ⓐ Ⓑ Ⓒ Ⓓ
57. Ⓐ Ⓑ Ⓒ Ⓓ
58. Ⓐ Ⓑ Ⓒ Ⓓ
59. Ⓐ Ⓑ Ⓒ Ⓓ
60. Ⓐ Ⓑ Ⓒ Ⓓ
61. Ⓐ Ⓑ Ⓒ Ⓓ
62. Ⓐ Ⓑ Ⓒ Ⓓ
63. Ⓐ Ⓑ Ⓒ Ⓓ
64. Ⓐ Ⓑ Ⓒ Ⓓ
65. Ⓐ Ⓑ Ⓒ Ⓓ
66. Ⓐ Ⓑ Ⓒ Ⓓ
67. Ⓐ Ⓑ Ⓒ Ⓓ
68. Ⓐ Ⓑ Ⓒ Ⓓ
69. Ⓐ Ⓑ Ⓒ Ⓓ
70. Ⓐ Ⓑ Ⓒ Ⓓ

PRACTICE TEST 1

Section I: Multiple-Choice Questions

Time: 55 Minutes
70 Questions

Directions: Each of the questions or incomplete statements below is followed by four suggested answers or completions. Select the one that is best in each case and then fill in the corresponding oval on the answer sheet.

Voyages of Zheng He

1. The map shown demonstrates that

   (A) Zheng He made several voyages across the Indian Ocean

   (B) the Silk Route had a maritime path

   (C) Christopher Columbus and Ferdinand Magellan could not have accomplished what they did without the aid of East Asian navigators

   (D) the Chinese were already aware that the Philippines held nothing of value

2. In the 1860s, Russia and the United States both accomplished the goal of

   (A) building a transcontinental railroad

   (B) directly electing senators to its Congress (United States) and Duma (Russia)

   (C) laying transoceanic telegraph cables

   (D) eliminating slavery

3. The basic ideological difference between Karl Marx and Mao Zedong is that

   (A) although Marx believed women should play an equal role in the development of a communist state, Mao believed women did not have an intellectual capacity equal to that of men

   (B) Marx felt that communism and capitalism could co-exist in a manner that Mao would never have tolerated

   (C) Marx felt that a communist state could exist as an island surrounded by capitalistic countries, while Mao felt pure communism could only exist if it were universal

   (D) Marx believed that an industrial working class would lead the revolution, while Mao believed a peasant class would lead it

GO ON TO THE NEXT PAGE

4. Which countries in northern Africa retained a significant Christian population during the spread of Islam?

   (A) Egypt and Morocco

   (B) Egypt and Ethiopia

   (C) Tunisia and Algeria

   (D) Ethiopia and Somalia

5. The major difference between Viking and Muslim expansion was

   (A) Viking expansion was motivated by the need to acquire natural resources whereas Muslim expansion was motivated by religious conversion

   (B) the Vikings invaded rural areas and the Muslims invaded urban areas

   (C) the Muslims forced religious conversion on those whom they defeated but the Vikings did not

   (D) the Muslims treated the defeated enemy harshly; the Vikings were much more conciliatory

6. Francis Xavier and Ignatius Loyola shared the trait of being

   (A) burned at the stake as a Catholic heretic

   (B) a Jesuit missionary

   (C) a missionary who followed the conquistadores, hoping to convert the "heathen" to Christianity

   (D) a leader in the European Scientific Revolution

7. The Mughal and Ottoman empires shared the trait of

   (A) having Muslim roots

   (B) being related to the Mongol "hordes"

   (C) eventually being conquered by Chinggis Khan

   (D) involvement in the fall of Constantinople

		Country #1		Country #2
Import Partners	South Korea	9.4%	Netherlands	20.3% (2012)
	Taiwan	8.0%	France	9.7%
	Japan	8.3%	Cameroon	9.1%
	United States	7.8%	South Korea	9.1%
	Australia	5.0%		
	Germany	4.8%		
GDP by Sector	Agriculture:	9.7%	Agriculture:	56.6%
	Industry:	45.3%	Industry:	14.5%
	Services:	45.0%	Services:	28.9%
Population Growth Rate		0.44%		2.13%
Literacy (over age 15 can read and write):	Total Population	95.1%	Total Population	56.6%

Source: CIA World Fact Book, 2013

GO ON TO THE NEXT PAGE

8. From the previous chart, we can conclude that "Country #1" is most likely

(A) China

(B) India

(C) the United States

(D) Central African Republic

9. The last colony on the mainland of the New World to become independent was

(A) the United States

(B) Brazil

(C) Canada

(D) Mexico

10. The Social Contract Theory in the West and the Mandate of Heaven in East Asia were similar in that

(A) they both relied on a civil service examination system

(B) they both justified revolution as a replacement for ineffective government

(C) they both justified the institution of slavery

(D) they both fell into disuse as their respective regions experienced an industrial revolution

11. What was shared by early 20th-century revolutionaries in China and Mexico?

(A) The Catholic Church supported the revolutionaries in both countries.

(B) The middle class rose in revolt against the aristocracy.

(C) Both revolutions were prompted by foreign invasion.

(D) Land reform was the goal.

12. In the 20th century, the greatest number of Muslims lived in

(A) the Middle East

(B) South Asia

(C) the Western Hemisphere and Europe

(D) South and Southeast Asia

Read the following passages from Hammurabi's Code and answer the questions that follow.

Law 1

If a man brings an accusation against another man, charging him with murder, but cannot prove it, the accuser shall be put to death.

Law 3

If he bears false witness concerning grain or money, he shall himself bear the penalty imposed in the case.

Law 23

If the robber is not captured, the man who has been robbed, shall make an itemized statement of his loss, and the city and the governor…shall compensate him for whatever was lost.

Law 129

If the wife of a man is caught lying with another man, they shall bind them and throw them into the water. If the husband of the woman wishes to spare the wife, then the king shall spare the subject.

Law 195

If a son strikes his father, they shall cut off his hand.

Law 221

If a physician sets a broken bone for a man or cures a sprained tendon, the patient shall pay five shekels of silver . . . a client pays three shekels . . . a slave's owner pays two shekels.

GO ON TO THE NEXT PAGE

Law 229

If a builder builds a house for a man and does not make . . . it sound, and the house . . . collapses and causes the death of the owner . . . the builder shall be put to death.

(A) "If a man brings an accusation against another man, charging him with murder, but cannot prove it, the accuser shall be put to death."

(B) "If he bears false witness concerning grain or money, he shall himself bear the penalty imposed in the case."

(C) "If the wife of a man is caught lying with another man, they shall bind them and throw them into the water. If the husband of the woman wishes to spare the wife, then the king shall spare the subject."

(D) "If a son strikes his father, they shall cut off his hand."

(E) "If a physician sets a broken bone for a man or cures a sprained tendon, the patient shall pay five shekels of silver . . . a client pays three shekels . . . a slave's owner pays two shekels."

(F) "If a builder builds a house for a man and does not make . . . it sound, and the house . . . collapses and causes the death of the owner . . . the builder shall be put to death."

(G) "If the robber is not captured, the man who has been robbed, shall make an itemized statement of his loss, and the city and the governor . . . shall compensate him for whatever was lost."

13. The previous laws state

(A) responsibility of the state to protect its citizens

(B) a general equality between the sexes

(C) a right of each citizen to own property

(D) a belief in civil disobedience

14. Which Judeo-Christian value is reflected in the above laws?

(A) "Render unto Caesar that which is Caesar's."

(B) "An eye for an eye."

(C) "And the meek shall inherit the earth."

(D) "Turn the other cheek."

15. Which of the following statements can be concluded from one of the above laws?

(A) The government was an early republic.

(B) This was an agriculture-based economy.

(C) The society recognized the existence of different classes.

(D) Males and females enjoyed equal status.

16. Hammurabi justified his code as having come from

(A) ancestors

(B) a tribal council of local chiefs

(C) the gods

(D) legal precedent

GO ON TO THE NEXT PAGE

Source: C. Cook and J Stevenson, *The Longman Handbook of Modern British History 1714-1980* (Longman, 1983) pp 191-2

17. These two charts graphing cotton traveling into and out of the United Kingdom demonstrate the economic practice of

(A) economic determinism

(B) mercantilism

(C) Ricardo's Iron Law of Wages

(D) Malthusian economics

18. The oldest of the following Mesoamerican civilizations is

(A) Toltec

(B) Incan

(C) Aztec

(D) Olmec

19. The cities of Xi'an (Chang'an) and Baghdad are historically connected by

(A) the Trans-Siberian Railroad

(B) the journeys of Ibn Battuta

(C) the journeys of Marco Polo

(D) the Silk Road

20. The Netherlands, southern Italy, the Philippines, and much of Iberia were actively controlled by which of the following European powers in the 16th century?

(A) England

(B) France

(C) Spain

(D) Portugal

21. More than anything else, what improved worldwide life expectancy between 1500 and 1750?

(A) The distribution of inexpensive medicines to combat viral and bacterial infection

(B) 250 years of relative worldwide peace

(C) The discovery of a practical and inexpensive system of water purification

(D) The mass dissemination of New World foods

GO ON TO THE NEXT PAGE

22. The European product in greatest demand in 19th-century Asia and Africa was

    (A) weaponry

    (B) cotton

    (C) alcohol

    (D) medicine

23. What product linked Great Britain, India, and China in the 19th century?

    (A) Silk

    (B) Tea

    (C) Clocks

    (D) Opium

A

B

C

24. The illustrations above represent three events that occurred in 20th-century China. Place the events represented in the correct chronological order, beginning with the earliest.

    (A) A, B, C

    (B) A, C, B

    (C) B, C, A

    (D) C, B, A

25. The connection between the Monroe Doctrine and the Brezhnev Doctrine is that

    (A) both supported the goals of the American Revolution

    (B) both justified a larger nation's claim to "protect" smaller nations

    (C) both justified imperialistic actions in Africa

    (D) both provided aid to European countries at the conclusion of WWII

26. What is being described by the following statements?

    • Believes events in Heaven and on Earth are directly connected

    • Says right to rule comes from heavenly powers

    • Says ruler is linked between Heaven and Earth

    • Similar to European concept of divine right

    • First used by the Zhou Dynasty

    (A) The Mandate of Heaven

    (B) Bushido

    (C) The Social Contract Theory

    (D) The teachings of Matteo Ricci

GO ON TO THE NEXT PAGE ⟹

27. What does each of the following have in common?

- Divine Right in Europe

- Aztec promotion of human sacrifice

- Songhay promotion of Islam

    (A) Rule by theocracy

    (B) The use of religious ideals to legitimize the ruling government

    (C) An attempt by an outside religion to infiltrate established values of a culture

    (D) A belief in animism

28. Which of the following prophets plays a prominent role in Christianity, Judaism, and Islam?

    (A) Mohammad

    (B) Abraham

    (C) Ahura Mazda

    (D) Jesus

29. The Divine Wind in East Asia and the Protestant Wind in Europe were similar in that they both

    (A) were monsoons that aided trade by providing winds that seasonally changed direction

    (B) frustrated people trying to invade island nations

    (C) inspired crusades in different parts of the world

    (D) encouraged Voyages of Exploration

30. The greatest manufacturing region in the world between 1000 and 1500 was in

    (A) Europe

    (B) the Middle East

    (C) China

    (D) India

31. Which of the following American crops most quickly became a staple in all of Eurasia?

    (A) Peanut

    (B) Corn (maize)

    (C) Potato

    (D) Tomato

32. The last country in the New World to abolish slavery was

    (A) Brazil

    (B) the United States

    (C) Mexico

    (D) Mauritania

33. England's biggest import in the 19th century was

    (A) rum

    (B) timber

    (C) slaves

    (D) cotton

34. Which of the following was the staple crop in 17th- to 19th-century Europe?

    (A) Onion

    (B) Potato

    (C) Rice

    (D) Beef

35. Which two naval powers dominated the Mediterranean Sea in the 16th century?

    (A) Spain and Portugal

    (B) Rome and Greece

    (C) Genoa and Venice

    (D) Italy and the Ottoman Empire

GO ON TO THE NEXT PAGE

Use the passage below to answer the four questions that follow.

Source: "The Worst Mistake In The History Of The Human Race" by Jared Diamond, *Discover Magazine*

Are 20th-century hunter-gatherers really worse off than farmers? Scattered throughout the world, several dozen groups of supposedly primitive people, like the Kalahari Bushmen, continue to support themselves that way. It turns out that these people have plenty of leisure time, sleep a good deal, and work less hard than their farming neighbors . . . . While farmers concentrate on high carbohydrate crops like rice and potatoes, the mix of wild plants and animals in the diet of surviving hunter-gatherers provides more protein and a better balance of other nutrients . . . . Archeologists studying the rise of farming have reconstructed a crucial stage at which we made the worst mistake in human history. Forced to choose between limiting population or trying to increase food production, we chose the latter and ended up with starvation, warfare, and tyranny.

36. What is Jared Diamond suggesting be traditionally thought of as the most dynamic development in human history?

(A) The development of agriculture

(B) The development of hunter-gatherer techniques

(C) The development of urbanization

(D) The domestication of beasts of burden

37. According to Diamond, which group of people has enjoyed the more successful existence?

(A) People who tend the herd

(B) People who forage in the natural environment

(C) People who plant the crops

(D) People who live in the cities

38. According to the passage, all of the following were fallout from the Agricultural Revolution except

(A) limited population growth

(B) disease

(C) gender inequality

(D) increased food production

39. Which of the following conclusions can correctly be drawn from the passage?

(A) There is evidence to suggest that hunter-gatherers led a more comfortable life than had formerly been believed.

(B) Jared Diamond is not respected by mainstream historians.

(C) The author is an archaeologist.

(D) Jared Diamond is a vegan.

40. What do the *latifundia* and the *yangban* have in common?

(A) They were the warrior classes in their respective countries.

(B) They were revolutions begun by the peasants in Greece and China.

(C) One is the untouchable class in India and the other is the lowest caste in Australia.

(D) They represented the landed gentry in their respective civilizations.

41. Aristotle's "Golden Mean" and China's "Middle Way" are similar in that both

(A) demanded loyalty to the state

(B) exalted the life of the peasant farmer

(C) emphasized the Four Noble Truths

(D) praised the avoidance of extremes

GO ON TO THE NEXT PAGE

42. A similarity between Zheng He and Vasco da Gama is both men

(A) sought to convert the "heathen" to their respective religions

(B) sought to militarily conquer the regions with which they came into contact

(C) claimed the land they "discovered" for their respective countries

(D) successfully journeyed to East Africa

43. The first European country to establish trading posts in Asia was

(A) Spain

(B) the Netherlands

(C) Portugal

(D) England

Use the following passage to answer the question that follows.

Formerly, the barbarian merchants brought foreign money to China; which being paid in exchange for goods, was a source of pecuniary advantage to the people of all the sea-board provinces. But latterly, the barbarian merchants have clandestinely sold opium for money, which has rendered it unnecessary for them to import foreign silver. Thus foreign money has been going out of the country, while none comes into it.

Xu Naji, administrator of the Sacrificial Court, advising the Chinese emperor to legalize opium production in 1836

44. Who are the earlier "barbarian merchants"?

(A) The Dutch

(B) The British

(C) The Japanese

(D) The Americans

The following passage comes from *Outlines of the World's History*, a high school history textbook written by William Swinton in 1874. Use it to answer questions 45–48.

The history of the civilized world is the history of the Aryan, Semitic, and Hamitic races. It is of interest to note that the race to which we belong, the Aryan, has always played the leading part in the great drama of the world's progress. The Hamitic nations, the Egyptians and Chaldeans, though they developed a peculiar type of civilization, yet grew up and remained in a great degree apart from the rest of the world, having no considerable influence on the main current of history. As to the Semites, there is one respect in which they have the greatest place in the story of mankind, namely, in religious development; for the three religions that have taught men that there is but one God—namely, the Jewish, the Christian, and the Mahom'etan—have all come from among them. But aside from this, the Semites do not make nearly so important or so conspicuous a figure in history as do the Aryans, or Indo—Europeans . . . . They have not, like the Aryans, been the planters of new nations and they have never attained a high intellectual development, or that progress in political freedom, in science, art, and literature, which is the glory of the Aryan nations.

45. Which of the following individuals would most likely have disagreed with this statement?

(A) Herbert Spencer

(B) Emilio Aguinaldo

(C) Adolf Hitler

(D) Richard Wagner

GO ON TO THE NEXT PAGE ⟩

46. What 19th-century "ism" played the greatest role in promoting the attitude expressed?

(A) Socialism

(B) Romanticism

(C) Utopianism

(D) Nationalism

47. Nineteenth-century readers who concurred with this passage would most likely agree with each of the following beliefs except

(A) imperialism

(B) the thesis of Rudyard Kipling's "White Man's Burden"

(C) Social Darwinism

(D) the idea of a world peacekeeping organization

48. When applying the principle of presentism, the historian must be careful to

(A) shelter Asians, Africans, and indigenous Latin Americans from passages that reference the prejudices of the past

(B) not judge the people of the past through the values of the present

(C) recognize the point of view in all of the documents

(D) not become too charitable to the less fortunate

49. Sweden, Spain, and Switzerland were comparable in the 20th century in that

(A) they switched sides during WWII

(B) each was on the winning side in WWI but lost territory to the peace treaty

(C) each lost all colonial possessions at the end of WWI

(D) each remained neutral during both WWI and WWII

Source: Herblock, Washington Post (1962)

50. What event is being contested in the Cold War-era cartoon depicted above?

(A) The SALT talks

(B) The Korean War

(C) The Cuban Missile Crisis

(D) The Vietnam War

51. What is the connection between Ashoka's relationship with Buddhism and Constantine's relationship with Christianity?

(A) Both felt threatened by their respective religions.

(B) Both used religion to unite the people.

(C) In order to subdue the regions they invaded, both had to outlaw these faiths.

(D) Both religions declined in popularity following each ruler's death.

GO ON TO THE NEXT PAGE →

52. In what part of the world would you most likely be excavating if you found an artifact that looked like the image shown above at a thousand-year old archaeological site?

(A) In Mesoamerica

(B) In the Middle East

(C) In East Africa

(D) In South Asia

53. The East Asian culture never conquered by the Mongols was

(A) Korea

(B) China

(C) Japan

(D) the Philippines

54. A mercantilist would most prefer to import

(A) timber

(B) rum

(C) firearms

(D) slaves

55. The period of Muslim rule in India was called the

(A) Mauryan Dynasty

(B) Gupta Dynasty

(C) Mughal Dynasty

(D) Reign of the Janissaries

56. The Sepoy Rebellion in India and the Boxer Rebellion in China share the common characteristic of a people

(A) wanting to overthrow the existing dynasty

(B) wanting to expel a foreign power

(C) wanting to import more opium into their country

(D) wanting to industrialize their country

57. Two rulers who remained neutral during the Cold War were

(A) Nehru of India and Nasser of Egypt

(B) Ataturk of Turkey and Begin of Israel

(C) Saddam Hussein of Iraq and King Hussein of Jordan

(D) Ho Chi Minh of Vietnam and Chiang Kai-shek of Taiwan

58. Which world region experienced the most dramatic decline in urban population at the conclusion of the classical era (c. 600 CE)?

(A) Pre-Columbian America

(B) Europe

(C) South Asia

(D) The Middle East

GO ON TO THE NEXT PAGE

59. The 12-century empire that extended from Korea to Eastern Europe was

   (A) the Mughal Empire
   (B) the Ottoman Empire
   (C) the empire of Alexander the Great
   (D) the Mongol Empire

60. Which East Asian products were supplied to Europe when traded for 16th-century New World silver?

   (A) Rice, tea, and elephant tusks
   (B) Teak, opium, and tomatoes
   (C) Silk, porcelain, and spices
   (D) Clocks, sake, and slaves

61. Which of the following European colonial powers gave its indigenous population the greatest freedom?

   (A) The Spanish
   (B) The British
   (C) The Portuguese
   (D) The French

62. Which one of the following diseases would most likely be found in a developed country in the 21st century?

   (A) Malaria
   (B) Cholera
   (C) Tuberculosis
   (D) Heart disease

63. The three people in the images shown above share the common quality of being

   (A) leaders of religious cults
   (B) scientists
   (C) romantic poets of the 18th century
   (D) advocates of European imperialism

64. A common cause of the decline of the Roman and Abbasid empires was

   (A) an exhaustion of natural resources
   (B) the demise of the Silk Road
   (C) malaria
   (D) a growing reliance on mercenary armies

GO ON TO THE NEXT PAGE ⇨

65. The river used by the Ottoman Empire to invade Europe was

(A) the Yangtze

(B) the Danube

(C) the Rhine

(D) the Ganges

66. The majority of people who lived in India during the Mughal Empire were

(A) Hindu

(B) Sikh

(C) Muslim

(D) Buddhist

67. How did goods typically travel in the Atlantic triangular trade of the 18th century?

(A) Raw goods to Africa, slaves to the New World, rum to Europe

(B) Guns to Africa, slaves to the New World, raw products to Europe

(C) Missionaries to Africa, slaves to the New World, finished products to Europe

(D) Raw goods to Africa, slaves to the New World, finished products to Europe

68. What determined current political boundaries in the Middle East?

(A) River flow

(B) Muslim leadership

(C) 19th-century wars

(D) European powers

69. The biggest hurdle to European hegemony in the 15th century was

(A) the Catholic Church

(B) the low level of technology in Europe

(C) constant wars with the Ottoman Turks

(D) frequent plagues

70. Which of the following accurately depicts a comparison between the Zhou and Han empires in China?

(A) Though Zhou China did not recognize the Mandate of Heaven, Han China was strongly influenced by it.

(B) Zhou China attempted to extend its influence into nomadic regions in a more dramatic fashion than did Han China.

(C) Neither dynasty practiced a reverence for its ancestors.

(D) Han China developed a more extensive long-distance trade pattern than did Zhou China.

IF YOU FINISH BEFORE TIME IS CALLED, YOU MAY CHECK YOUR WORK ON THIS SECTION ONLY. DO NOT TURN TO ANY OTHER SECTION IN THE TEST.   STOP

Section II

Part A: Document-Based Question

Mandatory reading period: 10 minutes
Suggested writing time: 40 minutes

Directions: The following question is based on the accompanying Documents 1 to 10. (The documents have been edited for purposes of this exercise.)

This question is designed to test your ability to work with and understand historical documents. Write an essay that:

- Has a relevant thesis and supports that thesis with evidence from the documents.

- Uses all of the documents.

- Analyzes the documents by grouping them in as many appropriate ways as possible; does not simply summarize the documents individually.

- Takes into account the sources of the documents and analyzes the authors' points of view.

- Explains the need for at least one additional type of document.

You may refer to relevant historical information not mentioned in the documents.

> **Prompt:** Analyze the impact of the growth of the McDonald's restaurant franchise around the world. Identify an additional relevant type of document and explain how it would help your answer to this question.

GO ON TO THE NEXT PAGE

DOCUMENT 1

Source: *The Economist* Magazine, 1986*

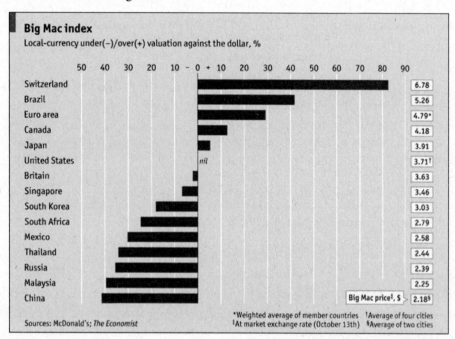

Big Mac index
Local-currency under(–)/over(+) valuation against the dollar, %

Country	Big Mac price, $
Switzerland	6.78
Brazil	5.26
Euro area	4.79*
Canada	4.18
Japan	3.91
United States	3.71†
Britain	3.63
Singapore	3.46
South Korea	3.03
South Africa	2.79
Mexico	2.58
Thailand	2.44
Russia	2.39
Malaysia	2.25
China	2.18§

Sources: McDonald's; *The Economist*
*Weighted average of member countries   †Average of four cities
‡At market exchange rate (October 13th)   §Average of two cities

In 1986, *The Economist* created the Big Mac Index as a light-hearted measure of the cost of living, using the base price of a Big Mac in the United States and comparing that to the prices of Big Macs in other countries.

DOCUMENT 2

Source: *The Baltimore Sun*, June 2, 1993

KREMLIN'S NEW NEIGHBOR MOSCOW'S 2ND MCDONALD'S FAST-FOOD CHAIN DEFIES ODDS

They ate nearly 11 million Big Macs and hungered for more. So yesterday, feeding Russia's seemingly insatiable appetite for all things American, McDonald's opened its second Moscow restaurant. McDonald's is, indeed, a grand spectacle. The first one was opened in 1990 and quickly became the world's busiest restaurant (40,000 to 50,000 customers every day).

Quotes about the restaurant abound: "I came to celebrate payday," "I feel like I've gone abroad," and "Success is possible in Russia."

GO ON TO THE NEXT PAGE ▷

DOCUMENT 3

Source: Thomas Friedman, *The Lexus and the Olive Tree*, 1996, p. 248

No two countries that both had McDonald's had fought a war against each other since each got its McDonald's. I'm not kidding: it was uncanny. Look at the Middle East: Israel had kosher McDonald's, Saudi Arabia had McDonald's, which closed five times a day for Muslim prayer, Egypt had McDonald's and both Lebanon and Jordan had become McDonald's countries. None of them have had a war since the Golden Arches went in. Where is the threat of war in the Middle East today? Israel-Syria, Israel-Iran and Israel-Iraq. Which three Middle East countries don't have McDonald's? Syria, Iran and Iraq.

DOCUMENT 4

Source: American Tourist in a McDonald's in South Africa, 1997

My wife and I were enjoying a hamburger in a spotless but relatively empty McDonald's in South Africa when one of the restaurant employees who had been sweeping the floor came over to us. Decked out in a recently ironed uniform, the shy girl, recognizing our Western accents, hesitatingly came up to us, greeted us with a warm smile and asked "Is our McDonald's as good as yours?"

DOCUMENT 5

The Times of London, August 1, 1998

THE PEOPLE LONGED FOR A LESS REMOTE MONARCH: YESTERDAY THEY MET HER

Those determined to portray the monarch as a people's queen could hardly have designed a more populist day out for her yesterday: she spent the morning in Ellesmere Port, shopping for kitchenware and a pair of trainers, sustaining herself with a visit to a drive-in McDonald's. Being the queen, she bought neither canvas shoes nor plastic washing-up bowl, and no Big Mac passed the royal lips. As the royal limousine drew up outside the burger bar, there seemed a momentary danger that the Queen might have to go inside to learn the mysteries of Quarter-Pounders and Chicken McNuggets, but she was spared and her visit was restricted to meeting the staff on the pavement outside.

* Mughal Emperor

GO ON TO THE NEXT PAGE

DOCUMENT 6

Source: *The Washington Post*, October 11, 1998

A McDonald's Promotion in Hong Kong, 1998

SNOOPY FAD TAKES HONG KONG BY STORM: THOUSANDS LINE UP OUTSIDE MCDONALD'S

HONG KONG—They began lining up at dawn, outside every branch in the city. Soon the lines grew to hundreds of people, stretching around city blocks. On a few occasions, police were called to keep order. What was the cause of this city-wide pandemonium? A run on a failing bank? A mad rush for visas, perhaps?

No, it was Snoopy. Not Snoopy Dogg, the rapper, but Snoopy, the world's most famous beagle, Charlie Brown's pooch from the Peanuts carton strip.

Every day for four weeks McDonald's offered three-inch Snoopy figurines for a mere six Hong Kong dollars—equivalent to about $.75—with the purchase of a McDonald's meal. Each day brought a Snoopy dressed in a different national costume – a Chinese Snoopy, a Mexican Snoopy, a Mongolian Snoopy, an American Snoopy in an Uncle Sam hat, as well as one in a cowboy hat with a pair of six-shooters around his waist.

DOCUMENT 7

Source: Interview in *Z Magazine* with Jose Bove, a French farmer and activist who had been protesting the construction of a McDonald's restaurant in Millau, France, 2001.

Jeffress: August 12, 1999, you and a group of farmers from your French union, the Confederation Paysanne, dismantled a McDonald's under construction just outside the city of Millau near Larzac. It was this action that brought you international attention. Would you talk about it?

BOVE: There are three or four of us who sat around in March 1999 talking about doing something symbolic, but there would have been no reason for the McDonald's protest if it hadn't been for the outrageous tariff placed on French cheese by the Americans because the French refused to let outlawed hormone-treated beef be imported from the States. The tariff meant that we lost our cheese market in the States. There was no political law against it, nothing to stop it, so one solution was to attack McDonald's as a symbol of malbouffe (bad food). This was not an anti-American action; it was anti–malbouffe. We were determined never to be trapped by the logic of being anti-American. This is a fight against free trade global capitalism. It's about the logic of a certain economic system, not an American system. It can be a struggle against any country, this one or that one. It's not against those who have an American passport.

GO ON TO THE NEXT PAGE

DOCUMENT 8

Source: Anti-capitalist protesters damage the sign of a McDonald's restaurant near Trafalgar Square in London, May 1, 2000.

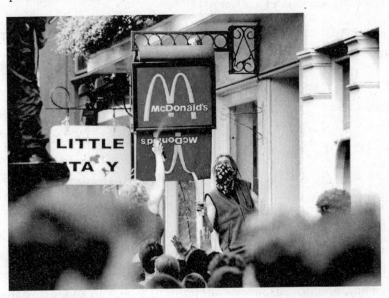

Photo Credit: ADRIAN DENNIS/AFP/Getty Images

DOCUMENT 9

Source: McDonald's Annual Report, 2012

McDonald's World Revenues (Company Operated Sales)
(Dollars in millions)

	2012	2011	2010
U.S.	$8,814	$8,529	$8,112
Europe	10,827	10,886	9,569
Asia, Pacific, Middle East, Africa	6,391	6,019	5,066
Other Countries and Corporate	1,535	1,572	1,328
TOTAL REVENUES	**27,567**	**27,008**	**24,075**

GO ON TO THE NEXT PAGE

DOCUMENT 10

Source: NPR Blog: The Salt, *Where In the World Are There No McDonald's?* by Jessica Naudziunas, August 2013

. . . McDonald's may seem to be everywhere, but there are still 105 countries without the fast food giant, from Ghana to Jamaica to Yemen to Tajikistan. And in six countries, McDonald's once had a presence, but due to economics, and sometimes politics, the franchises closed.

Still . . . McDonald's is well-represented overseas . . . . The company has 34,480 restaurants in 119 countries, including Cuba and France, where it's especially beloved, even by foreigners . . . .

It also sometimes maps onto politics. One of the most recent closures this May was in Macedonia after disputes between a franchisee and the American headquarters. And in the case of Bolivia, the government said they'd rather not have fries with that in 2002, when all McDonald's franchises there were closed . . . .

IF YOU FINISH BEFORE TIME IS CALLED, YOU MAY CHECK YOUR WORK ON THIS SECTION ONLY. DO NOT TURN TO ANY OTHER SECTION IN THE TEST.

STOP

Part B: Continuity and Change-Over-Time Question

Suggested writing time: 40 minutes

Directions: You are to answer the following question. You should spend five minutes organizing or outlining your essay. Write an essay that:

- Has a relevant thesis and supports that thesis with appropriate historical evidence.
- Addresses all parts of the question.
- Uses historical context to show continuity and change over time.
- Analyzes the process of continuity and change over time.

Prompt: Analyze continuity and change of the impact of technology on government in ONE of the following regions between 1450 and 1750.

- West Africa
- North America
- Latin America

Part C: Comparative Question

Suggested writing time: 40 minutes

Directions: You are to answer the following question. You should spend five minutes organizing or outlining your essay. Write an essay that:

- Has a relevant thesis and supports that thesis with appropriate historical evidence.
- Addresses all parts of the question.
- Makes direct, relevant comparisons.
- Analyzes relevant reasons for similarities and differences.

Prompt: Compare the spread of Islam and Christianity across Afro-Eurasia between 100 CE and 1450 CE.

IF YOU FINISH BEFORE TIME IS CALLED, YOU MAY CHECK YOUR WORK ON THIS SECTION ONLY. DO NOT TURN TO ANY OTHER SECTION IN THE TEST.

PRACTICE TEST 1: ANSWER KEY

1.	A	19.	D	37.	B	55.	C
2.	D	20.	C	38.	A	56.	B
3.	D	21.	D	39.	A	57.	A
4.	B	22.	A	40.	D	58.	B
5.	B	23.	D	41.	D	59.	D
6.	B	24.	B	42.	D	60.	C
7.	A	25.	B	43.	C	61.	D
8.	A	26.	A	44.	B	62.	D
9.	C	27.	B	45.	B	63.	B
10.	B	28.	B	46.	D	64.	D
11.	D	29.	B	47.	D	65.	B
12.	D	30.	C	48.	B	66.	A
13.	A	31.	B	49.	D	67.	B
14.	B	32.	A	50.	C	68.	D
15.	C	33.	D	51.	B	69.	B
16.	C	34.	B	52.	D	70.	D
17.	B	35.	D	53.	C		
18.	D	36.	A	54.	A		

PRACTICE TEST 1: ASSESS YOUR STRENGTHS

Question	Chapter
1	Chapter 4: 600 to 1450 CE
2	Chapter 6: 1750 to 1900 CE
3	Chapter 6: 1750 to 1900 CE and Chapter 7: 1900 CE to Present
4	Chapter 4: 600 to 1450 CE
5	Chapter 4: 600 to 1450 CE
6	Chapter 5: 1450 to 1750 CE
7	Chapter 4: 600 to 1450 CE
8	Chapter 7: 1900 CE to Present
9	Chapter 5: 1450 to 1750 CE and Chapter 6: 1750 to 1900 CE
10	Chapter 3: Up to 600 CE and Chapter 6: 1750 to 1900 CE
11	Chapter 7: 1900 CE to Present
12	Chapter 7: 1900 CE to Present
13	Chapter 3: Up to 600 CE
14	Chapter 3: Up to 600 CE
15	Chapter 3: Up to 600 CE
16	Chapter 3: Up to 600 CE
17	Chapter 6: 1750 to 1900 CE
18	Chapter 3: Up to 600 CE and Chapter 4: 600 to 1450 CE
19	Chapter 3: Up to 600 CE
20	Chapter 5: 1450 to 1750 CE
21	Chapter 5: 1450 to 1750 CE
22	Chapter 6: 1750 to 1900 CE
23	Chapter 6: 1750 to 1900 CE
24	Chapter 7: 1900 CE to Present
25	Chapter 6: 1750 to 1900 CE and Chapter 7: 1900 CE to Present
26	Chapter 3: Up to 600 CE
27	Chapter 4: 600 to 1450 CE
28	Chapter 3: Up to 600 CE and Chapter 4: 600 to 1450 CE
29	Chapter 4: 600 to 1450 CE and Chapter 5: 1450 to 1750 CE
30	Chapter 4: 600 to 1450 CE
31	Chapter 5: 1450 to 1750 CE
32	Chapter 6: 1750 to 1900 CE
33	Chapter 6: 1750 to 1900 CE
34	Chapter 5: 1450 to 1750 CE
35	Chapter 5: 1450 to 1750 CE
36	Chapter 3: Up to 600 CE

37	Chapter 3: Up to 600 CE
38	Chapter 3: Up to 600 CE
39	Chapter 3: Up to 600 CE
40	Chapter 3: Up to 600 CE
41	Chapter 3: Up to 600 CE
42	Chapter 4: 600 to 1450 CE and Chapter 5: 1450 to 1750 CE
43	Chapter 5: 1450 to 1750 CE
44	Chapter 6: 1750 to 1900 CE
45	Chapter 7: 1900 CE to Present
46	Chapter 6: 1750 to 1900 CE
47	Chapter 6: 1750 to 1900 CE
48	Chapter 6: 1750 to 1900 CE
49	Chapter 7: 1900 CE to Present
50	Chapter 7: 1900 CE to Present
51	Chapter 3: Up to 600 CE
52	Chapter 3: Up to 600 CE
53	Chapter 4: 600 to 1450 CE
54	Chapter 5: 1450 to 1750 CE
55	Chapter 4: 600 to 1450 CE
56	Chapter 6: 1750 to 1900 CE
57	Chapter 7: 1900 CE to Present
58	Chapter 3: Up to 600 CE and Chapter 4: 600 to 1450 CE
59	Chapter 4: 600 to 1450 CE
60	Chapter 5: 1450 to 1750 CE
61	Chapter 5: 1450 to 1750 CE
62	Chapter 7: 1900 CE to Present
63	Chapter 5: 1450 to 1750 CE and Chapter 6: 1750 to 1900 CE
64	Chapter 3: Up to 600 CE
65	Chapter 4: 600 to 1450 CE
66	Chapter 4: 600 to 1450 CE
67	Chapter 5: 1450 to 1750 CE
68	Chapter 7: 1900 CE to Present
69	Chapter 4: 600 to 1450 CE and Chapter 5: 1450 to 1750 CE
70	Chapter 3: Up to 600 CE and Chapter 4: 600 to 1450 CE

ANSWERS AND EXPLANATIONS

SECTION I

MULTIPLE-CHOICE ANSWERS

1. A

Zheng He made as many as seven long-distance sea voyages during his illustrious career. (B) is not validated by the map, and (C) and (D) are pure speculation.

2. D

Though the United States succeeded in constructing a transcontinental railroad in 1869, Russia did not complete the Moscow to Vladivostok railroad until 1916. The United States did not directly elect senators until the 20th century, and only the United States succeeded in laying a telegraph cable under the ocean within that time frame. However, Russia freed its serfs in 1861 and the Thirteenth Amendment eliminated slavery in the United States in 1865.

3. D

Both Marx and Mao believed in gender equality and both believed in the necessary universality of their beliefs. However, Marx believed the necessary proletarian revolution could only emerge in an industrialized society, whereas Mao saw the seeds of revolution emanating from the peasantry or farmers.

4. B

The Coptic Christian faith plays a dominant role in Ethiopia and a prominent role in Egypt. That faith's representation is significantly smaller in Somalia, Algeria, and Tunisia.

5. B

As a trading regime, the Muslims were more interested in what urban areas had to offer. The smaller numbers of the Vikings meant they were more focused on the booty that could be obtained from monasteries, convents, and smaller villages.

6. B

Though they were both Jesuit missionaries, the two men did not accompany the conquistadores. Neither were they treated as heretics or made inroads in the Scientific Revolution in Europe.

7. A

Both empires had Muslim roots; neither was conquered by any Khan or had any direct relationship to the Mongols. The Mughals had nothing to do with the fall of Constantinople.

8. A

The key here is to look at GDP by sector and literacy rates. Both India and the Central African Republic have at least half their population employed in agriculture, and both have literacy rates of less than 75 percent for the total population. Because the United States is already mentioned as a trade partner, the only possible answer is China.

9. C

France recognized American independence in 1778, Mexico won its independence in 1821, Brazil gained its independence from Portugal in 1824, and Canada became independent in 1867.

10. B

The Social Contract Theory makes no reference to a civil service exam and the Mandate of Heaven makes little reference to slavery. Also, the Industrial Revolution may have encouraged belief in the Social Contract Theory in the West, but it had little impact in the Far East. However, by definition, both endorsed the overthrow of corrupt government.

11. D

The inequitable distribution of land was a prime factor in motivating the "peasant" class in both countries.

12. D

The three most populous Muslim countries in the world in the last century were Indonesia, Pakistan, and India.

13. A

Several of these laws justify the authority of government as the agent of justice.

14. B

Several laws suggest that harm justifies harm, a common theme in the Old Testament.

15. C

Law 221 suggests the existence of classes.

16. C

Ancient rulers typically used the gods to justify their actions.

17. B

Economic determinism is part of Marxian communism and does not play a role here. Thomas Malthus was not an economist, and Ricardo's principle of keeping the worker subsistent would not have had a bearing on this chart. An important feature of mercantilism is the importation of raw goods and the exportation of finished products, which is exactly what these two charts show.

18. D

Olmec predates both Toltec and Aztec; Incan is not Mesoamerican.

19. D

Chang'an was the eastern terminus and Baghdad was a western terminus of the Silk Road.

20. C

Spain and Portugal make up the Iberian peninsula but Spain controlled the other regions at that time.

21. D

With the Columbian Encounter, the world discovered such revolutionary and calorie-rich foods as potatoes and corn. The world is still looking for

choice (C), and (A) did not happen within that time frame. The years 1500–1750 were no more peaceful than the 250 years that preceded them or the 250 years that followed (despite the dramatic impact of the two world wars during the 20th century).

22. A

Although each of these European products was traded to Asia and Africa during that period, the product in greatest demand by local Africans and Asians was weaponry.

23. D

Silk and clocks connected China and Great Britain but not India. Tea was a primary import to Great Britain from India, but not from China. Opium was collected by Great Britain in India and sold to China.

24. B

(A) represents the Great Leap Forward of the 1950s, (C) is the Cultural Revolution of the 1960s and 1970s, and (B) illustrates the state capitalism reforms of Deng Xiaoping from the late 1970s to the present.

25. B

The Monroe Doctrine was a statement to European powers to stay out of Latin American countries that had just become independent and the Brezhnev Doctrine was a statement to Western powers to stay out of the affairs of post–WWII eastern Europe.

26. A

Bushido is the Japanese code for its samurai warriors and not related to the correct answer, the Mandate of Heaven. Matteo Ricci and the Social Contract Theory are European and postdate the Zhou Dynasty.

27. B

European rulers sought to justify their actions by claiming a connection with God. The West African kingdom of Songhay gained legitimacy (and trade advantages) by converting to Islam, and the Aztec leaders demonstrated their power by endorsing sacrifices.

28. B
Mohammad is not important to the teachings of Christianity or Judaism, Jesus is not relevant to Islam, and Ahura Mazda is foreign to all three faiths. Only Abraham is mentioned in the important writings (Bible, Torah, and Quran) of all three faiths.

29. B
Both the Divine Wind and the Protestant Wind were storms that prevented the invasions of different island nations (the Divine Wind frustrated the Mongol invasions of Japan in the 13th century and the Protestant Wind prevented the Spanish invasion of England in the 16th century).

30. C
Urban areas in the Middle East were primarily trade centers, while India and Europe survived on agricultural production. China came closest to housing what would be considered a manufacturing center during that period.

31. B
By the end of the sixteenth century, resilient and adaptable corn could be found in Europe and East Asia.

32. A
Brazil abolished slavery in 1888. The United States ended the practice in 1865 and Mexico did so in 1829; some forms of slavery still exist in Mauritania (a country not located in the New World), the last country in the world to legally abolish slavery, which it did in 1981.

33. D
Far and away, cotton was needed to feed the textile mills of Liverpool and Manchester. Slavery was on the decline, as were imports of rum and timber.

34. B
Because so many calories could be harvested in a relatively small plant, the potato imported from the Americas quickly replaced all other nutrients as the dominant crop in Europe.

35. D
Both the Ottoman and the Italian empires competed for maritime dominance in the Mediterranean Sea during that period.

36. A
Diamond means to say that the nomadic lifestyle brought more leisure time and calories while settled communities brought disease, class conflict, and stress.

37. B
Choice (B) describes the life of the nomadic hunter-gatherers, while the other choices are related to agricultural production.

38. A
With agriculture comes a surplus of food production, which gives rise to the calamities of urbanization: social inequality, disease, and excessive population growth.

39. A
The only conclusion to be drawn from the passage is that Diamond presents an argument that hunter-gatherers may not have led the unpleasant life we once thought.

40. D
The *latifundia* and the *yangban* were the landowning classes in ancient Rome and Korea, respectively.

41. D
Aristotle would not have been familiar with the Four Noble Truths and didn't concern himself with loyalty to the state. Though both approaches respected the farmer, these terms refer to seeking the avoidance of extremes.

42. D
Zheng He tried to avoid military encounters (though he was prepared for such an event) and political takeovers; he was not motivated by the spread of religion. Both men did, however, make it to East Africa.

43. C

Portugal established a trading post at Calicut in 1498; the Dutch and English did not establish trading posts until their trading companies were formed in the 17th century. The Spanish invested their efforts in the Americas.

44. B

In the years before the Opium War, the Americans and the Dutch were minor players in trade negotiations with China, and China and Japan have rarely enjoyed trading with each other. In fact, China's complaint in this passage is one of the major causes of its war against Britain.

45. B

As a Filipino revolutionary in the early 1900s, Emilio Aguinaldo would have found this statement repugnant. In contrast, the other three placed Caucasians atop the racial pyramid and would have approved of Swinton's conclusions.

46. D

The vast majority of historians would agree that the dominant "ism" of the 19th century was nationalism. The supporters of each of the other three movements would pale in comparison.

47. D

The first three choices suggest a cultural pecking order. The idea of a world peacekeeping organization would not support such a pecking order.

48. B

Selection (B) gives the precise definition of presentism. In this case, to retain historical objectivity, historians should ask what prompted Swinton to make these statements rather than criticize him for them.

49. D

Because all three countries remained neutral during both world wars, (D) is the correct answer—(A) and (B) could therefore not possibly be correct. The three countries lost no colonial possessions as a result of the wars.

50. C

The cartoon depicts Soviet Premier Nikita Khrushchev, on the left, and American President John Kennedy, on the right, arm-wrestling over the Cuban Missile Crisis, a 1962 event that nearly resulted in the use of nuclear weapons. The SALT talks were an attempt to reduce armaments that came after Kennedy's presidency, while the Vietnam War did not relate to concern over nuclear usage. The Korean War predated both leaders.

51. B

Both men used religion to quell internal disputes within their respective empires.

52. D

Because this is an image of the Hindu god Shiva, it most likely would be found in South Asia.

53. C

The Mongols never conquered the Philippines, but it's not part of East Asia; they did successfully conquer Korea and China. Although they tried at least twice, the Mongols never successfully invaded Japan.

54. A

A mercantilist most wants to import raw goods that can be used to put citizens to work in factories producing manufactured products. They would not want rum, as it would discourage production, or slaves, as they would take the place of tax-paying citizens. Guns are already a manufactured product so would not be useful to a mercantilist.

55. C

The Janissaries lived in the Middle East and southeastern Europe. The Gupta and Mauryan dynasties appeared well before the Islamic faith was formed.

56. B

The sepoy sought to expel the British from India, while the Boxers hoped to dislodge several European powers from China.

57. A

Ataturk lived outside the time frame and Begin was always aligned with the West, as was King Hussein of Jordan. Ho Chi Minh was a loyal follower of communist ideology. The best answer is Nasser and Nehru, rulers of their respective countries in the 1950s.

58. B

As a generalization, urban centers in pre-Columbian America and South Asia experienced little change during this period, whereas the Middle East saw an increased movement of people to various urban areas. With the fall of the Western Roman Empire, however, Europe experienced a dramatic decline in urban populations.

59. D

The Mongols created the largest continuous land-based empire in history.

60. C

Rice would have been too bulky to ship in large quantities and tomatoes and slaves came from other parts of the world. It was East Asia that produced the silk, porcelain, and spices so much in demand by Europe.

61. D

Though none of the European colonial powers were particularly kind to natives, the French extended more autonomy to the local population than the other European colonists, extending rights of citizenship in some cases.

62. D

Though each is still present to some degree in both developed and developing countries, malaria, cholera, and tuberculosis have been effectively contained in developed countries. Of the four, heart disease remains the biggest threat in industrialized nations.

63. B

Left to right, the images are of Sir Isaac Newton, Sir Charles Darwin, and Dr. Marie Curie.

64. D

The Romans used more and more non-Italians in their ranks of leadership in an attempt to appease the "barbarians," while the Abbasids came to rely increasingly on the support of the Saljuq Turks.

65. B

The Danube flows from the Black Forest in present-day Germany to the Black Sea, and would have been used by the Ottomans.

66. A

Since religion was first recognized in South Asia, the followers of Hinduism have been the majority group.

67. B

European guns sent to Africa were used by the indigenous population to capture additional future slaves, who were transported across the "Middle Passage." The profits from the sale of the slaves were used to purchase raw goods, which were sold to factories in Europe.

68. D

Following World War I, European powers (Great Britain, in particular) determined politically advantageous names and geographic boundaries that often overlooked the actual layout of cultures, traditions, tribes, and ethnicities.

69. B

Until the end of the 15th century, European states lacked the technology (maritime and military) to branch out into uncharted waters. However, with the invention of the caravel and the combined use of the mobile cannon, the astrolabe, and the compass, Europeans were able to venture further and further into the unknown.

70. D

It was during the Han empire that the Silk Road was extended all the way to southwest Asia.

SECTION II

PART A: DOCUMENT-BASED QUESTION—STRONG SAMPLE RESPONSE

The McDonald's restaurant chain has enjoyed remarkable success in the last 65 years. However, this success has not been achieved without controversy. By looking at its economic impact, the way it has "Westernized" the rest of the world, and the anti-McDonald's reaction to its food and marketing techniques, we can better see the footprint McDonald's has left on the world scene.

The economic impact around the world can be seen most dramatically in Documents 1, 9, and 10. To imagine that the consumer price index of the world can be computed by comparing the price of a sandwich around the world is a testament to the power of McDonald's (Document 1). Though the "Economist" probably offered this tongue-in-cheek, as a British magazine it may also be looking at the McDonald's restaurant chain as another superficial and materialistic reflection of American culture. Document 10 mentions the global reach of McDonald's with restaurants in 119 countries, and Document 9 provides real dollar growth during a worldwide recession. Clearly, the franchise has had an impact around the world economically.

For better or worse, McDonald's has spread the values of the West, some of it by marketing and some by calorie consumption. The most amusing is the long lines at the restaurants in Hong Kong. That people would stand for hours to get a three-inch doll of an American icon shows how America is finding root around the world (Document 6). Of course, the popularity of the Moscow McDonald's (Document 2) and the "feeling like I've gone abroad" shows that McDonald's has eclipsed even Coca-Cola as America's ambassador of good will (Good Fill?). Just as the customer is satisfied by the Golden Arches so is the worker in the South African restaurant proud to be associated with an American institution (Document 4). To go from a broom-sweeping worker in South Africa to a limousine-riding monarch in England (Document 5), and both connected to McDonald's seems to capture the full democratic spirit of what the West hopes to convey—and lovin' it served your way! Though I imagine his thoughts have been discredited since he first made them in 1996, to suggest that no two countries that have McDonald's restaurants have ever gone to war against each other (Document 3) is perhaps less an indication of market strategy than the desire to establish restaurants in countries with solid political and economic bases. Nonetheless, the restaurants spread the image of Ronald McDonald.

However, though the Golden Arches may bring a smile to many faces, others see McDonald's in a very dim light. The image in Document 8 shows that there is a backlash against McDonald's and perhaps the info in Document 7 explains why. Bove explains that McDonald's strong-arm tactics really bring unwanted food to regions around the world. However, Bove may be as much motivated by a French culinary tradition and his own economic interests as the welfare of the people. It would be of value to hear from the person in charge of constructing the restaurant, not only to balance out the events but also to hear from people who are now out of a job. Still, there are some who would not be seen under the Golden Arches. Just as Queen Elizabeth would not enter the restaurant (Document 5), so Bolivia has also rejected the restaurant chain (Document 10).

To better gauge McDonald's impact on the world, it would be valuable to see a chart showing the number of different fast-food American restaurants around the world. This would show how unique McDonald's is when compared to restaurants such as KFC, Burger King, and Subway. Certainly, it can be debated whether the Nike logo, the dark silhouette of Mickey Mouse, or the Golden Arches is the more recognized symbol of America, Inc. But that McDonald's has impacted the world cannot be denied.

This is a strong essay, deserving of an 8. The thesis is included in the introductory paragraph; it addresses the question and provides three qualifiers, each of which headlines the following three paragraphs (1 point). It addresses all the documents and demonstrates understanding of each (1 point). All 10 documents are used as evidence (2 points) to support the thesis and three groupings are effectively provided (1 point). Two points of view are clearly presented in two documents (1 point) and there are two requests for additional documents (1 point). This student receives all seven basic core points. The essay receives 1 additional point in the expanded core because document requests are well done and are analyzed for the reasons they are needed to help answer the prompt.

WEAK SAMPLE RESPONSE

The McDonald's restaurant chain has seen much growth since its beginning. It can be seen as the American Dream come true. We can see this by looking at the economic, political, and cultural aspects of this growth.

Documents 2, 6, 9, and 10 talk about McDonald's economic successes. Even Document 2 is quoted as saying "Success is possible in Russia." Document 6 talks about long lines outside the restaurants in Hong Kong and Document 10 explains how large the restaurant chain is, with restaurants in 119 countries around the world. Document 9 provides the factual information by demonstrating the restaurant's continued financial success.

The political theme can be seen in Documents 1, 3, and 7. Document A shows the effect of one sandwich on different countries and Document 3 shows how McDonald's serves the cause of worldwide peace (I never knew it had that kind of impact!). Document 7 shows that not everyone agrees with what McDonald's is doing, sparking a revolt in France.

Finally, McDonald's is spreading the word of the West around the world. Document 4 shows how much South Africa wants to be like the West and Document 5 shows that even a British monarch can be curious about the Golden Arches. All is not peaches and cream, however, as some people find the food disgusting.

In conclusion, McDonald's has changed the world in many ways, culturally, economically, and politically.

No points can be awarded for the thesis primarily because the student has misunderstood the question. Though the student uses all the documents, no points can be awarded because he/she misunderstood Documents 1 and 3. Grouping the documents by categories of economics, politics and culture is not acceptable. There is no attempt at identifying point of view and there is no suggestion of an additional document. This student receives a score of 0.

PART B: CONTINUITY AND CHANGE-OVER-TIME QUESTION—STRONG SAMPLE RESPONSE

Between 1450 and 1750 (from the beginnings of European colonization to the beginnings of the Industrial Revolution), technology had a dramatic impact on the governance of regions within Latin America. Most of this impact was due to the colonization of the region by European powers. Technological innovations in weaponry, transportation, and methods of manufacture would change the way Latin America was governed during this time. Though there was a change in who controlled the reins of power, the devices used to maximize output perpetuated mass indemnity to the soil throughout this time period.

That which changed most dramatically during this time frame was who ruled. Well before the 15th century, the rulers were the indigenous aristocracy. Whether Meso or South America, the ruling elite spoke the same language and worshipped the same gods as the peasants of their region. Rulers may be overthrown by local invaders, but customs and practices remained intact. With the coming of the European invaders, however, all this changed. Ruling families were replaced by viceroys and a dramatic shift in governance began. Instead of worshipping a local ruler, farmers and miners now had to pay homage to a distant king, a monarch that demanded quotas. Whether it was the silver from Potosi or the "white gold" (sugar) from Brazil, the economy evolved from subsistence crops to cash crops.

To meet these quotas, government had to shift to a system of patronage and a bureaucratic pecking order. To this end, the mita system evolved where villages had to supply labor to the government for the purpose of refining the sugar or mining the precious metal. Within this an encomienda system developed that, though social and economic in origin, was political in effect in terms of determining who was in charge. Though the umbilical cord that connected the colony to its European colonial power was weakened by distance, there was no question that the throne in Europe expected to fill their coffers.

All this could not have been accomplished without technological developments. Though the European conquerors (conquistadors) were dramatically outnumbered, their weaponry more than evened the odds. From the armor worn by the horses, to the report of their blunderbusses, clearly the wooden swords of the indigenous population were no match for gunpowder. Of course, the European conquerors had to get to the New World and, once there, had to transport the goods (sugar, silver, gold, rum, timber, tobacco) back to the homeland and none of this could have been possible without technological innovations in navigation. The compass, astrolabe, and lateen sail had been around for some time but combining these devices with the caravel in the 15th century gave the Europeans the wherewithal to explore great distances away from the sight of land. With the fall of Constantinople, Europeans were actively seeking a way to gain precious resources without going through an Ottoman middle man.

Another technological development was the means to mass produce sugar. Historically, sugar was produced in a mortar-pestle device, forcing it to be relatively expensive. In the 15th century, however, a method was developed where sugar cane could be crushed by a device rotated by oxen. Thus, sugar could be produced en masse. Of course, due to the fact that sugar cane had to be harvested during a critically short period of time, producing refined sugar was a labor intensive project. Because large numbers of the indigenous population died due to the diseases imported by the Europeans, producing this sugar demanded the importation of slaves (also made possible by the trading of firearms to Africans who used them to capture future slaves from rival villages). This led to a new form of government based on economic exploitation of the indigenous population, a government theoretically run by a European monarch but in reality run by his representative (the viceroy) who in turn delegated responsibility for order and production to his peninsulares and creoles.

All did not change as the Europeans came in and exploited the people of this region. Throughout this time, peasants continued to serve an aristocracy, be it indigenous or foreign. Methods of production, often carried out with slave labor and such basic mechanical devices as the ox-drawn sugar cane grinder, guaranteed a huge inequity between those who owned the soil and those who worked the soil. The mita system, so actively harnessed by the Europeans, was also used by Aztec and Toltec rulers before them. An issue that would be so important to revolutionaries in this region in a later time period was the unequal distribution of land: an issue that seemed to also permeate the time frame 1450-1750.

So, we can see that were it not for technological innovation, the European invaders would have been frustrated in their attempts to colonize Latin America during the 1450-1750 time period. However, because of the use of weapons, navigational innovation, and new methods of production, the Europeans came into Latin America and dramatically changed government from one based on loyalty to a local aristocracy and monarch to one based on a foreign aristocracy and monarch. Throughout this time frame, however, the rich wore different clothes but the peasants still wore rags. While the throne was changed from local to distant, monarchs still ruled over a peasant class.

This is a very good essay. There is plenty of evidence to support a thesis that is both complete and analytical. Reference to change and continuity is addressed in the body of the essay and there are several examples of historical context. All points from the basic core are earned.

The strength of this essay lies in its evidence and analysis. Several links are made between technology's impact on how government changed in this region during the time frame. This essay receives a score of 9.

WEAK SAMPLE RESPONSE

Technology had a huge impact on how governments changed in Africa between 1450 and 1750. The bringing of guns to Africa by Europeans doomed traditional African village life and emptied the continent of young, hardworking men.

Europeans needed slaves to man their colonies in the New World. Because the Latin Americans were dying from disease, Africa seemed to provide the solution. But how to get the Africans out of Africa? Solution: give guns to some of the local tribes, let them defeat other rival tribes, and the spoils of victory will be selling (for more guns) slaves to Europeans.

Of course, this fighting had a dramatic impact on Africa. To begin, many villages ran out of men and they were not able to repopulate themselves. Also, because there were more guns there was more fighting and bitter rivalries emerged that exist to this day. All this resulted in the disappearance of government and the development of chaos in African villages.

Africa has never recovered from this.

This student gets one point for this essay. There is no thesis because there is no reference to West Africa ("Africa" does not distinguish among the regions) and because there is no attempt anywhere to talk about continuity. There is very little evidence—certainly not enough to get any points—and there is no real analysis. It's weak, but one point can be given at the beginning of the second paragraph for historical context. Finally, nowhere in this essay is there a connection between technology and governance.

PART C: COMPARATIVE QUESTION—STRONG SAMPLE RESPONSE

Many similarities and differences can be identified as the religions of Christianity and Islam spread across Afro-Eurasia between 100 and 1450. Though the growth of Christianity would essentially happen in the first half of this time frame and the growth of Islam would essentially happen in the second half, the success of each faith was meteoric with dramatic similarities and differences. The success of the spread of both faiths can be explained by the similarities of both spreading the faith with an evangelistic spirit (though they differed in the types of people used to spread this faith), the syncretic practicalities of adjusting their faith to incorporate the beliefs and practices of the local people, and the realities that as the two faiths spread more and more from their epicenters, there was a tendency for splinter groups to form. The two faiths differed in that the Islamic faith seemed to be more accommodating as it traveled to new lands. Also, Islam solved the problem of persecution as it was created while Christianity continued to be plagued by persecution during the early years of its existence as it attempted to spread its faith throughout the Roman Empire.

Both Islam and Christianity used missionaries to spread their faiths to distant lands. For Christians, these were missionaries pledged to the goal of conversion. For Muslims, these were soldiers and traders fully believing in their faith. In both instances, the believers in these two faiths successfully converted people to their faith. Though both faiths had their evangelists, the style of conversion may have been quite different. During this time, Muslims seemed to be more accommodating and tolerant of other faiths as they spread. There were, however, social and economic advantages to becoming Muslim: the Islamic faith at least officially tolerated other beliefs, especially those who were "people of the book." This is perhaps best reflected in West Africa after the 11th century. Successful traders and monarchs were Muslim with little pressure on others in the community to convert, though all recognized the economic advantage and many eventually did convert in Songhai and Mali. Christianity, on the other hand, frequently applied heavy-handed tactics. Textbooks love to talk about the "convert or die" tactics of Charlemagne.

Another similarity is that both faiths were syncretic as they moved away from their points of origin, meaning they adopted their faiths to accommodate the local customs. An example of this is that Christian missionaries spreading their faith in South Asia accepted the ascetic lifestyles practiced in that part of the world and made it a part of their religious practice upon returning to Europe. In the same manner, Muslim religious leaders made the practice of veiling observed in South Asia a more universal part of their religious expectations throughout Dar al-Islam.

Another similarity is how the faiths tended to fracture as they spread. As Islam spread into Persia, a serious conflict within its early leadership led to the creation of the Shi'a sect within the faith. Though Christianity has had several fractures in this time frame, most notably the Great Schism in the 11th century, I would like to talk about the early Nestorian break. In the early years of this time frame, as Christianity spread into Southwest Asia, there was a serious conflict over the nature of Christ. This break was philosophical in appearance but geographic in cause: the beliefs of Nestorius appealed more and more to the people of that part of the world. So, both religions as they spread further and further from their homeland in the early years had difficulty holding onto their flock.

A more subtle distinction between the two faiths lay in the role of persecution. Though both religions (indeed, perhaps all religions) were born in persecution, Islam seemed to resolve the issue more dramatically as their faith was born. Most of Islam's critics were eradicated when Mohammad returned to Mecca. Christian missionaries continued to face persecution even as they continued to spread their message throughout the Roman Empire. This persecution was not silenced until well into the fourth century, when Christianity was officially recognized as the imperial religion.

We can therefore see that the spread of Christianity and Islam during the time frame 100-1450 had the similarities of both having to endure splintering as they grew, both relying on the message of the evangelist to spread their teachings, and both accommodating the faiths of the local populace. Still, the spread of the two faiths were different in that Islam was more inclusive and accommodating, they used different agents to spread their faiths, and persecution played a different role.

This essay receives a score of 9. All components in the basic core are present and it receives additional expanded points because of its strong evidence, categories of investigation, and comparisons.

WEAK SAMPLE RESPONSE

The spread of Islam and Christianity were similar in that they both penetrated the same regions but different in that they used different methods to convert the places they conquered. Also, Christians had more time to do it.

One striking similarity is they have similar beliefs. Both Islam and Christianity are monotheistic and both were "born" in the same part of the world. This similarity in beliefs has caused them to compete for the same people that would be potential followers. This has caused them to not get along throughout history.

The differences lie in their methods of conversion. Christianity would send bishops over to the new lands and patiently convert the local population while Muslims would send merchants. One attracted people through the prospect of eternal redemption and the other promised a discount on goods sold.

We can see that the similarities lie in the lands visited but the differences lie in the methods of conversion.

This essay earns no points. The evidence is replete with factual inaccuracies, the thesis is inadequate—the region and time frame aren't mentioned—and there is no attempt to address the topic of religious spread. This essay receives a score of zero.

Practice Test 2 Answer Grid

1. Ⓐ Ⓑ Ⓒ Ⓓ
2. Ⓐ Ⓑ Ⓒ Ⓓ
3. Ⓐ Ⓑ Ⓒ Ⓓ
4. Ⓐ Ⓑ Ⓒ Ⓓ
5. Ⓐ Ⓑ Ⓒ Ⓓ
6. Ⓐ Ⓑ Ⓒ Ⓓ
7. Ⓐ Ⓑ Ⓒ Ⓓ
8. Ⓐ Ⓑ Ⓒ Ⓓ
9. Ⓐ Ⓑ Ⓒ Ⓓ
10. Ⓐ Ⓑ Ⓒ Ⓓ
11. Ⓐ Ⓑ Ⓒ Ⓓ
12. Ⓐ Ⓑ Ⓒ Ⓓ
13. Ⓐ Ⓑ Ⓒ Ⓓ
14. Ⓐ Ⓑ Ⓒ Ⓓ
15. Ⓐ Ⓑ Ⓒ Ⓓ
16. Ⓐ Ⓑ Ⓒ Ⓓ
17. Ⓐ Ⓑ Ⓒ Ⓓ
18. Ⓐ Ⓑ Ⓒ Ⓓ

19. Ⓐ Ⓑ Ⓒ Ⓓ
20. Ⓐ Ⓑ Ⓒ Ⓓ
21. Ⓐ Ⓑ Ⓒ Ⓓ
22. Ⓐ Ⓑ Ⓒ Ⓓ
23. Ⓐ Ⓑ Ⓒ Ⓓ
24. Ⓐ Ⓑ Ⓒ Ⓓ
25. Ⓐ Ⓑ Ⓒ Ⓓ
26. Ⓐ Ⓑ Ⓒ Ⓓ
27. Ⓐ Ⓑ Ⓒ Ⓓ
28. Ⓐ Ⓑ Ⓒ Ⓓ
29. Ⓐ Ⓑ Ⓒ Ⓓ
30. Ⓐ Ⓑ Ⓒ Ⓓ
31. Ⓐ Ⓑ Ⓒ Ⓓ
32. Ⓐ Ⓑ Ⓒ Ⓓ
33. Ⓐ Ⓑ Ⓒ Ⓓ
34. Ⓐ Ⓑ Ⓒ Ⓓ
35. Ⓐ Ⓑ Ⓒ Ⓓ
36. Ⓐ Ⓑ Ⓒ Ⓓ

37. Ⓐ Ⓑ Ⓒ Ⓓ
38. Ⓐ Ⓑ Ⓒ Ⓓ
39. Ⓐ Ⓑ Ⓒ Ⓓ
40. Ⓐ Ⓑ Ⓒ Ⓓ
41. Ⓐ Ⓑ Ⓒ Ⓓ
42. Ⓐ Ⓑ Ⓒ Ⓓ
43. Ⓐ Ⓑ Ⓒ Ⓓ
44. Ⓐ Ⓑ Ⓒ Ⓓ
45. Ⓐ Ⓑ Ⓒ Ⓓ
46. Ⓐ Ⓑ Ⓒ Ⓓ
47. Ⓐ Ⓑ Ⓒ Ⓓ
48. Ⓐ Ⓑ Ⓒ Ⓓ
49. Ⓐ Ⓑ Ⓒ Ⓓ
50. Ⓐ Ⓑ Ⓒ Ⓓ
51. Ⓐ Ⓑ Ⓒ Ⓓ
52. Ⓐ Ⓑ Ⓒ Ⓓ
53. Ⓐ Ⓑ Ⓒ Ⓓ
54. Ⓐ Ⓑ Ⓒ Ⓓ

55. Ⓐ Ⓑ Ⓒ Ⓓ
56. Ⓐ Ⓑ Ⓒ Ⓓ
57. Ⓐ Ⓑ Ⓒ Ⓓ
58. Ⓐ Ⓑ Ⓒ Ⓓ
59. Ⓐ Ⓑ Ⓒ Ⓓ
60. Ⓐ Ⓑ Ⓒ Ⓓ
61. Ⓐ Ⓑ Ⓒ Ⓓ
62. Ⓐ Ⓑ Ⓒ Ⓓ
63. Ⓐ Ⓑ Ⓒ Ⓓ
64. Ⓐ Ⓑ Ⓒ Ⓓ
65. Ⓐ Ⓑ Ⓒ Ⓓ
66. Ⓐ Ⓑ Ⓒ Ⓓ
67. Ⓐ Ⓑ Ⓒ Ⓓ
68. Ⓐ Ⓑ Ⓒ Ⓓ
69. Ⓐ Ⓑ Ⓒ Ⓓ
70. Ⓐ Ⓑ Ⓒ Ⓓ

PRACTICE TEST 2

Section I: Multiple-Choice Questions

Time: 55 Minutes
70 Questions

Directions: Each of the questions or incomplete statements below is followed by four suggested answers or completions. Select the one that is best in each case and then fill in the corresponding oval on the answer sheet.

1. Which of the following is true of both Mesopotamia and Egypt?

   (A) Both were organized into city-states.

   (B) Both were ruled by a military dicatorship.

   (C) Both used writing systems.

   (D) Both had monotheistic belief systems.

2. All of the following were characteristics of classical civilizations EXCEPT

   (A) social stratification.

   (B) extensive trade.

   (C) an organized bureaucracy.

   (D) democratic institutions.

3. Buddhism and Christianity have which of the following in common?

   (A) Belief in one god

   (B) A hierarchal organization

   (C) An emphasis on missionary activity

   (D) De-emphasis on rituals

4. Which of the following statements most accurately reflects a major difference between the fall of the Roman and Han Empires?

   (A) The effects of a decline in trade were more severe in Rome than in Han.

   (B) Only Rome suffered from major issues with government corruption.

   (C) While the Han had difficulty collecting taxes, the Roman Empire maintained an efficient tax collection system.

   (D) The spread of Buddhism had a large impact on the decline of Han, while Christianity had little impact on the decline of Rome.

GO ON TO THE NEXT PAGE

5. Dharma and karma are important concepts in which of the following two religions?

   (A) Judaism and Buddhism
   (B) Daoism and Confucianism
   (C) Hinduism and Islam
   (D) Buddhism and Hinduism

6. All of the following contributed to the Bantu Migration EXCEPT

   (A) animal domestication.
   (B) population pressure.
   (C) use of iron tools.
   (D) cultivation of bananas.

7. Which of the following statements best describes the political heritage of classical China?

   (A) Citizens are obligated to participate in the institution of government.
   (B) The emperor is to the state as the father is to the family.
   (C) The leader with the strongest army will wield the power.
   (D) The emperor should be questioned by his people.

8. Christianity spread to all of the following areas by 600 CE EXCEPT

   (A) the Middle East.
   (B) Western Europe.
   (C) East Africa.
   (D) East Asia.

9. After the expansion of Islam into West Africa,

   (A) the economy slowed.
   (B) a decentralized government developed.
   (C) civil war broke out.
   (D) trade increased.

10. According to Confucius, the most important role of the scholar-gentry class was to

   (A) found universities for teaching the young.
   (B) create a large bureaucracy.
   (C) rewrite the civil service exam.
   (D) promote harmony through the administration of the state.

11. Which of the following two religions have had the greatest impact on Japan through the centuries?

   (A) Daoism and Buddhism
   (B) Shinto and Buddhism
   (C) Animism and Hinduism
   (D) Christianity and Confucianism

12. In the time period 600 to 1450 CE, Dunhuang, Kashgar, and Samarkand were examples of

   (A) oasis towns on the Silk Road.
   (B) political capitals in East Africa.
   (C) economic centers on the Mediterranean Sea.
   (D) religious pilgrimage sites in South Asia.

GO ON TO THE NEXT PAGE ⟶

13. The collapse of empire was more negative in Western Europe than it was in the eastern Mediterranean or China because

(A) only Rome lost political control of the empire.

(B) continual waves of nomadic invasions made recovery difficult.

(C) the increase in Rome's population made feeding the population difficult.

(D) the Han dynasty in China was able to recover power.

14. Which of the following best describes the religious beliefs in Paleolithic society?

(A) Monotheistic

(B) Polytheistic

(C) Syncretistic

(D) Animistic

15. Which of the following had the most advanced naval technology in the time period 600 to 1450?

(A) Western Europe

(B) China

(C) West Africa

(D) India

16. Which of the following empires existed more than 500 years after the other four?

(A) Han

(B) Roman

(C) Gupta

(D) Song

17. All of the following were tributary states of China EXCEPT

(A) Korea.

(B) Tibet.

(C) Vietnam.

(D) India.

18. Why do historians know little about what led to the decline of the Indus Valley civilization?

(A) This river valley civilization left no written records.

(B) Its written records were destroyed by Mongol invaders.

(C) Its writing system has never been deciphered.

(D) It left written records which stop prior to its period of decline.

19. "The unexamined life is not worth living." This quotation was an important part of philosophy in which classical civilization?

(A) China

(B) India

(C) Southeast Asia

(D) Greece

GO ON TO THE NEXT PAGE

20. The term *Dar al-Islam* refers to

    (A) areas that share a common Muslim culture as a basis for society.

    (B) lands that are enemies of the Muslim religion.

    (C) religious leaders' influence in the community.

    (D) conquered areas that refuse to convert to Islam.

21. Which of the following did NOT facilitate commercial growth in the years 600–1450 CE?

    (A) The minting of coins

    (B) Government support of industry

    (C) The establishment of trade organizations

    (D) State-sponsored infrastructure projects

22. Which of the following is true of trade in the Indian Ocean during the time period 600 to 1450?

    (A) Europeans played a dominant role in the Indian Ocean.

    (B) Due to nomadic invasions, economic activity slowed considerably.

    (C) Chinese merchants were the only major participants in the trade.

    (D) Trade flourished with a mix of East African, South Asian, and Middle Eastern merchants.

23. The Ming dynasty halted the voyages of Zheng He because

    (A) the Chinese had a difficult time competing with European technology.

    (B) the Chinese had an unfavorable balance of trade.

    (C) the voyages were expensive and the world beyond China was deemed of little value.

    (D) the ships had been greatly damaged during earlier expeditions.

24. Which of the following statements is an accurate comparison of the Aztec and Mongol Empires?

    (A) Both groups expanded their empire by conquering and dominating neighboring areas.

    (B) The Aztecs collected taxes from their people, while the Mongols only demanded corvee.

    (C) The Mongols were far superior administrators than the Aztecs.

    (D) Trade was discouraged in both the Aztec and Mongol Empires.

25. The three statements below refer to which of the following?

    • Works of Leonardo da Vinci
    • Importance of the Medici family
    • Wealth of Mediterranean Sea trade

    (A) Northern Renaissance

    (B) Protestant Reformation

    (C) Enlightenment

    (D) Italian Renaissance

GO ON TO THE NEXT PAGE ⟹

26. Islam and Buddhism came into direct contact with each other during the time period 600 to 1450 in the region of

    (A) Western Europe.
    (B) East Africa.
    (C) Central Asia.
    (D) Eastern Europe.

27. In the time period 600 to 1450, the Mongols, Turks, and Vikings are all examples of

    (A) large empire builders.
    (B) nomadic people.
    (C) large organized bureaucracies.
    (D) skilled horsemen.

28. Which of the following describes the major impact of the Crusades on Western Europe?

    (A) European political dominance in the Middle East aided their development of shipping technology.
    (B) The exposure to Eastern goods and technology led to an increase in trade.
    (C) The feudal system was strengthened as a result.
    (D) The loss of the Crusades set Western Europe back economically hundreds of years.

29. The forced migration of enslaved Africans to the Americas in the 17th and 18th centuries resulted in

    (A) plantation-style agriculture in Southern Europe.
    (B) altered male-to-female ratios in Africa.
    (C) declining slave trading in the Middle East.
    (D) lower agricultural yields in the Caribbean and Latin America.

30. The Columbian Exchange caused all of the following EXCEPT

    (A) the population of Native Americans declined.
    (B) American foods were introduced to Europe.
    (C) European diseases were introduced to the Americas.
    (D) African diseases were introduced to Europe.

31. All of the statements below refer to which empire in the time period 1450 to 1750?

    • Lucrative trans-Saharan trade
    • All emperors were Muslim
    • Islamic universities at Timbuktu

    (A) Fatimid
    (B) Ottoman
    (C) Mughal
    (D) Songhay

GO ON TO THE NEXT PAGE

32. The photograph of the Taj Mahal above is representative of which type of architecture?

(A) Hindu

(B) Islamic

(C) Byzantine

(D) Chinese

33. As the Ottomans dominated much of the Middle East and North Africa during the time period 1450 to 1750, which of the following empires dominated South Asia?

(A) Safavid

(B) Delhi Sultanate

(C) Manchu

(D) Mughal

34. Women associated with the palace court of the Ottoman Empire wielded power by

(A) serving in administrative positions in the empire.

(B) selecting the vizier.

(C) influencing the sultan behind the scenes.

(D) speaking in public on political matters.

35. Which of the following contributed the most to the increase of the Atlantic slave trade?

(A) Industrialization

(B) Sugar plantations

(C) Absolute monarchies

(D) Laissez-faire capitalism

36. All of the following are crops from the New World that were introduced to Afro-Eurasia through the Columbian Exchange EXCEPT

(A) coffee.

(B) potatoes.

(C) manioc.

(D) maize.

GO ON TO THE NEXT PAGE

37. All of the following statements are true about Japan during the time period 1450 to 1750 EXCEPT that

(A) foreign trade was restricted by the government.

(B) the shogun ruled the country.

(C) Christians were persecuted.

(D) the economy declined.

38. Between 1450 and 1750, European interest in American colonies was primarily motivated by

(A) the need to escape the harsh European climate.

(B) its ability to spread democratic beliefs to a new area.

(C) the chance to make a large profit from cash crops.

(D) the ease of travel to the Americas.

39. A common feature of both Japanese and European feudalism was

(A) social mobility.

(B) political participation by all classes.

(C) a strong centralized authority.

(D) a strict social structure.

40. Which of the following places or empires had road systems similar to the Incan Empire and Tang dynasty?

(A) Rome and Persia

(B) Moscow and Kiev

(C) Athens and Sparta

(D) Egypt and Babylon

41. Neo-Confucianism refers to the

(A) rejection of Confucian beliefs during the Yuan dynasty.

(B) blending of Buddhist and Confucian ideas.

(C) spread of Confucianism to Japan.

(D) use of Confucianism to monitor economic relations.

42. All of the following were policies of Russia's Peter the Great EXCEPT

(A) increased foreign trade.

(B) the introduction of Western style of dress.

(C) improved technology.

(D) the use of Enlightenment ideas in the government.

43. A result of the political revolutions of the late 18th and 19th centuries was that they

(A) spread Enlightenment ideas through Europe and the Americas.

(B) strengthened European control over South America.

(C) prevented the formation of the nation-state.

(D) instituted Marxist ideas through Europe.

GO ON TO THE NEXT PAGE

44. Which of the following was NOT one of the basic ideals of Enlightenment thinkers?

(A) Popular sovereignty

(B) Freedom of speech

(C) Religious tolerance

(D) Equality for women

45. All of the following were key principles of the formation of the United States EXCEPT

(A) a written constitution.

(B) a federal government based on popular sovereignty.

(C) equality for all.

(D) three branches of government.

46. Which of the following events aided the success of the Latin American independence movements in the 1800s?

(A) German unification

(B) The Sepoy Mutiny

(C) Napoleon's invasion of Spain

(D) The Industrial Revolution

47. Simón Bolívar, Miguel de Hidalgo, and Jośe de San Martín are all examples of

(A) captains of industry.

(B) Spanish viceroys.

(C) leaders of slave revolts.

(D) revolutionary leaders.

48. Dominant power in Latin America during the late 1700s and early 1800s lay in the hands of the

(A) peninsulares.

(B) Creoles.

(C) middle class.

(D) mestizos.

49. Which of the following BEST represents a key idea of Karl Marx?

(A) The formation of trade unions would alleviate the problems of the industrial workers.

(B) The abuses of the capitalist system would be solved only if the system were overthrown.

(C) Democratic reforms would bring equality to the underprivileged.

(D) Factory owners need to give workers a minimum wage and health insurance.

50. All of the following were results of industrialization EXCEPT

(A) changes in working conditions.

(B) the family unit serving as an economic unit.

(C) greater opportunities for economic advancement.

(D) cheaper manufactured goods.

GO ON TO THE NEXT PAGE

51. All of the following statements describe developments in the Ottoman Empire in the time period 1750 to 1900 EXCEPT

(A) Europeans were exempt from following Ottoman law.

(B) Tanzimat reformers were inspired by Enlightenment thought.

(C) the Young Turk Party promoted reforms.

(D) the Islamic leadership, or ulama, supported the liberal reforms.

52. The Berlin Conference of 1884–1885 resulted in the

(A) division of Africa among European powers.

(B) creation of spheres of influence in China.

(C) redrawing of the map of Europe.

(D) colonization of India by the British.

53. Which of the following accurately describes the changes for middle- and working-class European women in the time period 1750 to 1900?

(A) Both middle- and working-class women achieved the right to vote.

(B) Working-class women labored in factories, and middle-class women followed the cult of domesticity.

(C) Middle-class women were paid more than working-class women for similar jobs.

(D) Working-class women were not as affected by the industrial revolution as middle-class women.

54. The 19th-century ideology of Social Darwinism promoted the notion that

(A) scientific processes could address all issues formerly only answered through religion.

(B) industrialization would lead to the eventual revolution of the working class.

(C) the domination of Europeans over subject peoples was an inevitable result of innate superiority.

(D) a ruler had an obligation to protect the natural rights of his citizens.

55. The Indian National Congress and the Pan-African Congress were important examples of

(A) economic alliances between countries in the developing world.

(B) nationalist organizations aimed at removing European control.

(C) international organizations with the goal of preventing Cold War conflicts.

(D) nongovernment organizations aimed at bringing industrialization to Asian and African countries.

56. The Boxer Rebellion was to China what the Sepoy Mutiny was to

(A) the Ottoman Empire.

(B) Japan.

(C) Korea.

(D) India.

GO ON TO THE NEXT PAGE

57. What late 20th-century issue in Latin America can be traced back to colonial times?

   (A) Urban crime

   (B) Uneven distribution of wealth

   (C) Agricultural overproduction

   (D) Theocratic rule

58. Japan's expansionism in Manchuria and China in the 1930s coincided with

   (A) its rapid industrialization.

   (B) closer ties with the United States.

   (C) the growing influence of the League of Nations.

   (D) the declining power of Japan's emperor.

"Homespun cloth delivers the poor from the bonds of the rich and creates a moral and spiritual bond between the classes and the masses. It restores to the poor somewhat of what the rich have taken from them."

"Nonviolence is a power which can be wielded equally by all—children, young men and women or grown-up people—provided they have a living faith in the God of Love and have therefore equal love for all mankind. When non-violence is accepted as the law of life it must pervade the whole being and not be applied to isolated acts."

59. These quotations come from which 20th-century leader?

   (A) Mao Zedong

   (B) Kwame Nkrumah

   (C) Ho Chi Minh

   (D) Mohandas Gandhi

60. Which of the following is a similarity between the Russian Revolution (1917) and the Chinese Revolution (1949)?

   (A) Both replaced corrupt monarchies.

   (B) Both involved a bloody civil war.

   (C) Both appealed primarily to the urban proletariat.

   (D) Both communist governments were overthrown within 25 years.

61. Many developing nations struggle with

   (A) low birthrates.

   (B) lack of natural resources.

   (C) no foreign aid.

   (D) a weak industrial base.

62. African and Asian nationalist movements in the 20th century were usually led by

   (A) urban factory workers.

   (B) aristocracy.

   (C) peasantry.

   (D) the educated class.

GO ON TO THE NEXT PAGE ▷

63. The Treaty of Versailles did not forge a lasting peace because the

   (A) Russians would not agree to the terms of the treaty.

   (B) treaty was solely influenced by Woodrow Wilson's Fourteen Points.

   (C) United States wished to punish the Germans for starting the war.

   (D) Germans were forced to accept total blame for the war and were severely punished.

64. Which of the following statements best defines genocide in the 20th century?

   (A) The trend toward liberalism in South Asia

   (B) The systematic murder of ethnic minorities

   (C) The rise of existentialist thought

   (D) The rapid industrialization of developing countries

65. Islam is the main religious faith associated with which of the following present-day nations?

   (A) Pakistan and Indonesia

   (B) Malaysia and Vietnam

   (C) Iran and South Africa

   (D) Bosnia and Romania

66. A global effect of World War I was

   (A) the economic and political isolation of Japan.

   (B) a 20-year period of economic stability.

   (C) the rise of nationalist movements in colonial areas.

   (D) the spread of communist regimes in Western Europe.

67. Which of the following statements accurately compares India's and Cuba's role in the Cold War?

   (A) Both nations were supporters of the Soviet Union.

   (B) Both nations refused to choose sides.

   (C) Cuba was a supporter of the Soviet Union, while India remained non-aligned.

   (D) Cuba was a supporter of the United States, while India supported the Soviet Union.

GO ON TO THE NEXT PAGE

68. Vladimir Lenin was to the Russian Revolution what Ayatollah Khomeini was to the

   (A) Zionist movement.
   (B) Egyptian nationalist movement.
   (C) Palestinian Liberation Organization.
   (D) Iranian Revolution.

69. Kwame Nkrumah, Jomo Kenyatta, and Frantz Fanon are all examples of

   (A) nationalist leaders.
   (B) communist leaders.
   (C) union leaders.
   (D) industrial capitalists.

70. Which of the following best describes the Israeli-Palestinian conflict in the latter half of the 20th century?

   (A) The international community ignored the issues of both sides.
   (B) Both sides had religious and historic claims to the same land.
   (C) The conflicts between European powers in the region continued.
   (D) The competition was over oil rights in the land.

IF YOU FINISH BEFORE TIME IS CALLED, YOU MAY CHECK YOUR WORK ON THIS SECTION ONLY. DO NOT TURN TO ANY OTHER SECTION IN THE TEST. **STOP**

Section II

Part A: Document-Based Question

Mandatory reading period: 10 minutes
Suggested writing time: 40 minutes

Directions: The following question is based on the accompanying Documents 1 to 10. (The documents have been edited for purposes of this exercise.)

This question is designed to test your ability to work with and understand historical documents. Write an essay that:

- Has a relevant thesis and supports that thesis with evidence from the documents.

- Uses all of the documents.

- Analyzes the documents by grouping them in as many appropriate ways as possible; does not simply summarize the documents individually.

- Takes into account the sources of the documents and analyzes the authors' points of view.

- Explains the need for at least one additional type of document.

You may refer to relevant historical information not mentioned in the documents

Prompt: Analyze the roles of women under communist rule in the Soviet Union and China. Identify an additional document and explain how it would help you analyze the roles of women during communism in the Soviet Union and China.

Historical Background: The Bolsheviks gained power in Russia in 1917, forming the Soviet Union. The Soviet Union, and specifically the Communist Party, remained in power until its collapse in 1991. In China, Mao Zedong and his Chinese Communist Party seized power in 1949. The Communist Party controls China up through the modern period.

DOCUMENT 1

Source: V.I. Lenin, leader of the Bolsheviks and instigator of communist revolution in Russia, from articles in the official Soviet newspaper *Pravda*, 1920.

The Soviet government was the first and only government in the world to abolish completely all the old, bourgeois, infamous laws which placed women in an inferior position compared with men and which granted privileges to men, as, for instance, in the sphere of marriage laws or in the sphere of the legal attitude to children. The Soviet government was the first and only government in the world which, as a government of the toilers, abolished all the privileges connected with property, which men retained in the family laws of all bourgeois republics, even the most democratic.

The proletariat cannot achieve complete freedom, unless it achieves complete freedom for women.

GO ON TO THE NEXT PAGE

DOCUMENT 2

Source: Emma Goldman, an American anarchist deported to Russia in 1920, from her memoirs *My Disillusionment in Russia*, 1923.

…the rations were distributed at the Commissary, but one had to fetch them himself. One day, while waiting my turn in the long line, a peasant girl came in and asked for vinegar. "Vinegar! who is it calls for such a luxury?" cried several women. It appeared that the girl was Zinoviev's servant. She spoke of him as her master, who worked very hard and was surely entitled to something extra. At once a storm of indignation broke loose. "Master! is that what we made the Revolution for, or was it to do away with masters? Zinoviev is no more than we, and he is not entitled to more."

DOCUMENT 3

Source: Grigory Shegl, teacher at the Moscow Art Institute and artist, official government poster, 1931.

Caption: Say goodbye to kitchen slavery!
Let the new life begin!

GO ON TO THE NEXT PAGE

DOCUMENT 4

Source: Krupskaya, V.I. Lenin's wife and a leader within the Bolshevik Party, preface to Lenin's *The Emancipation of Women*, 1933.

We in Russia no longer have the base, mean and infamous denial of rights to women or inequality of the sexes, that disgusting survival of feudalism and medievalism of the greedy bourgeoisie in every other country in the world without exception.

DOCUMENT 5

Source: Mao Zedong, Chairman of the Chinese Communist Party, excerpts from *The Selected Quotations of Mao Zedong* (known as the *Little Red Book*).

Introductory note to *Women Have Gone to the Labour Front*, 1955

In order to build a great socialist society it is of the utmost importance to arouse the broad masses of women to join in productive activity. Men and women must receive equal pay for equal work in production. Genuine equality between the sexes can only be realized in the process of the socialist transformation of society as a whole.

DOCUMENT 6

Source: Chinese poster used by the Chinese Communist Party (CCP), 1965.

Caption: Become a red seedling—Strike root, flower and bear seeds in the places the motherhood needs it most!

GO ON TO THE NEXT PAGE

DOCUMENT 7

Source: Shao Dangdi, Chinese grandmother and insurance agent, comments quoted in the American magazine *The New Republic*, March 2004.

After Liberation, women were made very equal.... The government promoted women's equality, but also it was necessary for family survival: you couldn't live on a single income. Now, you can.... Work units were required to maintain a rough gender balance in all departments and at all levels.... Now the workplace is so competitive. There are too many educated young people vying for too few positions, so employers pick the men first.

DOCUMENT 8

Source: Article in the official Chinese government's magazine *Women of China*, September 2004.

Career women, a modern meaning in its earliest usage, referred to female workers in the spinning, filature and tobacco production industries. As more women received educations and the women's liberation movement shook the last part of the 19th century, female teaching school graduates were able to become primary school teachers or nursery governesses. Women also became medical practitioners. In the 1920s and 1930, women could become teachers, library workers, editors and/or translators, accountants, lawyers, clerks, writers, actresses, shop assistants, operators, typists, stenographers and post employees. All those positions required education and skills.

Part B: Continuity and Change-Over-Time Question

Suggested writing time: 40 minutes

Directions: You are to answer the following question. You should spend five minutes organizing or outlining your essay. Write an essay that:

- Has a relevant thesis and supports that thesis with appropriate historical evidence.
- Addresses all parts of the question.
- Uses world historical context to show continuities and changes over time.
- Analyzes the process of continuity and change over time.

> **Prompt:** Analyze the continuities and changes in demography and the environment (for example, disease, animals, new crops, and population) in ONE of the following areas from 1450 to 1750.
>
> - The Americas
> - China
> - Europe
> - Sub-Saharan Africa

Part C: Comparative Question

Suggested writing time: 40 minutes

Directions: You are to answer the following question. You should spend five minutes organizing or outlining your essay. Write an essay that:

- Has a relevant thesis and supports that thesis with appropriate historical evidence.
- Addresses all parts of the question.
- Makes direct, relevant comparisons.
- Analyzes relevant reasons for similarities and differences.

> **Prompt:** Analyze the major similarities and differences in the spread of TWO of the following religions between 1000 BCE and 600 CE.
>
> - Judaism
> - Christianity
> - Buddhism

IF YOU FINISH BEFORE TIME IS CALLED, YOU MAY CHECK YOUR WORK ON THIS SECTION ONLY. DO NOT TURN TO ANY OTHER SECTION IN THE TEST.

PRACTICE TEST 2: ANSWER KEY

1.	C	25.	D	49.	B
2.	D	26.	C	50.	B
3.	C	27.	B	51.	D
4.	A	28.	B	52.	A
5.	D	29.	B	53.	B
6.	A	30.	D	54.	C
7.	B	31.	D	55.	B
8.	D	32.	B	56.	D
9.	D	33.	D	57.	B
10.	D	34.	C	58.	A
11.	B	35.	B	59.	D
12.	A	36.	A	60.	B
13.	B	37.	D	61.	D
14.	D	38.	C	62.	D
15.	B	39.	D	63.	D
16.	D	40.	A	64.	B
17.	D	41.	B	65.	A
18.	C	42.	D	66.	C
19.	D	43.	A	67.	C
20.	A	44.	D	68.	D
21.	B	45.	C	69.	A
22.	D	46.	C	70.	B
23.	C	47.	D		
24.	A	48.	A		

PRACTICE TEST 2: ASSESS YOUR STRENGTHS

Question	Chapter
1	Chapter 3: Up to 600 CE
2	Chapter 3: Up to 600 CE
3	Chapter 3: Up to 600 CE
4	Chapter 3: Up to 600 CE
5	Chapter 3: Up to 600 CE
6	Chapter 4: 600 to 1450 CE
7	Chapter 3: Up to 600 CE
8	Chapter 3: Up to 600 CE
9	Chapter 4: 600 to 1450 CE
10	Chapter 3: Up to 600 CE
11	Chapter 3: Up to 600 CE
12	Chapter 4: 600 to 1450 CE
13	Chapter 3: Up to 600 CE
14	Chapter 3: Up to 600 CE
15	Chapter 4: 600 to 1450 CE
16	Chapter 3: Up to 600 CE
17	Chapter 4: 600 to 1450 CE
18	Chapter 3: Up to 600 CE
19	Chapter 3: Up to 600 CE
20	Chapter 4: 600 to 1450 CE
21	Chapter 4: 600 to 1450 CE
22	Chapter 4: 600 to 1450 CE
23	Chapter 4: 600 to 1450 CE
24	Chapter 4: 600 to 1450 CE
25	Chapter 5: 1450 to 1750 CE
26	Chapter 4: 600 to 1450 CE
27	Chapter 4: 600 to 1450 CE
28	Chapter 4: 600 to 1450 CE
29	Chapter 5: 1450 to 1750 CE
30	Chapter 5: 1450 to 1750 CE
31	Chapter 5: 1450 to 1750 CE
32	Chapter 5: 1450 to 1750 CE
33	Chapter 5: 1450 to 1750 CE
34	Chapter 5: 1450 to 1750 CE
35	Chapter 5: 1450 to 1750 CE
36	Chapter 5: 1450 to 1750 CE

37	Chapter 5: 1450 to 1750 CE
38	Chapter 5: 1450 to 1750 CE
39	Chapter 4: 600 to 1450 CE
40	Chapter 5: 1450 to 1750 CE
41	Chapter 5: 1450 to 1750 CE
42	Chapter 5: 1450 to 1750 CE
43	Chapter 6: 1750 to 1900 CE
44	Chapter 6: 1750 to 1900 CE
45	Chapter 6: 1750 to 1900 CE
46	Chapter 6: 1750 to 1900 CE
47	Chapter 6: 1750 to 1900 CE
48	Chapter 6: 1750 to 1900 CE
49	Chapter 6: 1750 to 1900 CE
50	Chapter 6: 1750 to 1900 CE
51	Chapter 6: 1750 to 1900 CE
52	Chapter 6: 1750 to 1900 CE
53	Chapter 6: 1750 to 1900 CE
54	Chapter 5: 1750 to 1900 CE
55	Chapter 6: 1750 to 1900 CE
56	Chapter 6: 1750 to 1900 CE
57	Chapter 7: 1900 CE to Present
58	Chapter 7: 1900 CE to Present
59	Chapter 7: 1900 CE to Present
60	Chapter 7: 1900 CE to Present
61	Chapter 7: 1900 CE to Present
62	Chapter 7: 1900 CE to Present
63	Chapter 7: 1900 CE to Present
64	Chapter 7: 1900 CE to Present
65	Chapter 7: 1900 CE to Present
66	Chapter 7: 1900 CE to Present
67	Chapter 7: 1900 CE to Present
68	Chapter 7: 1900 CE to Present
69	Chapter 7: 1900 CE to Present
70	Chapter 7: 1900 CE to Present

ANSWERS AND EXPLANATIONS

SECTION I

MULTIPLE-CHOICE ANSWERS

1. C

Mesopotamia used cuneiform as its form of writing, and Egypt used hieroglyphics. Mesopotamia was organized into city-states, but Egypt was organized into kingdoms. Egypt's government was more centralized than was Mesopotamia's. Both cultures were polytheistic, not monotheistic.

2. D

Classical civilizations had all of the choices except democratic institutions. Although Greece and Rome had some elements of democracy, this was not a characteristic of most classical civilizations. The city-state of Athens had a direct democracy in which only citizens could vote and the republic of Rome had a government that elected its officials to govern. These democratic institutions were limited to a minority of the populations and were both relatively short-lived.

3. C

Both Buddhism and Christianity successfully spread because of their missionary activity. Since in both religions all could join and all were considered spiritually equal, each spread extensively. Unlike Buddhism, Christianity believes in one God. Christianity is considered a hierarchical religion, but not Buddhism. Both Christianity and Buddhism have rituals important to their practice.

4. A

In both empires, a decrease in trade occurred. However, the Roman Empire was more interdependent than the Han. As a result, the decrease in trade badly damaged the Roman Empire economically, while the Han was more self-sufficient. Both empires dealt with issues of government corruption and had difficulty collecting sufficient taxes. The spread of Christianity, it has

been argued, did cause a decrease in the feelings of loyalty to the Roman state, but Buddhism did not significantly spread to most of China until after the fall of the Han.

5. D

Hinduism and Buddhism both believe in the concepts of dharma and karma. Dharma is one's duty or role in life, and karma is what happens as a result of how well one does with his/her dharma.

6. A

The Bantu were a group that originated in West Africa. This agricultural society experienced population growth, which initiated migration. The use of iron tools and the cultivation of bananas allowed the Bantus to migrate farther and spread agriculture. Animal domestication was not a motivation to migrate.

7. B

According to Confucius, the basis of the state is the family. Since the ruler is the head of the state, he should model proper behavior for the state just as the father would model proper behavior for the family.

8. D

Christianity had some influence in all of the areas by 600 CE except East Asia. Christianity came to have some influence in East Asia, but not until after 600 CE. Trade routes, missionaries, and conquest in the classical period aided the spread of Christianity to the Middle East, Western Europe, and East Africa.

9. D

As a result of the spread of Islam into West Africa, the volume of trade along the trans-Saharan trade routes increased. Relationships were established with Muslim merchants and those relationships led to more trade. The economy grew rather than slowed, and a more centralized form of government developed. Centralized governments often kept order in their kingdoms, and thus decreased conflict.

10. D

Confucius believed that the civil servants taken from the scholar class would run the country for the emperor and would promote harmony in the empire.

11. B

Shinto and Buddhism have been the two most visible religions in Japan over the last thousand years. Shinto is native to Japan, while Buddhism came via China in the sixth century. Fewer than 1 percent of Japanese people are Christian. Daoism is native to China and not historically widespread in Japan.

12. A

Dunhuang and Kashgar are located in modern-day Western China, and Samarkand is located in Central Asia. These cities grew as a result of the Silk Road trade, supporting merchants and markets and aiding in the spread of religious beliefs, such as Buddhism.

13. B

After the fall of Rome, nomadic invasions continued, making it very difficult for the area to recover. As a result, a decentralized form of government developed that provided protection for its inhabitants. Both Rome and the Han lost political control of their respective empires. Rome's population decreased as a result of the spread of disease. The Han Empire did not recover power.

14. D

Paleolithic people most likely held animist beliefs, believing that spirit forces that existed in the natural world and influenced their lives. The people of later river valley civilizations were polytheistic, and monotheism first emerged with the development of Judaism. Syncretism refers to the blending of religious beliefs and practices.

15. B

During the time period 600 to 1450, China had developed advanced naval technologies, such as the compass and more advanced ships. During the Ming dynasty, massive ships were built and sent out to make voyages throughout the Indian Ocean. These ships were far superior to any used by other countries at that time.

16. D

The Song dynasty existed from 960 to 1279 CE in China. The other empires had all fallen by 600 CE.

17. D

China dealt with its neighboring areas by establishing a tributary relationship, in which the tributary states would have to recognize the superiority of China. Korea, Tibet, and Vietnam all had some form of a tributary relationship with China at some point in its history, but India never did.

18. C

Although the Indus Valley civilization had a writing system, it is yet to be deciphered, leaving the decline of this civilization as somewhat of a mystery.

19. D

This quote is attributed to Socrates and is representative of the Greek philosophical stress on the importance of the individual.

20. A

Dar al-Islam refers to the lands that were culturally influenced by the religion of Islam. When the political organization of Islam declined, the influence of Islam continued in this cultural area. By the year 1450, Dar al-Islam stretched from Western Europe to Eastern China.

21. B

Commercial growth during the years 600–1450 CE was facilitated by the minting of coins, the establishment of trade organizations such as the Hanseatic League, and by state-sponsored infrastructure projects such as the construction of the Grand Canal in China. Government support of industry would take place after the Industrial Revolution.

22. D

During the time period 600 to 1450, trade in the Indian Ocean flourished. It connected East China with East Africa and the many areas in between.

23. C

The ships of the Ming dynasty were far superior to any others on the sea, but the voyages were very expensive, and the trade that was generated was deemed of little value. The emperor cancelled the missions under pressure from Confucian scholars and instead focused on internal stability and defending the northern border from a possible Mongol return.

24. A

The Aztecs and the Mongols built their empires by conquering and dominating their neighbors. Both collected taxes. The Mongols were not particularly efficient administrators; instead, they often relied on their conquered people to administer the empire. Trade flourished in both areas.

25. D

Leonardo da Vinci, the Medicis, and the Mediterranean Sea trade all relate to the Italian Renaissance, the cultural rebirth that began in the late 14th century.

26. C

These two religions came in contact along the trade routes of Central Asia. Buddhism had spread to the region earlier from India through the Silk Road. Islam spread to Central Asia beginning in the eighth century and often overtook Buddhism as the dominant belief system.

27. B

All three groups were nomadic peoples who moved into neighboring areas. The Mongols and Turks were empire builders, but not the Vikings. The Turks later developed an organized bureaucracy in the Ottoman Empire, but the Mongols and Vikings were not

known for their bureaucratic expertise. While the Mongols and Turks were both skilled horsemen, the Vikings were more known for their seafaring skills.

28. B

As a result of the Crusades, Western Europe was reintroduced to the goods and technology of the Middle East. This led to an increase in trade and an increase in interaction with the outside world for Western Europe.

29. B

More men than women were enslaved in Africa during the period of the Atlantic slave system. As a result, the gender ratio in West Africa shifted to more women than men. The Middle East had a larger slave trade and agricultural productivity in the Caribbean, and Latin America increased during the 17th and 18th centuries. Plantation-style agriculture was never widespread in Southern Europe.

30. D

Although European diseases, like smallpox, spread to the Americas causing the death of millions of Native Americans, African diseases did not spread to Europe as a result of the Columbian Exchange. New foods were introduced from the Americas to Europe and to China, which led to population increase.

31. D

In the time period 1450 to 1750, the kingdom of Songhay controlled West Africa, during which these developments occurred. The Ottoman Empire dominated the Middle East and North Africa. The Fatimid dynasty was Muslim and in North Africa, but it was not based around Timbuktu. The Mughals dominated India. Great Zimbabwe developed power in East Africa.

32. B

The Taj Mahal was built during the Mughal Empire as a tomb for the Emperor Shah Jahan's wife. The Islamic-style architecture can be seen in the use of the dome and minarets.

33. D

During the time period 1450 to 1750, the Mughals conquered and ruled India. The Safavids ruled over Persia. The Delhi Sultanate ruled the northern part of India beginning in the 11th century. The Manchus ruled China.

34. C

The women of the palace court of the Ottoman Empire included the wives and concubines of the Ottoman sultan. Although their movement outside the harem was restricted, they often exhibited great influence over their husbands. By advising the sultan or pushing forward their choice for the next sultan, the women of the harem could exert significant influence.

35. B

The sugar plantation greatly increased the Atlantic slave trade because growing sugar was very labor intensive. In order to make a significant profit, plantation owners needed cheap labor to cultivate the sugar. The popularity of this cash crop led to a large increase in the demand for slaves in the Americas.

36. A

Potatoes, manioc, and maize were all unknown to Afro-Eurasia until after Columbus's voyages. Coffee had been grown and widely consumed, especially in the Middle East, centuries before 1492.

37. D

During the time period 1450 to 1750, Japan was ruled by the Tokugawa Shogunate, which heavily restricted foreign trade. The shogun ruled and the emperor was a figurehead. After gaining some initial conversions, the government banned the Christian missionaries and persecuted those who had converted. During this period of restricted foreign trade, internal trade increased and the economy prospered.

38. C

The ability to make large profits in cash crops drew many Europeans to the Americas in the hope of making their fortunes.

39. D

Under both Japanese and European feudalism, a strict social structure reinforced the system. Those born as serfs or peasants remained as such throughout their lives, as well as those lucky enough to be born as lords or daimyos.

40. A

As in the Tang dynasty, the Roman and Persian Empires both had extensive road systems. This encouraged trade and facilitated communication throughout the empires.

41. B

Neo-Confucianism developed during the Tang dynasty in response to the growing popularity of Buddhism in China. The incorporation of Buddhist beliefs and Confucian ideas became very influential in China and Japan.

42. D

Peter the Great wanted to westernize Russia by increasing foreign trade, Western style of dress, and technology. Peter was an absolute monarch who did not use Enlightenment ideas in the government.

43. A

The political revolution in the Americas and Europe led to a spread of Enlightenment ideas throughout these areas. As a result, Spanish and Portuguese power in South America decreased. Many nation-states were inspired by the ideas of the Enlightenment. Industrialization had a large impact on the spread of Marxist ideas and the political revolutions of the 19th century.

44. D

Enlightenment thinkers believed in the right of people to choose their government (popular sovereignty), freedom of speech, and religious tolerance, but often ignored the rights and equality of women.

45. C

Though the American state claimed that all were created equal, the reality was that the Constitution did not recognize the equality of women or slaves.

46. C

While Napoleon was building his European Empire in the early 1800s, he invaded both Spain and Portugal and deposed their rulers. This weakening of Spain and Portugal allowed the Latin American colonies to successfully fight for their independence from the European powers.

47. D

Simón Bolívar and José de San Martín led the revolutionary movements for independence in South America. Miguel de Hidalgo was a priest who led a peasant movement in Mexico.

48. A

The peninsulares, or those born in Europe, had the dominant power in Latin America in the early 1800s. The Creoles, descendents of Europeans, led independence movements in hopes of establishing power for themselves.

49. B

Marx wrote that the only way for the working class to overthrow the capitalist system was through a revolution. After the revolution, the proletariat would own the means of production.

50. B

The family unit had been an economic unit prior to industrialization, but was not so afterwards. As a result of industrialization, the prices for manufactured goods significantly decreased. As a result, the working class could now afford these goods. The improvement in working conditions occurred after government reforms demanded them. Some people were able to economically advance more than they could before industrialization.

51. D

Reforms and changes in the Ottoman Empire were often resisted by the ulama, or religious leadership. The incorporation of more Western ideas often undermined the authority of the ulama.

52. A

The Berlin Conference was a meeting of European powers called in order to avoid war. The European powers agreed to ground rules for the colonization of Africa, and as a result the map of almost all of Africa was carved up by European powers.

53. B

As working-class women entered the factories, middle-class women were often influenced by the ideal of the cult of domesticity. This ideal preached that the goal for women was to create a perfect household for their husbands and children.

54. C

Based on Charles Darwin's theories of evolution and survival of the fittest, Social Darwinists believed that Europeans had evolved to a higher level than those they were conquering. This was used as a justification for European imperialism.

55. B

The Indian National Congress was a group of educated Indians formed with the permission of the British in the late 19th century. This group helped to lead the nationalist movement in India under the leadership of Mohandas Gandhi. The Pan-African Congress first met in 1919 after World War I. It stressed African unity and helped to create nationalist movements, which came to eventually defeat the European colonial powers.

56. D

The Boxer Rebellion was an anti-foreign rebellion in China in 1900 that was forcefully put down by European powers. The Sepoy Mutiny occurred in 1857 in India, when sepoys (Indian troops who served the British army) rebeled after hearing a rumor that animal (cow or pork) fat was being used to grease ammunition cartridges for rifles. This offended both Hindu and Muslim sepoys. The mutiny was forcefully put down by the British, who then assumed full control of India as a colony.

57. B

Since the days of Spanish colonization, Latin America has had a small percentage of people controlling most of the wealth. To this day, the landed elites dominate political and military life. The area has historically had high birthrates, and until recently, a tendency toward right-wing military governments.

58. A

Japan's rapid industrialization created a need for more and more of the raw materials that it lacked. It moved into Korea and later Northeast China to get these materials. The successful annexation of Manchuria in 1931 weakened the prestige of the League of Nations and encouraged the militarists who were intensely loyal to the emperor.

59. D

Mohandas Gandhi believed in the forces of nonviolence and truth. He used these in the struggle against the British until India's independence in 1947. A part of that struggle involved the production and wearing of homespun clothing, which would help the poor and hurt the British textile industry.

60. B

The Russian Revolution was followed by a civil war between the Reds and the Whites. The Chinese Revolution also experienced a civil war, which occurred before the communist victory in 1949. The Russian Revolution overthrew Czar Nicholas, a corrupt monarch, but in China the monarchy had been overthrown 38 years earlier. The Russian Revolution appealed to industrial workers, but Mao in China targeted his revolutionary message to the rural peasantry. Both communist revolutions lasted much longer than 25 years.

61. D

Lack of capital has held many nations back from developing. Many poor nations have no lack of foreign aid or natural resources, but cannot find the money or technology needed to industrialize.

62. D

Asian nationalists (such as Ho Chi Minh) and African nationalists (such as Jomo Kenyatta) were well educated—even professionally trained in Europe—before becoming leaders in the colonies from which they came. Peasants were not able to communicate their political wishes, and if any aristocracy existed, they were often in league with the ruling colonial regime.

63. D

The European allies were looking to punish Germany after World War I, and even though American president Woodrow Wilson promoted "peace without victory" in his Fourteen Points, his wishes were largely ignored. Germany was forced to accept total blame for the war and pay large war reparations. This crippled the German economy and allowed for the rise of a fascist regime seeking to restore glory to the country.

64. B

In the 20th century, the act of genocide was carried out against many minority groups. Examples are the Armenians in Turkey in 1915, and the Jews in Eastern Europe during World War II.

65. A

Pakistan and Indonesia are both primarily Muslim nations.

66. C

As a result of the weakening of European power after World War I and the strengthening of the ideas of self-determination, nationalist movements rose in colonial areas such as Asia and Africa.

67. C

During the Cold War, Cuba, a communist nation, was a strong supporter and ally of the Soviet Union, much to the disappointment of its neighbor, the United States. India, on the other hand, was one of the leaders of the nonalignment movement in which nations refused to cater to one side or the other in the Cold War.

68. D

Lenin led the Bolsheviks to power in the Russian Revolution in 1917, and Ayatollah Khomeini led the Iranian Revolution in 1979. The latter revolution resulted in the creation of an Islamic fundamentalist state.

69. A

Kwame Nkrumah was a nationalist leader in Ghana. Jomo Kenyatta was the nationalist leader in Kenya, and Frantz Fanon led nationalist uprisings in French-controlled Algeria.

70. B

Both the Palestinians and the Israelis claim religious and historic ties to the same land. The international community has often been involved in attempting to help settle peace. European powers do not control this area anymore. Both sides have sat down to meet with varying degrees of success over the years.

SECTION II

PART A: DOCUMENT-BASED QUESTION—SAMPLE RESPONSE

Communist revolutions offered new economic opportunities for women in Russia and China. Previously, women had been restricted to traditional roles in both societies, but after the communist regimes came to power, women were viewed as playing a crucial part in building a strong socialist economy, and their liberation was seen as vital to realizing socialist ideals. It was preached that a true socialist revolution would only occur if equality of the sexes also occurred. The reality of these changes, however, was not so promising.

In Russia, women had very traditional roles, but after the communists came to power, were hailed as the builders of a new Russia. The leader of the Bolsheviks, V. I. Lenin, wrote in the official Soviet newspaper that the Soviet government was the first in the world to provide women with the same property rights as men (doc. 1). This document also connects the struggle for equality for women with the freedom of the working class. His position as the leader of the government heavily influenced his point of view. The article glorifies all the Soviet government had done for women in comparison to the "bourgeois republics." An official government poster (doc. 3) also glorifies the new position of women as it tells them to "say goodbye to kitchen slavery." The purpose of this poster is to motivate women to enter the workforce and participate in the building of a new and strong Russia. However, because both of these documents are advancing the point of view of the Soviet government, which had a vested interest in showing itself in the best possible light, these documents are biased and should be weighed against the accounts that describe the experiences of actual female Soviet citizens.

Women also reported on the changes going on in the Soviet Union. Emma Goldman, an American anarchist who was deported to Russia in the 1920s, writes about an instance in the ration line, when a young girl tries to get vinegar for her master, and the other women there remind her that he isn't entitled to it any more than they (doc. 2). The story demonstrates how women are beginning to stand up for themselves and no longer accepting an inferior social position. Lenin's wife, Krupskaya, herself a leader in the Bolshevik Party, reported that Russia no longer denies women their rights like every other country in the world (doc. 4). This excerpt is taken from the introduction to Lenin's book *The Emancipation of Women*; her purpose is clearly to glorify the change taking place for women in Russia (doc. 3). The changing roles of women in Russia would be more thoroughly analyzed if there were documentary evidence from a woman not politically connected, whose life had been transformed as a result of the revolution. It would also be helpful to have statistical evidence which analyzed the economic conditions of women before and after the revolution to judge the extent to which their lives had improved.

Similarly in China, the revolutionary government encouraged women to enter the workforce and help build a better and stronger nation. The Chairman of the Chinese Communist Party, Mao Zedong, wrote in his *Little Red Book* that women must be on equal footing with men in the workforce including receiving equal pay for equal work (doc. 5). His purpose seems to be to motivate women to contribute to the creation of a strong socialist economy, but it would be important to know to what degree these ideas were carried out. To what extent did women contribute to the Chinese economy and did they receive equal pay for equal work? A government poster also encourages women to participate in the economic strength of China. It shows an idealized woman happy as she works in the field to build a new China (doc. 6).

Shao Dangdi, however, is quoted in an American magazine in 2004 as saying that while women and men had equal footing in the workplace after the revolution, such is no longer the case (doc. 7). Now, in a more competitive workplace, men are often hired over women. According to this article, the capitalist changes occurring in China seemed to be hurting the economic roles of women. Written in the same year in an official Chinese government magazine, another article notes that the more women have gained rights to education, the greater their economic opportunities have been (doc. 8). However, as was the case with excerpt of the article by Lenin and the Soviet propaganda poster, these documents advance the point of view and bias of the Chinese government and need to be considered in light of the testimony of Chinese women. It would be helpful to hear from a woman who lived through the transition to the communist government to see if her economic role was truly transformed, and then to see if the capitalist changes of today are adding to or taking away from her economic opportunities.

There is no denying that women in Russia and China had greater economic opportunities as a result of their countries' communist revolutions. They entered the workforce and were hailed by the party as crucial members of society. It is harder to ascertain to what degree traditional values remained and how capitalist changes to these societies will further revolutionize the role of women.

Part B: Continuity and Change-Over-Time Question—Sample Response

As a result of the encounter with the Americas following Columbus's voyages in the late 15th century, the Americas were dramatically impacted by demographic and environmental changes. Demographically, the spread of disease led to a major decline in the native population, the migration of Europeans changed the social structure of the area, and the importation of African slaves transformed the society both socially and economically. Environmentally, the introduction of new crops and animals transformed the land and drastically changed the way people lived. People in the Americas, however, continued to farm the land throughout the 1450-to-1750 time period.

Before 1492, the Americas were a land settled by a diverse population. In Mexico, the Aztecs controlled a diverse empire, and in South America, the Incas had conquered their own large empire in the Andes Mountains. With the arrival of the Europeans, major demographic and environmental changes occurred. New diseases began to appear in the native population, particularly smallpox. Since the natives had no prior immunity to this disease, the results were devastating. The Europeans, on the other hand, had been exposed to the disease back home and were not as severely affected. The Aztec Empire lost 95 percent of its population within a century, and in this weakened state was easily controlled by its Spanish conquerors. Between 1500 and 1800, 100 million people died from the spread of smallpox to the Americas.

The new plantation economy set up by the Europeans established a system of forced labor, and since so many Native Americans were dying, the African slave trade was extended across the Atlantic Ocean to fulfill the demand for labor. The enslaved Africans, along with the Native American and European populations, made up a new social structure in American society—one based on race. The peninsulares, settlers from Spain or Portugal, made up the highest class (the Creoles were their descendants). Intermarriage led to new classes: the mestizos (a mix of Native American and European) and the mulattoes (a mix of African and European). The full-blooded Native American and Africans made up the lowest class.

Environmentally, America was transformed. New crops and animals never previously seen were introduced, altering the environment, economy, and diet of the people. In particular, animals such as horses, cattle, pigs, sheep, goats, and chickens were introduced. The Americas did not have any indigenous large draft animals, so the introduction of horses helped to transform farming which had developed in the Americas concurrently with the agricultural revolution in the rest of the world thousands of years ago and which had enabled highly advanced Native American civilizations to flourish up until the arrival of Europeans. Additionally, sugar cultivation was introduced; forests were cleared and plantations were set up to grow this profitable cash crop. However, native crops like corn, potatoes, and tobacco continued to be important economic commodities in the Americas. Additionally, natural resources like silver were mined in the mountains of Mexico and Peru using forced Native American labor. The profits from these resources greatly benefited the Spanish crown, but at the expense of Native Americans, and later the enslaved African populations.

The time period 1450 to 1750 was a time of dramatic change for the Americas. As the world was becoming more closely integrated, the Americas were brought into the global trade network. Demographically the population was dramatically changed by the destruction of the Native American population and the introduction of Europeans and Africans. Environmentally, the introduction of new crops and animals and the mining of natural resources, like silver, transformed the landscape of the Americas forever.

PART C: COMPARATIVE QUESTION—SAMPLE RESPONSE

Between the years 1000 BCE and 600 CE, new religious ideas began to arise from different civilizations, and a few were able to spread so vastly that they came to be widespread global movements. The introduction of long-distance trade during this period aided this religious growth. Christianity and Buddhism rose to be dominant world religions and their spread altered them significantly in similar ways. These religions had drastically different impacts on the Roman and Mauryan Empires, which they came to influence, respectively.

The spread of religion during the classical period took place mostly by way of missionaries. Buddhism, originating in India, was able to reach much of China, Japan, Korea, and Sri Lanka, along the Silk Road. Oasis cities along trade routes became Buddhist centers, where missionaries found many willing converts. Likewise, Christianity found its converts by promising salvation in heaven. Christianity, originating in Jerusalem and coming to dominate the Roman Empire, faced more difficulty as it spread, as its missionaries were not tolerated or embraced. In fact, many were persecuted. Despite these obstacles, Christianity spread from the Middle East to Africa, Asia, and Europe where it had significant impact on the cultures of these areas that continues to today.

With the spread of religion came the branching of religion. Buddhism was popular and accessible because it could assimilate to many cultures. Out of traditional Buddhism came the Theravada School (influential in Southeast Asia) and the Mahayana School (influential in China). Furthermore, Buddhism sometimes collaborated with Confucianist principles and Shinto deities. In Southwest Asia, Christians became ascetics and rejected materialism. Both Christianity and Buddhism began as reforms of pre-existing religions (from Judaism and Hinduism, respectively), but both spread and branched to be important distinct religions, which could fit the lifestyles of different peoples.

A religion can only truly grow to be a global movement when it infiltrates the government and affects aspects of life apart from spirituality. In the Mauryan Empire, Ashoka's conversion to Buddhism had a great effect on his people. Peace was encouraged throughout the empire; Ashoka practiced cultural pluralism and allowed conquered people to keep their own traditions, and the citizens were truly unified under a cultural authority. In great contrast was the influence Christianity had on the Roman Empire. Before the popularization of the religion by zealous missionaries and the conversion of the Emperor Constantine, Christians had been persecuted. But when Christianity grew to be the dominant religion of the area, it was the non-Christians who suffered persecution. Though some emperors declared divine right, ultimately government authority was weakened as people looked to God and salvation for their strength. Furthermore, this loss of government authority was exacerbated by economic problems caused by insufficient tax revenues, a situation made worse because the Church was exempt from paying taxes. Buddhism seemed much less controversial in India and actually succeeded in unifying the Mauryan Empire and its people. Conversely, Christianity caused chaos, upheaval, and disunity, and it contributed to the fall of the Roman Empire.

While Christianity and Buddhism did come to dominate the classical era by growing and spreading far beyond their centers of origin, they also greatly influenced the governments of which they became a part. Even today, they play a significant role in world history. When religion becomes a driving political force, the results can be overwhelming and sometimes tragic.

Practice Test 3 Answer Grid

1. (A) (B) (C) (D)
2. (A) (B) (C) (D)
3. (A) (B) (C) (D)
4. (A) (B) (C) (D)
5. (A) (B) (C) (D)
6. (A) (B) (C) (D)
7. (A) (B) (C) (D)
8. (A) (B) (C) (D)
9. (A) (B) (C) (D)
10. (A) (B) (C) (D)
11. (A) (B) (C) (D)
12. (A) (B) (C) (D)
13. (A) (B) (C) (D)
14. (A) (B) (C) (D)
15. (A) (B) (C) (D)
16. (A) (B) (C) (D)
17. (A) (B) (C) (D)
18. (A) (B) (C) (D)

19. (A) (B) (C) (D)
20. (A) (B) (C) (D)
21. (A) (B) (C) (D)
22. (A) (B) (C) (D)
23. (A) (B) (C) (D)
24. (A) (B) (C) (D)
25. (A) (B) (C) (D)
26. (A) (B) (C) (D)
27. (A) (B) (C) (D)
28. (A) (B) (C) (D)
29. (A) (B) (C) (D)
30. (A) (B) (C) (D)
31. (A) (B) (C) (D)
32. (A) (B) (C) (D)
33. (A) (B) (C) (D)
34. (A) (B) (C) (D)
35. (A) (B) (C) (D)
36. (A) (B) (C) (D)

37. (A) (B) (C) (D)
38. (A) (B) (C) (D)
39. (A) (B) (C) (D)
40. (A) (B) (C) (D)
41. (A) (B) (C) (D)
42. (A) (B) (C) (D)
43. (A) (B) (C) (D)
44. (A) (B) (C) (D)
45. (A) (B) (C) (D)
46. (A) (B) (C) (D)
47. (A) (B) (C) (D)
48. (A) (B) (C) (D)
49. (A) (B) (C) (D)
50. (A) (B) (C) (D)
51. (A) (B) (C) (D)
52. (A) (B) (C) (D)
53. (A) (B) (C) (D)
54. (A) (B) (C) (D)

55. (A) (B) (C) (D)
56. (A) (B) (C) (D)
57. (A) (B) (C) (D)
58. (A) (B) (C) (D)
59. (A) (B) (C) (D)
60. (A) (B) (C) (D)
61. (A) (B) (C) (D)
62. (A) (B) (C) (D)
63. (A) (B) (C) (D)
64. (A) (B) (C) (D)
65. (A) (B) (C) (D)
66. (A) (B) (C) (D)
67. (A) (B) (C) (D)
68. (A) (B) (C) (D)
69. (A) (B) (C) (D)
70. (A) (B) (C) (D)

PRACTICE TEST 3

Section I: Multiple-Choice Questions

Time: 55 Minutes
70 Questions

Directions: Each of the following questions or incomplete statements is followed by four suggested answers or completions. Select the one that is best in each case and then fill in the corresponding oval on the answer sheet.

1. Which of the following best describes slave populations in early societies such as Mesopotamia?

   (A) Slaves were generally an imported labor force made up of people of a different ethnic group than the free people.

   (B) Slaves were generally prisoners of war or people serving punishment for debt crimes.

   (C) Slaves were usually trained to provide services such as medical care and accounting to important families.

   (D) Slaves were not allowed to marry or have children.

2. Which of the following concepts was most emphasized in the religious life of China from the period 600 to 200 BCE?

   (A) The Buddhist Eightfold Path

   (B) Ancestor veneration

   (C) The Hindu caste system

   (D) The Sikh guidelines for truthful living

3. During the classical era, both Confucianism and Hinduism

   (A) included women in religious life by building convents as religious retreats

   (B) enforced patriarchal social patterns

   (C) were religions dominated by male priests

   (D) spread widely and rapidly through trade networks

4. Both the ancient Greek city-states and the Swahili city-states

   (A) were economically reliant on wealth generated by sea trade

   (B) were culturally diverse and home to numerous diasporic communities of merchants

   (C) frequently embarked on wars of conquest

   (D) were conquered by Alexander the Great during the third century BCE

GO ON TO THE NEXT PAGE

5. Which of the following is a motivation for the expansion of civilizations in regions such as Mesopotamia and the Nile Valley prior to 600 BCE?

(A) A desire for direct access to the Indian Ocean trade networks

(B) The need for access to iron ore for agricultural and military technology

(C) To obtain colonies in keeping with their mercantilist economic theory

(D) To engage in missionary work

6. One significant cause of both the Bantu migrations and the Polynesian migrations was

(A) the need for groups of hunter-gatherers to follow herds of large animals

(B) the development of double canoes and triangular sails that allowed more efficient travel

(C) forced migration through active slave trade networks

(D) population pressure and the need for resources

7. Historians often consider the year 600 CE to be a turning point in world history because

(A) it marks the beginning of an Axial Age and the founding of two major religions: Buddhism and Islam

(B) several centuries of environmental degradation resulted in severe weather patterns that year, including earthquakes and monsoons

(C) large empires including the Roman Empire collapsed and new political entities such as the Islamic Caliphates arose

(D) the invention of the astrolabe and the lateen sail allowed humans to engage in trade on the Atlantic and Pacific Oceans for the first time

8. Which of the following reinforced traditional expectations of women's roles in China?

(A) The expansion of the Chinese empire under Tang Empress Wu Zetian

(B) The proliferation of Buddhist convents in China

(C) The practice of foot binding during the Song dynasty

(D) Ban Zhao's call for the education of Chinese girls

9. The image above is an example of a mihrab, or prayer niche. Which direction would it face?

(A) East

(B) West

(C) Toward the center of the mosque

(D) Toward Mecca

GO ON TO THE NEXT PAGE ▷

10. During the Byzantine Empire, Emperor Justinian based the principles of his law code most directly on

(A) Hammurabi's Code

(B) the principles of human rights

(C) the Roman Twelve Tables of Law

(D) Islamic Sharia Law

11. Between 700 and 1000 CE, feudalism was the governmental form shared by which of the following two regions?

(A) Sub-Saharan Africa and Mesoamerica

(B) Northern Europe and the Middle East

(C) Northern Europe and Japan

(D) Sub-Saharan Africa and the Middle East

Arabia

12. The map shows important holy sites for which religion?

(A) Christianity

(B) Hinduism

(C) Buddhism

(D) Islam

13. What was one of the main reasons for the cessation of Zheng He's maritime expeditions in 1433?

(A) The government wanted to convert the treasure ships into warships for an impending war with Japan.

(B) The frequency of pirate attacks in the Indian Ocean made travel too dangerous.

(C) Chinese Confucian officials believed that the voyages brought China nothing of value.

(D) Devastating disease epidemics convinced Chinese officials to close the borders entirely.

14. Unlike Mongol rule in China under the Yuan Dynasty, Mongol rulers of the Golden Horde in Russia

(A) facilitated and encouraged trade

(B) used local rulers and bureaucrats to enforce laws and collect taxes

(C) refused to allow missionaries to visit and preach in their territory

(D) maintained certain Mongol cultural traditions

15. "Upon his arrival there, the Master worshipped the Bodhi tree and the image of the Buddha attaining enlightenment made by Maitreya Bodhisattva. After having looked at the image with deep sincerity, he prostrated himself before it . . . . "

—Huili, *A Biography of the Tripitaka Master*

This document describes the travels of Xuanzang, a Chinese Buddhist, to India. The purpose of the voyage was most similar to that undertaken by

(A) Marco Polo

(B) Mansa Musa

(C) European Crusaders

(D) Silk Road merchants

GO ON TO THE NEXT PAGE

16. The Inca and Aztec Empires were similar in that both

    (A) developed from Mayan civilization

    (B) acquired empires by means of military conquest

    (C) independently developed iron technology

    (D) had no system of regional trade

17. Great Zimbabwe and Calicut are examples of

    (A) cities that prospered because of their locations on long-distance trade routes

    (B) cities known for their monumental stone structures

    (C) walled cities that generated their wealth from agricultural production

    (D) cities that declined and collapsed due to environmental degradation

18. Which of the following assumptions underlay the Chinese tribute system?

    (A) China is the "middle kingdom," and all peoples beyond its borders are "barbarians"

    (B) Outsiders do not pose a threat to the security of the Chinese state

    (C) China has no use for any products or natural resources from outside its own borders

    (D) Foreign products and ideas are dangerous and should be avoided at all costs

19. Between 1400 and 1750, the political trend in Europe was toward

    (A) increasingly decentralized government.

    (B) democratic and Republican forms of government.

    (C) strong, centralized monarchies.

    (D) diplomacy rather than military resolutions to conflict.

"Sir, many of our people, keenly desirous of the wares and things of your Kingdoms, which are brought here by your people, and in order to satisfy their voracious appetite, seize many of our people, freed and exempt men, and they kidnap even nobles and the sons of nobles, and our relatives, and take them to be sold to the Whites who are in our Kingdoms."

—Nzinga Mbemba of the Kingdom of the Kongol

20. The quotation above comes from a 1526 letter to a Portuguese monarch from a king located on the

    (A) eastern coast of Africa

    (B) western coast of Africa

    (C) Pacific coast of Central America

    (D) Pacific coast of South America

21. Which of the following was a major motivation for European voyages of exploration in the 15th and 16th centuries?

    (A) The desire to promote free trade in Southeast Asia

    (B) An aim to take over the fur trade in Siberia

    (C) Efforts by Protestants to spread their faith

    (D) The desire to circumvent the Muslim monopoly on Indian Ocean trade

22. Which of the following is an example of a "trading-post empire" of the early modern era?

    (A) The American colonies under Great Britain

    (B) Portuguese bases in Africa and the Indian Ocean

    (C) The Incan Empire

    (D) The Ottoman Empire

GO ON TO THE NEXT PAGE

Although a Kingdom may be enriched by gifts received, or by purchase taken from some other Nations, yet these are things uncertain and of small consideration when they happen. The ordinary means therefore to increase our wealth and treasure is by Foreign Trade, wherein wee must ever observe this rule; to sell more to strangers yearly than wee consume of theirs in value. For suppose that when this Kingdom is plentifully served with the Cloth, Lead, Tin, Iron, Fish and other native commodities, we doe yearly export the overplus to foreign Countries to the value of twenty two hundred thousand pounds; by which means we are enabled beyond the Seas to buy and bring in foreign wares for our use and Consumptions, to the value of twenty hundred thousand pounds: By this order duly kept in our trading, we may rest assured that the kingdom shall be enriched yearly two hundred thousand pounds, which must be brought to us in so much Treasure; because that part of our stock which is not returned to us in wares must necessarily be brought home in treasure.

—Thomas Mun, England's Treasure by Foreign Trade, 1664

23. In this excerpt, Thomas Mun is discussing the economic philosophy known as

(A) mercantilism
(B) capitalism
(C) socialism
(D) feudalism

24. Why were the British in India unable to impose trade relationships through military force there, as the Dutch had done in Indonesia?

(A) The British navy was weaker than the Dutch navy.
(B) The Mughal Empire was a powerful presence on the Indian subcontinent.
(C) The British East India Company did not have access to an army.
(D) French traders already controlled the major ports on the west coast of India.

25. How did Japan's policies toward foreigners change from the mid-16th to the mid-17th century?

(A) At the beginning of the period, feuding Japanese warlords (daimyos) welcomed foreigners. By the end of the period, the powerful Tokugawa Shogunate had restricted and nearly eliminated contacts between Japan and the outside world.
(B) At the beginning of the period, Japan actively sought trade relationships with Europeans. By the mid-16th century, Japan had eliminated trade with Europeans in favor of trade with Muslim merchants.
(C) At the beginning of the period, the powerful Japanese emperor used his centralized control over the country to restrict trade. By the mid-16th century, his weakening power had opened up the opportunity for Christian missionaries to make significant inroads in Japan.
(D) Japan's policies toward foreigners changed very little in this period, although they were somewhat more open at the end of the period than they had been at the beginning.

GO ON TO THE NEXT PAGE

26. Which of the following best explains the movements of slaves shown on the map?

(A) Currents and wind patterns in the Atlantic Ocean made it difficult to transport slaves to North America.

(B) The slave trade did not exist before 1500.

(C) Plantation economies in Brazil and the Caribbean required the most intense labor in the Americas.

(D) Europe was only minimally involved in the slave trade because of moral opposition to the practice.

27. What was one of the major outcomes of the Protestant Reformation in the 15th and 16th centuries?

(A) The conversion of the majority of the French population to Protestantism

(B) A long period of religious warfare in Europe that caused significant destruction to the continent

(C) An increase in papal power in the Holy Roman Empire

(D) A decline in the overall number of Europeans practicing Christianity

28. In what ways were the Manchu rulers of the Chinese Qing Dynasty similar to the Mongol Rulers of the Yuan Dynasty?

(A) They both made intermarriage between the ruling ethnic group and their Chinese subjects illegal.

(B) They both supported and maintained the civil service examination system.

(C) They both received overwhelming support from the Chinese population.

(D) They both negotiated with the Russians to define borders and regulate trade.

29. Both Thomas Hobbes and John Locke

(A) believed that the best government should reflect human nature

(B) favored self-government

(C) believed that people are incapable of learning from their mistakes

(D) advocated a separation of powers between branches of government

To the shame of mankind, one knows that the laws of games are the only ones which everywhere are just, clear, inviolable and executed. Why is the Indian who gave us the rules of the game of chess willingly obeyed all over the world, and why are the popes' decretals, for example, to-day an object of horror and scorn? The reason is that the inventor of chess combined everything with precision for the satisfaction of the players, and that the popes, in their decretals, had nothing in view but their own interest. The Indian wished to exercise men's minds equally, and give them pleasure; the popes wished to besot men's minds....

—Voltaire, *Philosophical Dictionary*, "Laws"

GO ON TO THE NEXT PAGE →

30. This quotation is an example of

(A) the popularization of the game of chess during the eighteenth century in Europe

(B) the tendency of philosophes to support decrees of the Pope in France

(C) power struggles between French citizens and the French monarchy

(D) the questioning of traditional authority during the European Enlightenment

31. Which of the following was true of the French Revolution but not the American Revolution?

(A) It was caused by tensions in a colonial relationship with a distant imperial power.

(B) The wealthiest members of society were the main proponents of political change.

(C) Feudal obligations were the source of much of the discontent that lead to revolution.

(D) Enlightenment ideas provided the basis for much revolutionary rhetoric.

32. This image from a 1789 stamp has the caption "Be free and citizens." This abolitionist sentiment associated with the French Revolution was a direct cause of

(A) the Haitian Revolution

(B) the end of the Portuguese slave trade

(C) the abolition of slavery in Brazil

(D) the American Civil War

33. What is one of the major causes of the beginning of the Industrial Revolution in England?

(A) England had the most land of any European state.

(B) The lack of titles of nobility in England created unprecedented opportunities for upward social mobility and encouraged people to become capitalists.

(C) London was the center of the Enlightenment in the 18th century, which inspired the Industrial Revolution.

(D) The enclosure movement in England resulted in the decline of the small farm and the village commons, creating a large pool of mobile former agricultural workers who sought employment in factories.

34. In the graph above, the Y-axis represents the number of railroad lines in each country. Which of the following statements is supported by the graph?

(A) Great Britain had more railroads than any other country during the period 1840–1900.

(B) Great Britain led the world in railroads until 1880, when it was overtaken by Germany and later by Russia.

(C) Italy lacked the resources to produce good quality steel for its railroad lines.

(D) France and Austria built railroads primarily for transporting people rather than for transporting industrial goods.

GO ON TO THE NEXT PAGE

35. Which of the following systems represented an attempt by the Spanish to reform the harsh treatment of Native Americans working in mines and on plantations?

    (A) The encomienda system

    (B) The repartimiento system

    (C) Debt servitude

    (D) The Treaty of Tordesillas

36. Which of the following is a difference between feudal serfdom and chattel slavery?

    (A) Serfs were born into their status, whereas children of slaves in the United States were born free.

    (B) Serfs were generally literate, while slaves were generally illiterate.

    (C) A slave was personal property, whereas a serf was not personal property, but rather, was tied to the land on which he lived and worked.

    (D) Slaves often had their own plots of land from which they would feed themselves, whereas serfs were fed a share from the land they worked for their owners.

37. Which of the following was one of the hallmarks of the European Renaissance?

    (A) A new view of Man as a creative and rational being

    (B) A growing acceptance of atheism

    (C) A celebration of Chinese and Islamic art and rejection of Greco-Roman styles

    (D) A declining interest in international travel

38. What is an example of an early effort by a government to sustainably manage natural resources during the period 1450 to 1750?

    (A) The Tokugawa Shogunate's laws to restrict timbering operations

    (B) The British government's emissions restrictions to fight air pollution

    (C) The Ottoman Empire's efforts to reduce over-fishing in the Mediterranean region

    (D) The United States' designation of protected lands such as Yellowstone National Park

39. Which of the following Chinese innovations was essential to the Ottoman conquest of Constantinople in 1453?

    (A) Gunpowder

    (B) Movable type

    (C) Horse saddles

    (D) The lateen sail

GO ON TO THE NEXT PAGE

40. What historical process or event resulted in the redistribution of African territories as indicated on the previous map?

(A) The African slave trade of the 16th and 17th centuries

(B) The Seven Years War of 1754–1763

(C) The Berlin Conference of 1885

(D) African decolonization in the 20th century

41. Which of the following regions was least affected by Chinese and European maritime reconnaissance voyages in the period 1450–1750?

(A) The Indian Ocean region

(B) West Africa

(C) South America

(D) Oceania and Polynesia

42. One of the outcomes of the Taiping Rebellion in China was

(A) the criminalization of the opium trade in China

(B) the collapse of the Qing dynasty

(C) China's rapid industrialization

(D) a dramatically weakened economy

43. Built in 1883 in Tokyo, the building shown here is an example of

(A) westernization in Japan during the Meiji era

(B) architecture constructed in Japanese cities controlled by European trading companies

(C) palace buildings designed for Tokugawa shoguns

(D) Showa era department store architecture

44. One impact of World War I in Latin America was

(A) a population explosion as Americans migrated to Latin America to avoid the draft

(B) a population decline as many people volunteered to fight in the conflict, prompted by ideological sympathy

(C) a temporary economic boom because of demand for wartime products such as Chilean nitrates

(D) a temporary economic decline because of low international demand for luxury goods during World War I

GO ON TO THE NEXT PAGE

45. What was the impact of the Great Depression on colonial territories?

(A) Many of them were granted their independence because the governments of industrialized capitalist countries could no longer support them

(B) The impact was minimal because demand for raw materials continued during the Great Depression while demand for finished goods dropped

(C) The local economy was devastated because many colonies were tied to exporting products like rubber and cocoa, which were vulnerable to fluctuations in the world market

(D) Economic and social tensions caused many colonies to revolt and establish independent communist governments

46. This map illustrates the global distribution of raw material production in 1888. Which of the following statements does the map support?

(A) Coffee grows best near the Equator.

(B) Great Britain colonized Australia because of its rich gold resources.

(C) Furs were in great demand in North America.

(D) Construction of both the Panama and the Suez canals was underway in 1888.

Religions in Mauritius as a percentage of the population

Religion	Percent of Population
Hinduism	48.5%
Roman Catholicism	26.3%
Muslim	17.3%
Other or unspecified	7.8%

47. Which of the following statements provides an explanation for the religious distribution in Mauritius indicated by the chart?

(A) The island was unknown to traders in the Indian Ocean until it was discovered by the Portuguese in the 16th century.

(B) Large numbers of indentured servants from India migrated to the island in the 19th century.

(C) Efforts by Hindu missionaries to counter Muslim influence in the 10th and 11th centuries resulted in high conversion rates.

(D) British colonial governors in the 19th century encouraged native Mauritians to convert to Christianity.

GO ON TO THE NEXT PAGE

48. What was one major difference between the Russian and the Chinese communist revolutions?

(A) Russia focused on rapid industrialization, whereas China believed in a more gradual process.

(B) China developed a totalitarian political system dominated by the Communist Party, whereas Russia's system was more decentralized and relied on the support of local soviets.

(C) Support for the Russian Communist Party derived mainly from the cities, whereas support for the Chinese Communist Party was strongest in rural areas.

(D) Russia attempted to dismantle class and gender equality, whereas Confucian perspectives on gender persisted and became part of Chinese communist ideology.

49. This image is an example of

(A) anti-communist propaganda in Taiwan

(B) Maoist efforts to eliminate distinctions between rural and urban youth

(C) Lenin's vision for the education of Soviet youth

(D) attitudes toward gender equality resulting from the Chinese Cultural Revolution

50. The terms *glasnost* and *perestroika* are most closely associated with

(A) ahe People's Republic of China under Mao Zedong

(B) ahe Soviet Union under Gorbachev

(C) ahe Soviet Union under Stalin

(D) Cuba under Fidel Castro

51. Which of the following states sponsored massive industrialization in response to increasing Western European global dominance?

(A) The Ottoman Empire

(B) Russia

(C) China

(D) Japan

52. Which of the following is a cause of ethnic tensions in Africa that have, in some cases, led to violent conflict and genocide?

(A) Political borders created by Europeans that encompass unrelated and competing ethnic groups

(B) The lack of natural resources that can be sold on the global market

(C) The refusal of European powers to allow decolonization until the 1980s and 1990s

(D) Lack of attention paid to Africa by global organizations such as the United Nations

GO ON TO THE NEXT PAGE

53. Which of the following was true of the U.S.S.R. from 1922 until 1989?

    (A) The U.S.S.R. was an active participant in the League of Nations.

    (B) The U.S.S.R. was engaged in a Cold War with the United States.

    (C) A single party was in control of the government.

    (D) The economy was directed by a series of Five-Year Plans focused on rapid industrialization.

54. Which of the following was a major issue for feminists at the end of the 20th century, but not the beginning?

    (A) Equal pay for equal work

    (B) The right to vote

    (C) Access to education

    (D) Equality in marriage

55. Which of the following is an example of a global organization formed to encourage unrestricted trade relationships?

    (A) The EU

    (B) The United Nations

    (C) The WTO

    (D) OPEC

56. The progressive development of peoples is an object of deep interest and concern to the Church. This is particularly true in the case of those peoples who are trying to escape the ravages of hunger, poverty, endemic disease and ignorance . . . . The Church judges it her duty to help all men explore this serious problem, . . . and to impress upon them the need for concerted action at this critical juncture . . . .

    [S]ocial unrest has gradually spread throughout the world. The acute restlessness engulfing the poorer classes in countries that are now being industrialized has spread to other regions where agriculture is the mainstay of the economy . . . . Then there are the flagrant inequalities not merely in the enjoyment of possessions, but even more in the exercise of power . . .

    — .Encyclical of Pope Paul VI on the Development of Peoples, March 26, 1967l

    This selection from a 1967 papal encyclical illustrates a trend toward

    (A) increasing Catholic resistance to modern technology

    (B) the application of religious beliefs to political issues

    (C) papal support of socialist and communist governments

    (D) liberalization of Church policies toward contraception

57. The movement associated with this encyclical was called

    (A) Liberation Theology

    (B) Communitarianism

    (C) Christian Anarchism

    (D) Neo-Calvinism

The General Assembly proclaims this Universal Declaration of Human Rights as a common standard of achievement for all peoples and all nations, to the end that every individual and every organ of society, keeping this Declaration constantly in mind, shall strive by teaching and education to promote respect for these rights and freedoms and by progressive measures . . . .

Article 1

All human beings are born free and equal in dignity and rights. They are endowed with reason and conscience and should act towards one another in a spirit of brotherhood.

GO ON TO THE NEXT PAGE

58. The previous excerpt from the Universal Declaration of Human Rights is most similar to which 18th-century French document?

(A) The Declaration of the Rights of Man

(B) The Bill of Rights

(C) The Constitution of Medina

(D) The Magna Carta

59. This image illustrates the response of the Dadaist movement to the outcomes of which global conflict?

(A) The Thirty Years War

(B) The Franco-Prussian War

(C) World War I

(D) World War II

60. Which of the following is an example of an involuntary migration?

(E) The maritime migrations of the Polynesian peoples in the period 600 to 1450

(F) The migration of Italians to Argentina between 1850 and 1950

(G) The migration of Algerians to France in the postcolonial period

(H) The migration of Africans to Brazil and the Caribbean between 1550 and 1750

61. Which of the following is evidence of urban planning in Harappa and Mohenjo-Daro?

(A) A grid-like city layout with uniform housing

(B) Pottery and decorative items

(C) A writing system using approximately 400 symbols

(D) Metal tools of bronze and copper

62. Which of the following reflects the Daoist attitude toward war?

(A) It is better to submit to invaders than to engage in warfare.

(B) War should be used only for defensive purposes.

(C) War should be used as a tool to spread the beliefs of Daoism.

(D) Warriors should be revered as gods.

GO ON TO THE NEXT PAGE

But concerning their manners and superstitions, of the disposition and stature of their bodies, of their country and manner of fighting etc., he protested the particulars following to be true: namely, that they were above all men, covetous, hasty, deceitful, and merciless . . . . They think that all things are created for themselves alone . . . . They ride fast bound unto their horses, which are not very great in stature, but exceedingly strong, and maintained with little provender . . . . Vanquished, they ask no favor, and vanquishing, they show no compassion. They all persist in their purpose of subduing the whole world under their own subjection, as if they were but one man, and yet they are more than millions in number.

—A description of the Tatars [Mongols] from 1243

63. The most likely author of this source is a

(A) Mongol general, based on the effusive praise of their battle tactics

(B) Mongol soldier, because of the thorough knowledge of Mongol warfare

(C) European scholar, given the clear descriptions and slightly derisive tone

(D) defeated Russian prince, because of the angry and frustrated tone

64. Which of the following is an example of a new urban center that arose in Europe and was a significant trade center during the High Middle Ages?

(A) Rome

(B) Bruges

(C) Istanbul

(D) St. Petersburg

65. Which of the following was an outcome of new connections between the Eastern and Western hemispheres in the 16th century?

(A) Native Americans immediately developed immunities to European diseases.

(B) China began to trade directly with societies in Latin America.

(C) Food crops and animals were exchanged between the hemispheres.

(D) Portugal shifted its focus from its trading-post empires in Africa to the establishment of colonies in the Caribbean.

66. Which of the following was a response to anti-Semitism in the 19th century?

(A) Many European nations passed human rights legislation.

(B) The Zionist movement sought to establish a Jewish state in Palestine.

(C) Some European nations offered incentives for Jewish people to emigrate to the United States.

(D) Jewish people began to agitate for the right to vote.

GO ON TO THE NEXT PAGE

67. This image, produced in 1812, is an example of

(A) the participation of all social classes in the Industrial Revolution

(B) the use of newspapers to encourage the building of factories

(C) the movement of textile factories from Europe to colonial territories such as India

(D) violent reactions to the Industrial Revolution by groups that included the Luddites

68. Which of the following rebellions was supported by leaders of the Qing Dynasty in China?

(A) The Taiping Rebellion

(B) The Miao Rebellion

(C) The Dungan revolt

(D) The Boxer Rebellion

69. In both India and Africa, leaders of post-World War II independence movements were generally

(A) union leaders who believed in principles of nonviolence

(B) Europeans who believed that the colonial system was outdated and corrupt

(C) Indians and Africans who had received an education in Europe or the United States

(D) illiterate natives who resented the economic inequalities imposed by the Europeans

70. Which of the following was true of women during both the Russian and the Chinese revolutions?

(A) Women worked in factories.

(B) New marriage laws were written to eliminate arranged marriages.

(C) Lawmakers ignored issues such as maternity leave and child care.

(D) Women served in the army and in party leadership.

Section II

Part A: Document-Based Question

Mandatory reading period: 10 minutes
Suggested writing time: 40 minutes

Directions: The following question is based on the accompanying Documents 1–10. (The documents have been edited for purposes of this exercise.)

This question is designed to test your ability to work with and understand historical documents. Write an essay that:

- Has a relevant thesis statement and supports that thesis with evidence from the documents

- Uses all of the documents

- Analyzes the documents by grouping them in as many appropriate ways as possible and doesn't simply summarize the documents individually

- Takes into account the sources of the documents and analyzes the authors' points of view

- Explains the need for at least one additional type of document

You may refer to relevant historical information not mentioned in the documents.

Prompt: Analyze the processes associated with empire building in the Americas, Africa, and Asia from the early 16th century to the early 20th century. Identify an additional type of document and explain how it would help your analysis of these processes.

Historical Background: Empires expanded in all of the worlds' regions after 1500 CE and continued to emerge until the early 20th century. Empires formed and extended their control through a variety of means, and utilized a variety of governing structures.

GO ON TO THE NEXT PAGE ⟶

DOCUMENT 1

Source: Nzinga Mbenba (Afonso I), King of Kongo, letter to the King of Portugal, 1526

Sir, Your Highness should know that our Kingdom is being lost and it is necessary for you to act, since this is caused by the excessive freedom given to your agents and officials who come to our Kingdom to set up shops that sell goods that have been prohibited by us, and which are spread throughout our Kingdom to our vassals, whom we had in obedience, and who now do not comply because they have things in greater abundance than we ourselves; and it was with these things that we had them content and subjected under our control, so it is doing a great harm not only to the service of God, but the security and peace of our Kingdoms and State as well . . . .

That is why we beg of Your Highness to assist us by commanding your country's traders that they should not send either merchants or wares to Kongo . . . . Pray Our Lord in His mercy to have Your Highness under His guard and let you do forever the things of His service. I kiss your hands many times . . . .

From: *The Human Record: Sources of Global History*, vol. 1 (Boston: Houghton Mifflin, 2009), p. 433.

DOCUMENT 2

Source: Drawing by native artist of Spanish and their native allies fighting the Aztecs, *General History of the Things of New Spain*, 1585

GO ON TO THE NEXT PAGE

DOCUMENT 3

Source: Population estimates for Puerto Rico by ethnicity

Year	Europeans	Free Blacks	Mulattos*	Black Slaves	Natives
1530	10%	0%	0%	53.6%	36.4%
1600	55.6%	0%	16.6%	27.8%	
1775	40.4%	3.9%	46.7%	9%	
1795	38.4%	8.6%	34.5%	16%	2.5%
1815	47%	6.8%	36.9%	9.3%	
1860	51.5%	41.3%		7.3%	

From: "The Politics of Tanio Revivialism," Gabriel Haslip-Viera

DOCUMENT 4

Source: François Bernier, physician, *An Account of India and the Great Moghul*, France, 1665

Your Majesty, you have seen the maps of Asia and how great is the extent of the empire of the Great Mogul,* which is commonly called India . . . .

There are more than an hundred rajahs, or sovereigns, dispersed through the whole empire; . . . amongst whom there are about fifteen or sixteen that are very rich and powerful; . . . each of them is able in a very short time to raise and bring into the field twenty-five thousand horses, and better troops than the Mogul's . . . .

The Mogul is obliged to keep these rajahs in his service for several reasons: first, because the militia of the rajahs is very good and because there are rajahs who can bring into the field above twenty-five thousand men; second, to make sure all of the rajahs pay tribute, and serve in the army when the Mogul requires it; third, the Mogul may choose to nourish jealousies among them to keep them from organizing against him. This last tactic is done so that they will fight with one another very frequently.

* Mughal Emperor

GO ON TO THE NEXT PAGE

DOCUMENT 5

Source: Harry Verelst, Governor of Bengal for Britain's East India Company, Letter to the Company's Board of Directors in London, Delhi, India, 1769

The coming of the English to power in the Hindostan province of India occurred through a number of events distinguished by a series of fortunate and unforeseen occurrences; not the result of any fixed or connected plan. A colony of merchants influenced by principles of commerce, have acquired a political title and influence over the land, which in size, population, and revenue from trade may be compared to many of the most powerful states of Europe . . . . We see the increasing poverty of the country from the lack of circulation of money throughout. Since we have become governors here, however, the new policies we have made are designed to restore the equality of commerce, and the spirit of monopoly, promoted by the natives, shall be destroyed.

DOCUMENT 6

Source: National Legislative Assembly, Constitution, Paris, 1848

Preamble

In the presence of God and the name of the French people, the National Assembly proclaims:

I   France is a Republic . . . .

II   The French Republic is democratic, one and indivisible . . . .

IV   It is based on the principles of Liberty, Equality and Fraternity . . . .

Constitution

Chapter X—Special Provisions

Article 109 - The territory of Algeria and the colonies are declared French territory, and shall be governed . . . under this Constitution.

GO ON TO THE NEXT PAGE

DOCUMENT 7

Source: Russian Prince Ukhtomskii, *Travels in the East with Nicholas II, the Emperor of Russia,* 1891

The idea of invading a complex foreign civilization in Asia as a tool for the advancement of the selfish interests of modern, so-called civilized societies was repugnant to us. For more than two hundred years, the Russian government has remained at home in its own land; for our natural union with Turkestan and the region of the Amur* cannot be regarded as political annexations. We have remained at home while we watched the Pacific become the arena of western European advance against the people there, who have their own political constitutions and civilizations . . . .

These western strangers have dethroned and oppressed the East. Going there to live and make money, they do not find a home . . . . The natives of the Pacific areas are not treated as brothers in humanity by the western Europeans; for them the native land is one of voluntary exile, and the native people are considered miserable and inferior beings. The natives of this region gradually realize the true intent of these outrageous intruders, and repay them with intense hatred. Who but us Russians will protect them against the foreign foe?

DOCUMENT 8

Source: Winston Churchill, excerpt from *The River War: An Account of the Reconquest of the Sudan* on the British-Sudanese Battle of Omdurman, Britain, 1899

The moment was critical. It appeared to our cavalry commander that the Dervishes* would actually succeed, and their success would involve the total destruction of our corps of Camel cavalry. That could not, of course, be allowed . . . .

But at the critical moment our gunboat arrived . . . and began suddenly to blaze and flame from Maxim machine guns, quick-firing guns, and rifles. The range was short; the effect tremendous . . . . The river slopes of the Kerreri Hills, crowded with the advancing thousands of enemy forces, sprang up into clouds of dust and splinters of rock. The charging Dervishes sank down in tangled heaps. Even the masses in their rear paused. It was too much fire even for those in the back of their formation. The approach of another gunboat completed their fear. Our Camel Corps, hurrying along the shore, slipped past the fatal point of interception, and found safety.

GO ON TO THE NEXT PAGE

DOCUMENT 9

Source: Kisaburō Ohara, student, Keio University Japan, "A Humorous Diplomatic Atlas of Europe and Asia," 1904

English text reads in part: Black Octopus is the name newly given to Russia by a prominent Englishman. For the black octopus is so greedy that it stretches out its eight arms in all directions, and seizes everything that comes within its reach.

GO ON TO THE NEXT PAGE

DOCUMENT 10

Source: Komatsu Midori, an official with Japan's foreign ministry, "The Old People and the New Government," speech to Royal Asiatic Society, Seoul, Korea, 1912

Judging from the facts so far presented . . . , it is not unreasonable to conclude that the Japanese and Korean peoples formed for a long time one and the same nation. The recent annexation of Korea by Japan in 1910 is therefore not the incorporation of two different countries inhabited by different races, but, it may rather be said to be the reunion of two sections of one and the same nation after a long period of separation. Indeed it is nothing more nor less than the restoration of the natural state . . . .

Until our arrival Korea was constantly pressed and frequently attacked by her powerful neighbor, China. While the constant fear of foreign aggression made her timid; political corruption and social decline caused the country to decline and lag behind the progress of the times, until she became an object of pity and sympathy to the rest of the world . . . . The effect of this long standing evil state of things was clearly evident even in recent times. All its industries perished, and commerce in its true sense did not exist in Korea until we arrived.

IF YOU FINISH BEFORE TIME IS CALLED, YOU MAY CHECK YOUR WORK ON THIS SECTION ONLY. DO NOT TURN TO ANY OTHER SECTION IN THE TEST.

STOP

Part B: Continuity and Change-Over-Time Question

Suggested writing time: 40 minutes

Directions: Answer the following question. You should spend 5 minutes organizing or outlining your essay. Write an essay that:

- Has a relevant thesis and supports that thesis with appropriate historical evidence

- Addresses all parts of the question

- Uses a historical context to show continuity and change over time

- Analyzes the process of continuity and change over time

Prompt: Analyze factors contributing to continuities and changes in the urban centers of Sub-Saharan Africa from circa 1000 to 1600 CE.

IF YOU FINISH BEFORE TIME IS CALLED, YOU MAY CHECK YOUR WORK ON
THIS SECTION ONLY. DO NOT TURN TO ANY OTHER SECTION IN THE TEST.

STOP

Part C: Comparative Question

Suggested writing time: 40 minutes

Directions: Answer the following question. You should spend 5 minutes organizing or outlining your essay. Write an essay that:

- Has a relevant thesis and supports that thesis with appropriate historical evidence
- Addresses all parts of the question
- Makes direct, relevant comparisons
- Analyzes relevant reasons for similarities and differences

Prompt: Compare the impact of the belief systems on social structure in East Asia with the impacts of belief systems in ONE of the following regions, from the time the belief system originated to circa 600 CE.

- Middle East
- South Asia

PRACTICE TEST 3: ANSWER KEY

1.	B	19.	C	37.	A	55.	C
2.	B	20.	B	38.	A	56.	B
3.	B	21.	D	39.	A	57.	A
4.	A	22.	B	40.	C	58.	A
5.	B	23.	A	41.	D	59.	C
6.	D	24.	B	42.	D	60.	D
7.	C	25.	A	43.	A	61.	A
8.	C	26.	C	44.	C	62.	B
9.	D	27.	B	45.	C	63.	C
10.	C	28.	A	46.	A	64.	B
11.	C	29.	A	47.	B	65.	C
12.	D	30.	D	48.	C	66.	B
13.	C	31.	C	49.	D	67.	D
14.	B	32.	A	50.	B	68.	D
15.	B	33.	D	51.	D	69.	C
16.	B	34.	B	52.	A	70.	A
17.	A	35.	B	53.	C		
18.	A	36.	C	54.	A		

PRACTICE TEST 3: ASSESS YOUR STRENGTHS

Question	Chapter
1	Chapter 3: Up to 600 CE
2	Chapter 3: Up to 600 CE
3	Chapter 3: Up to 600 CE
4	Chapter 3: Up to 600 CE and Chapter 4: 600 to 1450 CE
5	Chapter 3: Up to 600 CE
6	Chapter 3: Up to 600 CE
7	Chapter 4: 600 to 1450 CE
8	Chapter 4: 600 to 1450 CE
9	Chapter 4: 600 to 1450 CE
10	Chapter 4: 600 to 1450 CE
11	Chapter 4: 600 to 1450 CE
12	Chapter 4: 600 to 1450 CE
13	Chapter 4: 600 to 1450 CE
14	Chapter 4: 600 to 1450 CE
15	Chapter 4: 600 to 1450 CE
16	Chapter 4: 600 to 1450 CE
17	Chapter 4: 600 to 1450 CE
18	Chapter 4: 600 to 1450 CE
19	Chapter 4: 600 to 1450 CE
20	Chapter 4: 600 to 1450 CE and Chapter 5: 1450 to 1750 CE
21	Chapter 5: 1450 to 1750 CE
22	Chapter 5: 1450 to 1750 CE
23	Chapter 5: 1450 to 1750 CE
24	Chapter 5: 1450 to 1750 CE
25	Chapter 5: 1450 to 1750 CE
26	Chapter 5: 1450 to 1750 CE
27	Chapter 5: 1450 to 1750 CE
28	Chapter 5: 1450 to 1750 CE
29	Chapter 5: 1450 to 1750 CE
30	Chapter 5: 1450 to 1750 CE
31	Chapter 6: 1750 to 1900 CE
32	Chapter 6: 1750 to 1900 CE
33	Chapter 6: 1750 to 1900 CE
34	Chapter 6: 1750 to 1900 CE
35	Chapter 5: 1450 to 1750 CE
36	Chapter 5: 1450 to 1750 CE

37	Chapter 5: 1450 to 1750 CE
38	Chapter 5: 1450 to 1750 CE
39	Chapter 5: 1450 to 1750 CE
40	Chapter 6: 1750 to 1900 CE
41	Chapter 5: 1450 to 1750 CE
42	Chapter 6: 1750 to 1900 CE
43	Chapter 6: 1750 to 1900 CE
44	Chapter 7: 1900 CE to Present
45	Chapter 7: 1900 CE to Present
46	Chapter 6: 1750 to 1900 CE
47	Chapter 6: 1750 to 1900 CE
48	Chapter 7: 1900 CE to Present
49	Chapter 7: 1900 CE to Present
50	Chapter 7: 1900 CE to Present
51	Chapter 6: 1750 to 1900 CE
52	Chapter 7: 1900 CE to Present
53	Chapter 7: 1900 CE to Present
54	Chapter 6: 1750 to 1900 CE Chapter 7: 1900 CE to Present
55	Chapter 7: 1900 CE to Present
56	Chapter 7: 1900 CE to Present
57	Chapter 7: 1900 CE to Present
58	Chapter 6: 1750 to 1900 CE Chapter 7: 1900 CE to Present
59	Chapter 7: 1900 CE to Present
60	Chapter 5: 1450 to 1750 CE
61	Chapter 3: Up to 600 CE
62	Chapter 3: Up to 600 CE
63	Chapter 4: 600 to 1450 CE
64	Chapter 4: 600 to 1450 CE
65	Chapter 5: 1450 to 1750 CE
66	Chapter 6: 1750 to 1900 CE
67	Chapter 6: 1750 to 1900 CE
68	Chapter 6: 1750 to 1900 CE
69	Chapter 7: 1900 CE to Present
70	Chapter 7: 1900 CE to Present

ANSWERS AND EXPLANATIONS

SECTION I

MULTIPLE-CHOICE ANSWERS

1. B

Slaves in early societies were often similar in ethnicity to free people in those same societies. Though occasionally slaves might receive special training, they were generally agricultural laborers or domestic servants. People in early societies became slaves as a result of warfare or debt.

2. B

Ancestor veneration was common practice in China during the Zhou Dynasty and beyond. Buddhism did eventually reach China, but was not heavily practiced prior to 200 BCE.

3. B

The five relationships of Confucianism included one between husband and wife. Hindu women were considered subordinate to men and were not allowed to read the sacred prayers. Hindu beliefs stated that only male Brahmins could reach *moksha*. These religious beliefs enforced social patterns that placed men above women in status.

4. A

The ancient Greek city-states were centered on trade networks of the Mediterranean Sea and relied heavily on revenues from trade for their economic prosperity. The Swahili city-states, located on the East African Coast, grew up around the Indian Ocean trade networks.

5. B

Mesopotamian civilizations such as the Assyrians, Babylonians, and Persians and Egyptian civilizations in the Nile Valley both required iron ore to produce large food surpluses and supply their militaries.

6. D

Both migrations were at least partially due to growing population and the endless quest for food and other resources. The development of canoes was more significant in the Polynesian region, whereas migrations in Africa were primarily land-based. The first and third choices were not significant causes of either migration.

7. C

By 600 CE, the classical civilizations had fallen and the world was recovering from their collapse. The arrival of Islam and the growth of the Islamic Caliphates fundamentally changed the religious and political makeup of Afro-Eurasia.

8. C

Foot binding was a sign of wealth and status among aristocratic Chinese families during and after the Song dynasty. Because the process was damaging to women's feet and limited their mobility, it reinforced social restrictions on elite women.

9. D

One of the Five Pillars of Islam requires Muslims to pray five times a day facing Mecca. Naturally, this direction changes depending on where a mosque is located.

10. C

Justinian saw himself as the inheritor of the Roman tradition, and as such based his law codes on the Roman Twelve Tables.

11. C

In Europe, the feudal system involved an exchange of land and military service between lords and their vassals. Peasants were generally serfs who were tied to the land and subject to the political authority of the lord. In Japan, power rested in the hands of the shogun, or supreme general, who managed regional military leaders known as *daimyo*. The freedom of Japanese peasants was also limited, especially if they could not produce enough to pay their taxes.

12.   D

Muhammad was born in Mecca and traveled to Medina to seek out willing converts to Islam. Later, Muhammad returned to Mecca and established a holy site there at the Kaaba.

13.   C

Confucian officials believed that China already produced everything it needed and that the treasure voyages were an unnecessary luxury. In addition, concerns over nomadic incursions in the North prompted refocused attention on internal security concerns.

14.   B

Khubilai Khan and his successors in China actively worked to separate the Chinese and the Mongols. Instead of using the Chinese examination system, the Mongols employed foreigners in the government administration. Conversely, the khanate of the Golden Horde allowed Russian rulers and bureaucrats to retain their positions, as long as they agreed to serve the Mongols and deliver taxes and other dues.

15.   B

Xuanzang traveled to India on a religious pilgrimage, just as Mansa Musa did when he visited Mecca in the 1300s. Marco Polo and the Silk Road merchants, on the other hand, were primarily traveling for the purposes of trade. Although the European Crusaders were on a religious mission, they were engaged in warfare, not a pilgrimage.

16.   B

Both the Inca and the Aztec Empires were military societies that expanded through the efforts of rulers and a warrior class. While Aztec culture was heavily influenced by Mayan culture, the Incas were isolated in the Andean highlands.

17.   A

Powerful city-states in West Africa included cities that prospered from the gold-salt trade across the Sahara. Islamic kings in these cities, such as Great Zimbabwe, taxed the trade and set regulations.

Calicut, a city on the coast of India, prospered because of its connection to the Indian Ocean trade routes.

18.   A

The Chinese tribute system was both a way to demonstrate Chinese power and wealth and a tactic to avoid unnecessary military engagements. Through the tribute system, the Chinese government would offer gifts to nomads to prevent incursions on their northern borders. The tribute system was also used in trade arrangements with foreigners from Southeast Asia and the Middle East.

19.   C

As Europe emerged from the Middle Ages, monarchs increasingly aimed for centralized control of their militaries and economies. Monarchs in France and England began to assert increasing power over feudal lords and developed more efficient systems of taxation.

20.   B

The Portuguese explorers traveled around the coast of Africa and set up numerous trading posts on the West Coast, including in the Kingdom of Kongo. Portuguese merchants were heavily involved in the slave trade in West Africa. In this excerpt, Nzinga Mbemba, also known as King Afonso I, asks the Portuguese king to curtail the damaging slave trade in his kingdom.

21.   D

Prior to the 15th century, the Indian Ocean trade was dominated by Muslim merchants, and most goods headed for Europe passed through Muslim Egypt via Venetian traders. For economic and religious reasons, the Portuguese hoped to bypass both the Venetians and the Muslims in order to purchase products from the East.

22.   B

"Trading-post empires" attempt to control commerce through force of arms but do not aim to capture large territories and populations. Early in the 15th century, Portugal began establishing trading-post empires on the African coast and in South and Southeast Asia. Their power began to decline by the late 1500s.

23. A

Thomas Mun argues that England should sell more products abroad than it purchases from foreign countries. If England maintained that balance, the surplus would be received in treasure, gold, or silver coin. Mercantilist economic theory held that countries should aim to end with a net profit in precious metals and could achieve that through trade, tariffs, and strategic use of colonial holdings.

24. B

Rather than imposing trading regulations on India through force, Britain used payments and bribes to the Mughal authorities or local rulers in order to gain access to the Indian market. The British East India Company did have an army, but it was not large enough to strong-arm the Mughals.

25. A

From 1467 to 1600, Japan was embroiled in bitter rivalries among various warlords (*daimyos*) who welcomed European traders in hopes of gaining an advantage through the use of their technology and other knowledge. In 1600, Tokugawa Ieyasu established the Tokugawa Shogunate and began a policy of restricted relationships with the outside world. Foreigners were not allowed to trade in Japanese ports, with a few small exceptions. Christian missionaries were expelled and the practice of Christianity was violently suppressed.

26. C

The wide arrows moving from Africa to Brazil and the Caribbean indicate that the largest numbers of slaves were transported in that direction. Sugar plantations in those colonies required intense and often dangerous labor, and slaves were considered the most efficient way to supply that labor. The map does not support the other answers.

27. B

Numerous wars and conflicts, including a civil war in Germany and the Thirty Years' War in the 17th century, were fought between Catholics and Protestants. Gradually, these conflicts took on more of a political nature. The Pope's power decreased in the Holy Roman Empire, where a number of princes officially converted their territories to Lutheranism following the 1555 Peace of Augsburg. However, France remained largely Catholic, and Europeans continued to follow one form or another of Christianity during this time period.

28. A

Both the Mongols and the Manchus were interested in preserving the purity of their ethnicity and culture. As a result, they did not allow intermarriage. The Mongols eliminated the civil service examination system, but the Manchus supported and continued it. Both were considered by the majority of the population to be illegitimate rulers.

29. A

Thomas Hobbes believed that people are incapable of learning from their mistakes and will always act in their own best interests. As a result, Hobbes argued that people are best governed by a Leviathan-like absolute monarch. John Locke, on the other hand, had a more positive view of human nature. Believing that people are naturally reasonable, he focused on self-government as the most rational political structure.

30. D

In this excerpt, Voltaire is suggesting that the leaders of the Catholic Church act only in their own interest, and that their decrees are not just or inviolable. Voltaire and other European philosophes emphasized the use of reason to justify human institutions, which undermined traditional authority derived from association with divine law.

31. C
Although serfdom was no longer present in late-18th-century France, many of the obligations and taxes of the feudal period continued to burden peasants at the time of the French Revolution. Unlike the American Revolution, France's revolution was primarily an internal struggle resulting from dramatic social divisions.

32. A
The French conception of human rights elucidated in the Declaration of the Rights of Man, coupled with a growing abolitionist movement, prompted talk about abolishing slavery in French territories in the first months of the French Revolution. Rumors that the French king had already declared an end to slavery prompted a massive slave revolt in Haiti in 1791, which escalated into a full-scale war for independence.

33. D
In the 18th century, large landowners sought to buy up land in order to experiment profitably with new technology and agricultural techniques. The resulting enclosure of village commons, along with the sale of small farms, freed up many individuals for factory labor.

34. B
The map shows that Germany surpassed Britain in 1880, and was itself surpassed by Russia by 1900. (A) contradicts the information shown on the map, and (C) and (D) can't be determined with the information provided.

35. B
The repartimiento system, like the encomienda system, required Native Americans to work for the Spanish. However, it promised them a fair wage for their labor. This system was rarely enforced in practice, and unfair treatment by the Spanish continued until decolonization.

36. C
Feudal serfs were tied to the land and, as such, were expected to work for their lords as well as provide for themselves, usually from a small plot of land designated for that purpose. Serfs were usually permanently indebted to their lords and almost always illiterate. In systems of chattel slavery, slaves were personal property to be bought or sold and received minimal provision as necessary to maintain their health. In both cases, children were born into the same status as their parents.

37. A
Though the Church was still quite powerful during the Renaissance, the growing power of merchant families and increasing interest in rediscovering the Greco-Roman past led to increasingly secular attitudes. New humanist philosophies depicted man as creative and rational, and the printing revolution supported a corresponding rise in literacy and interest in gaining knowledge.

38. A
Both the Tokugawa Shogunate and the French government under Louis XIV created laws to manage timber resources. The other answer choices are either untrue or are not relevant to the time period 1450 to 1750.

39. A
Constantinople was heavily fortified by strong walls and had previously been considered impregnable. The use of cannons, however, shifted the advantage to the side of the Ottomans, and Constantinople fell in 1453. It was renamed Istanbul.

40. C
The Berlin Conference invited European delegates to establish rules for the colonization of Africa. It cleared up territorial disputes among the various powers, but didn't involve African leaders in any way. The Berlin Conference completely redrew the map of Africa.

41. D
The Indian Ocean region was extensively impacted by Chinese maritime reconnaissance voyages, especially under Ming Admiral Zheng He. The Portuguese set up trading post empires in West

Africa, while the Spanish colonized large territories in South America. However, neither China nor Europe focused its resources on reconnaissance in the Pacific Ocean during this period.

42. D
The Taiping Rebellion occurred between 1850 and 1864. Based on a unique form of Christianity, it emphasized revolutionary change, socialist economics, and gender equality. The conflict between the Taiping and the imperial government resulted in a bloody civil war and disrupted the Chinese economy, severely weakening China.

43. A
This Renaissance-style building, called the Rokumeikan or "Deer-cry Hall," was built during the Meiji period and became a symbol of Japanese Westernization. The social and political changes during the Meiji period reflected a sense of inferiority vis-à-vis the West and were made with a view to catching up with Europe and the United States.

44. C
During World War I, Latin American countries were not directly involved in the fighting. However, increasing demand for raw materials was an economic boon to countries like Chile. After the war ended and demand fell, unemployment and strikes rose dramatically in Chile. As a result, many workers turned to the Chilean Communist Party.

45. C
Many colonial territories relied on exporting one or two main products. Global demand for rubber, for example, dramatically decreased during the depression, along with the market for car tires. Although the Depression caused political instability and extremism in many places, it did not immediately lead to wholesale independence movements.

46. A
The map indicates that coffee was produced in South Asia, equatorial West Africa, and northern

South America in the 1880s. We can't determine causes of colonization or demand for products by looking at this particular map. The Panama and Suez canals are indicated on the map; however, the Suez Canal was completed in 1869. The Panama Canal was begun by France in 1881 and completed by the United States in 1914.

47. B
In the 19th century, demand for cheap labor resulted in large migrations from South Asia to Mauritius to work on the British sugar plantations. This explains the large Hindu presence on the island, as Hinduism is not a missionary-based religion. Arab and Malay merchants had knowledge of the island as early as the 10th century, which is one explanation for the sizeable Muslim population. Though some Mauritians converted to Christianity, Roman Catholicism was more likely the result of the earlier Portuguese Roman Catholic influence than the later British Anglican influence.

48. C
The Russian Bolsheviks found most of their support in city soviets, which were generally councils made up of working-class individuals. China, on the other hand, was home to an enormous peasant population that favored communist policies such as land redistribution.

49. D
This image shows both male and female Red Guards participating in revolutionary activity. The female character is a good example of an "iron girl," with her short hair and her threatening posture; men and women were both seen as active participants in the revolution. Women were often depicted in masculine clothing, with short hair and severe features, performing traditional male work.

50. B
In the mid-1980s, Soviet leader Mikhail Gorbachev initiated policies that would ultimately lead to the dismantling of the U.S.S.R. Glasnost, or "openness," referred to a policy of cultural and intellectual freedom, leading to increased freedom for the press.

Perestroika, or "restructuring," introduced some aspects of capitalism into the economic system.

51. D
After the 1853 arrival in Japan of U.S. steamships, progressive members of the samurai class demanded that Japan modernize. After the overthrow of the Tokugawa regime, Japan built a modern infrastructure and rapidly industrialized.

52. A
Perhaps the best-known example of ethnic tensions connected to decolonization was in Rwanda, where hundreds of thousands of Tutsis were killed by the majority Hutus in 1994. In other areas, including South Africa, violent conflict arose from tensions between black and white societies.

53. C
During the entire period, the Communist party was directly in control of the U.S.S.R. The Five-Year Plans were policies implemented under the leadership of Stalin, whereas the League of Nations and the Cold War were in place only during a portion of the time period.

54. A
As early as 1848, at the assembly in Seneca Falls, women began to demand rights and privileges traditionally enjoyed by men, including political rights, equality in marriage, and access to education. These demands were, for the most part, realized by the 1920s and 1930s. The feminist movement of the 1970s focused on child care and equal pay for equal work.

55. C
The World Trade Organization was formed to promote unrestricted global trade. The other organizations are regional and serve other purposes besides promoting free trade.

56. B
This encyclical is connected to a movement in Roman Catholicism called Liberation Theology, in which the Church sees Jesus' message as a call to

political action. In this selection, Pope Paul VI calls for the Church to use its influence for the benefit of people suffering from political or economic oppression.

57. A
This encyclical is connected to a movement in Roman Catholicism called Liberation Theology, in which the Church sees Jesus' message as a call to political action. In this selection, Pope Paul VI calls for the Church to use its influence for the benefit of people suffering from political or economic oppression.

58. A
The Universal Declaration of Human Rights has its roots in the Declaration of the Rights of Man, a document developed during the course of the French Revolution that defines a set of universal rights for all human beings, not just French citizens. None of the other documents are 18th-century French documents.

59. C
Dadaism was a cultural and intellectual movement that reflected the chaos and irrationality of the modern world. Artists responded especially to the horrors of World War I and the perceived incompetence of governments such as the Weimar Republic in Germany. This particular image contains numerous direct references to "Dada," as well as images that reflect dress and styles of the era.

60. D
The migrations in choices (A), (B), and (C) are all voluntary migrations in search of raw materials or economic opportunity. The migration of Africans to Brazil and the Caribbean was a result of the Atlantic slave trade during that period.

61. A
Urban planning involves laying out streets and housing in an orderly manner. The presence of pottery, tools, and written language is common in early civilizations but not directly associated with urban planning.

62. B

Daoists believed in the way of nature and the concept of *wu wei* (to act by not acting). War was seen as a necessary evil for defensive purposes. The Han subscribed to this concept and used the Great Wall to protect against nomadic invaders.

63. C

The document refers to the Mongols as "covetous, hasty, deceitful, and merciless," which suggests that it is not a Mongol source. Although there are some negative attitudes toward the Mongols in the selection, the tone is not angry and frustrated. Rather, the author seems to be eager to record details of the Mongols' tactics and goals, since this document was written in 1243.

64. B

Bruges was located in Flanders on a river system. It became an important trading center for wool and textiles. Rome was still in a period of decline during the Middle Ages. Istanbul didn't get its name until the Ottomans conquered Constantinople in 1453. St. Petersburg was established in 1703 by Peter the Great.

65. C

The Columbian Exchange was one of the most significant environmental revolutions in history. For example, sugarcane moved from Europe to the Americas and became one of the most lucrative cash crops in the world. Conversely, potatoes traveled from the Americas to Afro-Eurasia, becoming the staple food in some places, including Ireland.

66. B

Ideas of nationalism in the 19th century caused many people to express hostility toward the Jews, who were a minority group in many European countries. In response, Theodor Herzl started the Zionist movement, whose goal was to establish a Jewish state in Palestine.

67. D

Some groups, among them the Luddites, saw the Industrial Revolution as threatening. As a result, they reacted by violently destroying factory equipment. The hammers in the image indicate that the individuals are breaking the frames, rendering this an anti-industrial image.

68. D

The anti-foreigner Boxer Rebellion was supported by Empress Dowager Cixi, who hoped to end foreign influence in China. After the defeat of the Boxers, the Qing Dynasty was forced to pay an indemnity to the United States, Russia, and Japan.

69. C

Many leaders of independence movements received a Western education. Mohandas Gandhi earned a law degree in London, and Kwame Nkrumah was educated in the United States.

70. A

In both Russia and China, rapid industrialization required a large labor force, and women started working in factories. Arranged marriage was done away with in China, but hadn't been an issue in Russia. Both Russia and China made laws that cared for pregnant women and mothers. Though women didn't hold positions of party leadership in either case, they did serve in the Russian Red Army.

SECTION II

PART A: DOCUMENT-BASED QUESTION—STRONG SAMPLE RESPONSE

Human societies have created empires since their early days. Imperial expansion took off in the early 16th century when the Europeans expanded across the Atlantic Ocean while at the same time land-based empires in Asia also grew as a result of gunpowder technology. Empires used strategies of conquest, colonization and trade relationships to form and extend their control and governed themselves through direct and indirect methods of control.

In both the early and later phases of expansion, empires used conquest to acquire territory and keep control. In the early 1500s, the Spanish invaded the Aztecs (Document 2). With advantages such as horses, which were not native to the Americas, and steel weapons, the Spanish allied with local societies opposed to Aztec rule. Document 2 shows a battle scene depicted by a native American artist in which the Aztecs fighters are losing. The Spanish went on to conquer and control all of lands of South America. In the late 19th century, the British also used technological advantages to expand their empire in Africa. Document 8 is an account of a battle in Sudan that demonstrates the awesome firepower of machine guns. The "blaze and flame from [the] Maxim guns" helped the British hold off Sudanese fighters and save their Camel Cavalry. The British would go on to control one of the largest swaths of territory in Africa. This document written by Winston Churchill might provide a glorified account of the battle. Churchill was from a wealthy British family and active in British politics, and so his sense of British nationalism likely underlies his portrayal of these events. Although they are from different time periods, both the Spanish conquest in the America and the British in Africa illustrate that superior military was a means of empire building. A document that might add to this analysis would be from a Chinese military official during the Opium wars between Britain and China. This would allow for the investigation of the role of industrialized technology when the outcome was not one of conquest of the entire country as happened against the Aztecs and Sudanese.

Colonists or settlers often followed conquest as seen in documents 3 and 6. Document 3 shows the population of Puerto Rico broken down by five ethnic groups—Europeans, Free Blacks, Mulattos, Black Slaves and Natives. From 1530 to 1795, the number of natives drops dramatically from 36.4% of the population to just 2.5%. In the same period, Europeans as a share of the population rise from 10 to 38.4% and by 1860 they are 51.5%. Document 6 is the constitution adopted by France in 1848 which makes "Algeria and the colonies" French territory and subject to government under the French constitution. The mention of colonies in this constitution indicates that either there was a sizeable French population present in them, or this was a symbolic statement for the benefit of France's European rivals. In the case of Algeria, there was a growing French population there, a fact that would contribute to the bloody independence movement in the mid 20th century as the "pied-noirs" violently resisted attempts to free Algeria from French control. I would like to see a population chart for Algeria similar to the one for Puerto Rico. This would allow me to examine if the rate of colonization of Algeria was similar to Puerto Rico.

A third way empires gained territory and control was through trade. Document 1 is a letter from the King of Kongo to the King of Portugal complaining about the behavior of Portuguese merchants in his country. These merchants are undermining the King's control because they sell goods to his vassals directly and the King is no longer able to dispense his largesse. This weakens the vassal relationships and shifts control away from the King of Kongo. As the King does not want to lose power, perhaps he is exaggerating when he accuses the Portuguese of having "excessive freedom" in Kongo in order to strengthen his case that the King of Portugal must act to rein in his people. From 1526 when the letter was written, the Portuguese did form a trading-post empire along the coasts of Africa, India and into the Spice Islands. The British also gained control in India through merchants (Document 5). In 1769, the Governor of Bengal wrote to the Directors of the British East India Company explaining how "a colony of merchants" had taken control of the government. Because of problems with the flow of money in the region, which disrupted trade and could lower profits for the British merchants, they began to implement laws that allowed money to move and trade and profits to flow. In both Asia and Africa, trade and commerce facilitated the formation of empires.

Empires sometimes governed themselves indirectly. Document 4 describes the structure of the Mughal Empire in which the emperor ruled local rajahs. The emperor will from time to time call on the rajahs to supply soldiers for his armies; the very definition of indirect control. Indirect rule poses a problem for the Mughal empire because some of the rajahs have better forces than the emperor, and there is always a chance that one or more of them might rise up against the emperor. The emperor must "nourish jealousies among them" so that they will focus more on fighting with each other than with the emperor. Indirect rule can often have this divide and conquer element to try and keep the empire stable and prevent challenges to imperial authority. This description from a French physician is addressed to the King of France, who in 1665 was Louis XIV. In an attempt to garner favor with the French King, Bernier might be presenting the circumstances of Mughal rule as more precarious than it actually is. It would be helpful to have a report from the Vizier, a head governing official in the Ottoman empire, which also ruled indirectly, to see if it faced similar challenges, and if it responded to them in the with similar divide and conquer tactics. In contrast to the indirect rule of the Mughals, France brought Algeria directly into its government structure in the 1848 constitution, and from that point on, Algeria was administered in the same manner as French territory on the European continent (Document 6). As far as the French government was concerned, there was no difference between Provence and Algeria.

Imperial expansion was sometimes prompted by the actions of other countries as Japan in document 10 and Russia in Document 7 illustrate. Komatsu Midori explains the annexation of Korea by Japan as the result of the low state to which Korea was reduced by pressure from China. Korea was lagging behind the rest of the world in its development and Japan stepped in to help as this was "the restoration of the natural state." In other words, according to Midori, the Korean and Japanese people were meant to be part of the same state. As an official with the Japanese foreign ministry, Midori is justifying the actions of Japan to take over Korea. His soothing language, "not unreasonable to conclude" and "the reunion of two sections of one and the same nation" is an attempt to obscure and gloss over what was a military event. Korean newspapers at the time might display a different perspective in their reports and accounts of Japan's takeover. It would helpful to have these to judge the significance of Chinese pressure as Midori asserts. Russia also notes the aggressive actions of other countries in East Asia. In 1891, Prince Uktomskii describes how Westerners have overthrown Asian governments, made the peoples subjects to their empires and treat them as "miserable and inferior beings." He offers Russia as the only country able to protect them from the Westerners. An interesting contrast to the Russians' view of themselves is provided in Document 9 from a Japanese college student. It is a map showing Russia as an octopus with its tentacles flowing both east and west. In the east near China, there is a face of man who looks like he is in pain as a tentacle comes close. The translated English text reads in part that the Russian octopus is greedy and its arms reach out in all directions to take whatever it comes across. Made in 1904 when Russia and Japan went to war against one another, this is certainly propaganda intended to rile up the Japanese people against Russia.

Empires built themselves through conquest, trading relationships, colonization, and propaganda. Once established they had to choose how much direct control to exert over their territory. Empires from the early 16th to the early 20th centuries exemplify the different choices empires made as they formed, expanded and governed.

This essay has a thesis that addresses the prompt with multiple categories of analysis earning this point. With five document groups—conquest (Documents 2 and 8), colonization (Documents 3 and 6), commerce (Documents 1 and 5), indirect rule (Documents 4 and 6), and competition (Documents 10, 7, and 9)—the essay earns the grouping point. The essay uses all 10 documents and the student clearly understands the meanings of all them, and also uses each of the 10 documents to support the argument of the essay, earning three points.

The essay contains three successful point-of-view analyses: of Documents 8 (Churchill), 1 (King of Kongo), and 4 (French physician), which earns the point for POV (only two analyses are needed to earn the core point). There is an unsuccessful POV attempt calling Document 9 propaganda without explaining the reasoning, so this is not awarded a point. The student makes three additional document requests, two of which are successful—the Chinese military official in the Opium Wars, and the Ottoman Vizier on indirect rule—and so earns this point.

Having earned all of the basic core points, the essay earns expanded core points for having five groups, because only three are required; a third POV analysis; a strong thesis; and a second successful request for additional documents.

The final score for this essay is 9 points.

WEAK SAMPLE RESPONSE

From the early 16th century to the early 20th century, Europeans formed empires in Africa, the Americas and Asia. Sometimes they conquered people with armies, sometimes with money. They built empires both overland and overseas.

In the Americas the Europeans fought and conquered the Aztecs (Document 2) and then began to colonize in the Caribbean (Document 3). In the battle drawn by the native artist, the Spanish are shown as bigger than the Aztecs and are on horses. Both of these portray their eventual dominance over the Aztecs. In Puerto Rico, the Europeans start as a small part of the population and end up over 50 percent. While there are a lot of slaves and natives at the start, by 1860 the Europeans dominate. In the Americas, the Europeans were able to conquer the natives and form an overseas empire.

In Africa, the Europeans conquered in some areas and took over through trade in others. In Sudan, the British fought using Maxim machine guns (Document 8) with great effect, while in Kongo, they used merchants to undermine the King's authority (Document 1). Because the Portuguese would sell to everyone, the king's subjects could get more from the Portuguese in "greater abundance" than from the King himself. Sometimes the Europeans made African colonies part of their government as the French did in their 1848 Constitution (Document 6). In Africa, Europeans had only maritime empires. A perspective that is not represented here is from European missionaries who were active in Africa during the 19th century. Memoirs or letters to family back home would describe the process of European empire building from the point of view of people who were in the ground before government officials and sometimes before military officials.

In Asia as well the Europeans took over through trading relationships. In Document 5, the British Governor of Bengal recounts how the British took over Hindustan. At the start, they were just a group of merchants but local laws interfered with trade and hence with their profits. They took control and made policies that were friendlier to commerce and trade. The government they took from was the Mughal empire, which is described in Document 4. Its decentralized structure, the emperor ruled through local leaders called Rajahs, meant that the British could pick off bits of the empire with ease. According to

Bernier, the Mogul had to work hard to keep the Rajahs in line, which he did by getting them to fight each other instead of him.

Also in Asia countries competed for influence and land. Russia is shown as a great, big octopus taking over Eurasia with its tentacles grabbing up land (Document 9). The Russians defend their actions in Document 7 saying that they are just protecting the native peoples from the Europeans who do not treat the Asians like brothers and who "are considered miserable and inferior beings." The Russians, so claims Russian Prince Uktomskii, are the only people who can protect the Asians from the West. Since he is a Russian Prince, and benefits from his country's expansion, he is praising his country and people. Similar to the Europeans, in East Asia, it is China that is seen as a menace (Document 10). According to Komatsu Midori, China has been so aggressive towards Korea, that Korea became "timid" and went into a decline that made her "an object of pity and sympathy to the rest of the world." Because of China's actions, the Japanese have annexed Korea to help restore the country to prosperity. In Asia, empires were mostly land-based as seen with the Mughals and Russia. Japan did create an overseas empire with its conquest of Korea.

Empires were built overland and overseas through conquest and trade. While it was mostly European countries that built empires, Asian countries also created them from the early 16th to the early 20th centuries.

The thesis does not address the prompt sufficiently to earn that point. The essay does use all of the documents and conveys understanding of the meaning of all of the documents enough to earn a point; however, it does not use evidence from enough documents to earn either of the evidence points.

It does contain four document groups, three of which address the process of empire building in regions: the Americas (Documents 2 and 3), Africa (Documents 8, 1, and 6), and Asia (Documents 5 and 4). The fourth group also addresses Asia by examining a separate process from the previous group, the role of competition in the process of empire building in Asia (Documents 9, 7, and 10). The essay earns the point for grouping in multiple ways.

The essay contains a successful additional document request for a memoir or letter from a European missionary during the nineteenth century to earn this point. The essay has only one successful point of view analysis for Document 7 and does not earn the point for POV.

The essay earns a score of 3.

PART B: CONTINUITY AND CHANGE-OVER-TIME QUESTION—STRONG SAMPLE RESPONSE

Cities developed to serve a variety of purposes, economic, cultural, and political. Cities formed organically in certain locations as a result of trade (caravansaries in Central Asia that grew into urban centers, such as Samarkand), as political capitals (the establishment of Persepolis by the Persian Empire), or as cultural centers of religion (Mecca), or education (Cairo). In sub-Saharan Africa during the period from 1000 to 1600 CE, urban centers in East Africa continued to function as trade centers as part of the Indian Ocean system; however, in West Africa new cities were created along the coast to take advantage of the emerging trade across the Atlantic Ocean.

Urban centers in East Africa had a significant economic role throughout the 1000 to 1600 time period. The city-states on the eastern coast of Africa formed as centers of trade across the Indian Ocean to cities along the western coast of India. Trading relationships were well established by 1000 and urban centers stretched along the coastline from Mogadishu in the north to Zanzibar and Sofala towards the south. All served as landing spots for traders riding the monsoon winds from cities like Calicut in South Asia, and later those traveling in junks from as far away as China, such as the explorer Zheng He. As a result of the interactions between Bantu-speaking Africans and Arab-speaking Muslims, a new language, Swahili, emerged. Swahili facilitated commercial relationships between African and Muslim merchants, and the urban centers of East Africa often referred to as the Swahili city-states. Even as Europeans, first the Portuguese and later the Dutch, entered the Indian Ocean trade network, the urban centers of East Africa maintained their significance as commercial city-states, and also their independence as city-states. Despite efforts by the Portuguese to establish dominance through the use of gun powder and cannons, in 1600 CE. Africans retained political control in these urban centers because, in the end, the Portuguese were more interested in trade than in conquest and administration of acquired territories. As the pace of trade and commerce picked up in the coastal areas throughout the time period, city-states located in interior regions, such as Zimbabwe, expanded their political control to form empires based on feeding the coastal trade with goods like slaves, gold and ivory. Urban centers of East Africa maintained their economic and cultural roles throughout the 1000 to 1600 time period, despite the arrival of Europeans.

In West Africa, urban centers experienced political and geographic changes from 1000 to 1600. Cities in this part of Africa had emerged to take advantage of the gold-salt trade across the Sahara. Cities such as Timbuktu and Jenne rested on a navigable river, the Niger, and facilitated the movement of gold mined farther south in exchange for salt brought by camel caravan from the north. As Islam spread along with this trade, Jenne developed as a cultural center featuring a large mosque, a university, and a lively publishing industry. In 1000 CE most urban centers in West Africa were city-states with minimal political structure, but as trade accelerated, political centralization emerged, first as part of the Kingdom of Ghana and later the Malian Empire. Along with its role in the gold-salt trade, Timbuktu became a political center of the Mali Empire, a role it maintained after the Mali Empire was defeated and replaced by Songhay. By 1600 cities in West Africa had been incorporated into larger political structures whereas in 1000 most of them had been independent city-states. A second change in the urbanization patterns of West Africa was the growth of cities in coastal areas—for example, Accra and Lagos. Urban centers on the Atlantic coast began to grow in importance after 1450, when European exploration in the Western hemisphere resulted in the Atlantic trade system. Port cities grew to facilitate the movement of slaves from interior regions where they had been captured for shipment across the Atlantic Ocean to the Americas. Even though by 1600 interior cities of West Africa continued to hold economic and cultural importance as part of Trans-Saharan trading relationships, urban centers along the Atlantic coast emerged as part of the new Atlantic trading network.

Urban centers of sub-Saharan Africa had fully developed by 1000 mostly in response to opportunities of trade and commerce. Their political status shifted in West Africa with the development of kingdoms and empires, while in East Africa they mostly remained autonomous city-states. During this time period, West Africa also experienced the emergence of cities in coastal areas when new trade opportunities arose, facilitated by the arrival of Europeans, while the cities of East Africa had been and continued to be vibrant along coastal areas, despite the arrival of Europeans.

This essay has a strong thesis statement located at the end of the introductory paragraph, earning this point. The author uses clear topic sentences in the second and third paragraphs to address continuity and change, respectively, and earns both addressing points. The essay provides evidence for both continuity and change to earn both evidence points.

The essay earns the point for global context by addressing it twice—once for the arrival of Europeans in sub-Saharan Africa, and later for the establishment of Trans-Atlantic trade. The essay also earns the point for analysis of the process of continuity (motives of the Portuguese) and change (emergence of kingdoms and empires in West Africa).

The essay earns two expanded core points for its plentiful evidence and its inclusion of analysis and global context for both continuity and change.

Final point total is 9.

WEAK SAMPLE RESPONSE

Cities developed after agriculture to form civilization, and it was not different in sub-Saharan Africa. Cities in sub-Saharan Africa also formed because of trade, and this stayed the same from 1000 to 1600 CE. What changed by 1600 was that the Europeans came and took control.

From Cairo in the North to the trading cities of the East, and of course, Timbuktu in the West, by 1000 CE there were already lots of cities located in Africa. Cities took advantage of trade to make money. For example, Timbuktu traded gold for salt. These cities were doing the same thing in 1600 because there was still trade going on, but by then Europeans had begun to explore the world, beginning along the West coast of Africa and then into the Indian Ocean. They had gunpowder and were able to easily defeat the Africans and take control of their cities. For a while, the Europeans stayed on the coasts but eventually they realized that they could make more money by inland. After a while, they had taken over the whole continent.

So while Africans lost control of their cities because of the Europeans, the cities remained involved in trade throughout the time period of 1000 to 1600 CE.

This essay does not have a thesis because the change cited in the first paragraph is inaccurate for the time period. The first paragraph does address continuity (trade being a factor for cities) and earns a point. The essay earns a point for addressing change in the second paragraph with mention of the Europeans coming to Africa; however, the discussion at the end of the paragraph about Europeans taking over cities and then the continent is not accurate. The essay has three pieces of evidence, which is not enough to earn a point.

Final point total is 2.

PART C: COMPARATIVE QUESTION—STRONG SAMPLE RESPONSE

After the development of agriculture, sedentary human societies became characterized by class and gender inequalities as job specialization and a new gendered division of labor emerged. Cultural patterns and belief systems reflected and reinforced the inequalities of their societies, functioning in part to make inequalities appear as part of the natural order of things. In both East Asia and South Asia, belief systems reinforced the inequality of the class structure of these societies. And while belief systems in both regions supported patriarchy, elements of East Asian belief systems also provided opportunities for women that did not exist in South Asia.

Belief systems supported class inequality in both East Asia and South Asia. By 600 CE, three belief systems existed in East Asia—Confucianism, Taoism, and Buddhism, which had spread from South Asia along the Silk Roads. Confucianism had the strongest impact on the class structure of China because intense study of Confucianism was required in order to perform well on the civil service exams. The exams served as the basis of the system used in China to develop, staff, and promote government bureaucrats, and this had the effect of creating an elite class in China that owed its success in part to the dominance of Confucian thought. Landowners also bought into Confucianism because families wanted sons to go into government service, and thus literacy, knowledge and training in Confucianism were essential. Government officials and landowners, together known as the scholar-gentry, were able to achieve and maintain high social status through Confucianism. Just as Confucianism played a central role in maintaining the status of elites in East Asia, Hinduism supported and reinforced the position and status of elites in South Asia. In fact, the origins of the South Asian class structure was religious because it was believed that body parts from the god Purusha had become the four Varnas that made up the South Asian social structure. Further up, the closer to the top of the body, the more important the Varna was considered. For example, the Brahmin, or priest class, had been formed from Purusha's mouth, while the peasants, or Sudra, had been made from his feet. In both South and East Asia, belief systems impacted the social structure because elites used religion to justify and maintain their high-ranking social positions. In South Asia, only the Brahmins could perform the public rituals required of Hindus, and in East Asia, with knowledge of Confucianism as the basis of the government exam system, only the scholar-gentry had sufficient time and money to afford the rigorous education required for success.

Although both regions had patriarchal societies, belief systems in East Asia provided women with some opportunities unlike South Asia. In South Asia, only men could preside over the necessary household rituals, which required a level of basic education. As they were excluded from performing religious rituals, women were therefore also excluded from education. The ideal Hindu woman as subservient to her husband as illustrated in the great Hindu epics, *Mahabharata* and *Ramayana*. In contrast in East Asia, elite women were expected to have a basic level of education so that they could raise sons properly. Although the society was patriarchal, elite women in East Asia were considered to have a significant role in raising their sons until they were old enough to go to school. Several elite women became Confucian scholars. Ban Zhao wrote about the proper roles and behavior for women, in *Lessons for Women*, using Confucian scholarship. Confucianism also emphasized the three submissions of women—first to her father, then to her husband, and following her husband's death to her son. In both South Asia and East Asia Buddhism did provide for an expanded role for women as nuns; however, the impact of Buddhism on the gender structure of South Asia was limited as leaders of the Gupta empire supported Hinduism against Buddhism, essentially stamping out Buddhism in its region of origin. As Buddhism spread to East Asia prior to 600 CE through trade routes women continued to have opportunities in Chinese society that were not available to them in South Asia.

As well as serving as a system of spirituality, belief systems often functioned as well to support and reinforce social structures that developed as a result of agriculture. In East and South Asia, the belief systems rationalized social inequality and kept elites in control. Hinduism also functioned to keep women subservient to men in South Asia and Buddhism and little impact on the patriarchal structure of the society. In contrast, Buddhism took much stronger hold in China, and was able to provide women with some relief in that patriarchal society.

The thesis is found in the last two sentences of the first paragraph, addressing a similarity and a difference in the impacts of belief systems on social structure in East Asia and one of the regions specified in the prompt. The essay addresses a relevant similarity between the two regions in the first sentence of the second paragraph, addresses a relevant difference in the first sentence of the third paragraph, and earns both points for addressing.

The essay has evidence for both regions, earning both of the evidence points.

The essay has three direct comparisons, two of which are in the second paragraph. The direct comparison at the end of the second paragraph is accompanied by an explanation of the similarity. Likewise, at the end of the fourth paragraph, the direct comparison is given with analysis of the difference. The essay earns the direct comparison point and the point for comparative analysis.

The essay is awarded two expanded core points for its multiple direct comparisons, comparative analysis of both similarity and difference, and the plentiful, specific and relevant evidence for both regions.

The essay earns 9 points.

WEAK SAMPLE RESPONSE

There were similarities and differences in the impacts of belief systems on the social structures of East Asia and the Middle East. Belief systems differed in their impact on class in the two regions but both East Asia and the Middle East were patriarchal societies.

In East Asia, Confucianism was used to test men who wanted to work for the government. If they could pass the civil service test that was based on Confucian texts, then they could get a job in the bureaucracy. These jobs were prestigious because they were important for the centralized political structure that the Han dynasty put in place and was used successfully to keep the country together until they lost the mandate of heaven. In the Middle East, the Persian Empire was in charge but it did not have a system to test people who wanted a government job, and the religions, Zoroastrianism and later Christianity, did not influence a person's social status. In the Middle East, owning land or being a merchant had more influence on social status than religion. Christians, in fact, were much more likely to be from a lower class because Christianity's emphasis on the equality of all believers appealed to lower class people. During the Roman Empire, the elites resisted Christianity until after the conversion of Emperor Constantine.

In China, women were seen as lowly, so lowly that eventually their feet were bound so that they could not walk without assistance. Confucianism said that women were to practice the three submissions to their fathers, husbands and sons. There was also patriarchy in the Middle East, but Zoroastrianism did not discriminate against women. Going back to the time of Mesopotamia, women had been veiled and lived in a secluded area of the house, a harem. As the first monotheistic, universal religion, Zoroastrianism believed that its adherents were equal in the eyes of god, Ahura Mazda. As the official religion of the Persian empire, Zoroastrianism was more important in its role as state religion than a role in the social structure. Christianity spread throughout the Middle East on trade routes, and like Zoroastrianism, Christianity also accepted the equality of all believers in the eyes of God. Unlike Zoroastrianism, Christianity did discriminate against women. Early on, women had played a role in religious ceremonies but as Christianity spread and became organized only men were allowed to be priests. When Christianity split Orthodox priests could marry, which they still cannot do in the Roman Catholic church. Islam did reinforce patriarchy because women had to be veiled in public.

Religion in East Asia and the Middle East contributed to male-dominated societies but only in East Asia did Confucianism help you get a government job and a better place in society.

The thesis in this essay doesn't work because it does not say how the belief systems differed in the impact, and it states a similarity without connecting it to both of the issues specified in the essay prompt. The essay does address differences twice and earns a point. The essay does not earn a point for addressing similarity because the essay addresses only similarity within the Middle East region, rather than between the impacts of belief systems in the Middle East and East Asia. The essay has plentiful evidence, especially for the Middle East, and earns both of these points. There is no direct comparison and no comparative analysis.

Final point total is 3.

Practice Test 4 Answer Grid

1. Ⓐ Ⓑ Ⓒ Ⓓ   19. Ⓐ Ⓑ Ⓒ Ⓓ   37. Ⓐ Ⓑ Ⓒ Ⓓ   55. Ⓐ Ⓑ Ⓒ Ⓓ

2. Ⓐ Ⓑ Ⓒ Ⓓ   20. Ⓐ Ⓑ Ⓒ Ⓓ   38. Ⓐ Ⓑ Ⓒ Ⓓ   56. Ⓐ Ⓑ Ⓒ Ⓓ

3. Ⓐ Ⓑ Ⓒ Ⓓ   21. Ⓐ Ⓑ Ⓒ Ⓓ   39. Ⓐ Ⓑ Ⓒ Ⓓ   57. Ⓐ Ⓑ Ⓒ Ⓓ

4. Ⓐ Ⓑ Ⓒ Ⓓ   22. Ⓐ Ⓑ Ⓒ Ⓓ   40. Ⓐ Ⓑ Ⓒ Ⓓ   58. Ⓐ Ⓑ Ⓒ Ⓓ

5. Ⓐ Ⓑ Ⓒ Ⓓ   23. Ⓐ Ⓑ Ⓒ Ⓓ   41. Ⓐ Ⓑ Ⓒ Ⓓ   59. Ⓐ Ⓑ Ⓒ Ⓓ

6. Ⓐ Ⓑ Ⓒ Ⓓ   24. Ⓐ Ⓑ Ⓒ Ⓓ   42. Ⓐ Ⓑ Ⓒ Ⓓ   60. Ⓐ Ⓑ Ⓒ Ⓓ

7. Ⓐ Ⓑ Ⓒ Ⓓ   25. Ⓐ Ⓑ Ⓒ Ⓓ   43. Ⓐ Ⓑ Ⓒ Ⓓ   61. Ⓐ Ⓑ Ⓒ Ⓓ

8. Ⓐ Ⓑ Ⓒ Ⓓ   26. Ⓐ Ⓑ Ⓒ Ⓓ   44. Ⓐ Ⓑ Ⓒ Ⓓ   62. Ⓐ Ⓑ Ⓒ Ⓓ

9. Ⓐ Ⓑ Ⓒ Ⓓ   27. Ⓐ Ⓑ Ⓒ Ⓓ   45. Ⓐ Ⓑ Ⓒ Ⓓ   63. Ⓐ Ⓑ Ⓒ Ⓓ

10. Ⓐ Ⓑ Ⓒ Ⓓ   28. Ⓐ Ⓑ Ⓒ Ⓓ   46. Ⓐ Ⓑ Ⓒ Ⓓ   64. Ⓐ Ⓑ Ⓒ Ⓓ

11. Ⓐ Ⓑ Ⓒ Ⓓ   29. Ⓐ Ⓑ Ⓒ Ⓓ   47. Ⓐ Ⓑ Ⓒ Ⓓ   65. Ⓐ Ⓑ Ⓒ Ⓓ

12. Ⓐ Ⓑ Ⓒ Ⓓ   30. Ⓐ Ⓑ Ⓒ Ⓓ   48. Ⓐ Ⓑ Ⓒ Ⓓ   66. Ⓐ Ⓑ Ⓒ Ⓓ

13. Ⓐ Ⓑ Ⓒ Ⓓ   31. Ⓐ Ⓑ Ⓒ Ⓓ   49. Ⓐ Ⓑ Ⓒ Ⓓ   67. Ⓐ Ⓑ Ⓒ Ⓓ

14. Ⓐ Ⓑ Ⓒ Ⓓ   32. Ⓐ Ⓑ Ⓒ Ⓓ   50. Ⓐ Ⓑ Ⓒ Ⓓ   68. Ⓐ Ⓑ Ⓒ Ⓓ

15. Ⓐ Ⓑ Ⓒ Ⓓ   33. Ⓐ Ⓑ Ⓒ Ⓓ   51. Ⓐ Ⓑ Ⓒ Ⓓ   69. Ⓐ Ⓑ Ⓒ Ⓓ

16. Ⓐ Ⓑ Ⓒ Ⓓ   34. Ⓐ Ⓑ Ⓒ Ⓓ   52. Ⓐ Ⓑ Ⓒ Ⓓ   70. Ⓐ Ⓑ Ⓒ Ⓓ

17. Ⓐ Ⓑ Ⓒ Ⓓ   35. Ⓐ Ⓑ Ⓒ Ⓓ   53. Ⓐ Ⓑ Ⓒ Ⓓ

18. Ⓐ Ⓑ Ⓒ Ⓓ   36. Ⓐ Ⓑ Ⓒ Ⓓ   54. Ⓐ Ⓑ Ⓒ Ⓓ

PRACTICE TEST 4

Section I: Multiple-Choice Questions

Time: 55 Minutes
70 Questions

Directions: Each of the questions or incomplete statements below is followed by four suggested answers or completions. Select the one that is best in each case and then fill in the corresponding oval on the answer sheet.

1. Which of the following correctly matches the river with the civilization that developed around it?

    (A) Nile: India
    (B) Yellow: Egypt
    (C) Tigris and Euphrates: Mesopotamia
    (D) Indus: China

2. The Twelve Tables and Hammurabi's Code are important examples of

    (A) written laws.
    (B) trade agreements.
    (C) political treatises.
    (D) religious doctrines.

3. In a patriarchal society,

    (A) the leader holds absolute power.
    (B) power resides with the men.
    (C) religious leaders dominate politics.
    (D) trade is severely restricted by the government.

4. All of the following are aspects of Chinese that were influenced by Daoism EXCEPT

    (A) medicine.
    (B) metallurgy.
    (C) gender roles.
    (D) architecture.

GO ON TO THE NEXT PAGE

5. Which of the following correctly matches the founder or prophet with his religion or philosophy?

   (A) Confucius: Daoism

   (B) Siddhartha Gautama: Zoroastrianism

   (C) Muhammad: Christianity

   (D) Abraham: Judaism

6. All of the following represent examples of Chinese Confucian filial piety EXCEPT

   (A) taking care of parents when they are ill.

   (B) showing love, respect, and support for parents.

   (C) honoring ancestors by carrying out sacrifices after their death.

   (D) respectfully pointing out errors parents make to help them improve.

7. All of the following statements describe important global developments during the time period 8000 BCE to 600 CE EXCEPT

   (A) in response to the growth in trade, systems of currency were developed.

   (B) the use of metallurgy allowed people to make stronger and more efficient weapons and tools.

   (C) the formation of nomadic empires led to the increase in trade along the Silk Road.

   (D) as civilizations developed, so did the need to keep records and communicate further; therefore, systems of writing developed.

8. Harrapa and Mohenjo-Daro were examples of

   (A) oasis towns along the Silk Road.

   (B) Greek city-states.

   (C) port cities along the Mediterranean Sea.

   (D) Indus River Valley cities.

9. The Roman Emperor Constantine influenced the spread of Christianity in the way that the Mauryan Emperor Ashoka influenced the spread of

   (A) Confucianism.

   (B) Hinduism.

   (C) Zoroastrianism.

   (D) Buddhism.

10. Which of the following statements most accurately compares the role of women in Christianity and Buddhism?

   (A) In both religions, women had an opportunity to follow an alternative life in the monastery.

   (B) In both religions, men were considered spiritually superior.

   (C) Christianity attracted many female converts initially, while Buddhism attracted very few.

   (D) Buddhist women were forbidden from reading the sacred prayers, but Christian women were encouraged to read the Bible.

GO ON TO THE NEXT PAGE

11. Which group in Confucianism can best be equated with the Brahmins in Hinduism?

    (A) Merchants

    (B) Scholar-gentry

    (C) Peasants

    (D) Rulers

12. All of the following represent major trade routes of the period from 600 BCE to 600 CE EXCEPT

    (A) Mediterranean sea lanes.

    (B) Atlantic Ocean sea lanes.

    (C) trans-Saharan caravan routes.

    (D) Eurasian silk roads.

13. "He (the superior man) does not mind not being in office; all that he minds about is whether he has qualities that entitle him to office. He does not mind failing to get recognition; he is too busy doing the things that entitle him to recognition." (Analects IV.14)

    The above quote from the Confucian Analects stresses the idea that

    (A) the emperor is close to the gods and should be treated as such.

    (B) proper behavior and respect for parents must always be considered.

    (C) the real leader focuses on work, rather than recognition.

    (D) a superior man always receives praise for a job well done.

14. All of the following represent significant global developments during the time period 600 to 1450 CE EXCEPT

    (A) trade and interaction were at their height during Pax Mongolia, the period when peace and order were established in the vast Mongol Empire.

    (B) one of the worst epidemic diseases in history—the Black Plague—spread during this period, due to the movement of people and their increased interaction.

    (C) major technological developments such as the compass, improved ship-building technology, and gunpowder helped to shape the development of the world.

    (D) European kingdoms reigned supreme as the dominant power during the time period, entering and then taking over the profitable Indian Ocean trade.

15. Which of the following ruled the Middle East and North Africa at the same time that the Tang dynasty ruled China?

    (A) Delhi Sultanate

    (B) Abbasid Caliphate

    (C) Ottoman Empire

    (D) Songhay Empire

GO ON TO THE NEXT PAGE

16. A significant consequence of the Mongol invasions was that

(A) Northern China was converted into steppe land for Mongol nomads.

(B) Western Europe took over 200 years to fully recover from the Mongol invasions.

(C) trade and communication along the Silk Road flourished.

(D) Mongol rule in India helped to incorporate the areas into the Indian Ocean trade network.

17. Ibn Battuta, Marco Polo, and Rabban Sauma are all examples of

(A) religious missionaries who helped to spread their religions along the Silk Road.

(B) travelers who were able to travel great distances and record their journeys.

(C) political diplomats who served the Mongol khan in various parts of the empire.

(D) merchants who profited from the open flow of trade during the Pax Mongolia.

18. Which of the following statements most accurately compares the leadership of the Roman Catholic Church and Eastern Orthodox Church?

(A) The pope was the head of both the Roman Catholic and Eastern Orthodox Churches.

(B) Local lords made religious decisions for the Roman Catholic Church, while the patriarch guided the Eastern Orthodox Church.

(C) The pope was the spiritual head and leader of the Roman Catholic Church, while the emperor and patriarch were co-heads of the Eastern Orthodox Church.

(D) Both religions allowed local communities to make religious decisions for them, as long as the head of the church was consulted first.

19. All of the following statements accurately describe the Chinese impact on Japan EXCEPT

(A) use of the civil service exam.

(B) importance of filial piety.

(C) spread of Buddhism.

(D) cultural practice of the tea ceremony.

GO ON TO THE NEXT PAGE

20. All of the statements below refer to which of the following?

    - Mansa Musa's pilgrimage to Mecca
    - Trans-Saharan trade route
    - Tolls collected on trade in gold and salt

    (A) Swahili Coast
    (B) Mali
    (C) Ethiopia
    (D) Great Zimbabwe

21. By 1450, Buddhism had spread to all of the following EXCEPT

    (A) China.
    (B) Japan.
    (C) Korea.
    (D) the Philippines.

22. Which of the following statements accurately compares the role of the Turks in India and in the Middle East?

    (A) In both areas, an organized force invaded and took over the existing empires.

    (B) The Turks formed the Delhi Sultanate and took control in India, while Turks gained power in the Abbasid Caliphate through military positions and power.

    (C) The Abbasids were easily defeated by Turkish invasions, while in India, the Turks had trouble establishing political control.

    (D) The Turks who invaded India converted to Hinduism, while the Turks who invaded the Middle East converted to Islam.

23. The Mongols were successful in creating the world's largest empire because

    (A) their military forces always outnumbered the opposition forces.

    (B) the spread of the Black Plague had significantly weakened the settled populations.

    (C) the civilizations that were conquered often had weak or declining political power.

    (D) the use of political negotiations eased the transfer of land into Mongol hands.

24. West Africa was greatly influenced by the trans-Saharan trade in the way that East Africa was influenced by the

    (A) Atlantic Ocean trade.
    (B) Mediterranean Sea trade.
    (C) Silk Road trade.
    (D) Indian Ocean trade.

GO ON TO THE NEXT PAGE

25. All of the following accurately describe the exchange of agriculture or technology during the time period 600 to 1450 EXCEPT

    (A) sugarcane originated in southwest Asia and spread to Europe as a result of the interaction during the Crusades.

    (B) gunpowder originated in China and spread to Persia, the Middle East, and eventually Europe, by way of the Mongols.

    (C) the Black Plague originated in the Mongol Empire and spread to the Middle East and Europe via the Silk Road trade.

    (D) smallpox, originating in Europe, spread to the Americas and caused the destruction of the Native American population.

26. Which of the following statements accurately compares the Incan and Roman Empires?

    (A) Both emperors claimed to be descendents of the sun god.

    (B) Both empires built effective road systems which aided communication and trade throughout their empires.

    (C) The Incan Empire had a tradition of representative government, while the Roman Empire claimed divine right.

    (D) Both empires declined due to nomadic invasions and a significant decrease in trade.

27. Which of the following is an accurate list of important trading cities in the time period 600 to 1450?

    (A) London, Baghdad, Delhi

    (B) Venice, Samarkand, Changan

    (C) Paris, Brussels, Cairo

    (D) Timbuktu, Rio de Janeiro, Beijing

28. The Latin American system of encomienda is most similar to the labor system of

    (A) the Aztec Empire.

    (B) Gupta India.

    (C) Medieval Europe.

    (D) Western Africa.

29. In its global impact outside of Western Europe, what is the most important result of the Catholic Reform movement of the 1500s?

    (A) The reassertion of Papal authority

    (B) The artistic movement of the Baroque

    (C) The founding of female monastic orders

    (D) The creation of the Jesuit missionary order

GO ON TO THE NEXT PAGE

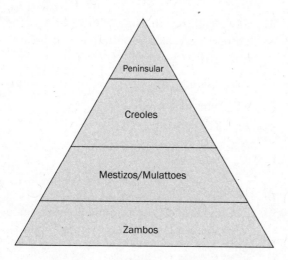

30. The chart above represents the social class structure in

(A) feudal Europe.

(B) Mughal India.

(C) the Incan Empire.

(D) Spanish America.

31. The purpose of the encomienda system was to

(A) eliminate the Native American population.

(B) prevent the Atlantic slave trade from increasing.

(C) supply Europeans with a steady supply of labor.

(D) give Native Americans economic opportunities.

32. Which of the following was NOT exchanged from the Americas to Europe?

(A) Tobacco

(B) Corn

(C) Cattle

(D) Potatoes

33. Which of the following most accurately describes the treatment of the Chinese by the Manchus?

(A) Chinese were forbidden from engaging in trade with the outside world.

(B) Chinese men were forced to wear their hair in a queue (ponytail).

(C) Chinese women were encouraged to marry Manchus.

(D) Confucian scholars were removed from government positions.

34. Which of the following statements most accurately describes the silver trade in the time period 1450 to 1750?

(A) Chinese demand for silver drove the trade.

(B) Spain was unable to attain the needed supply of silver.

(C) The Ottoman Empire served as the middleman in the trade.

(D) The Ming dynasty was strengthened due to the inflation caused by silver.

GO ON TO THE NEXT PAGE

35. During the time period 1450 to 1750, England rose as a dominant power in the Indian Ocean primarily because

(A) the English had defeated their major competitor, the Chinese, in the Opium War.

(B) of the use of joint-stock companies, allowing private investors to take risks and benefit from trade in the Indian Ocean.

(C) the Ottoman Empire had great difficulty retaining its position as the dominant power in the Indian Ocean.

(D) the Portuguese voluntarily withdrew their economic interests in the region.

36. The Mongols and the Ottomans shared all of the following characteristics EXCEPT

(A) administrative expertise.

(B) steppe diplomacy.

(C) interest in distant trading partners.

(D) autocratic leadership.

37. All of the following were indicators of the decline of the Qing dynasty during the 19th century EXCEPT

(A) a decline in foreign trade.

(B) famine and mass migrations.

(C) corruption and intrigue within the royal court.

(D) rebellions against the dynasty.

38. The ideological inspiration for the economic changes associated with the rise of capitalism came from

(A) Adam Smith.

(B) John Locke.

(C) Karl Marx.

(D) Jean-Jacques Rousseau.

39. The region most successful in keeping out Western European influence from 1600 to 1850 was

(A) Mesoamerica.

(B) sub-Saharan Africa.

(C) Japan.

(D) China.

40. Which of the following countries had global hegemony by 1800?

(A) China

(B) Great Britain

(C) Russia

(D) Japan

41. Which of the following is the most accurate statement about the Atlantic slave trade between 1450 and 1750?

(A) Slaves were brought to Europe to work in the mines.

(B) Most slaves were taken from the Saharan area.

(C) The trade was part of a larger triangular trade pattern.

(D) Most slaves were brought to work on rice plantations in North America.

GO ON TO THE NEXT PAGE ⇨

42. In the later half of the 19th century, Jewish people were most persecuted in

   (A) the Ottoman Empire.
   (B) Northern Europe.
   (C) North America.
   (D) Russia.

43. The earliest monotheistic religion was

   (A) Christianity.
   (B) Buddhism.
   (C) Islam.
   (D) Judaism.

44. Which of the following conclusions can best be supported by this map of the British Empire in the 19th century?

   (A) Indian independence was achieved from Britain by the end of the 19th century.
   (B) British imperial power was declining in the 19th century.
   (C) British influence was limited to the Americas in the 19th century.
   (D) The British Empire had spread throughout the world in the 19th century.

45. All of the following statements about how the development of the factory system affected labor are accurate EXCEPT

   (A) it concentrated labor in a single location.
   (B) it led to increasing specialization.
   (C) it led to improved working conditions.
   (D) it led to close supervision of workers.

46. A result of the competition for African colonies in the 19th century was

   (A) more rapid decolonization.
   (B) the Berlin Conference of 1885.
   (C) more cordial relations among European powers.
   (D) the reunification of Italy in 1870.

47. The Spanish were able to conquer the Incan Empire in part because

   (A) there was internal strife among the leadership.
   (B) Incan animistic religious beliefs existed.
   (C) other native groups helped them in the defeat.
   (D) no silver was found in South America.

GO ON TO THE NEXT PAGE

48. All of the following describe major global developments that occurred between 1450 and 1750 EXCEPT

    (A) the Columbian Exchange of goods, disease, and cultures spread throughout the world.

    (B) improvements in and the spread of shipping technologies and gunpowder weapons allowed European countries to begin their dominance of the world.

    (C) the inclusion of the Americas in the global trade network allowed a truly global economy to develop.

    (D) industrialization spread throughout Europe, changing the pace of work, the prices of goods, and the family unit.

49. During the time period 1750 to 1900, the developments below occurred in which country?

    - Taiping Rebellion
    - Opium War
    - Self-Strengthening Movement

    (A) Japan

    (B) Korea

    (C) India

    (D) China

50. How was the Taiping Rebellion different from most rebellions against imperial rule that occurred during the 1800s?

    (A) It was an anticolonial movement.

    (B) It was influenced by religious ideas.

    (C) It led to a new form of government.

    (D) It led the government to resist all reform.

51. All of the following statements about human migration in the 19th century are accurate EXCEPT

    (A) migrants tended to be male.

    (B) migrants created ethnic enclaves in their new lands.

    (C) migrants were attracted by the availability of non-manual labor.

    (D) migrants were not embraced by receiving societies.

52. The emancipation of the serfs in Russia in 1861 caused which of the following to happen?

    (A) Most serfs won political rights and were exempt from taxation.

    (B) Most serfs went on to successful careers as industrial capitalists.

    (C) Most serfs moved to cities to work in the factories.

    (D) Most serfs remained desperately poor.

53. Which of the following most significantly influenced both Italy and Germany in the 1800s?

    (A) Fascism

    (B) Democracy

    (C) Zionism

    (D) Nationalism

GO ON TO THE NEXT PAGE

54. All of the following describe major global developments in the time period 1750 to 1900 EXCEPT

    (A) with the development of industrialization, the world became more interdependent.

    (B) the way that people worked, lived, traveled, related to their families, communicated, and identified themselves changed for many people.

    (C) the industrialized nations, in search of raw materials and new markets, often colonized areas to protect economic interests.

    (D) the institution of slavery remained unchallenged throughout the period, and the plantation system dominated the economy of much of the world.

55. One effect of the West's cultural influence on Meiji Japan was that

    (A) Japanese literature was affected by European models, and writers experimented with Western verse.

    (B) Christianity replaced Buddhism and Shinto as the most popular religion in Japan.

    (C) the Japanese rejected Western fashion and hairstyles.

    (D) Confucian values were eliminated in Japan.

56. All of the following are examples of the new leisure opportunities enjoyed by the middle class in the late 19th century EXCEPT

    (A) the bicycle.

    (B) newspapers.

    (C) television.

    (D) theater.

57. Which of the following methods did Mohandas Gandhi (India) and Kwame Nkrumah (Ghana) use in their struggle for independence from the British?

    (A) Civil disobedience

    (B) Hunger strikes

    (C) Military force

    (D) Guerilla warfare

58. All of the following areas experienced acts of genocide in the 20th century EXCEPT

    (A) Rwanda.

    (B) Armenia.

    (C) Cambodia.

    (D) India.

59. In the 20th century, many newly independent African states

    (A) were able to industrialize quickly.

    (B) were plagued by ethnic tensions owing to the inherited colonial boundaries.

    (C) refused to take part in the United Nations.

    (D) successfully embraced democracy as the best form of government.

GO ON TO THE NEXT PAGE ⟩

60. All of the following accurately describe outcomes of World War I EXCEPT

    (A) Germany was economically and politically devastated. It had lost millions of men in the fighting and was forced to pay huge reparations to the Allies.

    (B) Japanese concessions in the treaties led to a surge of nationalism in China and a cultural and intellectual period known as the May Fourth Movement.

    (C) the use of the atomic bomb set up a technological stalemate known as the Cold War, in which the Soviet Union and the United States were the two dominant world powers.

    (D) in exchange for their help against the Central Powers, Arabs had been promised independence, but their land was carved into French and British mandates.

61. All of the following describe global developments of the time period 1900 to the present EXCEPT

    (A) the world's population grew from one billion people worldwide to over six billion.

    (B) the introduction of communist governments in various parts of the world challenged traditional social structure models, attempting to empower the working and peasant classes.

    (C) from the airplane to the atom bomb, the discoveries in math, science, and technology revolutionized how we live and communicate.

    (D) the nation-state first appeared and became a new concept of political identity.

62. NATO, OPEC, and EU are all examples of

    (A) nonalignment movements.

    (B) international organizations.

    (C) political parties.

    (D) government agencies.

63. The apartheid system in South Africa can be described as

    (A) a series of restrictive laws enacted with the goal of maintaining the separate societies of black and white.

    (B) the collaboration between black and white South Africans in the effort to remove British colonial rule.

    (C) the economic system which industrialized South Africa and focused on the mining of diamonds and gold.

    (D) the political party that encouraged widespread democracy and participation throughout South Africa.

64. All of the items below were policies during the rule of which communist leader?

    • Five-Year Plans

    • Collectivization

    • The Great Purge

    (A) Mao Zedong

    (B) Vladimir Lenin

    (C) Joseph Stalin

    (D) Karl Marx

GO ON TO THE NEXT PAGE

65. Since the 1980s, many countries in Latin America have moved politically toward

(A) communism.

(B) representative democracy.

(C) fundamentalism.

(D) totalitarianism.

66. In the Balfour Declaration of 1917, the

(A) United States supported the Palestinians' right to settle their homeland and govern as they chose.

(B) British government committed to support the creation of a homeland for Jews in Palestine.

(C) Russians declared the right to occupy the Middle East region in order to prevent the spread of capitalism to the area.

(D) Germans occupied the former Ottoman Empire, claiming the need for "Lebensraum" for German people.

67. Which two religious groups had continuous conflicts in India in the latter half of the 20th century?

(A) Christians and Hindus

(B) Buddhists and Muslims

(C) Sikhs and Buddhists

(D) Hindus and Muslims

68. Perestroika and glasnost were both policies that influenced

(A) decolonization in Africa.

(B) the fall of the Soviet Union.

(C) the Arab-Israeli conflict.

(D) the war on terror.

69. The statements below all describe which type of political system?

- A single party in charge of all government
- Ultra-nationalism and glorification of the state
- Militarism and glorification of war as the ultimate expression of power

(A) Democracy

(B) Absolute monarchy

(C) Anarchism

(D) Fascism

70. The stated goal of the nonalignment movement in the 1960s was to

(A) replace the United Nations.

(B) remain neutral during the Cold War.

(C) concentrate on domestic reforms.

(D) convince the United States to supply military aid.

Section II

Part A: Document-Based Question

Mandatory reading period: 10 minutes
Suggested writing time: 40 minutes

Directions: The following question is based on the accompanying Documents 1–6. (Some of the documents have been edited for the purpose of this exercise.)

This question is designed to test your ability to work with and understand historical documents. Write an essay that:

- Has a relevant thesis and supports that thesis with evidence from the documents.

- Uses all the documents.

- Analyzes the documents by grouping them in as many appropriate ways as possible; does not simply summarize the documents individually.

- Takes into account the sources of the documents and analyzes the authors' points of view.

- Explains the need for at least one additional type of document.

You may refer to relevant historical information not mentioned in the documents.

Prompt: Analyze the economic and social effects of the Spanish conquest of the Americas after 1492. Identify an additional type of document and explain how it would help your analysis of the economic and social effects of Spanish conquest of the Americas.

DOCUMENT 1

Source: Hernando Cortes, Spanish conquistador, Letters from Mexico, August 12, 1521.

On leaving my camp, I commanded Gonzalo de Sandoval to sail the brigantines (ships) in between the houses in the other quarter in which the Indians were resisting, so that we should have them surrounded, but not to attack until he saw that we were engaged. In this way they would have surrounded and so hard pressed that they would have no place to move save over the bodies of their dead or along the roof tops. They no longer could find any arrow, javelins or stones with which to attack us; and our allies fighting with us were armed with swords and bucklers, and slaughtered so many of them on land and in the water that more than forty thousand were killed or taken that day.

GO ON TO THE NEXT PAGE

DOCUMENT 2

Source: Bernardino de Sahagun, a Franciscan friar who was instrumental in preserving information about Aztec culture, *General History of the Things of New Spain*, 1519 to 1521.

After the previously mentioned hardships that befell the Spaniards in the year 1519, at the beginning of the year 1520 the epidemic of smallpox, measles, and pustules broke out so virulently that a vast number of people died throughout this New Spain. This pestilence began in the province of Chalco and last for sixty days. Among the Mexicans who fell victim to this pestilence was the lord Cuitlahuactzin, whom they had elected a little earlier. Many leaders, many veteran soldiers, and valiant men who were their defense in time of war, also died.

DOCUMENT 3

Source: Antonio Vasquez de Espinosa, a Spanish friar and missionary who sought to convert the Indians to Christianity, describes the silver mines of Potosí.

These Indians are sent out every year under a captain whom they choose in each village or tribe, for him to take them and oversee them for the year each had to serve; every year they have a new election, for as some go out, others come in. This works out very badly, with great losses and gaps in the quotas of Indians, the villages being depopulated; and this gives rise to great extortions and abuses on the part of the inspectors toward the poor Indians, ruining them and thus depriving the chief Indians of their property and carrying them off in chains because they do not fill out the mita assignment…

So huge is the wealth which has been taken out of this range since the year 1545, when it was discovered, up to the present year of 1628, which makes 83 years that they have been working and reducing its ores, and that merely form the registered mines, as appears from an examination of most of the account in the royal records, 326,000,000 pesos have been taken out.

DOCUMENT 4

Juan Ginés de Sepúlveda (1490–1573), a scholar and apologist for the Spanish treatment of the Indians in the Americas.

Turning then to our topic, whether it is proper and just that those who are superior and who excel in nature, customs, and laws rule over their inferiors, you can easily understand . . . if you are familiar with the character and moral code of the two peoples, that it is with perfect right that the Spaniard exercise their domination over those barbarians of the New World and its adjacent islands. For in prudence, talent, and every kind of virtue and human sentiment they are as inferior to the Spaniards as children are to adults, or women to men, or the cruel and inhumane to the very gentle, or the excessively intemperate to the continent and moderate . . .

GO ON TO THE NEXT PAGE

DOCUMENT 5

Bartolomé de las Casas, Dominican friar, *A Short Account of the Destruction of the Indies*, 1542.

As we have said, the island of Hispaniola was the first to witness the arrival of Europeans and the first to suffer the wholesale slaughter of its people and the devastation and depopulation of the land. It all began with the Europeans taking native women and children both as servants and to satisfy their own base appetites; then not content with what the local people offered them of their own free will (and all offered as much as they could spare), they started taking for themselves the food that natives contrived to produce by the sweat of their brows, (which was in all honesty little enough) . . . Some of them started to conceal food they had, others decided to send their women and children into hiding, and yet others took to the hills to get away from the brutal and ruthless cruelty that was being inflicted on them. . . .

DOCUMENT 6

Source: Engraving by Flemish engraver Theodor de Bry taken from a 16th-century Dutch edition of *A Short Account of the Destruction of the Indies* by Bartolomé de las Casas.

IF YOU FINISH BEFORE TIME IS CALLED, YOU MAY CHECK YOUR WORK ON THIS SECTION ONLY. DO NOT TURN TO ANY OTHER SECTION IN THE TEST.

STOP

Part B: Continuity and Change-Over-Time Question

Suggested writing time: 40 minutes

Directions: You are to answer the following question. You should spend five minutes organizing or outlining your essay. Write an essay that:

- Has a relevant thesis and supports that thesis with appropriate historical evidence.

- Addresses all parts of the question.

- Uses historical context to show continuity and change over time.

- Analyzes the process of continuity and change over time.

> **Prompt:** Analyze the continuities and changes in ONE of the following trade routes from 600 CE to 1750.
>
> - Trans-Saharan
>
> - Silk Road
>
> - Indian Ocean
>
> - Mediterranean Sea

Part C: Comparative Question

Suggested writing time: 40 minutes

Directions: You are to answer the following question. You should spend five minutes organizing or outlining your essay. Write an essay that:

- Has a relevant thesis and supports that thesis with appropriate historical evidence.

- Addresses all parts of the question.

- Makes direct, relevant comparisons.

- Analyzes relevant reasons for similarities and differences.

> **Prompt:** Analyze similarities and differences in the economic and political effects of TWO of the following social class structures from 600 to 1750 CE.
>
> - Hindu caste system
>
> - European feudalism
>
> - Japanese feudalism
>
> - Spanish American social structure
>
> - Traditional Confucian social structure

IF YOU FINISH BEFORE TIME IS CALLED, YOU MAY CHECK YOUR WORK ON THIS SECTION ONLY. DO NOT TURN TO ANY OTHER SECTION IN THE TEST.

STOP

PRACTICE TEST 4: ANSWER KEY

1.	C	25.	D	49.	D
2.	A	26.	B	50.	B
3.	B	27.	B	51.	C
4.	C	28.	C	52.	D
5.	D	29.	D	53.	D
6.	D	30.	D	54.	D
7.	C	31.	C	55.	A
8.	D	32.	C	56.	C
9.	D	33.	B	57.	A
10.	A	34.	A	58.	D
11.	B	35.	B	59.	B
12.	B	36.	A	60.	C
13.	C	37.	A	61.	D
14.	D	38.	A	62.	B
15.	B	39.	C	63.	A
16.	C	40.	B	64.	C
17.	B	41.	C	65.	B
18.	C	42.	D	66.	B
19.	A	43.	D	67.	D
20.	B	44.	D	68.	B
21.	D	45.	C	69.	D
22.	B	46.	B	70.	B
23.	C	47.	C		
24.	D	48.	D		

PRACTICE TEST 4: ASSESS YOUR STRENGTHS

Question	Chapter
1	Chapter 3: Up to 600 CE
2	Chapter 3: Up to 600 CE
3	Chapter 3: Up to 600 CE
4	Chapter 3: Up to 600 CE
5	Chapter 3: Up to 600 CE
6	Chapter 3: Up to 600 CE
7	Chapter 3: Up to 600 CE
8	Chapter 3: Up to 600 CE
9	Chapter 3: Up to 600 CE
10	Chapter 3: Up to 600 CE
11	Chapter 3: Up to 600 CE
12	Chapter 3: Up to 600 CE
13	Chapter 3: Up to 600 CE
14	Chapter 4: 600 to 1450 CE
15	Chapter 4: 600 to 1450 CE
16	Chapter 4: 600 to 1450 CE
17	Chapter 4: 600 to 1450 CE
18	Chapter 4: 600 to 1450 CE
19	Chapter 4: 600 to 1450 CE
20	Chapter 4: 600 to 1450 CE
21	Chapter 4: 600 to 1450 CE
22	Chapter 4: 600 to 1450 CE
23	Chapter 4: 600 to 1450 CE
24	Chapter 4: 600 to 1450 CE
25	Chapter 4: 600 to 1450 CE
26	Chapter 4: 600 to 1450 CE
27	Chapter 4: 600 to 1450 CE
28	Chapter 5: 1450 to 1750 CE
29	Chapter 5: 1450 to 1750 CE
30	Chapter 5: 1450 to 1750 CE
31	Chapter 5: 1450 to 1750 CE
32	Chapter 5: 1450 to 1750 CE
33	Chapter 5: 1450 to 1750 CE
34	Chapter 5: 1450 to 1750 CE
35	Chapter 5: 1450 to 1750 CE
36	Chapter 5: 1450 to 1750 CE

37	Chapter 6: 1750 to 1900 CE
38	Chapter 6: 1750 to 1900 CE
39	Chapter 5: 1450 to 1750 CE
40	Chapter 5: 1450 to 1750 CE
41	Chapter 5: 1450 to 1750 CE
42	Chapter 6: 1750 to 1900 CE
43	Chapter 3: Up to 600 CE
44	Chapter 6: 1750 to 1900 CE
45	Chapter 6: 1750 to 1900 CE
46	Chapter 6: 1750 to 1900 CE
47	Chapter 5: 1450 to 1750 CE
48	Chapter 5: 1450 to 1750 CE
49	Chapter 6: 1750 to 1900 CE
50	Chapter 6: 1750 to 1900 CE
51	Chapter 6: 1750 to 1900 CE
52	Chapter 6: 1750 to 1900 CE
53	Chapter 6: 1750 to 1900 CE
54	Chapter 6: 1750 to 1900 CE
55	Chapter 6: 1750 to 1900 CE
56	Chapter 6: 1750 to 1900 CE
57	Chapter 7: 1900 CE to Present
58	Chapter 7: 1900 CE to Present
59	Chapter 7: 1900 CE to Present
60	Chapter 7: 1900 CE to Present
61	Chapter 7: 1900 CE to Present
62	Chapter 7: 1900 CE to Present
63	Chapter 7: 1900 CE to Present
64	Chapter 7: 1900 CE to Present
65	Chapter 7: 1900 CE to Present
66	Chapter 7: 1900 CE to Present
67	Chapter 7: 1900 CE to Present
68	Chapter 7: 1900 CE to Present
69	Chapter 7: 1900 CE to Present
70	Chapter 7: 1900 CE to Present

ANSWERS AND EXPLANATIONS

SECTION I

MULTIPLE-CHOICE ANSWERS

1. C
The Tigris and Euphrates rivers surround the areas known as the Fertile Crescent, which developed into the Mesopotamian civilization. The Nile was in Egypt, the Indus in India, and the Yellow River in China.

2. A
The Twelve Tables were the written laws of the Roman Republic, and Hammurabi's Code from Mesopotamia was the first written collection of laws. Both were influential in the development of future laws.

3. B
A patriarchal society is one in which men hold the dominant power. Many traditional societies were patriarchal.

4. C
Daoism had a profound influence on many aspects of Chinese culture, including medical theory and practice, metallurgy, poetry, and architecture. However, it did not have any influence on gender roles.

5. D
Abraham is considered the founder of Judaism. He is also important in Christianity and Islam. Muhammad is the key prophet in Islam. The philosophy of Daoism is attributed to Laozi. Zoroaster is the founder of Zoroastrianism.

6. D
Filial piety is a Confucian belief that stresses respect for one's parents. One should never do anything that causes one's parent worry. Parents should be honored and not questioned, even if it is respectfully.

7. C
The great nomadic empires, namely the Mongols, were not a significant global development until the late-13th and 14th centuries, after the referenced time period.

8. D
Both of these cities were part of the Indus civilization, which was not discovered until the 1920s.

9. D
Ashoka was a emperor of the Mauryan dynasty in India who converted to Buddhism after fighting a bloody battle. He encouraged the spread of the religion by building roads and sending missionaries throughout India and beyond.

10. A
In both Christianity and Buddhism, women could live the life of a nun. For women living in a patriarchal society, this was an alternative to a more traditional life of wife and mother. In both religions, women were considered spiritually equal to men. Both religions attracted female converts.

11. B
The Brahmins in Hinduism are the highest caste of priests and scholars. In Confucianism, the highest and most well-regarded class is that of the scholar-gentry. The people in this class often studied Confucian teachings and attained jobs in the government after passing the civil service exam.

12. B
During the time period between 600 BCE and 600 CE, Mediterranean sea lanes, Indian Ocean sea lanes, Eurasian Silk Roads, and trans-Saharan trade routes comprised the world's major trade routes.

The sea lanes of the Atlantic Ocean did not figure in world trade until the 16th century CE.

13. C

The quote taken from the Confucian Analects states that a true leader is not overly concerned with recognition. A true leader focuses on the work itself.

14. D

From 600 to 1450, Europe was not a global world power; instead the area was in a period of recovery and restoration. After 1450, Europe began to get directly involved in the Indian Ocean trade, which helped it to become a world power.

15. B

The Tang dynasty ruled China in the 7th–10th centuries. At that same time, the Abbasid Caliphate ruled most of the Middle East and North Africa. The Delhi Sultanate ruled northern India in the 11th and 12th centuries. The Ottoman Empire ruled the Middle East and North Africa, but not until the 14th century. The Songhay Empire ruled West Africa in the 15th and 16th centuries.

16. C

The Mongols conquered the world's largest empire and in doing so, allowed the exchange of goods, culture, and technology to occur. The period, known as Pax Mongolia, witnessed a surge in trade and communication along the Silk Road.

17. B

Ibn Battuta was a Muslim scholar who traveled extensively in West Africa, the Middle East, and the Indian Ocean. Marco Polo was an Italian merchant who traveled from Venice to the Mongol Empire along the Silk Road. Rabban Sauma was a Nestorian Christian who traveled to Europe from the Mongol Empire on behalf of the Mongol khan. All three of these travelers recorded their journeys, which has helped to provide first-hand accounts of the history of the 13th and 14th centuries.

18. C

The Roman Catholic Church and the Eastern Orthodox Church split officially in the 11th century, though they had been growing apart for centuries. The pope remained the spiritual head and leader of the Roman Catholic Church, and the patriarch and the Byzantine emperor served as co-rulers of the Eastern Orthodox Church.

19. A

While Confucian ideas were very influential in Japan, the civil service exams were never adopted. Important government jobs were hereditary positions.

20. B

The kingdom of Mali, which ruled West Africa in the 13th and 14th centuries, gained great wealth from the tolls collected from the gold and salt traded along the trans-Saharan route. The religion of Islam was also very influential: The emperor Mansa Musa had converted to Islam and went on a pilgrimage to Mecca with an entourage of thousands.

21. D

Buddhism was influential in Tibet, China, Japan, and Korea by 1450, but it had not traveled as far as the Philippines.

22. B

The Turks who invaded India organized themselves into the Delhi Sultanate, which dominated most of northern India. In the Middle East, however, the Turks were often hired as mercenaries in the Abbasid army. Over time, their military power grew, and the sultan, ruler of the Turks, soon wielded more power than the caliph.

23. C

The Mongols were a powerful military force, but they never outnumbered the people they conquered. It was actually quite the opposite. What did help the Mongols conquer such large armies was that the civilizations they invaded were often declining in power. Some Mongols did convert to Islam, but that was something they learned from the conquered people.

24. D

The trade from the Indian Ocean greatly influenced East Africa. The wealth from the trade led to the rise of powerful city-states such as Sofala and Kilwa. These states are often referred to as Swahili city-states after their language, which was a blend of Bantu and Arabic. In the 900s, Islamic merchants traded gold, slaves, and ivory for pottery, glass, and textiles from Persia, India, and China. As the trade increased, so did the wealth of the city-states. Much like Ghana and Mali, these powerful city-states were governed by kings who taxed and controlled the trade. They built stone mosques and public buildings, and the ruling elite dressed in silk from China.

25. D

Smallpox was devastating to the American population, but not until after their encounter with Europeans in 1492.

26. B

The road systems that were built in these large empires greatly facilitated trade and communication. The Incan king alone claimed to be a descendent of the Sun God. The Roman republic did have a form of representative government. Both empires were brought down, partly by invasions, but the drop in trade was more significant in Rome and in the Incan Empire.

27. B

Venice was an important trading city along the Mediterranean Sea, Samarkand was an important oasis town along the Silk Road, and Changan was considered the start of the Silk Road trade in China. London, Paris, Brussels, Rio de Janeiro, and Beijing were not significant trading cities at that time.

28. C

For the encomienda system, Spanish landowners would control the land of the farmers, who were offered protection but were tied to the land. In these ways, the system was much like the feudal system that developed in Europe during the Medieval period.

29. D

The Society of Jesus, known as the Jesuit Order, was founded by Ignatius Loyola during the Catholic Reformation of the 16th century. The Jesuits sent Roman Catholic missionaries to Latin America, South Asia, and East Asia. The Jesuit missionaries were at times highly influential in the relations between European and non-European institutions in the 16th and 17th centuries. The Baroque artistic style, the authority of the Papacy, and female monastic orders all had influence in non-European areas but not in the direct way that the Jesuits did.

30. D

The social structure of Spanish America was based on race. At the top were the peninsulares, who had come directly from Europe. At the bottom were the zambos, who were a mix of Native American and African.

31. C

The early Spanish settlers in the Caribbean had a need for significant labor recruitment. The encomienda system gave Spanish settlers the right to demand labor in the mines and fields of native peoples. These laborers were worked hard and punished severely.

32. C

With the exception of cattle, all of the products were transferred from the Americas to Europe during the Columbian Exchange. Cattle went from Europe to the Americas, which at the time did not have large draft animals.

33. B

In order to separate the Chinese from themselves, the Manchus insisted that Chinese men wear their hair in a queue. This hairstyle involved shaving the top of the head and a long braid in the back. The ultimate sign of rebellion by the Chinese would be to cut off one's queue.

34. A

The great Chinese demand for silver drove the silver trade. The silver was supplied largely by Mexico, Peru, and Japan. The Spanish served as the middlemen transporting the silver to China. The Ming dynasty actually experienced serious problems with inflation as a result of the large influx of silver that flowed into China.

35. B
Unlike Portugal, whose government financed all of its expeditions in the Indian Ocean, Britain used joint-stock companies, in which investors—not the crown—funded the expeditions.

36. A
While the Ottomans were known for their administrative expertise, the Mongols were quite inefficient administrators who often relied on those they conquered to administer the empire.

37. A
China experienced an increase in foreign trade in the 19th century, though not necessarily a willing rise. The increase was often at the insistence of European powers. For example, the British participated in a lucrative opium trade with the Chinese in exchange for Chinese goods such as tea.

38. A
The writings of Adam Smith, in particular *The Wealth of Nation*, laid the ideological groundwork for the rise of capitalism. Locke and Rousseau were political philosophers of the Enlightenment. Karl Marx developed his socialist theories in response to the rise of capitalism and industrialization.

39. C
During the rule of the Tokugawa Shogunate, the Japanese closed their doors to outside interaction, and as a result, successfully avoided the intrusion of the West.

40. B
By 1800, Great Britain had emerged as the dominant world power. The industrial revolution and the building of an overseas empire led to Great Britain's power.

41. C
The Atlantic slave trade was part of a larger triangular trade network in which slaves were brought from Africa to the Americas. Cash crops were brought from the Americas to Europe, and goods such as gunpowder weapons were brought from Europe to Africa.

42. D
Jewish people in the villages of western Russia suffered vicious attacks known as pogroms in the last decades of the 1800s. Often these anti-Semitic raids were officially sanctioned by the Russian authorities. Anti-Semitism existed elsewhere, but did not take on the ruthless violence that existed in Russia.

43. D
Judaism is the earliest monotheistic religion. The Hebrews, or Jews, believe that they had a covenant with God, as his chosen people. In order to keep the covenant, Jews are asked to believe in only one God and follow the Ten Commandments.

44. D
According to the map, the British Empire had spread to most parts of the world in the 19th century. The expression "the sun never sets on the British Empire" refers to the fact that on each major continent the British had territorial influence. Indian independence was not achieved until 1947. European imperial power did not begin to decline until after World War I.

45. C
The factory system was a new way of organizing labor made necessary by the development of machines that were too large to fit in a worker's cottage and that could more efficiently use one power source. The drive for profits led to the use of interchangeable parts and the increasing specialization of labor to further increase efficiency. All of this was brought together under one roof, where it was easier for factory owners to supervise their workers. However, working conditions were hazardous and unhealthy, which led to the rise of the labor movement.

46. B
As European competition heated up, the potential for conflict seemed imminent. In response to this rising tension, German Chancellor Otto von

Bismarck called the Berlin Conference. Delegates (none of which were African) were invited to establish the ground rules for colonization of Africa, and it was decided that any European state could establish an African colony after it had notified the others.

47. C

To conquer the Incan Empire, the Spanish used advanced military technology. In addition, however, they allied themselves with native groups, many of whom were suffering from the effects of the smallpox epidemic.

48. D

Industrialization was a global movement, but it did not begin until after 1750.

49. D

The Taiping Rebellion (1850s) hoped to introduce reform to China. Internal disputes within the Taipings finally helped the Qing dynasty to defeat them, but it was a desperate 10-year struggle that exhausted the imperial treasury. Aggressive British traders began to import opium into China, and a customs dispute in Guangzhou led to the first Opium War in 1839. This resulted in two humiliating defeats for China and a series of disadvantageous treaties which gave Britain and other European nations commercial entry into China. In the 1860s and 1870s, with government-sponsored grants, local leaders promoted military and economic reform in China using the slogan, "Chinese learning at the base, Western learning for use." These leaders built modern shipyards, railroads, and weapon industries, and founded academies focused on the study of science. It was a great foundation, but the Self-Strengthening Movement only brought change to the surface. It also experienced resistance from the imperial government, in particular, the Empress Dowager Cixi.

50. B

The Taiping Rebellion differed from other rebellions against imperial rule that occurred in the 1800s in that it was influenced by religious ideas. It was not an anticolonial movement, but rather an internal rebellion within China against the Qing dynasty. It did not lead to a new form of government; however, the Qings did make some reforms including efforts at economic modernization.

51. C

The large-scale human migration of the 19th century led to a variety of consequences and actions. Migrants created ethnic enclaves such as Chinese migrants did in Southeast Asia, the Caribbean, North America, and South America. These migrants were not always welcomed in receiving societies, as evidenced by the U.S. Congress's passage of The Chinese Exclusion Acts. Moreover, because most of the work available to these migrants was difficult manual labor, these migrants tended to be male.

52. D

In 1861, Czar Alexander II abolished serfdom, and the government compensated landowners for the loss of land and serfs. The serfs gained their freedom and their labor obligations were gradually cancelled. They won very few political rights and had to pay a redemption tax for most of the land they received. Few serfs prospered and most were desperately poor. The emancipation led to little increase in agricultural production, as peasants continued to use traditional methods of farming. It did, however, create a large urban labor force for the newly industrialized empire.

53. D

Both Italy and Germany were formerly decentralized areas. In the 19th century, they were unified into new nations, thanks to a rise in nationalism, military victories, and political planning.

54. D

Slavery was indeed challenged during this period. Many 19th-century liberals in Europe and North America supported the abolition of this institution, as it openly conflicted with the Enlightenment ideals of liberty and equality. The slave trade ended officially in Great Britain in 1807, and in the United States in 1808—though a secret slave trade continued through much of the century. The emancipation of the slaves took much longer: British colonies emancipated slaves in 1833, French colonies in 1848, the United States in 1865, and Brazil in 1888.

55. A

As Japan was opening up to the industrialization of the West, it was also heavily influenced by Western culture. Japanese literature was affected by European models, and so writers began to experiment with Western verse. Architects and artists created large buildings of steel with Greek columns much like those seen in the West. Many Japanese also copied Western fashion and hairstyles. In spite of these powerful influences, though, Japan also continued to emphasize its own values.

56. C

As wages increased and work hours decreased in the industrial age, people were given new opportunities. A larger middle class led to an increase in the importance of leisure. The use of advertising communicated a sense of "needing things" to people. The bicycle, for instance, became the "must-have" item of the 1880s. Newspapers and theaters became popular in this new era of leisure and consumption. The television, however, was not introduced until the mid-20th century.

57. A

Both leaders used civil disobedience, like strikes or noncooperation, in their fight for independence from Great Britain.

58. D

India did not experience genocide in the 20th century, though ethnic conflict between Muslims and Hindus took place (and continues today).

59. B

As many African nations achieved their independence, they did so along the colonial borders established during imperialism. Unfortunately, the Europeans did not consult the Africans in drawing up these borders, and oftentimes, conflicting tribes or ethnic groups were at the borders of the same countries. This has led to conflict in many new nations.

60. C

The use of the atomic bomb was an outcome of World War II, not World War I.

61. D

The concept of the nation-state gained initial prominence in the 19th century with the unification of Italy and Germany, and the independence movements in North and South America. It continued to be an important political organization in the 20th century.

62. B

The North Atlantic Treaty Organization, the Oil Producing and Exporting Countries, and the European Union are all international organizations formed to achieve common goals with other nations.

63. A

Apartheid means separateness. In order to maintain its power, the minority white government enacted laws to separate blacks and whites in South Africa. Under this system, 87 percent of the territory was designated for white citizens, with the remaining part for black citizens.

64. C

Stalin instituted his Five-Year Plans in hopes of increasing industrial and agricultural productivity. Individual farms became collectivized, and those who refused collectivization were killed. The Russian people experienced tremendous oppression during Stalin's Great Purges of the 1930s. Thousands were tried and executed, and millions imprisoned.

65. B

Many Latin American countries have struggled politically and economically in the 20th century, but since the 1980s, many have been moving politically toward representative democracy.

66. B

Following World War I, the British held a mandate in Palestine, but had made conflicting promises to the Palestinian Arabs and the Jews. In the Balfour Declaration of 1917, the British government committed to support the creation of a homeland for Jews in Palestine and allowed Jews to migrate to Palestine during the mandate period. The Arab Palestinians, on the other hand, saw British rule and Jewish settlement as forms of imperial control.

67. D

Hindu and Muslim conflict dates back hundreds of years in India, but the conflict worsened after independence was granted to India and Pakistan (the Muslim-dominated area led by Muhammad Ali Jinnah). This division led to a mass migration of Muslim and Hindu refugees and terrible violence. Tension still exists today.

68. B

When Gorbachev came to power in 1985, he introduced a policy of perestroika ("restructuring"), which was the beginning of a market economy with limited free-enterprise and some private property. His policy of glasnost ("openness") encouraged people to discuss the strengths and weaknesses of the Soviet system. These changes and the weakness of the Soviet economy facilitated the fall of the Soviet Union.

69. D

Fascism, which was used by Hitler (Germany) and Mussolini (Italy), is a form of ultra-nationalism with an absolute leader and strong central government running the show.

70. B

The goal of the nonalignment movement was to remain neutral in the Cold War and not get dragged into the conflict between the United States and the Soviet Union. Nations such as India supported this movement, in hopes of standing on their own.

Section II

Part A: Document-Based Question—Sample Response

The European encounter with the Americas had a devastating impact both socially and economically on the native populations. Economically, the natives were taken advantage of and forced to perform labor. Socially, they were deemed inferior and were brutalized by the European conquistadors.

Economically, the natives suffered a huge loss of population and were pushed into forced labor. Bernardino de Sahagun, a Franciscan friar, reported the devastation that occurred to the native population as a result of smallpox (doc. 2). This excerpt from *General History of the Things of New Spain* demonstrates sympathy for the plight of the natives. He wrote that in "1520 the epidemic of smallpox, measles, and pustules broke out so virulently that a vast number of people died throughout New Spain." This major loss of population severely weakened the people and allowed them to be easily defeated and economically dominated by the Europeans. Additionally, the natives were forced to labor for the Europeans. Antonio Vasquez de Espinosa, a Spanish friar and missionary, described the silver mines of Potosí (doc. 3). He describes how the natives were forced to work for the mines and were often carried off in chains to their labor. Espinosa, a missionary interested in converting natives to Christianity, seems to be sympathetic and angry about their treatment. While the natives were toiling away in the mines, the Spanish were getting incredible wealthy. In the period of Espinosa's investigation over 300 million pesos of silver were taken out of the mines. The fact that both de Sahagun and Vasquez de Espinosa were Church officials and therefore connected to and aligned with the interest of the Spanish crown gives weight to their descriptions of the ravages of the smallpox epidemic and the brutality of the mita system. However, it still does not provide a complete picture of the impact of European contact. What is missing here is the voice of the native. It would be helpful to have a primary source that describes the economic situation before the encounter and a contrasting view after the encounter to truly judge the significance of the change.

Socially, the arrival of Europeans was equally devastating. The natives were viewed as inferior to the Europeans, enslaved, and brutalized. Hernando Cortes, a Spanish conquistador, describes his conquest of Mexico in 1521 (doc. 1). In it he describes how easily the natives were conquered and that other native groups aligned with the Spanish to aid in their defeat. Cortes's purpose in writing these letters is to glorify his own missions. Juan Gines de Sepulveda supplies a justification for the treatment of the native people, writing that the natives were clearly inferior in character and morals (doc. 4). He equates them with children, women, and the cruel and inhumane. Sepulveda's purpose is to justify the treatment of the natives by lowering them to a level beneath their European conquerors. Not all Europeans, however, were convinced that the natives deserved this inferior treatment. Dominican friar Bartolomé de las Casas wrote in *A Short Account of the Destruction of the Indies* in 1542 of the devastation and depopulation that the natives were suffering (doc. 5). His purpose was to get the attention of the Spanish king so he would end the abuses taking place. Las Casas did meet with some success when new laws were passed protecting native peoples, though these laws were not enforced and the horrific mistreatment continued unabated. It would be helpful to have some documentary evidence on the effects of las Casas's book, perhaps a copy of the new laws, or the testimony of a native before and after the laws were passed. Finally, an engraving by Flemish engraver Theodor de Bry shows the brutal Spanish burning a group of native people alive (doc. 6). However, because this engraving was produced to illustrate las Casas's book, it is undoubtedly biased against European actions and its accuracy can be called into question.

Economically and socially, the Americas were transformed by the Spanish conquest following 1492. This change was brought about by European advances in navigation, which spurred an era of exploration and an increased involvement in global trade. The Native American population suffered extremely negative consequences of forced labor and social inferiority, while many Spanish profited and rose to new levels of social significance.

PART B: CONTINUITY AND CHANGE-OVER-TIME QUESTION—SAMPLE RESPONSE

The Silk Road was the thriving trade route through much of the period 600 to 1750. From 600 to 1450, it served as the major thoroughfare for the exchange of goods, technology, and culture. From 1450 to 1750, trade along the road began to decline as the seaborne trade of the Indian Ocean took a higher prominence in global trade, yet it continued to be a major trade route until the mid-18th century.

By 600 CE, the Han dynasty had fallen in China, and a period of disorder followed, but China was eventually reunited by the Sui and then the Tang dynasties. The Tang and later Song dynasties revived trade along the Silk Road with the Islamic world. Buddhism spread, as did paper and gunpowder along the trade routes. Oasis towns like Kashgar and Samarkand grew and thrived because of the active trade route. When the Mongols conquered China and much of Asia, the Silk Road flourished even more, as the safety and security of the Pax Mongolia allowed for safe travel along the oasis towns of the Silk Road. Travelers such as Ibn Battuta and Marco Polo used these trade routes to travel extensively during this period. Continually, Europeans were receiving Asian goods after their long journeys on the Silk Road and paying high prices for them.

By 1450, however, the overland trade route became less important because more focus turned to the seas. The Indian Ocean, which had been an important trade route previously, became a key trading zone. Europeans, who had previously been receiving their Asian goods via the Silk Road, were now traveling around Africa to the Indian Ocean to trade these Asian products themselves. The new global trade network, with the inclusion of the Americas after 1492, was more driven by sea trade and as a result, the trade along the Silk Road began to decline.

The Silk Road was a dominant trade route throughout the time period 600 to 1450. The political stability and safety during this time period aided this thriving trade route. However, after 1450 the Europeans entered the Indian Ocean to get Asian goods for themselves via the sea trade. The rise of Europe and its involvement in global trade led to the decline in the Silk Road trade.

PART C: COMPARATIVE QUESTION—SAMPLE RESPONSE

Social structures serve the purpose of bringing stability to society. They set established roles and responsibilities in an effort to have a more organized and productive society. The social structures of traditional Confucianism and European feudalism had similar economic impacts in stabilizing society. Politically, however, Confucianism helped to create a more centralized society, while European feudalism supported decentralized society.

Economically, both traditional Confucianism and European feudalism helped to create financially stable societies. In feudalism the serfs were the lowest class and were bound to the land. This provided a laboring class of people who were not permitted to leave, therefore promoting economic stability. Economically, feudalism encouraged a self-sufficient system in which land was the primary form of wealth and extensive trade was not necessary. In Confucianism, the peasants were also a stable class of workers in this agriculturally based society. Additionally, merchants were considered lower than peasants because they didn't produce anything; rather they were seen as parasites who lived off the labor of others. Consequently, a merchant may have been economically wealthy, but considered socially low. The social/gentry class, like the European lords, controlled the land on which the peasants or serfs labored.

Politically, the impact of these social structures differed. Traditional Confucianism praised the emperor as the father of the people who set the example for the state, much the same way that the father sets the example for the son. Additionally, government positions, according to Confucius, should be based on merit. This led to the creation of the civil service examination system, in which students took exams based on Confucian thought to secure government jobs. Although only the landed gentry class could afford to be educated for such an exam, the opportunity for advancement did exist. As a result of this social structure, China had a highly centralized government in which all political decisions were made by the emperor and carried out by a highly trained bureaucracy that had the appearance of functioning as a meritocracy, but was really a bureaucratic elite. Feudalism, on the other hand, was decentralized and solely based on heredity. Lords inherited their land from their fathers and the land was passed down by generation. In feudalism, the king gave land to the lords in exchange for military service. This arrangement created a decentralized form of government where the king gave away much of his power (the land) to the noble class.

The nature of both Confucianism and European feudalism changed over time. However, both systems successfully created stable societies for China and Europe with economic production based on agriculture. Politically they differed, as Confucianism encouraged a more centralized government under the rule of a powerful emperor, and feudalism created a decentralized political system in which power was distributed to the noble class.

GLOSSARY

The AP World History course focuses on the "big picture" of history. It is not critical that you memorize names, dates, or events, yet the knowledge of certain world history vocabulary terms can be crucial in framing the analysis of world history. The terms presented here come primarily from the words used by the College Board to describe the important content material in AP World History.

GENERAL TERMS

Civilization

This term can be a loaded issue of historical debate. Who is civilized and who is not? Strictly speaking, a civilization is a form of culture that is characterized by cities, specialized workers, complex institutions, recordkeeping, and advanced technology. At times, however, the term has been used to separate those cultures considered advanced from those that did not "measure up," especially during the time of European imperialism.

Demography

The study of population dynamics. Demographics is important in the study of world history because population dynamics provide evidence of important historical trends, such as pandemics and migrations.

Diffusion

The spread of items from one place to another. In world history, the phrase *cultural diffusion* is used to describe the spread of ideas, such as religions.

Gender Roles

Describes the social roles that men and women adopt. Different cultures often have vastly different notions of gender roles. Even within a given society, gender roles may differ between different social groups, such as between the elites and the peasantry.

Historiography

The study of the way that historians write history. In one sense, it is the history of history. A person examining historiography would look at the way that a Marxist historian, for example, would frame the historical record differently than a person with an imperialist perspective.

Interregional

The connections between different regions of the world. Trade connections, for example, between South Asia and East Africa are an example of interregional connections.

Migration

The movement of people from one area to settle in another area. Migrations can be voluntary or forced, such as with the Atlantic slave trade.

Patriarchy

A social system in which the father is the head of the family or a system in which men dominate the social structure.

Periodization

The division of historical time into different periods. AP World History, for example, divides the course into six different periods of history. How history is divided is a matter of great debate since it, by nature, sets up different dates as the critical division points.

Technology

The way in which people adapt their knowledge to tools and inventions to meet their needs. The concept of technology in AP World History represents a major theme of the course.

UP TO 600 CE

Animism

Religious beliefs that maintain that spirits are animals, plants, and other objects in nature.

Caste System

The social system of the Aryans divided people into four castes, also known as Varnas. This caste system had a profound impact on the development of the Hindu religion. Each of the four main castes had specific roles to fulfill in society. The caste system led to a lack of social mobility in India.

Classical

Represents a period of great cultural significance in society before the modern age. In a limited form of usage, classical refers to the age of Athens in ancient Greece and to the time of the Roman Republic and Empire. The term *classical*, however, can also be applied to non-Mediterranean cultures, such as the Qin dynasty of China.

Filial Piety

A form of respect shown by children to their parents. Filial piety is a crucial concept in Confucian thought and can also be seen in the respect and veneration shown to elders and ancestors.

Monotheism

The religious belief in one God. Judaism, Christianity, and Islam all represent monotheist religions.

Neolithic Revolution

The term *Neolithic* means "new stone age." During the early years of the Neolithic period, which corresponds to the starting point of the AP World History course of 8000 bce, humans discovered agriculture and settled into fixed communities.

Nomadic

A way of life in which people do not have a settled home but rather move from place to place in order to support their livelihood. Pastoral nomads move in order to find places for their animals to forage; hunter-gatherer nomads seek out new areas for finding and hunting food.

Pastoral

Refers to a group that herds domesticated animals for their livelihood. Often, pastoral people are also nomadic.

Polygamy

A cultural trait in which one person is married to more than one spouse at a time.

Polytheism

Religious belief in more than one god. The ancient Greeks, for example, practiced polytheism.

Silk Road

The trade routes that linked the Mediterranean area of the Roman Empire with the Chinese Qin dynasty. Silk textiles and other precious trade goods traveled across the Silk Road about 2,000 years ago. Later, the Silk Road flourished under the Mongol period of the 13th century.

600 TO 1450 CE

Caliphate

Caliphs were the political—and to a certain extent religious—successors of Muhammad. The term *caliphate* refers to the political-religious state comprising the Muslim community and the lands and peoples under its control, which was ruled by a succession of caliphs following the death of Muhammad.

Crusades

Military excursions during the Middle Ages by the Christians of Western Europe with the objective of capturing the Holy Land from the Muslims. Christian crusader states were established along the eastern Mediterranean coast until later Muslim counter-attacks reconquered the area. The Crusades were also responsible for increasing the cultural and economic integration of Europe with the rest of the world.

Dar al-Islam

A term meaning "house of Islam" in Arabic. The Dar al-Islam is the expanse of the Islamic world. In the centuries that followed the death of Muhammad, Dar al-Islam stretched from the Iberian Peninsula of Western Europe to the far islands of Southeast Asia.

Feudalism

A social and political system in which lords are granted landed estates by a monarch in exchange for their loyalty, especially in military matters. Feudalism existed during the Medieval period in Western Europe and also in Japan during the age of the shoguns.

Indian Ocean Trade System

A network of trade established between the Indian subcontinent and the Swahili-speaking trade cities of Eastern Africa. Ocean-going merchants from the Arabian Peninsula used the regular patterns of the monsoon winds to travel back and forth carrying cargoes of textiles, spices, and precious metals. The domination of the Portuguese in the Indian Ocean during the 16th century ended the previous dynamics of this trade system.

Manorialism

Manorialism refers to the manor system, which was the economic system that supported the political system of European feudalism. The manor system was based on a set of rights and obligations between a lord and his serfs. Because European feudal manors were economically self-sufficient, Europe did not take a large part in global trade during this period.

Missionary

A person who spreads his or her religious belief to others. In several of the major world religions, such as Buddhism, Christianity, and Islam, missionaries . were vital in the spread of the faith.

Pandemic

A widespread outbreak of disease. Pandemics, such as the bubonic plague of the 14th century and the smallpox pandemic in the Americas after contact with the Europeans, caused global transformations.

Papacy

Referring to the authority of the Roman Catholic Pope, who is seen as the spiritual successor to Saint Peter. During the Medieval period, the papacy had great religious and political power over almost all of Western Europe.

1450 TO 1750

Absolutism

A style of government that came about in Europe during the 17th century. Absolute monarchs generally ruled a highly centralized state by concentrating power in their own hands. State-run armies, religions, and economic policy often supported the absolutist state. Louis XIV of France represents what many historians consider to be the epitome of absolutism. European absolute monarchs often used divine right theory—the assertion that their rule represented the will of God—to legitimize their rule.

Coercive Labor

Any labor system that involves force, such as various forms of slavery, serfdom, and indentured labor. Almost all civilizations relied on some form of coercive labor up to the 19th century.

Columbian Exchange

The biological exchange that occurred as a result of European involvement with the Americas following Columbus's voyage. Diseases, animals, and plants were transmitted from the Old World to the New World, vastly changing both.

Empire

A political unit in which groups of people, often in different countries, are controlled by a single ruler. Imperial systems are by nature expansionist.

Enlightenment

An intellectual movement centered in Western Europe during the 18th century. The Enlightenment focused on rational thought, order, and logic. These concepts had widespread impacts, such as on the American Revolution and the emancipation of slaves.

Harem

Strictly defined, a harem is the place within a Muslim palace where women were housed. Harems also refer to the women, typically concubines, who are attached to a powerful political ruler.

Neo-Confucianism

A movement to return to traditional Confucian values that occurred especially during the Song dynasty.

Reformation

The religious movement for reform of the Roman Catholic Church during the 16th century. The Reformation led to the creation of new Protestant Christian churches that sought authority separate from the Pope.

Renaissance

The period of intellectual and artistic "rebirth" that occurred first in Italy during the 14th and 15th centuries. During the Renaissance, many elite people sought inspiration in the ideals of classical times and focused on the ideas of humanism and individualism.

Scientific Revolution

A major period of change in scientific thought that occurred in Europe beginning in the 16th century. The scientific revolution was characterized by the use of observation and experimentation using the rational tools of the scientific method.

1750 TO 1900

Bourgeoisie

The middle class in European industrial society. During the French Revolution, the social group of mostly wealthy professionals and businessmen, who helped lead the initial phases of the revolution, were known as the bourgeoisie. Later, Karl Marx would consider the bourgeoisie to be the social class most responsible for the capitalist exploitation of the proletariat (working class).

Colonialism

Rule by one country over another country. In colonialism, raw materials and markets of the colony are often used to enrich the mother country.

Communism

A political and economic philosophy best represented by the thinking of Karl Marx during the 19th century. In communism, a violent revolution is needed in order to overthrow capitalism and create a society based on social equality.

Emancipation

The liberation of a group of people from the control of other people. Typically, emancipation relates to the liberation of people under a coercive labor system, such as slavery or serfdom. Emancipation may also refer to female emancipation, in which women achieve rights equal to those of men, including suffrage.

Ideology

A system of ideas or ways of thinking that guides the decisions of a group of people. Ideology generally involves issues of politics, but it also has economic, social, and cultural implications.

Imperialism

The process by which mostly European countries established political, economic, and social control over other parts of the world starting in the 16th century and reaching its height in the 19th century.

Industrialization

The development of a complex economic system using the factory system of production. Industrialization is one of the main characteristics of a modern society.

Marxism

A system of political and economic thought developed first by Karl Marx in the mid-19th century. Marxism emphasizes class struggle as the dominant force of social change and historical transformation.

Nationalism

A political belief that people should have loyalty to their nation (specifically the people they share a culture and history) rather than to a monarch or emperor. Often in nationalism, people see their own nation as having special aspects that separate and elevate their people in relation to people of other nations.

Social Darwinism

An intellectual movement that applied Charles Darwin's biological ideas of natural selection and the survival of the fittest to human societies. European Social Darwinists of the 19th century saw other parts of the world as weak and thus justifiably exploited.

1900 TO THE PRESENT

Apartheid

A governmental policy of racial separation that arose in South Africa during the middle of the 20th century. It was dismantled in the 1990s when black South Africans gained political representation.

Cold War

The period of conflict between the United States and its allies, and the Soviet Union and its allies. The Cold War began soon after World War II and ended in the last years of the 20th century.

Consumer Society

A society, especially in modern times, that expresses itself through the process of consumption of material goods. Issues such as the globalization of corporate brands and the role of multinational corporations in countries around the world are both indicators of the diffusion of the values of a consumer society.

Decolonization

The process by which former colonies become independent. Countries in South Asia and much of Africa became independent through decolonization during the middle of the 20th century.

Deforestation

The elimination of vast numbers of trees by logging operations as in Brazil and Indonesia or by individuals for firewood and construction material as in Haiti. Deforestation can have dramatic local environmental impacts, such as soil erosion. Widespread deforestation has been linked to broader ecological issues of a global nature such as global warming.

Demographic Transition

The shift to both lower birthrates and lower death rates, thus leading to stable population dynamics and increased longevity. Demographic transitions occur within countries that experience modernization and the advantages of modern medicine and lower child mortality.

Developing World

Parts of the world that have an economic system in which the process of industrial development is not advanced. Much of Africa, Asia, and Latin America is part of the developing world.

Fascism

A political system that emerged in Europe following World War I. Fascism combines ideas of extreme nationalism with authoritarian rule to oppose both liberal democracy and communism. Mussolini's Italy was the first fascist country.

Feminism

A social and political movement that views women as equal to men. Feminists demand equal rights and the elimination of patriarchal control.

Genocide

The planned, systematic killing of a group of people. The Nazi genocide of the Jews and other groups is known as the Holocaust. The 20th century also witnessed other acts of genocide, such as against the Armenians at the beginning of the century and in Rwanda at the end of the century.

Globalization

The process by which national boundaries become increasingly less important, as a result of economic, social, and cultural interactions between parts of the world.

Guerrilla War

A style of warfare that emphasizes irregular fighting units that use surprise attacks and unconventional methods.

Multinational Corporation

A company with operations in a variety of different countries. The late 20th century, with its rapid move toward globalization, saw a rise in influence of multinational corporations.

Non-aligned Nations

Countries that remained neutral during the Cold War conflict between the United States and the Soviet Union. For years, India was the symbolic leader among the non-aligned nations.

Pacific Rim

Those areas that surround the Pacific Ocean such as Taiwan and Singapore. The term is typically used to describe the new economic influence of the nations of East and Southeast Asia.

Popular Culture

Cultural issues of common identity that bind a group of people together. Film, music, and sports are all important aspects of modern popular culture. In recent years, popular culture has become increasingly globalized.

Third World

Strictly speaking, the Third World was the term used during the Cold War to describe those countries that were not Western allies of the United States or allies of the Soviet Union. Generally, it is applied to countries of the developing world, especially in Latin America, Africa, and Asia.

Urbanization

The process involved in the growth of cities and the areas surrounding them. Typically, urbanization occurs as part of the processes of industrialism and modernization. People migrate from rural areas or from other countries into rapidly growing urban centers so that they can take advantage of economic opportunity.